FOUNDATIONS OF HUMAN SOCIALITY

FOUNDATIONS OF HUMAN SOCIALITY

*Economic Experiments and Ethnographic
Evidence from Fifteen Small-Scale Societies*

Edited by

JOSEPH HENRICH, ROBERT BOYD,
SAMUEL BOWLES, COLIN CAMERER,
ERNST FEHR, AND HERBERT GINTIS

OXFORD
UNIVERSITY PRESS

This book has been printed digitally and produced in a standard specification
in order to ensure its continuing availability

OXFORD
UNIVERSITY PRESS

Great Clarendon Street, Oxford OX2 6DP

Oxford University Press is a department of the University of Oxford.
It furthers the University's objective of excellence in research, scholarship,
and education by publishing worldwide in

Oxford New York

Auckland Cape Town Dar es Salaam Hong Kong Karachi
Kuala Lumpur Madrid Melbourne Mexico City Nairobi
New Delhi Shanghai Taipei Toronto
With offices in
Argentina Austria Brazil Chile Czech Republic France Greece
Guatemala Hungary Italy Japan South Korea Poland Portugal
Singapore Switzerland Thailand Turkey Ukraine Vietnam

Oxford is a registered trade mark of Oxford University Press
in the UK and in certain other countries

Published in the United States
by Oxford University Press Inc., New York

Editorial selection and material © Joseph Henrich, Robert Boyd,
Samuel Bowles, Colin Camerer, Ernst Fehr, and Hebert Gintis 2004

The moral rights of the author have been asserted

Database right Oxford University Press (maker)

Reprinted 2009

ISBN 978-0-19-926205-2

PREFACE

The editors of this volume and the contributing authors would like to thank the many people who made this work possible. First, and foremost, we bestow our most heartfelt gratitude on the individuals and social groups from across the globe who participated in our experiments, answered our endless questions, and allowed us into their lives and homes.

We would also like to thank the John D. and Catherine T. MacArthur Foundation for the financial support that made this study possible, and especially Adele Simmons, former president of the MacArthur Foundation, for her vision and backing, both for this project and for the Preferences Network since its inception. Caren Grown and Kristin Butcher, the MacArthur Program Officers responsible for our research, also provided help and support in numerous ways. Nancy Staelens, our long-suffering Network Administrator, was invaluable and indefatigable, solving numerous problems (including convincing University of Massachusetts officials that we could not get signed receipts from illiterate peoples), and making sure everyone got reimbursed. Tracy Humbert helped organize the UCLA meetings. Suresh Naidu read a draft of the entire volume and provided many useful suggestions.

We have also benefited from the criticism and suggestions of a great many participants in seminars in which we have presented earlier versions of this work.

The authors' and editors' royalties have been assigned to Native People and Tropical Conservation, an organization that is working to to improve the lives of people in small-scale societies in Latin America and to preserve the cultural diversity that made our research possible. The urgency of their mission is suggested by the fact that in two cases a combination of long-term hardship and natural calamity destroyed the communities and people at two of our intended field sites (one on Nicaragua's Miskito coast and a second in highland Sulawesi). We hope that the pages that follow will contribute in however small a way to our shared vision of a world in which the beauty, dignity, and integrity of human life are enhanced by enduring and ever-changing cultural diversity.

January 2003

CONTENTS

LIST OF FIGURES

LIST OF TABLES

LIST OF CONTRIBUTORS

Michael S. Alvard
Department of Anthropology
4352 TAMU
Texas A & M University
College Station, TX 77843–4352

Abigail Barr
Centre for the Study of African Economies
University of Oxford
St. Cross Building
Manor Road
Oxford, OX1 3UL

Samuel Bowles
Santa Fe Institute
1399 Hyde Park Road
Santa Fe
New Mexico 87501
and University of Siena
Piazza S. Francesco 7
53100 Siena, Italy

Robert Boyd
Department of Anthropology
University of California, Los Angeles
405, Hilgard Avenue
Box 951361
Los Angeles, CA 90095–1361

Colin F. Camerer
Division of Humanities and Social Sciences
California Institute of Technology
Pasadena, CA 91125

Jean Ensminger
Department of Anthropology
California Institute of Technology
Pasadena, CA 91125

Ernst Fehr
Institute for Empirical Research in Economics
University of Zürich
Blümlisalpstrasse 10,
CH-8006, Zürich

Francisco J. Gil-White
Solomon Asch Center for
The Study of Ethnopolitical Conflict
University of Pennsylvania
3815 Walnut Street
Philadelphia, PA 19104-6196

Herbert Gintis
Santa Fe Institute
1399 Hyde Park Road
Santa Fe
New Mexico 87501

Michael Gurven
Department of Anthropology
University of New Mexico
Albuquerque, NM 87131

Joseph Henrich
Department of Anthropology
Emory University
Atlanta, GA 30322

Kim Hill
Department of Anthropology
University of New Mexico
Albuquerque, NM 87131-1086

Frank Marlowe
Associate Professor
Department of Anthropology
Peabody Museum
Harvard University
Cambridge, MA 02138

Richard McElreath
Department of Anthropology

UC Davis
One Shields Avenue
Davis, CA 95616-8522

John Q. Patton
Department of Anthropology
Washington State University

Natalie Smith
Harvard University
School of Public Health
Boston, MA 02115

David P. Tracer
Department of Anthropology and
Doctoral Program in Health and Behavioral Sciences
University of Colorado at Denver
Denver, CO 80217

1

Introduction and Guide to the Volume

Joseph Henrich, Robert Boyd, Samuel Bowles,
Colin F. Camerer, Ernst Fehr, and Herbert Gintis

HISTORY OF THE PROJECT

It is always hard to know when a new idea first comes into existence. Events always have antecedents, and those their antecedents, and so on back to the beginning of time. So it is with this project, which emerged through the work and efforts of many people, and draws on ideas from economics, anthropology, evolutionary biology, and psychology.

But stories have to begin somewhere, and the best place to begin this one is with the birth of the MacArthur Economics Networks. In 1993 Adele Simmons (then President of the MacArthur foundation) in collaboration with Sam Bowles, Kenneth Arrow, and Amartya Sen, initiated a series of research projects aimed at bringing together researchers from economics and other human sciences with the goal of promoting empirically grounded and transdisciplinary research in the social sciences. These were 'research networks' in the MacArthur Foundation's style, and brought ten to fifteen scholars together to work on some problem. One of these networks, founded by Herbert Gintis and Stanford economist Paul Romer and, since 1997, led by Gintis and Rob Boyd, focused on the 'nature and origin of preferences'. Although formal economic theory is silent about what people want, practicing economists typically assume that people's preferences are 'self-regarding' and 'outcome oriented'. In other words, people want stuff for themselves, and care only about their personal costs in getting what they want. There is much evidence, both from within economics, and from other disciplines, that this view of human nature misses a lot: people care both about other people, and about how social transactions occur—not just the outcomes. The goal of the Preferences Network was to bring together economists, anthropologists, psychologists, and other behavioral scientists to develop systematically richer models of preferences

according to which people take account of the effects of their actions
not only on themselves, but on others as well, and in which the
processes determining outcomes matter as well as the outcomes
themselves.

From the beginning, one focus of this Network has been the study
of these so-called social preferences, through the work of experimental
economics. Beginning in the early 1980s, a number of economists
began testing the predictions of economic theory in laboratories using
undergraduate subjects. In these experiments, subjects were asked to
make economic decisions in which real money was at stake, sometimes substantial sums. While some results were consistent with the
behavior of rational economic actors with standard (selfish) preferences, many were not. The Ultimatum Game, invented by the
German economist Werner Güth, is the canonical example. Two
subjects are given an endowment of money. One subject, the
'proposer', chooses a division of the stake. If the second subject, the
'responder', accepts, both players get the share that the proposer
suggested; if the responder rejects, neither player gets anything. The
game is anonymous, so there are no consequences for a player's
reputation. Economic theory predicts that extremely unequal offers
will be made and accepted. Rational selfish responders will accept any
offer since some money is better than none, and, knowing this,
proposers should make the smallest possible offer. However, this is
not what people actually do in the laboratory. Real people from many
societies frequently reject low offers, and proposers, who seem to
know this, typically propose a nearly equal division of the pot. This
behavior, and similar behavior in a variety of other experimental
games, suggest that people have 'social preferences'. They seem to
care about the nature of the transaction as well as the outcome, and
experimental economists have devoted a lot of effort to describing
these preferences.

Experimental economics played a big role in the Preferences
Network from the beginning because its membership included a
number of important researchers in the field, most notably Colin
Camerer, Catherine Eckel, Ernst Fehr, Daniel Kahneman, and
George Loewenstein. Many of the initial meetings of the network
were devoted to describing these results to other network members.
One network member, Rob Boyd, returned home from one of these
meetings and enthusiastically described these experimental results
to students in his graduate seminar in anthropology at the University

of California, Los Angeles. One of these students, Joe Henrich, was due to leave for his third summer of field work among the Machiguenga, a group of horticulturalists living in the tropical forests of southeastern Peru. Joe had the idea of running Ultimatum Game experiments in the field. Since all of the previous experiments had been done using students from urban, literate, market-based societies, there was no way of knowing whether the social preferences at work were a part of human nature, or a consequence of the particular cultures from which subjects were drawn. It seemed likely to most of us that the social preferences were universal, but until somebody did real cross-cultural experiments, we wouldn't know for sure.

Joe returned several months later (and some 20 pounds lighter) carrying very surprising results: the Machiguenga did not behave like the student subjects at all. The most common offer was 15 percent of the pot, and, despite many low offers, only one was rejected (Chapter 4). This result is especially surprising because the Machiguenga live in small villages in which people rarely interact with strangers—an environment many of us thought would lead to *more* concern for fairness and reciprocity, not less. Joe and Rob, with guidance from Colin, requested and received funding from the Preferences Network to run a high-stakes experiment with graduate students to control for some of the deviations from standard protocols and the large stakes. The result held—with graduate students dividing up $160 playing even more fairly than undergraduates dividing $10. The next year Joe Henrich and Natalie Smith, also a University of California, Los Angeles anthropology graduate student, spent another field season with the Machiguenga and did an experiment using a different game, the Public Goods Game, and also got results that indicated that the Machiguenga came to experiments with very different ideas than students about how to behave.

The obvious question at this point was: were the Machiguenga results anomalous in some fashion? Or, were they an indication of some substantial amount of cultural variation lurking outside the student-subject pools of the world's universities? To answer this question, Rob Boyd, who had by then replaced Paul Romer as co-director of the network, and Herb Gintis decided to organize and fund a program of cross-cultural experimental work. We invited a number of anthropologists to participate in a program of experimental research. We offered to fund a season of fieldwork at a site where the ethnographers already had done extensive work during which they would conduct one or two experiments. The project began with a two-day meeting at University of California, Los Angeles. The first day was a crash course in game theory and experimental economics conducted by Colin, Catherine, Ernst, and Sam, and the second day was devoted to improving and adapting the methods that Joe had used with the Machiguenga. The meeting went extremely well, with none of the misunderstanding and squabbling that often characterizes interdisciplinary meetings. There was also a memorable conversation at dinner in which the anthropologists one by one regaled the group with vivid descriptions of the grossest thing they had had to eat in the field. After the meeting, three other researchers, Kim Hill, Mike Gurven, and Abigail Barr, joined the project.

Eighteen months later we reassembled again to report and discuss results. Two fieldworkers had been unable to complete the experiments: (1) because Hurricane Andrew had destroyed his field site in eastern Nicaragua; and (2) because of drought and famine at his field site in central Sulawesi. The rest brought back a treasure trove of interesting and challenging results that are the subject of this volume.

A second round of experiments is currently underway, now funded by the National Science Foundation in the United States. Led by Joe Henrich and Jean Ensminger, this second round both improves on the methodologies used in this first project (based on our experience) and expands into new theoretical areas. In seventeen small-scale societies, we are doing Dictators Games, Strategy-Method Ultimatum Games, and Third-Party Punishment Games (see Chapter 2 for descriptions), as well as some other games with smaller subgroups (Social Network data and Trust Games). We are also gathering more detailed measures of market incorporation, community cooperation, income, wealth, and education from all groups involved. The participants include many of the same researchers as in the first project: David Tracer (Papua New Guinea), Francisco Gil-White (Mongolian), Richard McElrearth (Tanzania), Michael Gurven (Bolivian Amazon), Abigail Barr (Ghana), John Patton (Ecuadorian Amazon), Frank Marlowe (Tanzania), Jean Ensminger (Kenya), and Joe Henrich (Fiji). In addition, we've added new members of our team: Jeff Johnson (Siberia), Laban Gwako (Kenya), Caroline Lesogrol (Kenya), Guillero de la Pena (Mexico), Alex Bolyantas (New Ireland, Papua New Guinea), Clark Barrett (Ecuadorian Amazon), and Juan Camilo Cardenas (Columbia).

GUIDE TO THE VOLUME

The work in this project is rooted in the logic of game theory and the practices of experimental economics. This material will be familiar to economists, and to many other scholars, especially those in political science and evolutionary anthropology. However, we believe that the results will be of interest to a much wider audience who will not be familiar with game theory or experimental economics. These readers should start with Chapter 3. Here Colin Camerer and Ernst Fehr provide a user-friendly introduction to the fundamentals of behavioral game theory, and procedures and conventions of experimental economics. Readers familiar with game theory and experimental economics should begin with Chapter 2.

In Chapter 2, the editors (with Richard McElreath) summarize and compare the results from all fifteen field sites. We draw two lessons from the experimental results: first, there is no society in which experimental behavior is even roughly consistent with the canonical model of purely self-interested actors; second, there is much more variation between groups than has been previously reported, and this variation correlates with differences in patterns of interaction found in everyday life. We believe that our results bear on fundamental questions about human behavior and society: what is the nature of human motivations, and how are these motivations shaped by the societies in which people live? As a consequence, reviewers of our work have strongly recommended that we expand our discussion of its larger implications. The problem is that our results are relevant to a wide range of disciplines in the human sciences, and reviewers from different disciplines have made wildly different recommendations. Thus, paradoxically, the fact that this work bears on important matters of interpretation caused us to stick fairly close to the data, and limit our discussion to its implications for rational actor and similar models of human behavior. A proper scholarly treatment of the many connections between our research and that of social and cultural anthropologists, social psychologists, sociologists, political scientists, and historians would be both far too lengthy, and well beyond the competence of the present editors.

In the remaining Chapters 4–14, the fieldworkers provide in-depth information on their field sites and methods, and discuss

Table 1.1. Fieldworkers, field sites and methods, and theoretical issues

Chapter and author	Country and group(s)	Experiments	Key topics
4. Patton	Ecuador: Achuar and Quichua	Ultimatum Game	Status, coalitions, local ethnic variation low offers—few rejections
5. Henrich and Smith	Peru, Chile, and USA: Machiguenga, Mapuche, and US Controls	Ultimatum Game, Public Goods Game	Variation, context, student controls, low offers—few rejections
6. Marlowe	Tanzania: Hadza	Ultimatum Game, Dictator Game	Behavioral ecology, local group size, local variation, low offers—high rejections
7. Gurven	Bolivia: Tsimane	Ultimatum Game, Public Goods Game	Market integration, local variation, Ultimatum Game–Public Goods Game comparisons—no rejections
8. Tracer	Papua New Guinea: Gnau and Au	Ultimatum Game	Market integration, local ethnic variation, hyper-fair offers—rejections
9. Gil-White	Mongolia: Torguuds and Kazakhs	Ultimatum Game	Ethnicity, in-group out-group, methods—few rejections
10. Barr	Zimbabwe: Shona	Ultimatum Game, Trust Game	Resettlement effects, local variation, trust
11. McElreath	Tanzania: Sangu	Ultimatum Game	Farmer-herder variation, responder analyzes
12. Ensminger	Kenya: Orma	Ultimatum Game, Dictator Game, Public Goods Game	Market integration, context, wage labor effects—few rejections
13. Hill and Gurven	Paraguay: Ache	Ultimatum Game, Public Goods Game	Context, Public Goods Game–Ultimatum Game comparisons, anonymity effects—no rejections
14. Alvard	Indonesia: Lamalera	Ultimatum Game	Hyper-fair offers, context

theoretical issues relevant to their particular cases. Table 1.1 lists these chapters, summarizing the key topics discussed in each. We think that the diversity of disciplines and theoretical perspectives is one of the strengths of this volume. Project fieldworkers came from a range of theoretical perspectives, including rational choice theory, human behavioral ecology, evolutionary psychology, and cultural evolutionary theory. This diversity is reflected across the chapters. Other than requiring certain analyses and checking that terminology was used uniformly throughout the chapters, no effort has been made to produce a unified theoretical interpretation. There is no party line here, and some authors suggest interpretations that are quite different from those of the editors.

2

Overview and Synthesis

Joseph Henrich, Robert Boyd, Samuel Bowles,
Colin F. Camerer, Ernst Fehr, Herbert Gintis, and
Richard McElreath

The 1980s and 1990s have seen an important shift in the model of human motives used in economics and allied rational actor disciplines (e.g. Caporael *et al.* 1989). In the past, the assumption that actors were rational was typically linked to what we call the *self-ishness axiom*—the assumption that individuals seek to maximize their own material gains in these interactions and expect others to do the same. However, experimental economists and others have uncovered large and consistent deviations from the predictions of the textbook representation of *Homo economicus* (Roth 1995; Fehr and Gächter 2000; Gintis 2000*a*; Camerer 2003). Literally hundreds of experiments in dozens of countries using a variety of experimental protocols suggest that, in addition to their own material payoffs, people have social preferences: subjects care about fairness and reciprocity, are willing to change the distribution of material outcomes among others at a personal cost to themselves, and reward those who act in a pro-social manner while punishing those who do not, even when these actions are costly. Initial skepticism about the experimental evidence has waned as subsequent experiments with high stakes and with ample opportunity for learning failed to substantially modify the initial conclusions.

This shift in the view of human motives has generated a wave of new research. First, and perhaps most important, a number of authors have shown that people deviate from the selfishness axiom and that this can lead to radical changes in the kinds of social behavior that result. For example, Fehr and Gächter (2002) have shown that social preferences leading to altruistic punishment can have very important effects on the levels of social cooperation (Ostrom *et al.* 1992). Second, a number of authors have formulated new models of individual utility functions and other behavioral foundations consistent with the evidence from across a variety of experimental settings (Charness and Rabin 1999; Falk and Fishbacher 1999; Fehr and Schmidt 1999). Finally, these empirical results have motivated a number of attempts to explain the long-term evolutionary success of non-selfish behaviors (Caporael *et al.* 1989; Simon 1990; Sober and Wilson 1994; Gintis 2000*b*, 2003*a*, *b*; Boyd *et al.* 2001; Gintis, Smith, and Bowles 2001; Henrich and Boyd 2001).

Nevertheless, fundamental empirical questions remain unanswered. Are the violations of the selfishness axiom seen in experiments the evidence of universal social preferences? Or, are social preferences modulated by economic, cultural, and social environments? If the latter, which economic and social conditions are involved? Is reciprocal behavior better explained statistically by individuals' attributes such as their sex, age, and relative wealth, or by the attributes of the group to which the individuals belong? Are there cultures that approximate the canonical account of purely self-regarding behavior? Existing research cannot answer such questions because virtually all subjects have been university students, and while there are some cultural differences among student populations throughout the world, these differences are small compared to the full range of human, social, and cultural environments. This work has focused on a far too narrow slice of humanity to allow generalizations about the human species.

A vast amount of ethnographic and historical research suggests that social preferences *are* likely to be influenced by the economic, social, and cultural environment. Humans live in societies with different forms of social organization and institutions, different kinship systems, and diverse ecological circumstances; varying degrees of market integration demonstrate quite different kinds of social behavior. Many of these behavioral patterns *do* seem to reflect local context, circumstances, and culture. However, while ethnographic and historical methods provide rich contextualized details about the lives of individuals and the practices of groups, they can only yield circumstantial evidence about human motives. As the longstanding, fundamental disagreements within the cultural and historical disciplines attest, many different models of human action are consistent with the ethnographic and historical record. True, people live in a dizzying variety of societies. How can we be sure that such differences are evidence for differences in people's motivations. Perhaps they result from differences in ecology and technology? Or, perhaps to historically contingent institutional differences? Without experiments, it is difficult to choose among the many possible hypotheses. In particular, anonymous one-shot experiments allow us to distinguish clearly between behaviors that are instrumental towards achieving other goals (reputations, long term reciprocity, and conformance with social rules for expediency sake) and behaviors that are valued for their own sake.

Accordingly, we undertook a large cross-cultural study of behavior in several standard experimental games (Ultimatum Games, Public Goods Games, and Dictator Games) in which social preferences had been observed in student subjects. Our goal was to use these experiments in combination with ethnographic data to explore the motives that underlie the diversity of human sociality. Twelve experienced field researchers (ten anthropologists, an economist, and a psychologist) recruited subjects from fifteen small-scale societies (from twelve countries on four continents and New Guinea) exhibiting a wide variety of economic and cultural conditions. Our sample consists of three foraging societies, six that practice slash-and-burn horticulture, four nomadic herding groups, and two sedentary, small-scale agricultural societies. Our games were played anonymously, and for real stakes (the local equivalent of one or more days' wages). Both theoretically and methodologically our results pose more questions than they answer. Nevertheless, our data illuminate the nature of human nature, the potential importance of culture, and the appropriateness of the assumption of self-interest that underpins much of social science. This chapter provides an overview and synthesis of the data.[1]

The results of this project, described in detail below, can be summarized in five points: first, there is no society in which experimental behavior is consistent with the canonical model from economics textbooks; second, there is much more variation between groups than has been previously reported; third, differences between societies in Market Integration and the importance of cooperation explain a substantial portion of the behavioral variation between groups; fourth, individual-level economic and demographic variables do not explain behavior within or across groups; and fifth, experimental play often mirrors patterns of interaction

---

[1] Those unfamiliar with game theory or experimental economics may find it useful to begin with Chapter 3.

found in everyday life. Below we first describe the experimental methods used and give brief descriptions of the societies studied. We then present and interpret our results.

THE CROSS-CULTURAL BEHAVIORAL EXPERIMENTS PROJECT

Early cross-cultural economics experiments (Roth *et al.* 1991; Cameron 1999) showed little variation among societies: whether in Pittsburgh, Ljubliana, Yogyakarta, or Tokyo, university students played these games in much the same way. However, in 1996 an anomalous experiment finding broke the consensus: the Machiguenga, slash-and-burn horticulturalists living in the southeastern Peruvian Amazon, behaved much less pro-socially than student populations around the world (Henrich 2000). What then appeared as 'the Machiguenga outlier' sparked curiosity among a group of behavioral scientists: was this simply an odd result, perhaps due to the unusual circumstances of the experiment, or had Henrich tapped real behavioral differences, perhaps reflecting the distinct economic circumstances or cultural environment of this Amazonian society? The cross-cultural behavioral experiments project sought answers to these and many more questions. Here we present the findings thus far. A second round of experiments is currently underway.

The experiments

The field researchers performed three different kinds of economics experiments: Ultimatum Game, a bargaining game, Public Goods Game, and Dictator Game. Every field worker did the Ultimatum Game, several administered some form of the Public Goods Game and three did the Dictator Game. Below, we briefly describe these three games, although interested readers should see Kagel and Roth (1995) and Davis and Holt (1993) for details.

The ultimatum game

The Ultimatum Game is a simple bargaining game that has been extensively studied by experimental economists. In this game, subjects are paired, and the first player, often called the 'proposer', is provisionally allotted a sum of money, the 'pie'. The proposer then can offers any portion of the pie to a second person, often called the 'responder'. The responder, knowing both the offer and the total amount of the pie, then has the opportunity either to accept or reject the proposer's offer. If the responder accepts, he or she receives the amount offered and the proposer receives the remainder (the pie minus the offer). If the responder rejects the offer, then neither player receives anything. In either case, the game ends; the two subjects receive their winnings and depart. Players typically receive payments in cash and remain anonymous to other players, but not to the experimenters (although experimental economists have manipulated both of these variables). In the experiments described here, players were anonymous, and the games involved substantial sums of the appropriate currency. If one assumes that players maximize their income and this is known by all, then responders should accept any positive offer because something is better than nothing. Knowing this, proposers should offer the smallest non-zero amount possible. In every experiment yet conducted the vast majority of subjects have violated this prediction.

The dictator game

The Dictator Game is played exactly like the standard Ultimatum Game, except that the responder is not given an opportunity to accept or reject the offer. The proposer merely dictates the division. In the Dictator Game, positive offers cannot result from a fear of rejection. Thus, when used in conjunction with the Ultimatum Game, this experimental tool allows researchers to determine whether proposers make positive offers out of a 'sense of fairness' or from a 'fear of rejection'.

Public goods games

Public goods experiments are designed to investigate how people behave when individual and group interests conflict. We used two variants: the 'Voluntary Contributions' format and the 'Common-Pool Resources' format, the only difference being that in the former, subjects may contribute to the common good and in the latter may refrain from withdrawing from the common resource for private gain. In the Voluntary Contributions version, players receive some initial monetary endowment. They then have the opportunity to anonymously contribute any portion of their endowment (from zero to the full endowment) to the group fund. Whatever money is in the group fund after all players have had an opportunity to contribute is increased by 50 percent (or sometimes doubled), and then distributed equally among all players regardless of their contribution. The payoff structure of the Common-Pool Resources version is identical, except that instead of receiving an endowment, players can make limited withdrawals from the group fund. Whatever remains in the fund (the common pool) after everyone has withdrawn is increased by 50 percent or doubled, and distributed equally among all group members. The game is not repeated. Free riding is thus the dominant strategy for the selfish subjects—contributing as little or withdrawing as much as possible maximizes their monetary payoffs no matter what the other players do. Thus, selfish players should contribute zero to the group fund (or withdraw their limit in the Common-Pool Resources format).

Ethnographic description

Figure 2.1 shows the locations of each field site, and Table 2.1 provides some comparative ethnographic information about the societies discussed here. In selecting these locations, we included societies both sufficiently similar to the Machiguenga to offer the possibility of replicating the original Machiguenga results, and sufficiently different from one another to provide enough economic and cultural diversity to allow an exploration of the extent to which

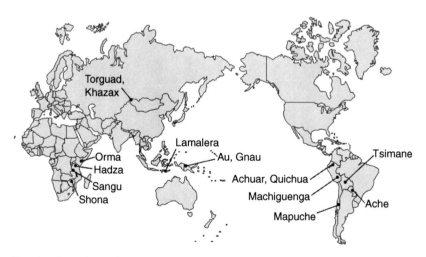

FIG. 2.1. Locations of the societies mentioned in the text

Table 2.1. Ethnographic summary of societies

Group	Language family	Environment	Economic base	Residence	Complexity	Researcher	Settlement Size	Payoffs to Cooperation	Anonymity	Market Integration
Machiguenga	Arawakan	Tropical forest	Horticulture	Bilocal semi-nomadic	Family	Henrich, Smith	250	1	5	4
Quichua	Quichua	Tropical forest	Horticulture	Sedentary/Semi-nomadic	Family	Patton	187	1	1	2
Achuar	Jivaroan	Tropical forest	Horticulture	Sedentary/Semi-nomadic	Family plus extended ties	Patton	187	1	1	2
Hadza	Khoisan/Isolate	Savanna-woodlands	Foraging	Nomadic	Band	Marlowe	75	4	1	1
Ache	Tupi-Guarani	Semi-tropical woodlands	Horticulture/Foraging	Sedentary-nomadic	Band	Hill, Gurven	300	6	3	4
Tsimane	Macro-panoan Isolate	Tropical forest	Horticulture	Semi-nomadic	Family	Gurven	93	1	4	3
Au	Torricelli/Wapei	Mountainous tropical forest	Foraging/Horticulture	Sedentary	Village	Tracer	300	3	2	5

						Tracer				
Gnau	Torricelli/Wapei	Mountainous tropical forest	Foraging/Horticulture	Sedentary	Village	Tracer	300	3	2	5
Mapuche	Isolate	Temperate plains	Small scale farming	Sedentary	Family plus extended ties	Henrich	80	2	6	6
Torguuds	Mongolian	High latitude desert, seasonally-flooded grassland	Pastoralism	Transhumance	Clan	Gil-White	1000	2	9	8
Kazakhs	Turkic	High-latitude desert, seasonally-flooded grassland	Pastoralism	Transhumance	Clan	Gil-White	1000	2	9	8
Sangu	Bantu	Savanna-woodlands, seasonally-flooded grassland	Agro-Pastoralists	Sedentary or Nomadic	Clan-Chiefdom	McElreath	250	5	6	8
Orma	Cushitic	Savanna-woodlands	Pastoralism	Sedentary or Nomadic	Multi-Clan Chiefdom	Ensminger	500	2	10	9
Lamalera	Malayo-Polynesian	Island tropical coast	Foraging–Trade	Sedentary	Village	Alvard	1219	7	8	7
Shona	Niger-Congo	Savanna-woodlands	Farming	Sedentary	Village	Barr	480	5	10	8

behaviors covary with local differences in the structures of social interaction, forms of livelihood, and other aspects of daily life.

In Table 2.1, the 'Economic Base' column provides a general classification of the production system in each society. *Horticulturalists* rely primarily on slash-and-burn agriculture, which involves clearing, burning, and planting small gardens every few years. All the horticulturalists included in this study also rely on a combination of hunting, fishing, and gathering. We have classified the Ache economic base as *Horticulture/Foraging* because they were full-time foragers until about 28 years ago, and still periodically go on multi-week foraging treks, but have spent much of the last few decades as manioc-based horticulturalists. The Au and Gnau of Papua New Guinea are classified as *Foraging/Horticulture* because, despite planting slash and burn gardens, they rely heavily on harvesting wild sago palms for calories, and game for protein. Unlike foragers and horticulturalists, *Pastoralists* rely primarily on herding livestock, often cattle. *Agro-pastoralists* rely on a combination of small-scale sedentary agriculture and herding. We labeled the Orma, Mongols, and Kazakhs as pastoralists because most people in these groups rely entirely on herding, although some members of all three groups do some agriculture. The Sangu are labeled *Agro-pastoralists* because many Sangu rely heavily on growing corn, while others rely entirely on animal husbandry (consequently, in some of our analyses we separate Sangu herders and Sangu farmers).

The 'Residence' column classifies societies according to the nature and frequency of their movement. *Nomadic* groups move frequently, spending as little as a few days in a single location, and as long as a few months. *Semi-nomadic* groups move less frequently, often staying in the same location for a few years. Horticultural groups are often semi-nomadic, moving along after a couple of years in search of more abundant game, fish, wild foods, and fertile soils. *Transhumant* herders move livestock between two or more locations in a fixed pattern over the course of a year, often following the good pasture or responding to seasonal rainfall patterns. *Bilocal* indicates that individuals maintain two residences and spend part of the year at each residence. The Machiguenga, for example, spend the dry season living in villages along major rivers, but pass the wet season in their garden houses, that may be located three or more hours from the village. Classifications of the form *Bilocal–*

Semi-nomadic indicate that the Machiguenga, for example, were traditionally semi-nomadic, but have more recently adopted a bilocal residence pattern. Similarly, the Ache are classified as *Sedentary–Nomadic* because of their transition from nomadic foraging to sedentary horticulture.

The 'Language Family' column provides the current linguistic classification for the language traditionally spoken by these societies, and is useful because linguistic affinity provides a rough measure of the cultural relatedness of two groups. The classification of the Mapuche, Hadza, Tsimane, and New Guinean languages require special comment. There is no general agreement about how to classify Mapuche within the language groups of South America—it is often regarded as a linguistic isolate. Similarly, although it was once thought that Hadza was a Khoisan language, distantly related to the San languages of southern Africa, agreement about this is diminishing. The Tsimane language resembles Moseten (a Bolivian group similar to the Tsimane), but otherwise these two languages seem unrelated to other South American languages (except perhaps distantly to Panoan). Finally, because of the linguistic diversity of New Guinea, we have included both the language phylum for the Au and the Gnau, Torricelli, and their local language family, Wapei.

The 'Complexity' column refers to the anthropological classification of societies according to their political economy (Johnson and Earle 2000). *Family-level* societies consist of economically independent families that lack any stable governing institutions or organizational decision-making structures beyond the family. Societies classified as *Family plus extended ties* are similar to family-level societies, except that such groups also consistently exploit extended kin ties or non-kin alliances for specific purposes such as warfare. In these circumstances decision-making power is *ad hoc*, ephemeral, and diffuse, but high status males often dominate the process. *Bands* consist of both related and unrelated families that routinely cooperate in economic endeavors. Decision-making relies heavily on group consensus, although the opinions of high status males often carry substantial weight. *Clans* and *villages* are both corporate groups of the same level of complexity, and both are usually larger than bands. *Clans* are based on kinship, tracked by lineal descent from a common ancestor. Decision-making power is often assigned based on lineage position, but prestige or achieved status may play a role. *Villages* operate on the same scale of social and political organization as clans, but consist of several unrelated extended families. Decision-making is usually vested in a small cadre of older, high-status men who may compete fiercely for prestige. At a larger scale of organization, *Multiclan corporate* groups are composed of several linked clans, and are governed by a council of older high-status men—assignment to such councils is often jointly determined by lineal descent and achieved prestige. Multiclan corporations sometimes act only to organize large groups in times of war or conflict, and may or may not play important economic role. Often larger than multiclans corporations, *Chiefdoms* are ruled by a single individual or family and contain several ranked clans or villages. Rank of individuals, clans, and villages usually depends on real or customary blood relations to the chief. Economic organization and integration in chiefdoms are more intense than in multiclan corporate groups, and chiefs usually require subjects to pay taxes or tribute. Such payments allow for the large-scale construction of irrigation works, monuments, and public buildings, as well as the maintenance of standing armies. The column labeled 'SS' gives the size of settlements for each of the groups and provides a second measure of social complexity.

The remaining columns, payoffs to cooperation, anonymity, and Market Integration refer to rankings we constructed on the basis of our own and others' ethnographic investigations; we explain these below.

EXPERIMENTAL RESULTS

Because our comparative data on the Ultimatum Game is much more extensive than for the Public Goods Game and Dictator Game, we primarily focus on the Ultimatum Game results.

Substantial cross-cultural variability

The variability in Ultimatum Game behavior across the groups in our study exceeds that in the entire empirical literature. Prior work comparing Ultimatum Game behavior among university students from Pittsburgh, Ljubljana (Slovenia), Jerusalem, Tokyo (Slonim and Roth 1998; Roth *et al.* 1991; Roth 1995), and Yogyakarta (Java, Indonesia) (Cameron 1999) revealed little variation between

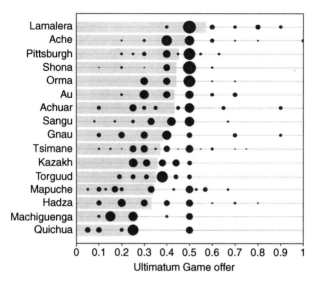

FIG. 2.2. A Bubble Plot showing the distribution of Ultimatum Game offers for each group

Notes: The diameter of the bubble at each location along each row represents the proportion of the sample that made a particular offer. The right edge of the lightly shaded horizontal gray bar is the mean offer for that group. Looking across the Machiguenga row, for example, the mode is 0.15, the secondary mode is 0.25, and the mean is 0.26.

groups. In contrast, Figure 2.2 summarizes our Ultimatum Game results from fifteen different societies. While mean Ultimatum Game offers in experiments with student subjects are typically between 42 and 48 percent, the mean offers from proposers in our sample span a range from 25 to 57 percent—both below and above the typical behavior (Table 2.2 presents additional details). While modal Ultimatum Game offers are consistently 50 percent among university students, in our sample modes vary from 15 to 50 percent.

The behavior of responders in the Ultimatum Game (Figure 2.3) is also much more variable than previously observed. In some groups, rejections are extremely rare, even in the presence of low offers, while in others, rejection rates are substantial, including frequent rejections of 'hyper-fair' offers (i.e. offers above 50 percent). Among the Kazakh, Quichua, Ache, and Tsimane, we observe zero rejections after 10, 14, 51, and 70 proposer offers, respectively. And, while the offers to the Ache were mostly equitable, 47 percent of offers to Tsimane and 57 percent of the offers to

TABLE 2.2. Ultimatum Game experiments

Group	Sample size	Stake	Mean	Mode (% sample)[a]	Rejections	Low rejections[b]
Lamalera[c]	19	10	0.57	0.50 (63)	4/20 (sham)[d]	3/8 (sham)
Ache	51	1	0.48	0.40 (22)	0/51	0/2
Shona (resettled)	86	1	0.45	0.50 (69)	6/86	4/7
Shona (all)	117	1	0.44	0.50 (65)	9/118	6/13
Orma	56	1	0.44	0.50 (54)	2/56	0/0
Au	30	1.4	0.43	0.3 (33)	8/30	1/1
Achuar	14	1	0.43	0.50 (36)	2/15[e]	1/3
Sangu (herders)	20	1	0.42	0.50 (40)	1/20	1/1
Sangu (farmers)	20	1	0.41	0.50 (35)	5/20	1/1
Sangu	40	1	0.41	0.50 (38)	6/40	2/2
Shona (unresettled)	31	1	0.41	0.50 (55)	3/31	2/6
Hadza (big camp)	26	3	0.40	0.50 (35)	5/26	4/5
Gnau	25	1.4	0.38	0.4 (32)	10/25	3/6
Tsimane	70	1.2	0.37	0.5/0.3 (44)	0/70	0/5
Kazakh	10	8	0.36	0.38 (50)	0/10	0/1
Torguud	10	8	0.35	0.25 (30)	1/10	0/0
Mapuche	31	1	0.34	0.50/0.33 (42)	2/31	2/12
Hadza (all camps)	55	3	0.33	0.20/0.50 (47)	13/55	9/21
Hadza (small camps)	29	3	0.27	0.20 (38)	8/29	5/16
Quichua	15	1	0.25	0.25 (47)	0/14[f]	0/3
Machiguenga	21	2.3	0.26	0.15/0.25 (72)	1	1/10

[a] If more than one mode is listed, the first number is the most popular offer and the second number is the second most popular, etc. The % in parentheses is the total proportion of the sample at the mode(s). For example, for the Machiguenga 72% of the sample offered either 0.15 or 0.25.

[b] This is the frequency of rejections for offers equal to or less than 20% of the pie.

[c] In Lamalera, Alvard used pack of cigarettes instead of money to avoid the appearance of gambling. Cigarettes can be exchanged for goods/favors.

[d] Instead of giving responder the actual offers, Alvard gave 20 'sham' offers that range from 10 to 50% (mean sham offer = 30%). These are the frequency of responses to sham offers.

[e] Patton randomly paired Quichua and Achuar players, and as a result there were fourteen Achuar proposers and fifteen Achuar responders.

[f] Patton randomly paired Quichua and Achuar players, and as a result there were fifteen Quichua proposers and fourteen Quichua responders.

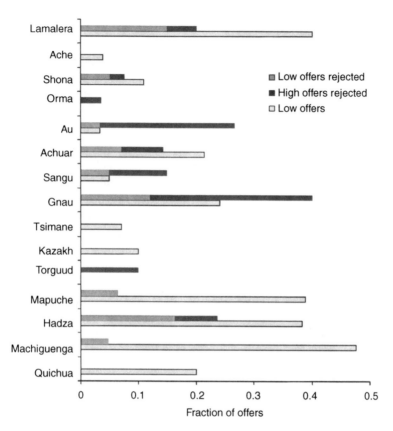

FIG. 2.3. Summary of Ultimatum Game responders' behavior

Notes: The lightly shaded bar gives the fraction of offers that were less than 20% of the pie. The length of the darker shaded bar gives the fraction of all Ultimatum Game offers that were rejected. The length of gray part of the darker shaded bar gives the number of these low offers that were rejected as a fraction of all offers, while the black section of this bar gives the number of high offers rejected as a fraction of all offers. The low offers plotted for the Lamalera were sham offers created by the investigator.

Quichua were at or below 30 percent—yet all were accepted. Similarly, Machiguenga responders rejected only one offer, despite the fact that over 75 percent of their offers were below 30 percent of the pie. At the other end of the rejection scale, Hadza responders rejected 24 percent of all proposer offers and 43 percent (9/21) of offers of 20 percent and below. Unlike the Hadza and other groups who preferentially rejected low offers, the Au and Gnau of Papua New Guinea rejected both unfair *and* hyper-fair offers with nearly equal frequency, a seemingly odd finding which will presently provide considerable insight into the relationship between experimental behavior and daily life. University student responders fall towards the upper end of the rejection scale (with more rejection than average), but still reject less than some groups like the Au, Gnau, Sangu farmers, and Hadza, all of whom rejected positive offers with greater frequency than (e.g.) the Pittsburgh subjects in Roth *et al.* (1991).

As in the Ultimatum Game, Voluntary Contributions and Common-Pool Resources games, which we will collectively call Public Goods Game, also show much greater variation than previously found in Public Goods Games run in industrialized societies, and all these results conflict with the predictions of self-regarding models under standard assumptions. Typical distributions of Public Goods Game contributions from university students have a 'U-shape' with the mode at full defection (those who contribute zero) and a secondary mode at full cooperation (those who contribute everything to the group). The mean contribution is usually between 40 and 60 percent. Table 2.3 shows that our cross-cultural data provides some interesting contrasts with this pattern. The Machiguenga, for example, have a mode at full defection, but lack any fully cooperative contributions—which yields a mean contribution of 22 percent. Both the Aché and Tsimane experiments yielded means between 40 and 60 percent, like folks from industrialized societies, but, unlike industrial societies, they show unimodal distributions with peaks at 50 and 66.7 percent, respectively. Their distributions resemble *inverted* American distributions with few or no contributions at full free riding and full cooperation. Like the Ache and Tsimane, the Orma and Huinca have modes near the center of the distribution, at 40 and 50 percent respectively, but they also show secondary peaks at full cooperation (100 percent)—and no contributions at full defection. Interestingly, the Orma and Huinca distributions resemble the first round of a finite, repeated Public Goods Game done with university students (similar to Fehr and Gächter 2000, for example; see Henrich and Smith, Chapter 5, this volume).

Violations of the selfishness axiom

In one way or another, the selfishness axiom was violated in every society we studied across all three different experimental games

TABLE 2.3. Summary of public good experiments

Group	Format[a]	Group size	MPCR[b]	Sample size	Stake[c] size	Mean	Mode[d] (% sample)	% full cooperation	% full defection
Machiguenga	Common-Pool Resources	4	0.375	21	0.58	0.22	0 (38)	0	38
Swiss[e] strangers	Voluntary Contributions	4	0.375	120	0.1	0.33	0 (45)	14	45
Mapuche	Voluntary Contributions	5	0.40	12	0.33	0.34	0.1 (42)	0	0
Michigan	Common-Pool Resources	4	0.375	64	0.58	0.43	0 (33)	26	33
Tsimané	Voluntary Contributions	4	0.50	134	0.75	0.54	0.67 (17)	1.5	5
Swiss partners	Voluntary Contributions	4	0.375	96	0.1	0.55	1 (24)	24	9.60
Huinca	Voluntary Contributions	5	0.40	12	0.33	0.58	0.5 (25)	17	0
Orma	Voluntary Contributions	4	0.50	24	0.5	0.58	0.40 (37)	25	0
Ache	Voluntary Contributions	5	0.40	64	1	0.65	0.40 (30)	3.1	1.6

[a] Our public goods experiments have two formats with identical payoff structures. In Common-Pool Resources games, each player simultaneously withdraws between zero and some fixed amount from a common pot. Whatever remains in the pot after all the players have withdrawn is increased and distributed equally among all players. In Voluntary Contributions games, players are each endowed with some amount of money. Players then contribute any amount they want, between zero and their endowment, to a common pot (or a 'project'). The amount total contributed to the common pot is increased and distributed equally among all players.

[b] Marginal per capita return.

[c] Stakes sizes are standardized to one-day wage in the local market, so this column is the endowment received by each player divided by one-day's wage.

[d] The % in parentheses is the total proportion of the sample at the mode.

[e] The Swiss data comes from Fehr and Gächter (2000). The 'Swiss' row represents data from the first five rounds of a 'strangers' treatments' in which players never played with the same people more than once. We aggregated this data because the individual rounds were indistinguishable from one other. From the same study, the 'Swiss partners' data is the first round of a ten round game in which players repeatedly played with the same players through all ten rounds.

(Dictator Game, Ultimatum Game, and Public Goods Game). Focusing on the Ultimatum Game, either proposer or responder behavior violated the axiom, or both. Responder behavior was consistent with selfish motives in several groups, but, like university students, Au, Gnau, Sangu farmers, and Hadza subjects rejected positive offers contrary to the prediction of the selfishness axiom. However, as shown in Figure 2.3, responders from the Ache, Tsimane, Machiguenga, Quichua, Orma, Sangu herders, and Kazakhs all have rejection rates of less than 5 percent, roughly consistent with the canonical model. For some groups these low rejection rates are uninformative because all the offers were near 50 percent (e.g. the Ache and Sangu), so no one in the group received low offers. However, proposers in several groups provided numerous low offers that were virtually never rejected. The self-interest axiom accurately predicts responder behavior for about half of our societies, even though it generally fails to predict the responder behavior of university students.

Proposer behavior was consistent with income maximizing behavior among only two groups, Hadza and Sangu Farmers. Among university subjects, it is generally thought that offers are fairly consistent with expected income-maximizing strategies *given* the distribution of rejections across offers (Roth *et al.* 1991). This was not the case in most of the groups we studied. In four groups (Ache, Tsimane, Kazakhs, and Quichua) we could not estimate the income-maximizing offer because there were no rejections. Nevertheless, as discussed above, it seems likely that the substantially lower offers would have been accepted. In two groups (Au and Gnau) the Income-Maximizing Offer could not be established because responders from these groups did not preferentially accept higher offers, which is perhaps an even more striking violation of the selfishness axiom.

For all but one of the remaining societies, estimated Income-Maximizing Offer is higher than observed mean offer.[2] The Income-Maximizing Offer is a useful measure of the frequency with which low offers were rejected. If rejections are few, or if their likelihood of being rejected is not strongly related to the size of the offer, the

[2] A the probability of the rejection as a function of the size of the offer was estimated for each group using logistic regression, and the income maximizing offer was calculated from using this estimate. Due to the small number of rejections some of these estimates are not very precise. For more details see McElreath this volume.

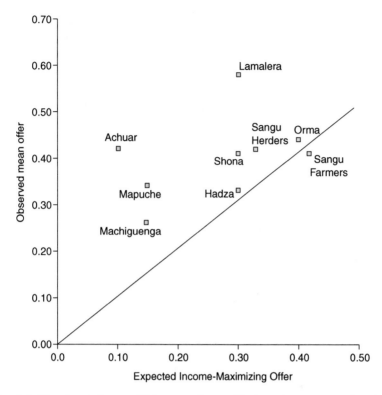

FIG. 2.4. The observed mean Ultimatum Game offer in various groups plotted against the expected Income-Maximizing offer estimated from observed distribution of rejections

Notes: All but one of the points lie above the 45 degree line which gives the expected mean offer under the assumption that people are expected income maximizers. We were unable to estimate the Income-Maximizing Offer for societies with no rejections (Quichua, Tsimane, Ache, Kazakhs), or societies in which rejections bore no systematic relationship to offer (Au, Gnau, Torguuds).

Income-Maximizing Offer will be low (e.g. the Machiguenga). If substantial offers are frequently rejected, the Income-Maximizing Offer will be high (e.g. Sangu farmers). Figure 2.4 compares Income-Maximizing Offer's (calculated from responder data) to actual mean offers (from proposers). The mean offers made by the Sangu (farmers) was slightly less than their Income-Maximizing Offer, and the mean offers made by Hadza and Orma were a little greater than their Income-Maximizing Offer's (but, in both groups responder behavior violates the selfishness axiom). For the other groups, mean offers were all substantially above the Income-Maximizing Offer, ranging from Sangu herders whose mean offers were 130 percent of the Income-Maximizing Offer to the Achuar whose mean offers were 400 percent of the Income-Maximizing Offer. We conclude that the behavior of proposers in our groups generally does not match the prediction based on the selfishness axiom.

It is possible that high offers are consistent with a more conventional extension of the selfishness axiom, namely risk aversion. It is a common (though not universal) observation that people prefer a certain amount of money to a gamble with the same expected payoff. Economists model this behavior by assuming that people seek to maximize their expected utility, and that utility is a concave function of income (diminishing returns). For example, suppose a subject estimates that an offer of 40 percent of the pie will be accepted for sure, and that an offer of 10 percent will be accepted with probability $\frac{2}{3}$. If she were risk averse, she could value the certainty of keeping 60 percent of the pie more than the $\frac{2}{3}$ chance of keeping 90 percent (and a $\frac{1}{3}$ chance of getting nothing). In this case the expected monetary gain is the same for the two offers (60 percent of the pie), but the *expected utility* of the certain outcome is greater. Thus, a highly risk averse subject might make a high offer even if the probability of rejection of a low offer is small.

There are two reasons to doubt that risk aversion explains proposer behavior in our samples. First, the degree of risk aversion necessary to explain the behavior we observed is much higher than is typically seen in gambles for the kinds of stakes used in our experiments. To determine if utility maximization by risk averse proposers could explain our observations, we transformed the game payoffs into utilities using varying levels of risk aversion, and for each group estimated the degree of risk aversion sufficient that the observed mean offer would be utility maximizing.[3] The Hadza and the Sangu farmers were approximately expected income maximizers, and thus their offers are consistent with expected utility maximization for risk neutral individuals. But for the other groups—Orma, Sangu herders, Machiguenga, Mapuche, and

---

[3] See the Appendix of this volume. We modeled risk aversion by expressing a subject's utility as one's payoff raised to the exponent r where an individual for whom $r < 1$ is risk averse, $r = 1$ risk neutral, and $r > 1$ risk preferring. We then found the r for which the observed mean offer maximized the expected utility of the proposers, where the expectation is taken over all possible offers and the estimated likelihood of their being rejected.

Shona—the implied levels of risk aversion are implausible. Even for the least extreme case, the Shona, the necessary degree of risk aversion necessary to make their behavior consistent with expected utility maximization implies that they would be indifferent between an even chance that an offer of one out of ten dollars would be accepted (an expected payoff of US \$4.5) and getting 4 cents with certainty.[4] Clearly, an individual with this level of risk aversion would be unable to function in an uncertain environment. Second, risk aversion was measured directly in the Mapuche and the Sangu by offering subjects a series of risky choices (Henrich and McElreath 2002; Henrich and Smith, Chapter 5, this volume). In both societies, subjects were risk preferring, not risk averse, a fact that casts further doubt on the risk aversion interpretation. We conclude that our offers are not explained by risk aversion in the usual sense intended by economists.

It is quite possible that high offers reflected a desire to avoid rejections in some sense not consistent with the canonical model (e.g. fear that a rejection would be considered an insult or a desire to avoid conflict in the group). These possibilities are discussed below and in several of the following chapters.

Additional evidence against the selfishness axiom comes from our three Dictator Game experiments: the results here are more transparent than for the Ultimatum Game because the proposer is simply giving money away with no possibility of rejection. In each of the three groups in which the Dictator Game was played, offers deviate from the typical behavior of university students and from the predictions of self-regarding models. Mean offers among the Orma, Hadza, and Tsimane, respectively, were 31, 20, and 32 percent of the pie. These mean Dictator offers are 70, 60, and 86 percent of the corresponding mean Ultimatum Game offers for these groups. And, few or none of the subjects in these societies offered zero, while the modal offer among university students is typically zero.

---

[4] Because the numbers of rejections are small, some of our estimates of risk aversion are very imprecise. Accordingly one might worry that more reasonable estimates of risk aversion might fit the data nearly as well as the best fit. To test for this possibility, we computed the difference between likelihood of the best-fit value of r and 0.81, the value estimated by Tversky and Kahneman (1992) for laboratory data on risky decision-making. For some data sets the difference was small, and others quite large. Moreover, there is a positive but nonsignificant correlation between deviation of observed behavior from the Income-Maximizing Offer and this measure of the precision of the estimate of r. Thus, it seems unlikely that risk aversion can be a complete explanation for our observations.

Finally, the results from all six of our Public Goods Games also conflict with the selfishness axiom, with means ranging from 22 percent among the Machiguenga to 65 percent among the Ache (Table 2.3). Except for the Machiguenga (and student populations), no group has more than 5 percent full defectors.

EXPLAINING DIFFERENCES IN BEHAVIOR ACROSS GROUPS

We first attempted to determine whether any attributes of individuals were statistically associated with proposer offers across our sample. One reflection of the diversity of the societies in our study is the paucity of quantifiable individual-level variables that are available and meaningful across the populations we studied. Among the measured individual attributes that we thought might statistically explain offers were the proposer's sex, age, level of formal education, and their wealth relative to others in their group.[5] In pooled regressions using all offers we found that none of these individual measures predicted offers once we allowed for group level differences in offers (by introducing dummy variables for each of our groups). Since the group dummies account for about 12 percent of the variance of individual offers, we conclude that group differences are important. However, for the moment we remain agnostic about the role of individual differences. Our pooled regression tested for common effects of these variables across all the groups and hence does not exclude the possibility that the individual differences we have measured may predict behaviors in different ways from group to group. We return to this possibility below.

We speculated that the large between-group differences in offers might reflect differences among groups in the ways that group-members typically interact in the pursuit of their livelihood, in governance of their common affairs, and in other respects. In our efforts to understand why groups might vary so much in their game play, we ranked our societies in six categories: First, Payoffs to

---

[5] Relative wealth was measured by the in-group percentile ranking of each individual, with the measure of individual wealth varying among groups: for the Orma and Mapuche we used the total cash value of livestock, while among the Au, Gnau, and Machiguenga we used total cash cropping land. Estimates using relative wealth were restricted to proposers in the seven groups for which we have wealth data.

Cooperation—what is the potential benefit to cooperative as opposed to solitary or family-based productive activities? Groups like the Machiguenga and Tsimane are ranked the lowest because they are almost entirely economically independent at the family level—no one's economic well-being depends on cooperation with non-relatives. In contrast, the economy of the whale hunters of Lamalera depends on the cooperation of large groups of non-relatives. Second, Market Integration—do people engage frequently in market exchange? Hadza were ranked low because their life would change little if markets suddenly disappeared. Others, like the Orma herders are ranked higher because they frequently buy and sell livestock, and work for wages. Third, Anonymity—how important are anonymous roles and transactions? While many Achuar of the Ecuadorian Amazon never interact with strangers, the Shona of Zimbabwe frequently interact with people they do not know and may never see again. Fourth, *privacy*—how well can people keep their activities secret from others? In groups like the Au, Gnau, and Hadza, who live in small villages or bands and eat in public, it's nearly impossible to keep secrets and it's quite difficult to hide anything of value. Among the Hadza, simply having pants substantially increases privacy because they have pockets (which is a reason for their popularity among some Hadza). In contrast, Mapuche farmers live in widely scattered houses and maintain strict rules about approaching another's house without permission, so privacy is substantial. Fifth, *sociopolitical complexity*—how much does centralized decision-making occur above the level of the household? Because of the importance in the anthropological literature of the conventional classifications of societies by their political complexity (Johnson and Earle 2000), we ranked our societies from family level through chiefdoms and states. And sixth, *settlement size*—what is the size of local settlements? This value ranged from less than 100 in among the Hadza to more than 1,000 for the Lamalera.

Before we began the collective analysis we ranked the groups along the first four dimensions (all but Sociopolitical Complexity and Settlement Size) using the following procedure: during a meeting of the research team, we had a lengthy discussion of the underlying attributes that each dimension was designed to capture. Then, the field researchers lined up and sorted themselves by repeatedly comparing the characteristics of the group that they studied with their two neighbors in line, switching places if necessary, and repeating the process until no one wanted to move.[6] Our Sociopolitical Complexity rankings were generated by both Henrich (who was not blind to our experimental results) and, Allen Johnson, an outside expert on societal complexity, who was blind to our results. Henrich's and Johnson's rankings correlated 0.9, and explain nearly identical amounts of the variation in mean Ultimatum Game offers. The subjective nature of the resulting ordinal measures is quite clear. Actual Settlement Sizes were measured by the fieldworkers, and then ranked to be compatible with other ranked variables.

We assume that these indices are exogenous in the sense that the behavioral patterns generated by our experimental subjects are not also causes of the aspects of groups we have captured in our indices. It is for this reason, for example, that we sought to measure the *potential* Payoffs to Cooperation—viewed as a characteristic of the local ecology rather than the amount of cooperation actually practiced which depends on choices of the inhabitants. While plausible, this assumption could be false. Societies adhering to a norm of egalitarian sharing, for example, often sustain the custom of eating in public, a practice that makes the food sharing process transparent, minimizes monitoring costs, and reduces the likelihood of conflicts over divisions. Thus, across a sample of groups, generous proposer offers reflecting a group norm of sharing might vary inversely with the degree of privacy as we have measured it, but the causal relationship would be from the sharing norm to privacy rather than the reverse.

As can be seen in Table 2.4, four of these indices, Market Integration, Anonymity, social complexity, and Settlement Size, are highly correlated across groups suggesting that they may all result from the same causal factors. The correlation of each of these variables with the potential Payoffs to Cooperation is very small, suggesting that this ranking measures a second set of causal factors. In retrospect, this should not have been surprising. An increase in social scale is associated with a shift to market based economy, and an increase in Anonymity. However, within small scale societies with similar levels of social complexity, there is a wide range of economic systems with varying levels of cooperation. To capture

---

[6] This procedure was suggested by Abigail Barr who had used it in her fieldwork.

TABLE 2.4. Correlation matrix among predictor variables

	PC	AN	MI	PR	SS
SC	0.242	0.778	0.913	0.374	0.670
PC	—	− 0.063	0.039	− 0.320	0.165
AN		—	0.934	0.743	0.664
MI			—	0.644	0.731
PR				—	0.328
SS					—

TABLE 2.5. Regression coefficients and statistics

	Unstandardized beta coefficients		Standardized beta coefficients	t-statistic	Sig.
	β	Std. error	β		
(Constant)	0.261	0.036		7.323	0.000
PC	0.021	0.007	0.528	2.922	0.011
AMI	0.012	0.005	0.448	2.479	0.027

SC = Socio-Political Complexity; PC = Payoffs to Cooperation; AN = Anonymity; PR = Privacy; SS = Settlement Size; MI = Market Integration; AMI = Aggregate Market Integration

the causal effects of this nexus of variables, we created a new index of 'aggregate market integration' by averaging the ranks of Market Integration, Settlement Size, and Sociopolitical Complexity. (We did not include Anonymity because it is so similar to Market Integration; including it only changes the results slightly.)

We estimated ordinary least squares regression equations for explaining group mean Ultimatum Game offer using the Payoffs to Cooperation and Aggregate Market Integration. Both their normalized regression coefficients are highly significant and indicate that a standard deviation difference in either variable results in roughly half a standard deviation difference in the group mean offers (Table 2.5, Figure 2.5). Together, these two variables account for 47 percent of the variation among societies in mean Ultimatum Game offers. All regressions using Payoffs to Cooperation and one of the other predictors (Anonymity, Market Integration,

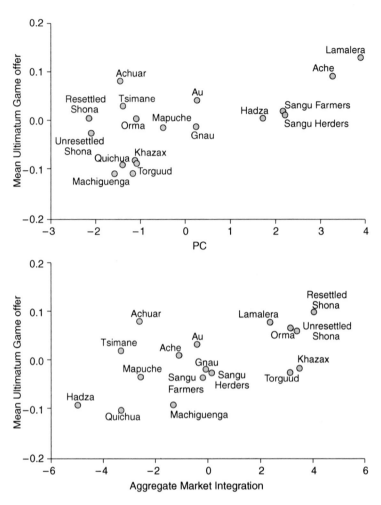

FIG. 2.5. Partial regression plots of mean Ultimatum Game offer as a function of indexes of Payoffs to Cooperation and Market Integration

Notes: The vertical and horizontal axes are in units of standard deviation of the sample. Because Aggregate Market Integration and Payoffs to Cooperation are not strongly correlated, these univariate plots give a good picture of the effect of the factors captured by these indexes on the Ultimatum Game behavior.

Sociopolitical Complexity, and Settlement Size) yielded a significant positive coefficient for Payoffs to Cooperation and a positive, near significant coefficient for the other variable. If we use the Income-Maximizing Offer as a predictor of the Ultimatum Game offers along with Payoffs to Cooperation and Aggregate Market Integration, its coefficient is smaller (in magnitude), negative and insignificant, while the coefficients of Payoffs to Cooperation and Aggregate Market Integration remain large and close to significance (even though now there are only nine cases), suggesting that the effects of economic structure and cultural differences captured by Payoffs to Cooperation and Aggregate Market Integration do not substantially influence offers through the Income-Maximizing Offer.

The same two variables (Payoffs to Cooperation and Aggregate Market Integration) also predict the group average Income-Maximizing Offer; the effect sizes are large (normalized regression coefficients about one half) but very imprecisely estimated (significant only at the 20 percent level). Taken at face value, these estimates suggest that the subjects' expectation that low offers will be rejected covaries with both the benefits of cooperation and Aggregate Market Integration.

Our analysis of the individual level responder data across all groups reveals some of the same basic patterns observed in the proposer data. A responder's age, sex, and relative wealth do not affect an individual's likelihood of rejecting an offer. What does matter is the proportion of the stake offered, and the responders' ethnolinguistic group.

EXPLAINING INDIVIDUAL DIFFERENCES WITHIN GROUPS

In contrast to the surprising power of our group level measures in statistically explaining between-group differences in experimental behaviors, our individual level variables explain little of the variation between individuals in experimental play. With a few group-specific exceptions, nothing that we measured about the individuals other than their group membership (or village, camp, or other subgroup membership) predicted experimental play. It is possible, of course, that the unexplained within group variance in experimental behaviors reflects subjects' lack of comprehension of the game or errors in experimental play that are unrelated to measures like age, education, or wage labor participation. We return to this issue below, when we discuss concerns about our experimental methods. Here we summarize our findings concerning individual attributes and experimental play.

Sex, wealth, and age do not account for any significant portion of the variance in game play *within* groups. However, sex was marginally significant among the Tsimane, where males offer 10 percent more than females. And among the Hadza, women's Ultimatum Game offers strongly increased with camp population size, but camp size was not important to men's offers. Conversely, in the Dictator Game, it was the offers of Hadza men that increased with camp size—although this may be an artifact (Marlowe, Chapter 6, this volume). As in the Ultimatum Game, Public Goods Game data from five societies also reveal no significant effects of sex, except among Ache men who contribute a bit more than women. Similarly, wealth, in any form (e.g. cash, cows, land), does not predict game behavior. In several circumstances, multiple measures of wealth (e.g. animal wealth, cash, and land wealth) were gathered and analyzed, as well as an aggregate measure. In these within-group analyses, wealth emerged as significant only once in twelve different data sets (including both Ultimatum Game and Public Goods Game datasets). The exception arises from an all-male Public Goods Game among the Orma. Controlling for age, education, income, and residence pattern (sedentary versus nomadic), wealth was the only significant predictor of contributions in a multivariate linear regression, with a standard deviation difference in wealth predicting well over half a standard deviation difference in contributions—we make sense of this finding below.

Several researchers also gathered and analyzed measures of the number of years of formal schooling subjects had. Analyzing Ultimatum Game data from the Sangu, Orma, Mapuche, Au, and Gnau, we find that the extent of schooling does not account for any significant portion of the variation in offers in either bivariate analyses or multivariate regression that controlled for sex, age, and wealth. Among the Tsimane, the extent of formal education emerges as marginally significant in a multivariate regression involving age, village, sex, Spanish-speaking ability, trips to the nearest market town, and Wage Labor participation. More educated Tsimane offer less in the Ultimatum Game game. However, we find no effect of formal education on Public Goods Game play in the Tsimane. Thus, while schooling effects may exist in a few cases, they are not particularly strong or consistent across games or societies.

Although our group level measure of Market Integration has impressive statistical power, individual level measures of market exposure do not explain any significant proportion of the variation within groups. To assess market exposure, some of the researchers gathered data on individuals' participation in Wage Labor, their reliance on cash cropping, and their competence in the national language. Wage Labor participation shows no significant relation to offers in the Ultimatum Game in five of the six groups in which it was tested—the Tsimane, Ache, Gnau, Au, Machiguenga, and Mapuche. In these groups, individuals who participate in Wage Labor make offers that are indistinguishable from those who do not. Public Goods Game data from the Orma, Ache, Machiguenga, and Tsimane also indicate that Wage Labor does not affect game play. The only clear exception to the Wage Labor pattern occurs in the Orma Ultimatum Game data, where individuals who have participated in Wage Labor make significantly higher offers than those who had not.

In societies based on agriculture, another measure of Market Integration is the amount of land an individual (or household) devotes to cash cropping, as opposed to subsistence cropping. We have cash cropping data from three societies. Among the Machiguenga, land (in hectares or as a proportion of total land) devoted to cash cropping is highly correlated with Ultimatum Game offers; its normalized partial regression coefficient when age, sex, and Wage Labor are controlled remains substantial, though its significance level is marginal. Neither cash cropping land nor the proportion of land devoted to cash cropping is significantly related to Ultimatum Game offers for the Au and Gnau. However, among the Au (but not the Gnau) multivariate regressions show that land devoted to *subsistence* cropping positively predicts Ultimatum Game offers, controlling for sex, age, Cash Cropping Land, and Wage Labor.

In many places, an individual's degree of competence in the national language may also represent a measure of Market Integration, or at least of market exposure. Unfortunately, we only have language data from one society, the Tsimane. Comparing the sample of the most fluent Spanish speakers (who are also the most likely to be educated outside the village) against all others, more fluent speakers offered more in the Ultimatum Game than less fluent speakers. However, using multivariate regression to control for village membership, sex, age, visits to San Borja, years of formal education, and participation in Wage Labor, we find no relationship between

Spanish-speaking ability and Ultimatum Game offers. Furthermore, in the Tsimane Public Goods Game, competence in the national language also does not predict contributions, using the same controls.

As is the case for all of our individual level data, except for age and sex, these measures capture individual behaviors that may well be endogenous with respect to the beliefs or preferences our experiments measure. Because it is possible that these measures are the consequence rather than the cause of individual behavioral differences, we were also able to use geographical measures of proximity to market opportunities as exogenous instruments for measuring market exposure in three groups: Tsimane, Au, and Gnau. However, none of these were significant predictors of proposer behavior.

Given that we sought individual level statistical associations for a number of variables in fifteen societies and found just a handful of estimates suggesting substantial effects, we conclude that, other than group membership, the individual level facts we have collected about our subjects do not consistently predict how individuals will behave. This does not mean that within-group variation in subjects' behavior cannot be explained; rather, it suggests that the explanation may be group-specific and/or that we may not have collected the appropriate individual information. It is also possible that variation within groups is explained by individual genetic differences uncorrelated with our regressors (Sherman *et al.* 1997), even though variation between groups probably results entirely from economic, social, or cultural differences.

LOCAL GROUP EFFECTS

Our analysis suggests that group effects may be important, and this opens the question of how to define a group. In the above analyses, we used ethnolinguistic markers to define group membership, but non-ethnolinguistic regional groupings, or smaller local groupings (e.g. villages) may be more appropriate. Our data allow several comparisons. Such small-scale tests allow us to control for a number of variables, including climate, language, regional/national economy, local buying power of the game stakes, and local history. In the Bolivian Amazon, the effects of Market Integration and local groups were explored by performing the Ultimatum Game and Public Goods Game in five different communities at different distances from the market town of San Borja, the only source of commercial goods, medicines, and Wage Labor opportunities. Like the Machiguenga, the Tsimane live in small communities scattered along a major riverine drainage system. In this situation, physical distance (in travel time along the river) from San Borja acts as an exogenous proxy measure for the extent of market contact of different Tsimane communities. The results indicate that a community's distance from San Borja is unrelated to Ultimatum Game or Public Goods Game behavior. Interestingly, the best predictor for Ultimatum Game proposer behavior and Public Goods Game contributions is what community one is from, *independent* of the community's distance from San Borja and population size. So, Tsimane lifeways matter, but small differences in both individual-level measures of Market Integration and community-level market variables apparently do not. Among the Tsimane, the relevant group for predicting Ultimatum Game and Public Goods Game behavior appears to be smaller than the ethnolinguistic group.

As with the Tsimane, we were surprised to find a number of cases in which group membership effects were strong even in the absence of geographical isolation, suggesting that the processes that generate behavioral differences among groups can maintain differences between frequently interacting, intermixing, and even intermarrying groups. In Chile, Mapuche farmers and non-Mapuche Chilean townspeople, locally called Huinca, have lived side by side, intermarried, and interacted for about 100 years. Yet, the Mapuche and the Huinca behave quite differently in a single-shot Public Goods Game. The Mapuche contributed a mean of 33 percent to the pot, while the Huinca offered an average of 58 percent. Moreover, in Ecuador the Achuar and Quichua of Conambo, who interact and intermarry frequently, play the Ultimatum Game quite differently—Achuar proposers offered a mean of 43 percent while Quichua offered only 25 percent. This difference is especially notable as Quichua and Achuar subjects were randomly paired, so the proposers from the two groups faced the same probability of rejection. As mentioned above, the single biggest predictor of both Ultimatum Game and Public Goods Game offers among the Tsimane was village membership. In Tanzania, Hadza from the biggest camp (which was three times larger than the next largest camp) played the Ultimatum Game much more like university students than Hadza from the four smaller camps, despite the fact that camps are ephemeral social units and camp membership is quite fluid. For the

Hadza, camp population size turns out to be the best predictor of Ultimatum Game offers—the larger the camp, the higher the mean Ultimatum Game offer. Finally, although Sangu herders and farmers make similar Ultimatum Game offers, farmers reject offers significantly more frequently than herders. Yet, Sangu often change from farmer to herder and back again in the course of one lifetime.

Interestingly, however, in some of our other research locations group membership displayed no predictive power. In Mongolia, Torguud Mongols and Kazakhs are separated by deep cultural and historical differences, yet they play the Ultimatum Game similarly. In Papua New Guinea the Au and Gnau, who speak mutually unintelligible languages and show differing degrees of market incorporation, played the Ultimatum Game in the same unusual manner (making and frequently rejecting offers of more than half the pie). In Zimbabwe, resettled Shona live in villages that were made up of strangers at their inception two decades ago, while unresettled Shona live in villages comprised of families that have lived side by side for generations. Nonetheless, there are only slight differences in Ultimatum Game behavior among resettled and unresettled groups.

In general, the micro-level variation we observed contrasts with the Ultimatum Game results from the United States and Europe in which university students, who speak different languages and live thousands of miles apart, behave quite similarly. Of course, it is possible that variation exists within contemporary societies, but this variation is not represented in university populations. However, experiments with subjects outside of universities in western societies have thus failed to uncover behavioral patterns in the Ultimatum Game much different from those observed among university students, although Dictator Game behavior appears quite different (Smith 2001).

EXPERIMENTAL BEHAVIOR AND EVERYDAY LIFE

Group-level measures of economic and social structure statistically explain much of the between-group variance in experimental play. This suggests that there might be a relationship between behavior in our games and common patterns of interaction in daily life. In a number of cases the parallels are quite striking, and in some cases our subjects readily discerned the similarity, and were able to articulate it. The Orma, for example, immediately recognized that the Public Goods Game was similar to the *harambee*, a locally initiated contribution that Orma households make when a community decides to construct a public good such as a road or school. They dubbed the experiment 'the *harambee* game' and gave generously (mean 58 percent with 25 percent full contributors).

Recall that among the Au and Gnau of Papua New Guinea many proposers offered more than half the pie, and many of these offers were rejected. The rejection of seemingly generous offers may have a parallel in the culture of status-seeking through gift-giving found in Au and Gnau villages, and throughout Melanesia. In these groups, accepting gifts, even unsolicited ones, implies a strong obligation to reciprocate at some future time. Unrepaid debts accumulate, and place the receiver in a subordinate status. Further, the giver may demand repayment at times, or in forms (political alliances), not to the receiver's liking—but the receiver is still obliged to respond. Consequently, excessively large gifts, especially unsolicited ones, will frequently be refused because of concern about the obligation to reciprocate.

Among the whale hunters on the island of Lamalera of Indonesia, 63 percent of the proposers in the Ultimatum Game divided the pie equally, and most of those who did not offered more than half (the mean offer was 57 percent of the pie). In real life, when a Lamalera whaling crew returns with a whale or other large catch, a specially designated person meticulously divides the prey into pre-designated parts allocated to the harpooner, crew members, and others participating in the hunt, as well as the sailmaker, members of the hunters' corporate group, and other community members (who make no direct contribution to the hunt). Because the size of the pie in the Lamalera experiments was the equivalent of 10 days' wages, making an experimental offer in the Ultimatum Game may have seemed like dividing a whale.

Similarly, in Paraguay the Ache regularly share meat. During this sharing, the hunters responsible for the catch commonly forgo their share, while the prey is distributed equally among all other households. There is no consistent relationship between the amount a hunter brings back and the amount his family receives (Kaplan and Hill 1985). Successful hunters often leave their prey outside the camp to be discovered by others, carefully avoiding any hint of boastfulness. When asked to divide the Ultimatum Game pie, Ache proposers may have perceived themselves as dividing the game they or a male member of their family had acquired, thereby leading 79 percent of the Ache proposers to offer either half or 40 percent, and 16 percent to offer more than 50 percent, with no rejected offers.

By contrast, the low offers and high rejection rates of the Hadza, another group of small-scale foragers, are not surprising in light of numerous ethnographic descriptions of these people (Woodburn 1968; Marlowe 2002; Blurton-Jones, personal communication). Although the Hadza extensively share meat (and other foods to a lesser degree), they do not do so without complaint; many look for opportunities to avoid sharing. Hunters sometimes wait on the outskirts of camp until nightfall so they can sneak meat into their shelter without being seen. It seems the Hadza share because they fear the social consequences that would result from not sharing. Cooperation and sharing is enforced by a fear of punishment that comes in the form of informal social sanctions, gossip, and ostracism. Many Hadza proposers attempted to avoid sharing in the game and many of them were punished by rejection. Thus, we find two foraging peoples—the Ache and the Hadza—at opposite ends of the Ultimatum Game spectrum in both proposers' offers and responders' rejections; their contrasting behaviors seem to reflect their differing patterns of everyday life, not any underlying logic of hunter-gatherer life ways.

Similarly, the life ways of our two family-level societies are reflected in their game behavior. Both the Machiguenga and Tsimane live in societies with little cooperation, exchange, or sharing beyond the family unit. Ethnographically, both show little fear of social sanctions and seem to care little about public opinion. The Machiguenga, for example, did not even have personal names until recently—presumably because there was little reason to refer to people outside of one's kin circle. Consequently, it's not surprising that in anonymous experimental interactions both groups made low Ultimatum Game offers. Given that the Tsimane Ultimatum Game offers vary from village to village, it would be interesting to know if these differences reflect village-level differences in real prosocial behavior.

Like many other small-scale agriculturalists, the Mapuche's relations with their neighbors are characterized by mutual suspicion, envy, and fear of being envied. The Mapuche believe that illness, death, and bad luck are caused by the malevolent magic of spiteful neighbors and acquaintances, or sometimes merely by the unintentional power of envious others. Material wealth and good fortune result from trickery, taking advantage of others, and making deals with spirits—not from hard work, courage, or intelligence. Households keep secrets if they can, and many norms are maintained by fear of social sanctions, not general goodwill. This pattern of social interaction and cultural beliefs is consistent with the Mapuche's postgame interviews in the Ultimatum Game. Unlike University of California, Los Angeles students, Mapuche proposers rarely claimed that their offers were influenced by a sense of fairness. Instead, most proposers based their offers on a fear of rejection. Even proposers who made hyper-fair offers claimed that they feared rare spiteful responders, who would be willing to reject even 50/50 offers.

Discussions of experimental behavior and everyday life commonly address the real world predictive power of experimental play (Loewenstein 1999). Our concern here has been more modest: to determine if there might be analogous patterns of behavior in the experiments and in the daily life of our subjects. In many societies it appears that there are and that our subjects were aware of the parallels in some cases. But this modest observation begs the causal question: why did our subjects behave as they did?

DISCUSSION

Research methods

It is possible that the diversity of behaviors we observe is an artifact of our experimental methods in these unusual settings. The problems we faced in this respect are different in degree, not in kind, from those confronting any attempt to make inferences about behavioral patterns from experimental data in university laboratories. We were especially mindful of the fact that individual differences in experimental play may arise from a combination of dispositional differences and differences in the way the experimental situation itself is framed. Such framing effects may have been quite strong in our case because of the oddity of the experimental situation to most of our subjects, who have had little experience with abstract games. Moreover, for many of our subjects it is unusual to interact with anyone from outside their own ethnolinguistic community, as the experimenters were. Although the considerations raised below highlight some of the difficulties of cross-cultural experimental work, we think the experienced fieldworkers who administered the experiments anticipated and addressed these difficulties for the most part.

First, the administration of the experiments in novel settings may have given rise to misunderstandings, often rooted in different implicit assumptions. For example, in a pregame pilot study, some Mongolian subjects believed that by accepting Ultimatum Game offers they would be taking money away from the experimenter, while other subjects, even after being clearly told otherwise, did not believe that they would actually be paid real money. The Mongolian results reported here are from a second round of experiments in which these confusions were eliminated by painstaking, repeated instruction and testing. In most cases, experimenters tested subjects for game comprehension before the experiments were implemented, and excluded those who had difficulty grasping the game. In several cases, experimenters used postgame interviews to probe for possible misunderstandings and faulty assumptions. Among the Mapuche, players were ranked according to how well they understood the strategic nature of the game, and how well they were able to do the mathematical calculations involved. After excluding those with inadequate understanding and computational competence, the behavior of the remaining players was not statistically related to their ranking. Similarly, among the Hadza, each player was scored according to the number of practice examples it took for them to learn the game (i.e. to give correct answers to hypothetical test examples). Among Hadza men this measure is unrelated to both Ultimatum Game proposer and responder behavior, but for women comprehension is positively and significantly correlated with offer size. We do not know if the covariation of comprehension and experimental behavior among Hadza women represents the effect of comprehension *per se*, and hence, represents a problem of experimental design or implementation, or results from the association of comprehension with other correlates of game play for women, such as camp size (a strong predictor of Hadza women's offers).

Another methodological problem in interpreting the cross-cultural results comes from possible experimenter bias. In several cases, the relationship between the experimenter and the participants is much closer, more personal, and longer lasting than in typical university-based experiments. Consequently, it is possible that ethnographers may bias the results of these experiments in different ways than experimenters usually affect the results. Henrich (2000) attempted to control for some of this effect by replicating the Machiguenga Ultimatum Game protocol with University of California, Los Angeles anthropology graduate students. In this control, Henrich and his subjects were all known to one another, had interacted in the past, and would interact again in the future. His results were quite similar to typical Ultimatum Game results in high stakes games among university students, and substantially different from the Machiguenga. This is certainly not a complete control for experimenter bias, but it does control for some elements of the bias. To test for experimenter bias across our samples, we examined the relationship between the time each experimenter had spent in the field prior to administering the games and the mean Ultimatum Game of each group, but found no consistent pattern in the data. Nonetheless, we cannot entirely exclude the possibility that some of the observed between-group differences are the result of differences among the experimenters and the manner in which the experiments were implemented. Our next round of experiments further addresses this concern.

Third, the fact that most, but not all, of our experiments were played for money is likely to have affected experimental behavior. In most societies, money is a powerful framing device: the fact that substantial sums of money are changing hands is a strong cue about the nature of the interaction. We see no reason to think that our subjects were any less eager to pick up cues about appropriate behavior in these experimental situations than university students. In Lamalera, for example, packs of cigarettes were used instead of money to avoid the appearance of gambling—cigarettes are highly valued and can be exchanged for money or favors. We do not know if the many hyper-fair offers made by these whale hunters would have been observed had the pie been denominated in money, or how experimental play might have been affected had the pie been denominated in whale meat. Ethnographic evidence suggests that distinct sharing rules pertain to different goods—meat and honey are meticulously shared among the Ache, for example, but goods purchased with money and manioc are not. Experimental play with university students and other data suggest that the means by which a valued resource is acquired influences how it is divided, perhaps because different means of acquisition cue different sharing rules. Goods acquired by chance may be governed by sharing rules that do not apply to goods acquired by labor, and it seems likely that the experimental pie would be seen as a good acquired by chance. Our subsequent work will explicitly examine the effect of different mediums of exchange on game play.

Fourth, some ethnographers had to modify the standardized game procedures. Three researchers instructed their subjects in large groups on how to play the games, rather than in the one-on-one scenarios employed by the other ethnographers (note, this variant makes no difference for university students) (Henrich 2000; Henrich and Smith, Chapter 5, this volume). In another case, to facilitate the game explanation, Hill used explicit analogies to real life social interactions to clarify the games.

And fifth, in an effort to collect rejection data, Alvard and Gil-White made sham offers to responders, instead of presenting the actual proposers' offers. It's unclear how these methodological differences may have influenced the overall results, although among US university students, behavior in both the Ultimatum Game and Public Goods Game is not very sensitive to such methodological modifications.

Some have suggested that the common violations of the canonical model in these one-shot games arose because the subjects simply had no experience with one-shot interactions in their own lives, and thus treated these games *as if* they were repeated. Had the subjects interpreted these experiments in this way, they might have imagined being in the role of responder in some subsequent round, possibly paired with the same partner, and made generous offers (or rejected low offers) to affect the subsequent behavior of this imagined future partner. However, we do not find this interpretation compelling for several reasons. First, extensive postgame interviews by several of our researchers indicate that our subjects did comprehend the one-shot aspect of the games. Second, in some experimental comparisons between one-shot and repeated games, most university students demonstrate clear strategic adjustments as they move from one-shot to repeated contexts (e.g. in gift exchange games, Gächter and Falk 2001), indicating that they can perceive a difference—although this does not occur in the Ultimatum Game (Roth *et al.* 1991). Nevertheless, this shows that subjects can, in general, recognize the difference between one-shot and repeated games. Third, when opportunities for reputation-building are incorporated into a series of one-shot Ultimatum Game plays, university students make predictable strategic adjustments compared to a series of one-shot games without reputation-building (Fehr and Gächter 2000), which again indicates that they can perceive the difference. Finally, it is important to remember that half of our societies generated mean Ultimatum Game offers between the predictions of the canonical model (near zero) and university students. So, if people make generous offers in one-shot games because they believe (in some sense) that they are playing a repeated game, then university students must understand the one-shot nature of the game *less* well than the uneducated people in our small-scale societies. Such a claim would be particularly odd, given that university students participate in real one-shot interactions much more frequently than most of our subjects. For these reasons, we believe our results are neither experimental artifacts nor were they caused by our subjects' inability to distinguish between one-shot and repeated interactions.

Interpretation

Our data suggest that these between-group behavioral differences, which all violate the selfishness axiom, are the product of the patterns of social and economic interaction that frame the everyday lives of our subjects. There are at least four ways that patterns of social interaction could have these effects (Bowles 1998).

Task performance effects   Economic and social institutions structure the tasks people must perform to make a living, and to remain in 'good standing' in the relevant community. There is ample evidence from experiments, industrial sociology, and ethnography, that commonly performed tasks affect values, and that these values are generalized far beyond the immediate domains of task performance. In experimental work, Sherif (1937) and others have shown that the performance of cooperative tasks (in which success depends on the efforts of many and the rewards are shared) induces positive sentiments toward those with whom one cooperates, while competitive tasks produce the opposite effect. From sociology and ethnography, the degree of autonomy one exercises in making a living, for example, is strongly associated with child rearing values in industrial societies (Kohn 1990) and simple societies (Barry, Child, and Bacon 1959).

Framing and situational construal   Economic and social institutions are situations in the social psychological sense and thus have framing and other situation construal effects (Ross and Nisbett 1991). Economists typically represent a choice situation by a set of feasible actions, beliefs concerning the consequences of actions, and an evaluation of the consequences according to exogenous preferences. But the institutions that define feasible actions may also alter beliefs about consequences of actions and the evaluation of these consequences. For example, a market-oriented society may develop distinct cognitive capacities and habits. The fact that almost everything has a price in market-oriented societies provides a cognitive simplification not available to people in societies where money plays a lesser role: namely, allowing the aggregation of disparate objects using a monetary standard as in '$50 of groceries'. To take another example, extensive market interactions may accustom individuals to the idea that interactions with strangers may be mutually beneficial. By contrast, those who do not customarily deal with strangers in mutually advantageous ways may be more likely to treat anonymous interactions as hostile or threatening, or as occasions for the opportunistic pursuit of self-interest. Experiments in industrial societies have shown that contextual cues can significantly change the contributions of undergraduates in social dilemmas. For example, Pillutla and Chen (1999) used two versions of a Public Goods Game—one construed as a joint investment and the other as a contribution to a social event. Players contributed significantly more to the social event than to the investment despite the fact that the two versions had the same payoff structure. Similarly, Hayashi *et al.* (1999) showed that simple framing differences strongly affect rates of cooperation in an otherwise identical two-person Prisoner's Dilemma, and that these effects depend on whether one is from Japan or the United States.

Relationship-specific investments   The structure of social interactions affects the benefits and costs of reputation building and other relationship-specific investments and thereby alters the evolution of common norms and the degree of social ties. Societies differ markedly in the frequency of interaction with known individuals and the degree to which interactions are governed by complete contracts as opposed to informal guarantees related to trust and reputation. We know from experiments, for example, that trust and interpersonal commitment often arise where contracts are incomplete, but not under complete contracting (Kollock 1994; Brown, Falk, and Fehr 2001); these patterns appear to be replicated in actual exchange situations such as the international diamond market (Bernstein 1992) and the market for raw rubber in Malaysia (Siamwalla 1978). If trust and commitment are important parts of one's livelihood, these sentiments may be generalized to other areas of life or evoked in situations which appear similar to everyday life.

Effects on the process of cultural transmission The structure of social interactions affects the process of cultural learning, as it affects who meets particular cultural models (individuals to learn from), under which conditions, and with what information about the available behavioral alternatives, their prevalence in the relevant social group, and the degree of success or other experiences of those following differing behavioral rules. For example, in some societies in which schooling plays a significant role in child-rearing, teachers are often 'high prestige' cultural models very often representing the behavioral patterns of a socially dominant group, while in societies in which schooling plays a lesser role, the cultural models may be more locally representative and dispersed.

Our interpretation of these cases reflects an underlying causal model in which preferences and beliefs are endogenous. According to our view, behaviors in a given situation are the result of individuals' *beliefs* about the relationship between actions and consequences and the *preferences* with which they evaluate these consequences. The structure of everyday social interactions affects both beliefs and preferences. The reason is that who we meet when we do particular tasks with particular payoffs influences both the kinds of information we deploy when we update our beliefs and the experiences that lead us to reaffirm or revise our preferences.[7] The updating of beliefs and preferences may respond to the relative payoffs of those holding distinct beliefs and preferences— the successful may be copied. Or, it may be sensitive to the frequency with which one imitates individuals holding distinct beliefs and preferences—learning may be conformist. In combination,

[7] For a more extended discussion see Bowles (1998), Boyd and Richerson (1985), and the works cited therein.

such forms of social learning, as well as individual learning, will produce groups with different combinations of beliefs and preferences (which can occur even in the absence of structured social interaction).

We are convinced that local economic and social structures are reflected in the experimental behaviors we observed, and we think it is reasonable that the connection between local conditions and behaviors can be illuminated by the learning model sketched above. However, we are unclear about some important details of how local situations influence behaviors. Two plausible interpretations come to mind. Perhaps different social and physical environments foster the development of differing generalized behavioral dispositions that are applicable across many domains, as might be the case using the above reasoning concerning task-performance or investment in reputation-building. For example, Lamalerans may be generally more 'altruistic' or 'fair-minded' than the Machiguenga or Quichua. In our experimental situations, such dispositions could account for the statistical relationships between group economic and social characteristics and experimental outcomes. In contrast, our abstract game structures may cue one or more highly context specific behavioral rules, as is suggested by the situational framing examples given above concerning the use of money. According to this interpretation, our subjects were first identifying the kind of situation they were in, seeking analogs in their daily life, and then acting in an appropriate manner. In this case, individual differences result from the differing ways that individuals frame a given situation, not from generalized dispositional differences. The diverse societies in our sample clearly differ markedly in their everyday analogs to the experimental situation, and this would explain both the magnitude of group differences and the statistical association between group-level economic and social structure, and experimental behavior.

These two approaches are difficult to distinguish empirically, and our dataset does not help us judge their relative importance. But in at least one set of our experiments, the two interpretations support quite different sets of predictions. The context-specific approach predicts that behavior when playing different games (e.g. Ultimatum Game and Public Goods Game) will be similar if the game seems similar to the subjects—such that the different games cue the same behavioral rules. By contrast, the dispositional approach predicts similarity of play in games in which a particular disposition would influence play. If situational cues explain experimental play, we might not observe any correlation between subjects' offers unless the two games evoked the same situational cues in the subjects. It is generally difficult to derive any testable hypotheses from this reasoning in part because the cueing process is obscure.

However, one of our cases allows an illuminating distinction between the two. Recall that the Orma made a connection between the Public Goods Game and their customary practice, the *harambee*. The Orma believe that wealthy households should make larger contributions to the *harambee* than poor households. The Orma did not perceive a similar connection between the *harambee* and the Ultimatum Game. Multivariate regressions involving wealth, age, education, and income indicate that wealth is the only significant predictor of Public Goods Game contributions. The more wealth a person has the more they contribute to the common pool, just like in the real *harambee*. Wealth, however, is not a significant predictor of Ultimatum Game offers in either multivariate or bivariate analyses. The importance of wealth for Public Goods Games, but not for Ultimatum Games, is consistent with predictions from the context-specific approach.

The many other cases in which one or more of our experimental situations appeared similar to common social interactions, do not allow us to distinguish between the dispositional and situational interpretations.

CONCLUSION

We summarize our results as follows. First, the selfishness axiom is not supported in *any* society studied, and the canonical model fails in a variety of new ways. Second, there is considerably more behavioral variability across groups than had been found in previous research. Third, group-level differences in economic organization and the degree of Market Integration explain a substantial portion of the behavioral variation across societies: the higher the degree of Market Integration and the higher the Payoffs to Cooperation, the greater the level of prosociality found in experimental games. Fourth, individual-level economic and demographic variables do not explain behavior either within or across groups.

Fifth, behavior in the experiments is generally consistent with economic patterns of everyday life in these societies.

We believe that the degree of variability observed in our cross-cultural sample of societies, and the persistent failure of the selfishness axiom, bears directly on related research emerging in economics (Fehr and Gächter 2000), economic sociology (Kollock 1994), and political science (Ostrom 1998, 2000). In economics, for example, the building blocks of new theories posit preferences such as a sense of fairness, a devotion to reciprocity, an aversion to inequality, a concern for relative payoffs, and a taste for punishment (e.g. Bolton and Ockenfels 1999; Charness and Rabin 1999; Fehr and Schmidt 1999). However, our results suggest that the student populations examined by most experimental social scientists may represent a very limited sample from a quite diverse population of human societies.

It is tempting to react to the widespread experimental evidence of non-selfish behaviors by replacing the *selfishness axiom* with some equally simple and universal assumption about human behavior. If *Homo economicus* has failed the experimental test, maybe *Homo altruisticus*, *Homo reciprocans*, or some other simplified version of a panhuman nature will do better. The diversity of behaviors we have observed leads us to doubt the wisdom of this approach. It is not only the case that behaviors differ markedly among groups; within-group variability is marked as well. Our evidence leads us to recognize two fundamental types of behavioral heterogeneity: between-group heterogeneity, which is apparently closely related to group differences in social structure and culture, and within-group heterogeneity, which is for the most part unexplained in our study, but which is strongly suggestive of the coexistence within groups of distinct dispositions, situationally cued mental models, or other behavior-producing constructs.

Two central problems are raised by our research. First, our work, along with hundreds of other experiments published in the last two decades, raises an evolutionary puzzle: what accounts for the success and persistence of behavior that violates the selfish axiom? We do not doubt that selfish motives are both common and essential to understanding human behavior. The challenge is to understand how and why unselfish behaviors and motives could evolve in the face of the material advantages accruing to selfish individuals. We think that long-run evolutionary processes governing the distribution of genes and cultural practices could have resulted in a substantial fraction of each population acting in certain situations (and perhaps generally) to forgo material payoffs in order to share with others or to punish unfair actions, as did our experimental subjects. A number of recent models have shown that under conditions that appear to approximate the ancestral environments of human populations, prosocial behavior (carried in either genes or culture) can proliferate (Gintis 2003*a*, *b*; Boyd *et al.* 2003; Henrich and Boyd 2001; Bowles and Gintis 2004; Bowles *et al.*, in press). But the evolutionary puzzle posed by the violations of the selfishness axiom on the broad canvas of cultural variation in our sample is far from resolved.

The second question raised by our study is: why did members of different groups behave so differently? Why is there so much variation between human groups, considering we do not observe this degree of variation among most university students or in other animal species? Addressing this question will require theories that explain why and how different dispositions, different sets of contextual rules, or different modes of processing information spread in different groups and how they are maintained. A central task of any such account is to understand why behavioral patterns appear to covary with economic and social structures in the ways we have observed. Failure to recognize the extent of human diversity and the range of processes that have generated the human mosaic may lead large sections of social science to an empirically false and culturally limited construction of human nature.

REFERENCES

Barry, H., Child, I. L., and Bacon, M. K. (1959). 'Relation of child training to subsistence economy', *American Anthropologist*, *61*, 51–63.

Bernstein, L. (1992). 'Opting out of the legal system: Extralegal contractual relations in the diamond industry', *Journal of Legal Studies*, *21*, 115–57.

Bolton, G. E. and Ockenfels, A. (1999). 'A theory of equity, reciprocity and competition', *American Economic Review*, *90*, 166–94.

Bowles, S. (1998). 'Endogenous preferences: The cultural consequences of markets and other economic institutions', *Journal of Economic Literature*, *36*, 75–111.

Bowles, S., Choi, J.-K. and Hopfensitz, A. 'The coevolution of individual behaviors and group level institutions', *Journal of Theoretical Biology.* (In press.)

——and Gintis, H. (2004). *The Evolution of Strong Reciprocity: Theoretical Population Biology.*

Boyd, R. and Richerson, P. J. (1985). *Culture and the Evolutionary Process.* Chicago, IL: University of Chicago Press.

——Gintis, H., Bowles, S., and Richerson, P. (2003). Evolution of altruistic punishment', Proceedings of the National Academy of Sciences, *100,* 6: 3531–5.

Brown, M., Falk, A., and Fehr, E. (2001). 'Contractual incompleteness and the nature of market interactions', Working Paper no. 38, Institute for Empirical Research in Economics, University of Zürich.

Camerer, C. (2003). *Behavioral Game Theory: Experiments on Strategic Interaction.* Princeton, NJ: Princeton University Press.

Cameron, L. (1999). 'Raising the stakes in the ultimatum game: Experimental evidence from Indonesia', *Economic Inquiry, 37,* 47–59.

Caporael, L., Dawes, R. M., Orbell, J. M., and van de Kragt, A. J. (1989). 'Selfishness examined: Cooperation in the absence of egoistic incentives', *Behavioral and Brian Sciences, 12,* 683–97.

Charness, G. and Rabin, M. (1999). *Social Preferences: Some Simple Tests and a New Model.* Berkeley: University of California Press.

Davis, D. D. and Holt, C. A. (1993). *Experimental Economics.* Princeton, NJ: Princeton University Press.

Falk, A. and Fischbacher, U. (1999). *A Theory of Reciprocity.* Institute for Empirical Economic Research, University of Zurich.

Fehr, E. and Gächter, S. (2000). 'Fairness and retaliation: The economics of reciprocity', *Journal of Economic Perspectives, 14,* 159–81.

——and Schmidt, K. M. (1999). 'A theory of fairness, competition, and cooperation', *Quarterly Journal of Economics, 114,* 817–68.

Gächter, S. and Falk, A. (2001). 'Reputation or reciprocity? Consequences for labour relation', *Scandinavian Journal of Economics, 104,* 1–25.

Gintis, H. (2000a). *Game Theory Evolving.* Princeton, NJ: Princeton University Press.

——(2000b). 'Strong reciprocity and human sociality', *Journal of Theoretical Biology, 206,* 169–79.

——(2003a) 'Hitchhikers guide to altruism: Genes, culture and the internalization of norms', *Journal of Theoretical Biology, 220,* 4: 407–18.

——(2003b) 'Solving The Puzzle of Prosociality', *Rationality and Society, 15,* 2: 155–87.

——Smith, E. A., and Bowles, S. (2001). 'Costly Signaling and Cooperation', *Journal of Theoretical Biology, 213,* 103–19.

——Bowles, S., Boyd, R., and Fehr, E. (2004). *Moral Sentiments and Material Interests: On the Foundations of Cooperation in Economic Life* (Cambridge, MA: MIT Press).

Hayashi, N., Ostrom, E., Walker, J. M., and Yamagishi, T. (1999). 'Reciprocity, trust, and the sense of control', *Rationality and Society, 11*, 27–46.

Henrich, J. (2000). 'Does culture matter in economic behavior? Ultimatum game bargaining among the Machiguenga of the Peruvian Amazon', *American Economic Review, 90*, 973–79.

—— and Boyd, R. (2001). 'Why people punish defectors. Weak conformist transmission can stabilize the costly enforcement of norms in cooperative dilemmas', *Journal of Theoretical Biology, 208*, 79–89.

—— and McElreath, R. (2002) 'Are peasants risk averse decision-makers', *Current Anthropology, 43*(1), 172–81.

Johnson, A. and Earle, T. (2001). *The Evolution of Human Societies: From Foraging Group to Agrarian State*, 2nd edn. Stanford, CA: Stanford University Press.

Kagel, J. H. and Roth, A. E. (1995). *Handbook of Experimental Economics*. Princeton, NJ: Princeton University Press.

Kaplan, H. and Hill, K. (1985). 'Food sharing among Aché foragers: Tests of explanatory hypotheses', *Current Anthropology, 26*, 223–46.

Kohn, M. (1990). 'Position in the class structure and psychological functioning in the U.S., Japan, and Poland', *American Journal of Sociology, 95*, 964–1008.

Kollock, P. (1994). 'The emergence of exchange structures: An experimental study of uncertainty, commitment, and trust', *American Journal of Sociology, 100*, 313–45.

Loewenstein, G. (1999). 'Experimental economics from the vantage point of view of behavioural economics', *Economic Journal, 109*, F25–F34.

Ostrom, E. (1998). 'A behavioral approach to the rational choice theory of collective action', *American Political Science Review, 92*, 1–21.

—— James Walker, and Ray Gardner (1992) 'Covenant with and without a sword: Self-governance is possible', *American Political Science Review, 86*, 2: 404–17.

—— (2000). 'Collective action and the evolution of social norms', *Journal of Economic Perspectives, 14*, 137–58.

Pillutla, M. M. and Chen, X. P. (1999). 'Social norms and cooperation in social dilemmas: The effects of context and feedback', *Organizational Behavior and Human Decision Processes, 78*, 81–103.

Ross, L. and Nisbett, R. E. (1991). *The Person and the Situation: Perspectives of Social Psychology*. Philadelphia, PA: Temple University Press.

Roth, A. E. (1995). 'Bargaining Experiments', in J. Kagel and A. Roth (eds), *The Handbook of Experimental Economics*, Princeton, NJ: Princeton University Press.

—— Prasnikar, V., Okuno-Fujiwara, M., and Zamir, S. (1991). 'Bargaining and market behavior in Jerusalem, Ljubljana, Pittsburgh, and Tokyo: An experimental study', *American Economic Review, 81*, 1068–95.

Sherif, M. (1937). 'An experimental approach to the study of attitudes', *Sociometry*, *I*, 90–8.

Sherman, S. L., DeFries, J. C., Gottesman, I. I., Loehlin, J. C., Meyer, J. M., Pelias, J., Rice, J., and Waldman, I. (1997). 'Recent developments in human behavioral genetics: Past accomplishments and future directions', *American Journal of Human Genetics*, *60*, 1265–75.

Siamwalla, A. (1978). 'Farmers and middlemen: Aspects of agricultural marketing in Thailand', *Economic Bulletin for Asia and the Pacific*, *39*, 38–50.

Simon, H. A. (1990). 'A mechanism for social selection and successful altruism', *Science*, *250*, 1665–67.

Slonim, R. and Roth, A. E. (1998). 'Learning in high stakes ultimatum games: An experiment in the Slovak Republic', *Econometrica*, *66*, 569–96.

Smith, N. (2001). Ethnicity, Reciprocity, Reputation and Punishment: An Ethnoexperimental Study Among the Chaldeans and Hmong of Detroit. Unpublished dissertation, University of California, Los Angeles.

Sober, E. and Wilson, D. S. (1994). 'Reintroducing group selection to the human behavioral sciences', *Behavioral and Brain Sciences*, *17*, 585–654.

Tversky, A. and Kahneman, D. (1992). 'Advances in prospect theory: Cumulative representation of uncertainty', *Journal of Risk and Uncertainty*, *5*, 297–323.

Woodburn, J. (1968). 'An introduction to the Hadza ecology', in R. B. Lee and I. De Vore (eds), *Man the Hunter*, Chicago, IL: Aldine, pp. 49–55.

3

Measuring Social Norms and Preferences Using Experimental Games: A Guide for Social Scientists

Colin F. Camerer and Ernst Fehr

INTRODUCTION

The purpose of this chapter is to describe a menu of experimental games that are useful for measuring aspects of social norms and social preferences. Economists use the term 'preferences' to refer to the choices people make, and particularly to tradeoffs between different collections ('bundles') of things they value—food, money, time, prestige, and so forth. 'Social preferences' refer to how people rank different allocations of material payoffs to themselves *and* others. We use the term 'self-interested' to refer to people who do not care about the outcomes of others. While self-interest can be a useful working assumption, experimental research of the 1980s and 1990s have shown that a substantial fraction of people in developed countries (typically college students) also care about the payoffs of others. In some situations, many people are willing to spend resources to reduce the payoff of others. In other situations, the same people spend resources to increase the payoff of others.

As we will see, the willingness to reduce or increase the payoff of relevant reference actors exists even though people reap neither present nor future material rewards from reducing or increasing payoffs of others. This indicates that, in addition to self-interested behavior, people sometimes behave as if they have altruistic

This paper was prepared for the MacArthur Foundation Anthropology project meeting. This research was supported by NSF SBR9730364. Thanks to Sam Bowles, Jean Ensminger, and Joe Henrich for comments, and Natalie Smith for sharing figures from her paper. Ernst Fehr acknowledges support from the Swiss National Science Foundation (project number 1214-05100.97), the Network on the Evolution of Preferences and Social Norms of the MacArthur Foundation, and the EU-TMR Research Network ENDEAR (FMRX-CTP98-0238). Colin Camerer acknowledges support of the Preferences Network and NSF grant SES-0078911.

preferences, and preferences for equality and reciprocity.[1] Reciprocity, as we define it here, is different from the notion of reciprocal altruism in evolutionary biology. Reciprocity means that people are willing to reward friendly actions and to punish hostile actions *although the reward or punishment causes a net reduction in the material payoff of those who reward or punish.* Similarly, people who dislike inequality are willing to take costly actions to reduce inequality, although this may result in a net reduction of their material payoff. Reciprocal altruism typically assumes that reciprocation yields a net increase in the material payoff (e.g. because one player's action earns them a reputation which benefits them in the future). Altruism, as we define it here, means that an actor takes costly actions to increase the payoff of another actor, *irrespective of the other actor's previous actions.* Altruism thus represents unconditional kindness while reciprocity means non-selfish behavior that is conditioned on the previous actions of the other actor.

Reciprocity, inequality aversion, and altruism can have large effects on the regularities of social life and, in particular, on the enforcement of social norms. This is why the examination of the nature of social preferences is so important for anthropology and for social sciences in general. There is, for example, an ongoing debate in anthropology about the reasons for food-sharing in small-scale societies. The nature of social preferences will probably have a large effect on the social mechanism that sustains food-sharing. For example, if many people in a society exhibit inequality aversion or reciprocity, they will be willing to punish those who do not share food, so no formal mechanism is needed to govern food-sharing. Without such preferences, formal mechanisms are needed to sustain food-sharing (or sharing does not occur at all). As we will see there are simple games that allow researchers to find out whether there are norms of food-sharing, and punishment of those who do not share.

In the following we first sketch game theory in broad terms. Then we describe some basic features of experimental design in economics. Then we introduce a menu of seven games that have proved useful

---

[1] We defer the question of whether these *preferences* are a stable trait of people, or tend to depend on situations. While many social scientists tend to instinctively guess that these preferences are traits of people, much evidence suggests that cross-situational *behavior* is not very consistent at the individual level. Note, however, that behavioral variations across situations do not imply that preferences vary across situations because individuals with fixed preferences may well behave differently in different situations (see section on 'Theories of Social Preferences').

in examining social preferences. We define the games formally, show what aspects of social life they express, and describe behavioral regularities from experimental studies. The behavioral regularities are then interpreted in terms of preferences for reciprocity, inequity aversion, or altruism. The final sections describe some other games anthropologists might find useful, and draw conclusions.

GAMES AND GAME THEORY

Game theory is a mathematical language for describing strategic interactions and their likely outcomes. A game is a set of strategies for each of several players, with precise rules for the order in which players choose strategies, the information they have when they choose, and how they rate the desirability ('utility') of resulting outcomes. Game theory is designed to be flexible enough to be used at many levels of detail in a broad range of sciences. Players may be genes, people, groups, firms, or nation-states. Strategies may be genetically coded instincts, heuristics for bidding on the e-Bay website, corporate routines for developing and introducing new products, a legal strategy in complex mass tort cases, or wartime battle plans. Outcomes can be anything players value—prestige, food, control of Congress, sexual opportunity, returning a tennis serve, corporate profits, the gap between what you would max-imally pay for something and what you actually pay ('consumer surplus'), a sense of justice, or captured territory.

Game theory consists of two different enterprises: (1) using games as a language or taxonomy to parse the social world; and (2) deriving precise predictions about how players will play in a game by assuming that players maximize expected 'utility' (personal valuation) of consequences, plan ahead, and form beliefs about other players' likely actions. The second enterprise dominates game theory textbooks and journals. Analytical theory of this sort is extremely mathematical, and inaccessible to many social scientists outside of economics and theoretical biology. Fortunately, games can be used as a taxonomy with minimal mathematics because understanding prototypical games—like those discussed in this chapter—requires nothing beyond simple logic.

The most central concept in game theory is Nash equilibrium. A set of strategies (one for each player) form an equilibrium if each player is choosing the strategy which is a best response (i.e. gives the highest expected utility) to the other players' strategies. Attention is focused on equilibrium because players who are constantly switching to better strategies, given what others have done, will generally end up at an equilibrium. Increasingly, game theorists are interested in the dynamics of equilibration as well, in the form of evolution of populations of player strategies (Weibull 1995); or learning by individuals from experience (e.g. Fudenberg and Levine 1998; Camerer and Ho 1999).

Conventions in economic experimentation

At this point, it is useful to describe how experimental games are typically run (see Friedman and Sunder 1994; Davis and Holt 1993; Camerer 2003 for more methodological details). Experimental economists are usually interested initially in interactions among anonymous agents who play once, for real money, without communicating. This stark situation is not used because it is lifelike (it's not). It is used as a benchmark from which the effects of playing repeatedly, communicating, knowing who the other player is, and so forth, can be measured by comparison.

In most experiments described below, subjects are college undergraduates recruited from classes or public sign-up sheets (or increasingly, email lists, or websites) with a vague description of the experiment (e.g. 'an experiment on interactive decision-making') and a range of possible money earnings. The subjects assemble and are generally assigned to private cubicles or as groups to rooms. Care is taken to ensure that any particular subject will not know precisely whom they are playing. If subjects know with whom they are playing, their economic incentives may be distorted in a way the experimenter does not understand (e.g. they may help friends earn more) and there is an opportunity for postgame interaction which effectively changes the game from a one-shot interaction to a repeated interaction.

The games are usually described in plain, abstract language, using letters or numbers to represent strategies rather than concrete descriptions like 'helping to clean up the park' or 'trusting somebody in a faraway place'. As with other design features, abstract language is used not because it is lifelike, but as a benchmark against which the effects of more concrete descriptions can be

measured. It is well-known that there are framing effects, or violations of the principle of description invariance—how the experiment is described may matter. For example, in Public Goods
Games, players who are asked to take from a common pool for
their private gain typically behave differently than subjects who are
asked to give to the common pool by sacrificing (Andreoni 1995).
Subjects generally are given thorough instructions, encouraged to
ask questions, and are often given a short quiz to be sure they
understand how their choices (combined with choices of others) will
determine their money earnings. Economists are also obsessed with
offering substantial financial incentives for good performance, and
many experiments have been conducted which show that results
generalize even when stakes are very large (on the order of several
days' or even months' wages).

Since economists are typically interested in whether behavior
corresponds to an equilibrium, games are usually played repeatedly
to allow learning and equilibration to occur. Because playing
repeatedly with the same player can create different equilibria, in
most experiments subjects are rematched with a different subject
each period in a 'stranger' protocol. (In the opposite, 'partner' protocol, a pair of subjects know they are playing each other repeatedly.)
In a design called 'stationary replication', each game is precisely like
the one before. This is sometimes called the 'Groundhog Day' design,
after a movie starring Bill Murray in which Murray's character re-
lives the same day over and over. (At first he is horrified, then he
realizes he can learn by trial and error because the events of the day
are repeated identically.)

After subjects make choices, they are usually given feedback on
what the subject with whom they are paired has done (and sometimes feedback on what all subjects have done), and compute their
earnings. Some experiments use the 'strategy method' in which
players make a choice conditional on every possible realization of a
random variable or choice by another player (e.g. in a bargaining
game, subjects might be asked whether they would accept or reject
every offer the other player could make. Their conditional decision
is then enacted after the other player's offer is made). At the end of
the experiment, subjects are paid their actual earnings plus a small
'show up' fee (usually US$3–$5). In experimental economics, there
is a virtual taboo against deceiving subjects by actively lying about
the experimental conditions, such as telling them they are playing

another person when they are not (which is quite common in social psychology). A major reason for this taboo is that, for successful experimentation, subjects have to believe the information that is given to them by the experimenter. In the long run deception can undermine the credibility of the information given to the subjects.

The seven examples we will discuss are Prisoner's Dilemma, public goods, ultimatum, dictator, trust, gift exchange, and third-party punishment games. Table 3.1 summarizes the definitions of the games (and naturally occurring examples of them), the predictions of game theory (assuming self-interest and rational play), experimental regularities, and the psychological interpretation of the evidence.

Prisoners' dilemma and public goods games

Figure 3.1 shows payoffs in a typical Prisoner's Dilemma. The rows and columns represent simultaneous choices by two players. Each cell shows the payoffs from a combination of row and column player moves; the first entry is the row player's payoff and the second entry is the column players payoff. For example, (T, S) in the (Defect, Cooperate) cell means a defecting row player earns T when the column player cooperates, and the column player earns S.

Mutual cooperation provides payoffs of H for each player, which is—by definition of a Prisoner's Dilemma—better than the L payoff from mutual defection. However, if the other player plays C, a defector earns the T(emptation) payoff T, which is better than reciprocating and earning only H (since $T > H$ in a Prisoner's Dilemma). A player who cooperates against a defector earns the S(ucker) payoff, which is less than earning L from defecting. Since $T > H$ and $L > S$, both players prefer to defect whether the other player cooperates or not. So mutual defection is the only Nash (mutual best-response) equilibrium.[2] This equilibrium is

---

[2] It is important to note the distinction between outcomes that are measured in field data or paid in experiments, and the utilities or personal valuations attached to those rewards. Game theory allows the possibility that players get utility from something other than their own rewards (e.g. they may feel pride or envy if others earn lots of money). In practice, however, we observe only the payoffs players earn. For the purpose of this chapter, when we assume 'self-interest' we mean that players are solely motivated to maximize their own measured earnings in dollars (or food, or some other observed outcome).

TABLE 3.1. Seven experimental games useful for measuring social preferences

Game	Definition of the game	Real life example	Predictions with rational and selfish players	Experimenta regularities, references	Interpretation
Prisoner's Dilemma Game	Two players, each of whom can either cooperate or defect. Payoffs are as follows: 		Cooperate	Defect
Cooperate	H,H	S,T
Defect	T,S	L,L | $H > L, \; T > H, \; L > S$	Production of negative externalities (pollution, loud noise), exchange without binding contracts, status competition.	Defect.	50% choose to cooperate. Communication increases frequency of cooperation. Dawes (1980).[a]	Reciprocate expected cooperation.
Public Goods Game	n players simultaneously decide about their contribution g_i, $(0 \le g_i \le y)$ where y is players' endowment; each player i earns $\pi_i = y - g_i + mG$ where G is the sum of all contributions and $m < 1 < mn$.	Team compensation, cooperative production in simple societies, overuse of common resources (e.g. water, fishing grounds).	Each player contributes nothing, that is, $g_i = 0$.	Players contribute 50% of y in the one-shot game. Contributions unravel over time. Majority chooses $g_i = 0$ in final period. Communication strongly increases cooperation. Individual punishment opportunities greatly increase contributions. Ledyard (1995).[a]	Reciprocate expected cooperation.

TABLE 3.1. *Continued*

Game	Definition of the game	Real life example	Predictions with rational and selfish players	Experimenta regularities, references	Interpretation
Ultimatum Game	Division of a fixed sum of money S between a proposer and a responder. proposer offers x. If responder rejects x both earn zero, if x is accepted the proposer earns $S - x$ and the responder earns x.	Monopoly pricing of a perishable good; '11th hour' settlement offers before a time deadline.	Offer $x = \epsilon$ where ϵ is the smallest money unit. Any $x > 0$ is accepted.	Most offers are between 0.3 and 0.5S. $x < 0.2S$ rejected half the time. Competition among proposers has a strong x-increasing effect; competition among responders strongly decreases x. Güth, Schmitterbert and Schwartze (1982),[b] Camerer (2003).[a]	Responders punish unfair offers; negative reciprocity.
Dictator Game	Like the UG but the responder cannot reject, that is, the 'proposer' dictates $(S - x, x)$.	Charitable sharing of a windfall gain (lottery winners giving anonymously to strangers).	No sharing, that is, $x = 0$.	On average 'proposers' allocate $x = 0.2S$. Strong variations across experiments and across individuals. Kahneman, Knetsch, and Thaler (1986),[b] Camerer (2003).[a]	Pure altruism.

Game	Description	Real-world analogue	Standard prediction	Results	Summary
Trust Game	Investor has endowment S and makes a transfer y between 0 and S to the trustee. Trustee receives $3y$ and can send back any x between 0 and $3y$. Investor earns $S-y+x$. Trustee earns $3y-x$.	Sequential exchange without binding contracts (buying from sellers on e-Bay).	Trustee repays nothing: $x=0$. Investor invests nothing: $y=0$.	On average $y=0.5S$ and trustees repay slightly less than $0.5S$. x is increasing in y. Berg Dickhaut, and McCabe (1995),[b] Camerer (2003).[a]	Trustees show positive reciprocity.
Gift Exchange Game	'Employer' offers a wage w to the 'Worker' and announces a desired effort level $\hat{e}$. If worker rejects $(w, \hat{e})$ both earn nothing. If Worker accepts, he can choose any e between 1 and 10. Then Employer earns $10e - w$ and Worker earn $w - c(e)$. $c(e)$ is the effort cost which is strictly increasing in e.	Noncontractibility or nonenforceability of the performance (effort, quality of goods) of workers or sellers.	Worker chooses $e=1$. Employer pays the minimum wage.	Effort increases with the wage w. Employers pay wages that are far above the minimum. Workers accept offers with low wages but respond with $e=1$. In contrast to the UG competition among workers (i.e. responders) has no impact on wage offers. Fehr, Kirchsteiger, and Riedl (1993).[b]	Workers reciprocate generous wage offers. Employers appeal to workers' reciprocity by offering generous wages.
Third-Party Punishment Game	A and B play a DG. C observes how much of amount S is allocated to B. C can punish A but the punishment is also costly for C.	Social disapproval of unacceptable treatment of others (scolding neighbors).	A allocates nothing to B. C never punishes A.	Punishment of A is higher, the less A allocates to B. Fehr and Fischbacher (2001a).[b]	C sanctions violation of a sharing norm.

Note: [a] Denotes survey papers. [b] denotes papers that introduced the respective games.

	Cooperate (C)	Defect (D)
Cooperate (C)	H, H	S, T
Defect (D)	T, S	L, L

FIG. 3.1. Prisoner's Dilemma

Note: (Assumption: $T > H > L > S$).

inefficient because mutual cooperation would render both players better off.

Public goods games have an incentive structure similar to Prisoner's Dilemma games.[3] Every player is best off by contributing nothing to the public good, but contributions from everyone would make everyone better off.[4]

The following experiment illustrates a typical Public Goods Game. There are n subjects in a group and each player has an endowment of y dollars. Each player can contribute between zero and y dollars to a group project. For each dollar that is contributed to the group project, *every* group member (including those who contributed nothing) earns $m < 1$ dollars. The return m thus measures the marginal *private* return from a contribution to the group project (i.e. the amount of her investment which a specific individual gets back, in the form of her share of the public good). Since a subject benefits from the contributions of the others it is possible to free ride on these contributions. The parameter m also obeys the condition $mn > 1$. The product mn is the total marginal return for the *whole group* from a contribution of one more dollar. For each dollar that is kept by a subject, that subject earns exactly one dollar. The total material payoff π of a subject that contributes g dollars is, therefore, given by $\pi = y - g + mG$ where G is the sum of the contributions of all n group members.[5] Self-interested subjects should contribute nothing to the public good, regardless of how much the

[3] There is a huge literature on Public Goods Games. For a survey see Ledyard (1995).

[4] In the general case players in the Public Goods Game have an incentive to contribute inefficiently little to the good. In most experimental applications players had an incentive to contribute nothing.

[5] In the general case players may have unequal endowments y_i and they may derive unequal benefits m_i from the public good G. m_i may also depend nonlinearly on G. The material payoff of player i can then be expressed as $\pi_i = y_i - g_i + m_i(G)G$. However, for anthropology experiments it is advisable to keep material payoff functions as simple as possible to prevent that subjects are confused. A particularly simple case is given when the experimenter doubles the sum of contributions G and divides the total $2G$ among all $n > 2$ group members.

other subjects contribute. Why? Because every dollar spent on the group project costs the subject one dollar but yields only a *private* return of $m < 1$. This means that, in equilibrium, all self-interested subjects will contribute nothing to the public good. A group of self-interested subjects earns y dollars in this experiment because $G = 0$. But since the total return for the group mn is larger than one, the group as a whole benefits from contributions. If all group members invest their entire endowments y, then $G = ny$ which means each subject earns mny rather than y (which is better because mn is larger than one). Thus, contributing everything to the group project renders all subjects better off relative to the equilibrium of zero contributions, but an individual subject does even better by contributing nothing.

The Prisoner's Dilemma and Public Goods Games are models of situations like pollution of the environment, in which one player's action imposes a harmful 'externality' on innocent parties (cooperation corresponds to voluntarily limiting pollution), villagers sharing a depletable resource like river water or fish in a common fishing ground with poor enforcement of property rights (e.g. Ostrom 2000), and production of a public utility like a school or irrigation system that noncontributing 'free riders' cannot be easily excluded from sharing. Note also that contributions in public goods games are often in the form of time rather than money—for example, helping to clean up a public park or standing watch for village security. Low rates of voluntary cooperation and contribution in these games might be remedied by institutional arrangements like government taxation (which forces free riders to pay up), or informal mechanisms like ostracism of free riders. (Of course, if ostracism is costly then players should free ride on the ostracism supplied by others, which creates a second-order public good problem.) Also, when Prisoner's Dilemma and Public Goods Games involve players who are matched together repeatedly, it can be an equilibrium for players to all cooperate until one player defects. Sometimes the experimenter wants to allow for stationary replication but, at the same time, wants to prevent the existence of equilibria that involve positive contribution levels. This can be achieved by changing the group composition from period to period such that no player ever meets another player more than once.

In the Prisoner's Dilemma, self-interested subjects have an incentive to defect. In the Public Goods Game, when $m < 1$, the self-interest hypothesis predicts zero contributions. In experiments, however, subjects in one-period Prisoner's Dilemma games cooperate about half of the time. In one-period Public Goods Games, they contribute an average of a half of their endowment, but the distribution is typically bimodal with most subjects contributing either everything or nothing. Higher values of the private return m lead to higher contributions. Similar effects are obtained in the Prisoner's Dilemma. An increase in the value of H, relative to T, increases the rate of cooperation. Interestingly, pre-play communication about how much players intend to contribute, which should have no effect in theory, has a very strong positive impact on cooperation levels in both the Prisoner's Dilemma and Public Goods Games (Ledyard 1995; Sally 1995).

When the Public Goods Game is repeated for a finite number of periods, interesting dynamic contribution patterns emerge. Irrespective of whether subjects can stay together in the same group or whether the group composition changes from period to period, subjects initially contribute as much as they do in one-period games, but contributions decline substantially over time. Approximately 60–80 percent of all subjects contribute nothing in the final period and the rest contribute little.[6] The first ten periods of Figure 3.2 show the dynamic pattern of average contributions in a standard Public Goods Game like the one described above. Another important fact is that about half the subjects are 'conditional cooperators'—they contribute more when others are expected to contribute more and do contribute more (Croson 1999; Fischbacher, Gächter, and Fehr 2001). Conditional cooperation is not compatible with pure self-interest, but consistent with a preference for behaving reciprocally. The studies cited above also indicate that

---

[6] Initially, many experimentalists interpreted this as a victory of the self-interest hypothesis (Isaac, McCue, and Plott 1985). It was thought that at the beginning of the experiment subjects do not yet fully understand what they rationally should do (even though the incentive to free ride is usually transparent and is often pointed out very explicitly in the instructions) but over time they learn what to do and in the final period the vast majority of subjects behave self-interestedly. This interpretation is wrong. Andreoni (1988) showed that if one conducts a 'surprise' second Public Goods Game after the final period of a first game, subjects start the new game with high contribution levels (similar to initial levels in the first game). If players had learned to free ride over time, this 'restart' effect would not occur; so the dynamic path that is observed is more likely to be due to learning by conditional cooperators about the presence and behavior of free riders, rather than simply learning that free riding is more profitable. Camerer and Weigelt (1988) observed the same kind of restart effect in repeated trust games.

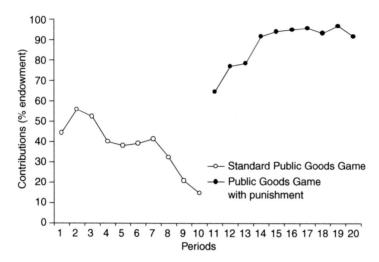

FIG. 3.2. Average contributions over time in Public Goods Game with a constant group composition

Source: Fehr and Gächter (2000).

about a third of the subjects are purely self-interested, and never contribute anything.

Why do average contributions decline over time? A plausible explanation is that each group has a mixture of subjects who behave selfishly and others who behave reciprocally. The reciprocal subjects are willing to cooperate if the other group members co-operate as well. However, in the presence of selfish subjects who never contribute, reciprocal subjects gradually notice that they are matched with free riders and refuse to be taken advantage of by them.[7]

The unraveling of cooperation over time raises the question of whether there are social mechanisms that can prevent the decay of cooperation. A potentially important mechanism is social ostracism. In a series of experiments, Fehr and Gächter (2000) introduced a punishment opportunity into the Public Goods Game

[7] The existence of conditional cooperators may also explain framing effects in public goods and Prisoner's Dilemma games (see Ross and Ward (1996)). If, for example, a Prisoner's Dilemma game is described as the 'Wall Street' game, subjects are likely to have pessimistic expectations about the other players' cooperation. Conditional cooperators are, therefore, likely to defect in this frame. If, in contrast, the Prisoner's Dilemma is described as a 'Community' game, subjects probably have more optimistic expectations about the cooperation of the other player. Hence, the conditional cooperators are more likely to cooperate in this frame.

(see also Yamagishi 1966). In their game there are two stages. Stage one is a Public Goods Game as described above. In stage two, after every player in the group has been informed about the contributions of each group member, each player can assign up to ten punishment points to each of the other players. The assignment of one punishment point reduces the first-stage income of the punished subject by 10 percent but it also reduces the income of the punisher. (The punishment is like an angry group member scolding a free rider, or spreading the word so the free rider is ostracized—there is some cost to the punisher, but a larger cost to the free rider.) Note that since punishment is costly for the punisher, the self-interest hypothesis predicts zero punishment. Moreover, since rational players will anticipate this, the self-interest hypothesis predicts no difference in the contribution behavior between the standard Public Goods Game and the game with a punishment opportunity. In both conditions zero contributions are predicted.

The experimental evidence rejects this prediction.[8] In contrast to the standard Public Goods Game, where cooperation declines over time and is close to zero in the final period (see the first ten periods in Figure 3.2), the punishment opportunity causes a sharp jump in cooperation (compare period 10 with period 11 in Figure 3.2) and a steady increase until almost all subjects contribute their whole endowment. The sharp increase occurs because free riders often get punished, and the less they give, the more likely punishment is. Cooperators feel that free riders take unfair advantage of them and, as a consequence, they are willing to punish the free riders. This induces the punished free riders to increase cooperation in the following periods. A nice feature of this design is that the actual rate of punishment is very low in the last few periods—the mere threat of punishment, and the memory of its sting from past punishments, is enough to induce potential free riders to cooperate.

The results in Figure 3.2 are based on a design in which the same group of players are paired together repeatedly (the 'partner' protocol). When the group composition changes randomly from period to period or when subjects are never matched with the same group members again (the 'stranger' protocol), cooperation levels are lower than in the partner design, but the dynamic pattern is similar

---

[8] In the experiments subjects first participated in the standard game for ten periods. After this they were told that a new experiment takes place. In the new experiment, which lasted again ten periods, the punishment opportunity was implemented.

to Figure 3.2. Interestingly, the punishment pattern is almost the same in the partner and the stranger protocol. This means that, in the partner protocol, the strategic motive of inducing future cooperation is not an important cause of the punishment.

The Public Goods Game with a punishment opportunity can be viewed as the paradigmatic example for the enforcement of a social norm. Social norms often demand that people give up private benefits to achieve some other goal. This raises the question of why most people obey the norm. The evidence above suggests an answer: some players will punish those who do not obey the norm (at a cost to themselves), which enforces the norm.

Another mechanism that causes strong increases in cooperation is communication (Sally 1995). If the group members can communicate with each other, the unraveling of cooperation frequently does not occur. Communication allows the conditional cooperators to coordinate on the cooperative outcome and it may also create a sense of group identity.

While Prisoner's Dilemma and Public Goods Games capture important components of social life, they cannot typically distinguish between players who are self-interested, and players who would like to reciprocate but believe pessimistically that others will not cooperate or contribute. Other games are useful for separating out these different types of players. Three other games have proved useful in separating these two explanations and measuring a wider range of social preferences—ultimatum, dictator, and trust games.

Ultimatum Games

Ultimatum Games represent a form of take-it or leave-it bargaining (Güth, Schmittberger, and Schwarze 1982). One player, a proposer, can make only one proposal regarding the division of a fixed amount of money S between herself and a responder. The responder can accept the offer x, or reject it, in which case neither player earns anything. If the responder accepts, he earns x and the proposer earns $S - x$. In theory, self-interested responders will accept any positive offer, and proposers who anticipate this should offer the smallest possible positive amount (denoted by ε in Table 3.1).

The Ultimatum Game measures whether responders will negatively reciprocate, sacrificing their own money to punish a proposer who has been unfair. In dozens of experiments under different

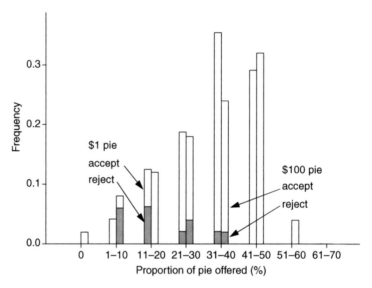

FIG. 3.3. Offers and rejections in $10 and $100 Ultimatum Games
Source: Hoffman, McCabe, and Smith (1996).

conditions in many different countries, responders reject offers less than 20 percent of *S* about half the time. proposers seem to anticipate this negative reciprocity and offer between 30 and 50 percent of *S*. A typical distribution of offers is given in Figure 3.3, which shows the data from Hoffman, McCabe, and Smith (1996).

Figure 3.4 shows offers from experiments with four groups University of California, Los Angeles graduate students; students from University of Iowa; employees from a large firm in Kansas City (see Burks *et al.* 2001), and Chaldeans, who are Catholic Iraqis in Detroit (see Smith 2000). The offers and rejection rates are generally quite robust across (developed) cultures, levels of stakes (including $100–$400 in the United States and 2–3 months' wages in other countries), and changes in experimental methodology (see Camerer 2003). There are weak or unreplicated effects of demographic variables like gender, undergraduate major (economics majors offer and accept less), physical attractiveness (women offer more than half, on average, to more attractive men), age (young children are more likely to accept low offers), and autism (autistic adults appear to be unable to imagine what others might find acceptable so they offer very little; see Hill and Sally 2002). Creating

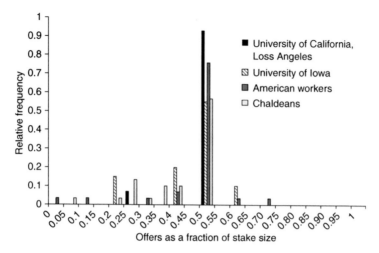

FIG. 3.4. Distribution of ultimatum offers

a sense of entitlement by letting the winner of a trivia contest be the proposer also leads to lower offers and more frequent acceptances.

An important finding is that competition on the side of the responders or the proposers causes large shift in proposals and agreements (Roth *et al.* 1991; Fischbacher, Fong, and Fehr 2003). In case of two responders, for example, who simultaneously accept or reject the offer *x* of a single proposer, the average offer decreases to 20 percent of *S*. Competition among the responders induces them to accept less, and proposers anticipate this and take advantage by offering less. When proposers compete, by making simultaneous offers to a single responder who accepts the single best offer, the average accepted offer rises to 75 percent of *S*.

At a first glance the fact that responders reject less and proposers offer more under competitive conditions seems to indicate that the preference for reciprocity is weaker in this situation. But people may have precisely the same kinds of social preferences in two-player and multiplayer games with competition, but act more self-interestedly when there is competition because doing so actually satisfies their preferences. How? Note that a negatively reciprocal responder is willing to punish a proposer for an unfair proposal. Under competitive conditions, however, a responder can only punish the proposer if the other responder(s) also reject a given offer. With competition, punishment of the proposer is a public good that is only produced if *all* responders reject. Since there is always a positive probability to be matched with a self-interested responder, who accepts every positive offer, the reciprocal responder's rejection becomes futile. Hence, there is less advantage to rejecting under competition, even if one has a strong preference for reciprocity. Competition essentially makes it impossible for players to express their concern about reciprocity. Consequently, evidence of the self-interested behavior in the face of competition does not cast doubt on evidence of reciprocity in other domains.

The fact that proposers offer on average 40 percent of *S* might be due to altruism, a preference for sharing equally, or to a fear that low offers will be rejected ('strategic fairness'). Although rejection rates are lower under competitive conditions there is still a significant rate of rejection. Thus, even under competitive conditions proposers have reason to fear that very low offers are rejected. Dictator games help separate the fear-of-rejection hypothesis from the other explanations mentioned above because the responder's ability to reject the offers is removed.

Dictator Games

A Dictator Game is simply a proposer division of the sum *S* between herself and another player, the recipient (Kahneman, Knetsch, and Thaler 1986; Forsythe *et al.* 1994). Self-interested proposers should allocate nothing to the recipient in the Dictator Game. In experiments with students, proposers typically dictate allocations that assign the recipient on average between 10 and 25 percent of *S*, with modal allocations distributed between 50 percent and zero (see Figure 3.5, from Smith 2000). These allocations are much less than student proposers offer in Ultimatum Games, though most players do offer something. Comparing dictator with bilateral Ultimatum Games shows that fear of rejection is *part* of the explanation for proposers' generous offers, because they do offer less when there can be no rejection. But many subjects offer something in the Dictator Game, so fear of rejection is not the entire explanation. Moreover, the Chaldeans and the employees from Kansas City offer roughly the same in the Ultimatum Game and the Dictator Game.[9]

[9] Unfortunately, there are so far not many experiments with non-student populations. It is therefore not clear to what extent the results from the Chaldeans (Smith 2000) and from the Kansas City workers (Burks *et al.* 2001) represent general patterns in non-student populations.

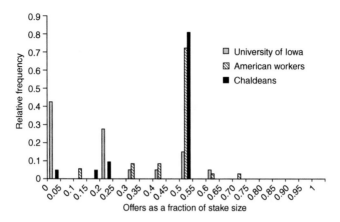

FIG. 3.5. Dictator Game allocations

The Dictator Game is a 'weak situation' because there is typically no strong norm for a reasonable allocation, so average allocations can change dramatically with changes in the experimental design. At one extreme, when experimenters take pains to ensure to subjects that their individual decisions cannot be identified by the experimenter (in 'double-blind' experiments), self-interest emerges more strongly (among students): About 70 percent of the proposers allocate nothing and the rest typically allocate only 10–20 percent of *S* (Hoffman *et al.* 1994). At the opposite extreme, when the eventual recipient of the proposer's allocation gives a short description of him or herself which the proposer hears, the average allocation rises to half of *S*, and allocations become more variable (Bohnet and Frey 1999). Many proposers give nothing and others give the entire amount, as if proposers make an empathetic judgment about the recipient's deservingness. These two extremes simply illustrate that dictator allocations can be strongly influenced by many variables (in contrast to ultimatum offers, which do not deviate too far from 30–50 percent in most previous experiments with students).

Trust and gift exchange games

Dictator games measure pure altruism. An interesting companion game is the 'trust game' (see also Camerer and Weigelt 1988 and Berg, Dickhaut, and McCabe 1995). In a trust game an investor and trustee each receive an amount of money *S* from the experimenter.

The investor can invest all or part of her money by sending any amount y, between zero and S, to the trustee. The experimenter then triples the amount sent, so that the trustee has $3y$ (in addition to her initial allocation of S which is hers to keep). The trustee is then free to return anything between zero and $3y$ to the investor. The payoff of the investor is $S - y + z$ and the payoff of the trustee is $3y - z + S$ where z denotes the final transfer from the trustee to the investor. For example, suppose S is \$10 and the investor invests \$7, keeping \$3. The \$7 investment triples to \$21. If the trustee repays \$10 and keeps \$11 for herself, then the investor gets a total of \$3 + \$10, or \$13, and the trustee gets \$10 + \$11, or \$21. Note that if investors do not invest, then together the two players earn $2S$. If the investor invests everything, the players earn $4S$ (the trustee's S plus the tripled investment of $3S$); so there is a large mutual gain from trust. The trust game is essentially a Dictator Game in which the trustee dictates an allocation, but the amount to be allocated was created by the investor's initial investment.

In theory, self-interested trustees will keep everything and repay $z = 0$. Self-interested investors who anticipate this should transfer nothing, that is, $y = 0$. In experiments in several developed countries, investors typically invest about half the maximum on average, although there is substantial variation across subjects. Trustees tend to repay slightly less than y so that trust does not quite pay. The amount trustees repay increases with y, which can be interpreted as positive reciprocity, or a feeling of obligation to repay more to an investor who has exhibited trust.

Positive reciprocity like the one that shows up in the trust game has important implications for the enforcement of informal agreements and incomplete contracts. Most social relations are not governed by explicit contracts but by implicit informal agreements. Moreover, when explicit contracts exist they are often highly incomplete, which gives rise to strong incentives to shirk (Williamson 1985). Economic historians like North (1990) have argued that differences in societies' contract enforcement capabilities are probably a major reason for differences in economic growth and human welfare, and Knack and Keefer (1997) find that countries with high measured trust (from surveys) have higher economic growth.

To see the role of reciprocity in the enforcement of contracts, consider the following variant of the gift exchange game (Fehr, Kirchsteiger, and Riedl 1993). In the gift exchange game subjects are in the role of employers or buyers and of workers or sellers, respectively.[10] An employer can offer a wage contract that stipulates a binding wage w and a desired effort level $\hat{e}$. If the worker accepted this offer, the worker is free to choose the actual effort level e between a minimum and a maximum level. The employer always has to pay the offered wage irrespective of the actual effort level. In this experiment effort is represented by a number e between one and ten. Higher numbers represent higher effort levels and, hence, a higher profit π for the employer and higher effort costs $c(e)$ for the worker. Thus, the lowest effort level gives the worker the highest material payoff but the highest material payoff for the employer is given at the maximal effort level. Formally, the profit π from the employment of a worker is given by $\pi = 10 \times e - w$ and the monetary payoff for the experimental worker is $u = w - c(e)$. The crucial point in this experiment is that selfish workers have no incentives to provide effort above the minimum level of $e = 1$ irrespective of the level of wages. Employers who anticipate this behavior will, therefore, offer the smallest possible wage such that the worker just accept the contract offer. Reciprocal workers will, however, honor at least partly generous wage offers with non-minimal, generous, effort choices. The question, therefore, is to what extent employers do appeal to workers' reciprocity by offering generous contracts and to what extent workers honor this generosity.

It turns out that in experiments like this many employers indeed make quite generous offers. On average, the offered contracts stipulate a desired effort of $\hat{e} = 7$ and the offered wage implies that the worker receives 44 percent of the total income that is generated if the worker indeed performs at $e = 7$. Interestingly, a relative majority of the workers honor this generosity. Most of them do not fully meet the desired effort level but they choose levels above $e = 1$. A minority of the workers (about 30 percent) always choose always the minimal effort. The average effort is $e = 4.4$—substantially above the selfish choice of $e = 1$. Moreover, there is also a strong positive correlation between effort and wages, indicating positive reciprocity. A typical effort–wage relation is depicted in Figure 3.6. Thus, although shirking exists in this situation the evidence suggests that in response to generous offers, a relative majority of the people

---

[10] In the following we stick to the employer–worker framing although the experiment could also be presented in a buyer–seller frame. The gift-exchange experiment has been conducted in both frames with virtually the same results.

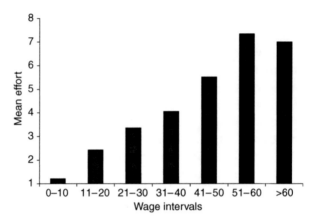

FIG. 3.6. Effort–wage relation in the gift exchange game
Source: Fehr, Gächter, and Kirchsteiger (1997).

are willing to put forward extra effort above what is implied by purely pecuniary considerations.

Similar to the Ultimatum Game the regularities in the gift exchange game are quite robust with regard to stake levels. In experiments in which subjects earned on average between two and three times their monthly incomes the same wage and effort patterns prevail. Another important result is obtained if there is competition between the workers—similar to the responder competition in the Ultimatum Game. While in the Ultimatum Game with responder competition proposers make much lower offers compared to the bilateral case, competition has *no* impact on wages in the gift exchange game. The reason for this striking result is that it does not pay for employers to push down wages because reciprocal workers respond to lower wages with lower effort levels.

Third-party punishment games

Many small scale societies are characterized by extensive food-sharing. A simple game to examine whether food sharing is a social norm that is enforced by social sanctions has been conducted by Fehr and Fischbacher (2001*a*). The game is called 'third-party punishment game' and has three players. The game between player A and player B is just a Dictator Game. Player A receives an endowment of 100 tokens of which he can transfer any amount to player B, the recipient. Player B has no endowment and no choice to make. Player C has an endowment of fifty tokens and observes the transfer of player A. After this player C can assign punishment points to player A. For each punishment point assigned to player A player C has costs of one token and player A has costs of three tokens. Since punishment is costly a self-interested player C will never punish. However, if there is a sharing norm player C may well punish player A if A gives too little.

In fact, in the above experiments player A is never punished if they transferred fifty or more tokens to player B. If they transferred less than fifty tokens the punishment was stronger, the less player A transferred. In case that player A transferred nothing she received on average nine punishment points from player C, that is, the payoff of player A was reduced by twenty-seven tokens. This means that in this three-person game it was still beneficial, from a selfish point of view, for player A to give say, nothing compared to an equal split. If there is more than one player C, who can punish player A, this may, however, no longer be the case.

Another interesting question is to what extent cooperation norms are sustained through the punishment of free riders by third parties. We have already seen that in the Public Goods Game with punishment strikingly high cooperation rates can be enforced through punishment. In this game each contribution to the public good increases the payoff of each group member by 0.4. Thus, if a group member free rides instead of cooperation she directly reduces the other group members' payoff. In real life there are, however, many situations in which free riding has a very low, indeed almost imperceptible, impact on the payoff of particular other individuals. The question then is, whether these individuals nevertheless help enforcing a social norm of cooperation. In case they do a society greatly magnifies its capability of enforcing social norms because every member of a society acts as a potential policemen.

It is relatively easy to construct cooperation games with punishment opportunities for third (unaffected) parties. Fehr and Fischbacher (2001a), for example, have conducted Prisoner's Dilemmas in which a member of the two-person group, who played the Prisoner's Dilemma, observes a member of some other group, who also played the Prisoner's Dilemma. Then the member of the first group can punish the member of the second group. Thus, each member could punish and could be punished by somebody outside

their own two-person group. It was ensured that reciprocal punishment was not possible, that is, if subject A could punish subject
B, subject B could not punish A but only some third subject C. It
turns out that the punishment by third parties is surprisingly strong. It
is only slightly weaker than second-party (within group) punishment.

THEORIES OF SOCIAL PREFERENCES

Within economics, the leading explanation for the patterns of
results described above is that agents have social preferences
(or 'social utility') which take into account the payoffs and perhaps
intentions of others. Roughly speaking, social preference theories
assume that people have stable preferences for how money is allocated (which may depend on who the other player is, or how the
allocation came about), much as they are assumed in economics to
have preferences for food, the present versus the future, how close
their house is to work, and so forth.[11]

Cultural anthropologists and evolutionary psychologists have
sought to explain the origin of these preferences. One idea is that in
the Environment of Evolutionary Adaptation or ancestral past,
people mostly engaged in repeated games with people they knew.
Evolution created specialized cognitive heuristics for playing
repeated games efficiently. It is well-known in game theory that
behavior which is optimal for a self-interested actor in a one-period
game with a stranger—such as defecting or free riding, accepting all
ultimatum offers—is not always optimal in repeated games with
partners. In a repeated Ultimatum Game, for example, it pays to
reject offers to build up a reputation for being hard to push around,
which leads to more generous offers in the future. In the unnatural
habitat view, subjects cannot 'turn off' the habitual behavior shaped
by repeated game life in the Environment of Evolutionary Adaptation when they play single games with strangers in the lab. An

---

[11] A different interpretation is that people have rules they obey about what to do—
such as, share money equally if you haven't earned it (which leads to equal-split offers
in the Ultimatum Game) (Güth 1995). A problem with the rule-based approach is that
subjects do change their behavior in response to changes in payoffs, in predictable ways.
For example, when the incremental payoff from defecting against a cooperator (denoted
T–H above) is higher, people defect more often. When a player's benefit m of the public
good is higher, they contribute more. When the social return from investing in a trust
game is lower, they invest less. Any rule-based account must explain why the rules are
bent by incentives. A theory with flexible rules will probably end up looking like a theory
of social preferences which explicitly weighs self-interest against other dimensions.

important modification of this view is that evolution did not equip all people with identical hard-wired instincts for playing games, but instead created the capacity for learning social norms. The latter view can explain why different cultures would have different norms.

As is common in evolutionary explanations, the unnatural habitat theory assumes the *absence* of a module or cognitive heuristic that could have evolved but did not—namely, the capacity to distinguish temporary one-shot play from repeated play. If subjects had this ability they would behave appropriately in the one-shot game. In principle it is testable whether people have the ability to distinguish temporary one-shot play from repeated play. Fehr and Fischbacher (2003) did this in the context of the Ultimatum Game (cf. Camerer *et al.* 2002, in repeated Trust Games).

They conducted a series of ten Ultimatum Games in two different conditions. In both conditions subjects played against a different opponent in each of the ten iterations of the game. In each iteration of the baseline condition the proposers knew nothing about the past behavior of their current responders. Thus, the responders could not build up a reputation for being 'tough' in this condition. In contrast, in the reputation condition the proposers knew the full history of the behavior of their current responders, that is, the responders could build up a reputation for being 'tough'. In the reputation condition a reputation for rejecting low offers is, of course, valuable because it increases the likelihood to receive high offers from the proposers in future periods.

If the responders understand that there is a pecuniary payoff from rejecting low offers in the reputation condition one should observe higher acceptance thresholds in this condition. This is the prediction of the social preferences approach that assumes that subjects derive utility from both their own pecuniary payoff and a fair payoff distribution. If, in contrast, subjects do not understand the logic of reputation formation and apply the same habits or cognitive heuristics to both conditions, one should observe no systematic differences in responder behavior across conditions. Since the subjects participated in both conditions, it was possible to observe behavioral changes at the individual level. It turns out that the vast majority (slightly more than 80 percent) of the responders increase their acceptance thresholds in the reputation condition relative to the baseline condition. This contradicts the hypothesis that subjects do not understand the difference between one-shot and repeated play.

The above experiment informs us about the proximate mechanisms that drive responder behavior in the Ultimatum Game. Whatever the exact proximate mechanisms will turn out to be, a hypothesis that is based on the story that subjects do not really understand the difference between one-shot and repeated play seems to be wrong. A plausible alternative hypothesis is that responders face strong emotions when faced with a low offer and that these emotions trigger the rejections. These emotions may be the result of repeated game interactions in our ancestral past and may not be fine-tuned to one-shot interactions. For modeling purposes, behaviorally relevant emotions can be captured by appropriate formulations of the utility function. This is exactly what theories of social preferences do.

The challenge for all the social preference theories (and evolutionary explanations of their origins) is to explain a lot of results in different games with one model, and make new predictions which survive attempts at falsification. For example, why players contribute in the standard Public Goods Game at first, then stop contributing; why they punish and contribute in the Public Goods Game with punishment opportunities; why responders reject unfair offers; why proposers in the Dictator Game give away money; why many trustees repay trust; why third parties punish defection in the Prisoner's Dilemma and unfair allocations in the Dictator Game and why competition causes more unequal divisions in Ultimatum Games but has no impact in gift exchange games.

Two flavors of models have been proposed—models of inequality-aversion and models of reciprocity. In inequality-aversion theories, players prefer more money and also prefer that allocations be more equal. Attempting to balance these two goals, players will sacrifice some money to make outcomes more equal. For example, in the theory of Fehr and Schmidt (1999), the players' goals are formalized as follows. Let x_i denote the material payoff of player i and x_j the material payoff of player j. Then, the utility of player i in a two-player game is given by $U_i(x) = x_i - \alpha_i(x_j - x_i)$ if player i is worse off than player j $(x_j - x_i \geq 0)$, and $U_i(x) = x_i - \beta_i(x_i - x_j)$ if player i is better off than player j $(x_i - x_j \geq 0)$. α_i is a constant that measures how much player i dislikes *disadvantageous* inequality (envy) while β_i measures how much i dislikes *advantageous* inequality (guilt). When α_i and β_i are zero players, i is self-interested. Fehr and Schmidt also assume that, in general, players dislike advantageous inequality less

	Cooperate (C)	Defect (D)
Cooperate (C)	2, 2	0, 3
Defect (D)	3, 0	1, 1

FIG. 3.7. Representation of Prisoner's Dilemma in terms of material payoffs

	Cooperate (C)	Defect (D)
Cooperate (C)	2, 2	$0 - 3\alpha,\ 3 - 3\beta$
Defect (D)	$3 - 3\beta,\ 0 - 3\alpha$	1, 1

FIG. 3.8. Utility representation of Prisoner's Dilemma in Figure 3.7

than disadvantageous inequality, that is, $0 \leq \beta_i \leq \alpha_i$ and $\beta_i < 1$. For α_i they assumed no upper bound.[12]

An important ingredient of this theory is that the population of players is assumed to be heterogeneous—some people act purely selfishly and some are inequality-averse. This model predicts all the regularities mentioned above: small offers in the Ultimatum Game are rejected by envious players with a positive α and positive allocations in Dictator Games occur when guilty players have a positive β. A positive β also explains why trustees repay some money to investors in the trust game and why players who expect that the other player(s) cooperate in Prisoner's Dilemma and Public Goods Games reciprocate cooperation rather than defecting or free riding. The theory is consistent with the fact that in the Ultimatum Game with responder competition the responders reject much less than in the bilateral Ultimatum Game and why, in the gift-exchange game, responder competition does not matter. It also is consistent with (third party) punishment in the Prisoner's Dilemma, the Dictator Game and the Public Goods Game. For a quick illustration, consider the Prisoner's Dilemma in Figure 3.7. Note that the numbers in Figure 3.7 represent material payoffs and not utilities.

In Figure 3.8 we show the utilities that are attached with the material payoffs of Figure 3.7 if both players have identical preferences with $\alpha > 0$ and $\beta > 0$. In Fehr and Schmidt's theory, if player 2 (the column player) is expected to cooperate, player 1 (the

---

[12] In the general n-person case the utility function of Fehr and Schmidt is given by $U_i(x) = x_i - \alpha_i \frac{1}{n-1} \sum_{j \neq i} \max\{x_j - x_i, 0\} - \beta_i \frac{1}{n-1} \sum_{j \neq i} \max\{x_i - x_j, 0\}$. The term $\max\{x_j - x_i, 0\}$ denotes the maximum of $x_j - x_i$ and 0. It measures the extent to which there is disadvantageous inequality between player i and j.

row player) faces a choice between material payoff allocations (2,2) and (3,0). The social utility of (2,2) is $U_1(2,2) = 2$ because there is no inequality. The social utility of (3,0), however, is $U_1(3,0) = 3 - 3\beta$ because there is inequality that favors the row player. Therefore, player 1 will reciprocate the expected cooperation of player 2 if $\beta > \frac{1}{3}$ [13] (i.e. if player 1 feels sufficiently 'guilty' from defecting). If player 1 defects and player 2 cooperates, the payoff of player 2 is $U_2(3,0) = 0 - 3\alpha$: if player 2 defected instead the utility would be 1. This means that player 2 will always reciprocate defection because cooperating against a defector yields less money and more envy.[14] Figure 3.8 shows that if $\beta > 1/3$, there are two (mutual best response) equilibria: (cooperate, cooperate) and (defect, defect). In utility terms, inequality-averse players no longer face a Prisoner's Dilemma. Instead, they face a coordination or assurance game with one efficient and one inefficient equilibrium (the same as the 'stag hunt' game described below). If the players believe that the other player cooperates, it is rational for each of them to cooperate, too.

Inequality-averse players are thus conditional cooperators. They cooperate in response to (expected) cooperation and defect in response to (expected) defection. The theory is, therefore, also consistent with framing effects in the Prisoner's Dilemma (and in Public Goods Games). If the framing of the game makes players more optimistic about the other players' cooperation, then inequality-averse players will cooperate more.

Inequality-aversion theories are simplified because they include only the other players' material payoffs into the calculation of social utility. Reciprocity theories include other players' actions and, in particular, the intention behind the action, as well. In one important formal reciprocity theory (Rabin 1993), player A forms a judgment about whether another player B has sacrificed to benefit (or harm) her. A likes to reciprocate, repaying kindness with kindness, and meanness with vengeance.

---

[13] Note that if the temptation payoff is raised from 3 to T, then a player cooperates if $\beta > (T-2)/T$. Since the latter expression converges to 1 as T grows larger, a player with a fixed β who cooperates at a T near 2 will switch to defection at some point as T grows large; so the model predicts the correct (empirically observed) response to the change in payoff structure.

[14] This also means that if a selfish and an inequality-averse player are matched, and the inequality-averse player knows that the other player is selfish, the unique equilibrium is (defect, defect). The reason is that the inequality-averse player knows that the other player will defect and, hence, she will defect, too.

In the Prisoner's Dilemma Figure 3.7, for example, suppose the row player is planning to cooperate. Then the column player's choice essentially determines what the row player will get. Since row's possible payoffs are 2 and 0, let's take the average of these, 1, to be a 'fair' payoff. By choosing to cooperate, the column player 'awards' the row player the payoff of 2, which is 'nice' because it's greater than the fair payoff of 1.[15] Rabin proposes a utility function in which niceness has a positive value and meanness has a negative value, and players care about their own dollar payoffs and the product of their own niceness and the niceness of the other player. Thus, if the other player is nice (positive niceness), they want to be nice too, so the product of nicenesses will be positive. But if the other player is mean (negative niceness), they want to be negative, too, so the product of nicenesses will be positive. While Rabin's theory is more analytically difficult than other theories, it captures the fact that a single player may behave nicely or meanly depending on how they expect to be treated—it locates social preferences and emotions in the combination of a person, their partner, and a game, rather than as a fixed personal attribute.

There are also hybrid models that combine the notions of reciprocity with models of social preferences based on own and other players' material payoffs. Charness and Rabin (2002) proposed a hybrid model in which players care about their own payoffs, and about a weighted average of the lowest payoff anybody receives (a 'Rawlsian' component) and the sum of all payoffs (a 'utilitarian' component). Their theory has a hidden aversion to inequality through the emphasis on the lowest payoff. In addition, players also care about the actions of the others. Falk and Fischbacher (1998) proposed a model that combines reciprocity and inequality aversion. Both the model of Charness and Rabin and of Falk and Fischbacher explain some data that Fehr–Schmidt's theory cannot explain. This increase in explanatory power comes, however, at a cost because these models are considerably more complicated.

There are an increasing number of experiments that compare predictions of competing theories. One important result of these experiments is that there is clear evidence for reciprocity beyond inequality-aversion (as anticipated by Rabin 1993). Players do not

---

[15] The degree of niceness is formalized by taking the difference between the awarded and fair payoffs, normalized by the range of possible payoffs. In this example, niceness is $(2 - 1)/(2 - 0) = \frac{1}{2}$.

only care about the allocation of material payoffs. They also care about the actions and the intentions of the other players.

Regardless of which models are most accurate, psychologically plausible, and technically useful, the important point for social scientists is that a menu of games can be used to measure social preferences, like the extent to which people weigh their monetary self-interest with the desire to reciprocate (or limit inequality), both negatively (in Ultimatum Games) and positively (in Trust Games), and with pure altruism (in Dictator Games). Dozens of experiments in many developed countries, with a wide range of instructions, subjects, and levels of stakes, have shown much regularity. And simple formal theories have been proposed which can account for findings that appear to be contradictory at first blush (e.g. sacrificing money to harm somebody in an Ultimatum Game, and sacrificing to help somebody in Prisoner's Dilemma or Trust Games). Exploring behavior in these games in a much wider range of cultures, at various stages of economic development and with varying patterns of sharing norms, governance structures, and so forth, will undoubtedly prove interesting and important. In addition, anthropological studies in remote field sites will serve as an important empirical reminder for economists and psychologists who currently study these games about how very narrow the range of cultures they study is.

WHY DO GAME EXPERIMENTS? AND WHICH GAMES?

A central advantage of experimental games is comparability across subject pools (provided great care is taken in controlling for differences in language, purchasing power of outcomes, interactions with experimenters, and so forth). While comparability is clearly not perfect, it is surely as good as most qualitative measures. A further advantage is replicability. The fact that experiments are replicable is a powerful tool for creating consensus about the fact and their interpretation in the scientific community.

In fact, experiments conducted in the field by anthropologists may actually have two large advantages compared to lab experiments in Western countries that usually (though not always) use college students as experimental subjects. First, since anthropologists are in the field for long periods of time, the cost of collecting data is rather low. (Most contributors to this volume often noted that the experiment was unusually fun for participants, probably more so than for college students raised in a world of Nintendo, 500-channel cable TV, and web surfing.) Second, the amount of funds budgeted by granting agencies in developed countries for subject payments typically have extraordinary purchasing power in small-scale societies. As a result, it is easy for anthropologists to test whether people behave differently for very large stakes, such as a week or month of wages, compared to low stakes. Such comparisons are important for generalizing to high-stakes economic activity, but are often prohibitively expensive in developed countries.

Games impose a clear structure on concepts that are often vague or fuzzy. Social scientists often rely on data like the General Social Survey, in which participants answer questions such as, 'In general, how much do you trust people?' on a 7-point Likert scale. It would be useful to have questions about trust that are more concrete, tied to actual behavior, and likely to be interpreted consistently across people (see Glaeser *et al.* 2000). A question like 'How much of $10 would you place in an envelope, knowing it will be tripled and an anonymous person will keep as much as they like and give the rest back to you?' is arguably a better survey question—it is more concrete, behavioral, and easy to interpret. Note that anthro-pologists also study their subjects much more carefully than experi-mental psychologists and economists do, so they often have lots of behavioral data to correlate with behavior from experimental games.

Of course, games are reductions of social phenomena to some-thing extremely simple, but they can always be made more complex. A painter who first sketches a line drawing on a blank canvas has reduced a complex image to two dimensions of space and color. But the line drawing reduction is also a platform on which more com-plex images can be restored (e.g. it can be painted over to give the dimension of color and the illusion of depth).

From a technical point of view it is often useful to apply the so-called strategy method in experiments. In the Ultimatum Game, for example, a strategy for the responder stipulates a Yes or No response *for each possible offer*. A simple way of eliciting a responder strategy is the elicitation of the responder's minimal acceptable offer, x^{min}. If the actual offer is below x^{min}, it is rejected, if it is above x^{min}, it is accepted. This method has the big advantage that the experimenter not only knows the responder's response to the actual offer but also to all other feasible offers. Very often most offers in the Ultimatum Game are close to the equal split so that there are no rejections. In this case the experimenter learns little about the willingness to accept or reject low offers unless the strategy method is applied.

In simple societies the strategy method may sometimes be too complicated for the subjects. In this case it is advisable to restrict the set of feasible offers. For example, in the Ultimatum Game the experimenter may only allow a 90 : 10 offer and a 50 : 50 offer, and the responder then has to indicate his response to both potential offers before he knows the actual offer. For similar reasons as in the Ultimatum Game, the strategy method, is of course, also useful in many other games like, for example, the trust or the third party punishment game. Knowing the trustee's response to all feasible investments in the Trust Game, or player C's punishment of player A for all feasible transfers player A can make to player B in the third-party punishment game, provides a lot more information compared to the usual method.

The experimental games described in this chapter are line draw-ings, to which richness can be added. For example, most of the games we described are only played once without communication (the soundtrack of life is muted) and without mutual identification of who the other players are (like the Magritte painting 'The Lovers' in which two people kiss with their heads shrouded in cloth). Conducting experiments this way is obviously not a deliberate choice to model a world in which people don't talk and only meet hooded strangers (although it might be appropriate for nearly anonymous internet transactions). Instead, this baseline design is a stark control condition that can be used to study the effect of communication, by comparing results in the control condition with experiments in which communication is allowed (turning up the soundtrack volume) and mutual identification is allowed (removing the hoods).

Other games social scientists might find useful

While the games described above have been studied most widely (including by anthropologists; see this volume) other games or treatments might also be of interest. This section describes four of them.

	Stag	Rabbit
Stag	2, 2	0, 1.5
Rabbit	1.5, 0	1, 1

FIG. 3.9. The 'stag hunt' or assurance game

Measuring moral authority in dictator games As noted above, the Dictator Game is a weak situation in the sense that a wide variety of treatment variables—instructions, entitlement, experimental control for 'blindness' to individual allocations, identification of recipients, etc.—affect allocations significantly. The fact that preferences are malleable suggests a way to measure moral authority, which was very cleverly suggested by Carolyn Lesorogol. Collect a group of subjects. Have a person A suggest a way the subjects should play the Dictator Game. Then have the subjects play. The extent to which subjects adhere to A's recommendation is a measure of A's moral authority or ability to create norms which are adhered to. (Lesorogol used this method to see whether traditional authority, of village elders, had declined after land privitization.)

Coordination: Assurance and threshold public goods games Figure 3.9 shows a game called 'stag hunt', also known as an 'assurance game' or Wolf's Dilemma. The game is identical to the Prisoner's Dilemma in structure except for one crucial difference: It is better to reciprocate cooperation, because the material payoff to defecting when the other player cooperates is lower than the material payoff from cooperating. If there are strong synergies or 'complementarities' from the cooperative choices of two players, or if free riders are punished after they defect, then the Prisoner's Dilemma game is transformed into stag hunt.[16]

The game is called stag hunt after a story in Jean-Jacques Rousseau about hunters who can choose to hunt a large stag with others, which yields a large payoff if everyone else helps hunt the stag, or can hunt for rabbit on their own. An example familiar to anthropologists is hunting for large animals like whales (see Alvard,

---

[16] Recall that when players are inequality-averse the PD, when represented in social utility terms, is transformed into an assurance game. From an experimental viewpoint, this is, however, different from an assurance game where the payoffs are monetary. While the experimenter has full control over the monetary payoffs we can never be sure about the preferences of the players.

Chapter 14, this volume), in which the marginal hunter's presence can be crucial for a successful hunt. Stag hunt is a 'coordination game' because there is more than one Nash equilibrium, and players would like to find a way to coordinate their choices on one equilibrium rather than mismatch. Since stag is a best-response to hunting stag, (stag, stag) is an equilibrium; but so is (rabbit, rabbit).

Stag hunt is closely related to 'threshold' Public Goods Games (also called the 'volunteer's dilemma'). In these games there is a threshold of total contribution required to produce the public good. If n-1 players have contributed, then it pays for the nth player to pitch in and contribute, since her share of the public good outweighs the cost of her marginal contribution.

The central feature of the Prisoner's Dilemma is whether the other player has social preferences that induce her to cooperate (acting against her self-interest) *and* whether the player himself gets social utility from reciprocating cooperation. Stag hunt is different: because players get a higher *material* payoff from reciprocating the cooperative choice (stag), all they need is sufficient assurance that others will hunt stag (i.e. a probability of playing stag above $\frac{2}{3}$, which makes the expected payoff from stag higher than the expected payoff from rabbit) to trigger their own stag choice. The Prisoner's Dilemma game is about cooperativeness; how cooperative is player 1 *and* how cooperative does he expect player 2 to be. Stag hunt is solely about perceptions of whether others are likely to cooperate. Experiments with coordination games like stag hunt show that, perhaps surprisingly, the efficient (stag, stag) outcome is not always reached. Preplay communication helps. Social structure has an interesting effect: if a population of players are matched randomly each period, the tendency to play stag is higher than if players are arrayed on a (virtual) circle and play only their neighbors each period. Stag hunt could be useful to measure whether a culture has a norm of playing 'stag' when the cooperative action is risky.

Status in bargaining Figure 3.10 shows a game called 'battle of the sexes'. In this game, two players simultaneously choose a strategy

	R	C
R	3, 1	0, 0
C	0, 0	1, 3

FIG. 3.10. Battle of the Sexes Game

we have labeled R and C. If the players mismatch, they get nothing. If they match on R, the row player gets the higher payoff of 3 and the column player gets 1. The payoffs are opposite if they match on C. The game is called battle of the sexes after a hoary story about a husband and wife who would like to attend an event together, but the husband prefers boxing while the wife prefers ballet.

Battle of the sexes is a classic 'mixed-motive' game because the players prefer to agree on something than to disagree, but they disagree on what to agree on. Alternatively, think of the game as a bargaining game in which the players will split 4 if they can agree how to split it (but it must be uneven, 3 : 1 or 1 : 3) and earn nothing otherwise.

In experiments with payoffs like Figure 3.10, players tend to choose their preferred strategy (row chooses R, column chooses C) around 65 percent of the time, which means they mismatch more than half the time (see Camerer 2003: ch. 7). Since mismatches yield nothing, the game cries out for some social convention or coordinating device which tells players which one of them gets the larger payoff; in principle, the player who gets less should go along with the convention since getting 1 is better than mismatching and getting nothing.

Any commonly understood variable which produces consistent matches in a pair of players can be interpreted as an indicator of status. A striking illustration of this is Holm's (2000) experiments on battle of the sexes and gender. He ran experiments in which men and women played battle of the sexes games (simultaneously, with no communication) with players of the same sex and opposite sex. Take the row player's view. When women played with men, the women (in the row player position) were more likely to play C and men (in the row player position) where more likely to play R, compared to when they played with subjects of the same gender. The players played as if they all respected a social convention in which women get the smaller share and the men the larger share. Remarkably, women actually earned a larger average payoff playing against men than playing against other women! The reason for this is that earning 1 with a high probability is better than trying to earn 3 but mismatching very frequently.

We interpret these results as evidence that males have status. An agreed-upon status variable has two interesting effects in these games: It increases collective gains (by minimizing mismatches); and it creates greater wealth for the high-status group than for the low-status group. The latter effect, of course, can spark a self-fulfilling spiral in which, if wealth itself creates status, the rich get status and get richer, too.[17]

Since concepts of hierarchy, privilege, and status are central in anthropology (and in sociology), games like battle of the sexes which reveal status relations (and show their economic impact) could prove useful. Game-theoretic revelation of status also provides a way for economists to comprehend such concepts, which do not fit neatly into primitive economic categories like preferences and beliefs.

Shared understanding and cultural homogeneity in matching games
In 1960, Schelling drew attention to simple 'matching games', in which players choose an object from some category, and earn a fixed prize if their objects match. For example, subjects who are asked to choose a place and time to meet in New York City often choose noon at Grand Central Station, or other prominent landmarks like Central Park or the Statue of Liberty. Careful experiments by Mehta, Starmer, and Sugden (1994) show the same effect. Asked to name a mountain, 89 percent of subjects picked Mt Everest; naming a gender, 67 percent picked 'man'; naming a relative, 32 percent picked 'mother' (20 percent picked 'father'); asked to pick a meeting place in London, 38 percent picked Trafalgar Square; and so forth.

From a game-theoretic viewpoint, matching games with a large choice set have lots and lots of equilibria. Schelling's point was that shared world knowledge often picks out a psychologically prominent 'focal' point. A focal point is the right choice if 'everybody knows' it's the right choice. The extent of shared understanding can be measured by how well subjects match. We suggest this as a measure of cultural homogeneity. For example, Los Angeles is a diverse patchwork of local communities of wildly varying ethnicity. Asked to choose a meeting place in LA (playing the game with their own ethnic or geographical community), Koreans might choose the

---

[17] An alternative interpretation is that Battle of Sexes play reflects the extent to which the aggressiveness of the other player is common knowledge. If all women believe that men are more aggressive, it pays for them to give in. Yet, if wealth creates status, than the greater aggressiveness of men ultimately also confers status.

corner of Western and Wilshire (the heart of 'Koreatown'), those from south beach might choose 'The Strand' (a boardwalk by the ocean), Hollywood Hills trendies would choose Skybar, and so forth. The fact that most readers haven't heard of all these 'famous' places is precisely the point. The degree to which a group coordinates on a culturally understood meeting place seems like a good measure of overall cultural homogeneity. (If they do not agree, they aren't a group—at least not a group with shared cultural knowledge.)

Weber and Camerer (2003) use matching games, with a linguistic twist, to study endogenous development of culture and cultural conflict. In their experiments, a pair of subjects are each shown sixteen pictures which are very similar (e.g. scenes of workers in an office). One subject is told that eight of the pictures have been selected as targets. This subject, the director, must describe the pictures to the second subject, so that the second subject chooses the correct pictures as quickly as possible. (They earn money for accuracy and speed.) Since the subjects have never seen these pictures before, they must create a homemade language to label the pictures. Because they are under time pressure, with repeated trials they create a very pithy 'jargon' to describe the distinctive features of a picture as briefly as possible. Their homemade language is one facet of culture (albeit designed to accomplish a specific purpose—commonly understood labeling of novel objects). Cultural conflict can be studied by combining two separate groups, whose jargon tend to be different.

These paradigms can be used to measure or create shared understanding, with economic incentives to reveal shared understanding or create it quickly. These could prove useful in anthropology too for measuring cultural homogeneity and dimensions of shared perception.

CONCLUSIONS

Game theory has proved useful in a wide range of social sciences in two ways: by providing a taxonomy of social situations which parse the social world; and by making precise predictions about how self-interested players will actually play. Behavior in experiments which carefully control players' strategies, information, and possible payoffs shows that actual choices often deviate systematically from the game-theoretic prediction based on self-interest. These deviations are naturally interpreted as evidence of social norms (what players expect and feel obliged to do) and social preferences (how players feel when others earn more or less money). This evidence is now being used actively by economists to craft a parsimonious theory of social preferences that can be used to explain data from many different games in a simple way that makes fresh predictions. Since anthropologists are often interested in how social norms and preferences emerge, evolve, and vary across cultures, these games could provide a powerful tool for doing empirical anthropology. In addition to measuring social preferences and social norms experimental games may also be used for measuring moral authority, players beliefs about other players' actions in coordination games, cultural homogeneity, and status effects in bargaining.

REFERENCES

Andreoni, James (1988). 'Why free ride? Strategies and learning in public goods experiments', *Journal of Public Economics, 37*, 291–304.
—— (1995). 'Warm-glow versus cold-prickle: the effects of positive and negative framing on cooperation in experiments', *Quarterly Journal of Economics, 110*, 1–22.
Berg, Joyce, Dickhaut, John, and McCabe, Kevin (1995). 'Trust, reciprocity and social history', *Games and Economic Behavior, 10*, 122–42.
Bohnet, Iris and Frey, Bruno S. (1999). 'Social distance and other-regarding behavior in dictator games: Comment', *American Economic Review, 89* (March), 335–9.
Burks, Stephen, Carpenter, Jeffrey, and Verhoegen, Eric (2002). 'Comparing students to workers: The effect of stakes, social framing, and demographics on bargaining outcomes', Middlebury Working Paper. http://community.middlebury.edu/jcarpent/papers.html
Camerer, Colin F. (2003). *Behavioral Game Theory: Experiments on Strategic Interaction*. Princeton, NJ: Princeton University Press.
—— and Ho, Teck (1999). 'Experience-weighted attraction (EWA) learning in normal-form games', *Econometrica, 67*, 827–74.
—— —— Chong, Kuan, and Weigelt, Keith (2002). 'Strategic teaching and equilibrium models of repeated trust and entry games', Caltech working paper, October.
http://www.hss.caltech.edu/camerer/camerer.html
—— and Weigelt, Keith (1988). 'Experimental tests of a sequential equilibrium reputation model', *Econometrica, 56*, 1–36.

Charness, Gary and Rabin, Matthew (2002). 'Understanding social preferences with simple tests', *Quarterly Journal of Economics, 117,* 817–69.

Croson, Rachel T. A. (1999). 'Theories of altruism and reciprocity: Evidence from linear public goods games', Discussion Paper, Wharton School, University of Pennsylvania.

Davis, Douglas and Holt, Charles (1993). *Experimental Economics.* Princeton, NJ: Princeton University Press.

Dawes, Robyn M. (1980). 'Social dilemmas', *Annual Review of Psychology, 31,* 169–93.

Falk, Armin and Fischbacher, Urs (1998). *A Theory of Reciprocity,* Institute for Empirical Research in Economics, University of Zurich, Working Paper No. 6.

Fehr, Ernst and Fischbacher, Urs (2001a). *Third Party Norm Enforcement,* Institute for Empirical Research in Economics, University of Zurich, Working Paper No.106.
http://www.unizh.ch/iew/wp/iewwp106.pdf

———— (2003). 'The nature of human altruism-proximate patterns and evolutionary origins', *Nature* (in press).

——— Gächter, Simon, and Kirchsteiger, Georg (1997). 'Reciprocity as a contract enforcement device', *Econometrica, 65,* 833–60.

—— and Gächter, Simon (2000). 'Cooperation and punishment in public goods experiments', *American Economic Review, 90,* 980–94.

—— and Schmidt, Klaus M. (1999). 'A theory of fairness, competition and co-operation', *Quarterly Journal of Economics, 114,* 817–68.

—— Kirchsteiger, Georg, and Riedl, Arno (1993). 'Does fairness prevent market clearing? An experimental investigation', *Quarterly Journal of Economics, CVIII,* 437–60.

Fischbacher, Urs, Fong, Christina, and Fehr, Ernst (2003). *Fairness and the Power of Competition,* Institute for Empirical Research in Economics, University of Zurich, Working Paper No. 133.
http://www.unizh.ch/iew/wp/iewwp133.pdf

—— Gächter, Simon, and Fehr, Ernst (2001). 'Are People Conditionally Cooperative?—Evidence from Public Goods Experiments', *Economic Letters, 71,* 397–404.

Forsythe, Robert L., Horowitz, Joel, Savin, N. E., and Sefton, Martin (1994). 'Fairness in simple bargaining games', *Games and Economic Behavior, 6,* 347–69.

Frey, Bruno and Bohnet, Iris (1997). 'Identification in democratic society', *Journal of Socio-Economics, 26,* 25–38.

Friedman, Daniel and Sunder, Shyam (1994). *Experimental Methods—A Primer for Economists.* Cambridge: Cambridge University Press.

Fudenberg, Drew and Levine, David (1998). *The Theory of Learning in Games.* Cambridge, MA: MIT Press.

Glaeser, Edward, Laibson, David, Scheinkman, Jose, and Soutter, Christine (2000). 'What is social capital? The determinants of trust and trustworthiness', *Quarterly Journal of Economics, 115*, 811–46.

Güth, Werner, Schmittberger, Rolf, and Schwarze, Bernd (1982). 'An experimental analysis of ultimatum bargaining', *Journal of Economic Behavior and Organization, III*, 367–88.

—— (1995). 'On the construction of preferred choices—The case of ultimatum proposals', Discussion Paper Economic Series No. 59, Humboldt University Berlin.

Hill, Elisabeth and Sally, David (2002). *Dilemmas and Bargains: Theory-of-Mind, Cooperation, and Fairness.* University College London Working Paper.

Hoffman, Elisabeth, McCabe, Kevin, and Smith, Vernon (1994). 'Preferences, property rights, and anonymity in bargaining games', *Games and Economic Behavior, 7*, 346–80.

—————— (1996). 'On expectations and monetary stakes in ultimatum games', *International Journal of Game Theory, 25*, 289–301.

Holm, Hakan J. (2000). 'Gender Based Focal Points', *Games and Economic Behavior, 32*(2), 292–314.

Isaac, Mark R., Walker, James M., Williams, Arlington W. (1994). 'Group size and the voluntary provision of public goods', *Journal of Public Economics, 54*, 1–36.

—— McCue, Kenneth F., and Plott, Charles R. (1985). 'Public goods provision in an experimental environment', *Journal of Public Economics, 26*, 51–74.

Kahneman, Daniel, Knetsch, Jack L., and Thaler, Richard (1986). 'Fairness as a constraint on profit seeking: Entitlements in the market', *American Economic Review, 76*, 728–41.

Knack, Steven and Keefer, Philip (1997). 'Does social capital have an economy payoff? A cross-country investigation', *Quarterly Journal of Economics, 112*, 1251–88.

Ledyard, John (1995). 'Public goods: A survey of experimental research', in Alvin Roth and John Kagel (eds), *Handbook of Experimental Economics*, Princeton, NJ: Princeton University Press.

Mehta, Judith, Starmer, Chris, and Sugden, Robert (1994). 'The nature of salience—an experimental investigation in pure coordination games', *American Economic Review, 84*, 658–73.

North, Douglass (1990). *Institutions, Institutional Change and Economic Performance.* Cambridge: Cambridge University Press.

Ostrom, Elinor (2000). 'Collective action and the evolution of social norms', *Journal of Economic Perspectives, 14*, 137–58.

Rabin, Matthew (1993). 'Incorporating fairness into game theory and economics', *American Economic Review, 83*(5), 1281–302.

Ross, Lee and Ward, Andrew (1996). 'Naive realism in everyday life: Implications for social conflict and misunderstanding', in E. S. Reed,

E. Turiel, and T. Brown (eds), *Values and Knowledge*, Mahwah, NJ: L. Erlbaum Associates, pp. 103–35.

Roth, Alvin E., Prasnikar, Vesna, Okuno-Fujiwara, Masahiro, and Zamir, Shmuel (1991). 'Bargaining and market behavior in Jerusalem, Ljubljana, Pittsburgh, and Tokyo: An experimental study', *American Economic Review, 81*, 1068–95.

Sally, David (1995). 'Conversation and cooperation in social dilemmas: A meta-analysis of experiments from 1958–1992', *Rationality and Society, 7*, 58–92.

Schelling, Thomas (1960). *The Strategy of Conflict*. Cambridge, MA: Harvard University Press.

Smith, Natalie (2000). 'Ultimatum and dictator games among the Chaldeans of Detroit', Talk to MacArthur Foundation Anthropology Project, December 4, 2000.

Weber, Roberto, and Camerer, Colin F. (2003). 'Cultural conflict and merger failure: an experimental approach', *Management Science, 49*(4), 400–15.

Weibull, Jörgen (1995). *Evolutionary Game Theory*. Cambridge, MA: MIT Press.

Williamson, Oliver (1985). *The Economic Institutions of Capitalism*. New York: Free Press.

Yamagishi, Toshio (1986). 'The provisioning of a sanctioning system as a public good', *Journal of Personality and Social Psychology, 5*, 110–16.

4

Coalitional Effects on Reciprocal Fairness in the Ultimatum Game: A Case from the Ecuadorian Amazon

John Q. Patton

INTRODUCTION

In this chapter, data are reported from an Ultimatum Game played in the community of Conambo in the summer of 1998. Conambo is located in a remote corner of the Ecuadorian Amazon. Its members comprise two ethnic/political groups who share common hunting, fishing, gathering, and horticultural lifeways, but who play the Ultimatum Game differently, coming to different conclusions as to what constitutes a fair offer. In the pages to follow, I will provide a brief theoretical background for this study; describe some of the differences and similarities of the two groups that comprise Conambo; present the Ultimatum Game data; and argue that differences in performance in the game are due to differences in coalitional stability, perceptions of trust, and needs to maintain reputation. In making this argument, I will first present data used to estimate average alliance strengths for the dyadic relationships between individual proposers in the Ultimatum Game and the other members of the community and report a significant positive correlation between alliance strengths and the amounts offered by proposers in the game. Second, the alliance strength data will be used to define coalitional boundaries, and coalitional differences in Ultimatum Game performance will be examined. Third, I will present meat-sharing data collected in a previous field season (1992–93) to argue that the Ultimatum Game data corresponds with patterns of cooperative behavior in Conambo. I will conclude by arguing that coalitional differences in performance in the Ultimatum Game reflect different perceptions of trust. Members of the less stable coalition have lower expectations that acts of cooperation will be reciprocated in the future. This difference in trust results in different judgments as to what offers to propose in the Ultimatum Game, and to differences in the importance of maintaining a reputation as a fair player.

THE ULTIMATUM GAME AND RECIPROCAL FAIRNESS

The theoretical context of this study is dealt with in detail in the introductory chapters of this volume. The goal of this section is to provide emphasis to some aspects of this context that are relevant to this case study and the conclusions drawn below while avoiding undue redundancy.

The anomaly of equitable play in the cross-cultural results of Ultimatum Games has led some game theorists to shift from models of *Homo economicus* to descriptions of the behavior of *Homo reciprocans* where the logic of 'reciprocal fairness' take precedence over selfish self-maximizing behaviors (e.g. Fehr and Gächter 1998). This relabeling of motivation for Ultimatum Game players implies that rules for reciprocity are innate. To state that reciprocal fairness is an aspect of human nature is to argue that the social contexts for the evolution of cooperation favored those individuals who engaged in cooperative equitable exchanges over those less inclined toward cooperative exchanges; that is, those who were asocial or engaged in selfish behaviors. The logic of reciprocal fairness would have been selected for in our evolutionary past as long as the long-term benefits derived from direct and indirect cooperative exchanges outweighed the short-term costs of equitable exchanges or foregoing the benefits of pursuing selfish self-maximizing behaviors at the expense of others.

Some models of the evolution of reciprocal fairness suggest that reputation effects are important, at least in some contexts. Providing false cues that one can be trusted is not likely to be a sustainable strategy within enduring social contexts, and an individual's success in instigating and maintaining social contracts for equitable exchange would be influenced by his or her ability to provide believable cues to others that he or she is a reciprocator, could be trusted, and would not defect on social contracts. The evolutionary context for reciprocal fairness is likely one in which anonymity, and social interactions that resemble single-shot games, are rare (although see Fehr and Henrich 2003 for a counter argument). Generous offers in the Ultimatum Game may reflect not only a logic of reciprocal fairness, but also that strategies for invoking this logic are not easily overruled by a conscience understanding that the game is anonymous and non-repeated, or that proposers do not fully trust the stated conditions of the game; that is, the perceived cost of assuming anonymity and non-opportunity for retribution is high. This 'illogical' invocation of reciprocal fairness suggests that reputation effects were an important aspect of the context for the evolution of adaptations for cooperative equitable exchanges, and recent modeling from the perspective of evolutionary game theory suggests that the evolution of reciprocal fairness within the context of the Ultimatum Game is linked to reputation effects (Nowak, Page, and Sigmund 2000).

The Machiguenga (Henrich and Smith, Chapter 5, this volume) were the first tribal society to play the game and their lack of conformity with the other samples indicates that reciprocal fairness may be strategic and conditional. The question is, what are the social or environmental conditions that evoke reciprocal fairness? Or better put, what are the conditions of Machiguenga life, as represented by Henrich and Smith's sample, that evokes the decision not to play the Ultimatum Game in a reciprocally fair way? In addition, why are the Machiguenga less concerned, compared with the other populations, about providing cues of selfish play; that is, less concerned about their reputation and conditioning future and existing social contracts?

CONAMBO

In 1998, when the Ultimatum Game was played, the community of Conambo had a population of 187 Achuar (a Jivaroan language) and Quichua speakers, living along the banks of the Conambo River. The headwaters of the Conambo River begin at the eastern slope of the Ecuadorian Andes and end where it joins with the Rio Pindo at the border with Peru (Figure 4.1). The current border with Peru was established in 1942 with the Protocol of Rio de Janeiro of 1942 after an armed conflict between Ecuador and Peru over oil reserves. As a result, Ecuador lost almost half of its territory to Peru, and the people living along the Conambo River, along with others in the Ecuadorian Amazon, lost important access to river trade routes

F<small>IG</small>. 4.1. Location of Conambo

to the south. For the Achuar, who were concentrated to the west of the Conambo River, this loss of trade was devastating. The Achuar had been receiving carbines and ammunition from trade with people living in Peru and with these arms had established a balance of power with the Shuar who lived to the west of them. The Shuar were the subject of Harner's well-known ethnography *The Jivaro: People of the Sacred Waterfalls* (1972). The Shuar lived closer to Spanish-speaking settlers and had access to black powder muzzle-loading shotguns. When trade to the south was cut off, the balance of power shifted toward the Shuar, who found a ready market for shrunken Achuar heads to supply the world's museums and collectors (cf. Ross 1984). The Achuar, fleeing head-taking raids, expanded to the south into Peru and toward the east into the Conambo River valley. The Achuar in Conambo and along the Rio Pindo represent the Achuar's eastern frontier.

By the time the Achuar reached the Conambo River, the Zaparos who lived in the valley had been all but wiped out. During the

sixteenth and seventeenth centuries, disease and enslavement
reduced the Zaparos from perhaps 100,000 or more (Whitten
1981: 138–39) to around 20,000, with some Zaparoan groups
completely annihilated (Sweet 1969). The Conambo River valley
was one of the last strongholds for the Zaparos until a measles
epidemic in the 1930s fragmented the last Zaparo settlements. The
epidemic triggered witchcraft accusations and the remaining
Zaparos were further decimated in feuds. Today, only four native
speakers of Zaparo remain along the Conambo River and the Rio
Pindo. They are some of the last speakers of the Zaparo language,
along with a group of about twenty who fled the area to relocate
along the Rio Curaray (1991 census, Paymal and Sosa 1993: 186).

When Achuar people moved into the Conambo River Valley to
flee the head-taking raids, it was largely depopulated. The majority
of remaining Zaparos intermarried with the Achuar and Quichua
speakers from other areas. Quichua, the lingua franca throughout
the region, was the only language in common for these mixed
households. The Quichua speakers in Conambo refer to themselves
ethnically as Quichua, but most can within a generation or so trace
their heritage directly to Achuar and Zaparo ancestry. This process
of ethnic formation of Ecuadorian Jungle Quichua from Achuar–
Zaparo intermarriage has a recent history in Conambo but is the
tail end of an ongoing process that probably began during the early
colonial period of the seventeenth century (Whitten 1976: 7).

The most obvious difference between the Achuar and Quichua
in Conambo is language; most of the Achuar are also fluent in
Quichua but few Quichua speak Achuar. There are some differences
in house style. More Achuar have oval roofs and more Quichua
have A-frame roofs. There are also subtle differences in how women
decorate pottery that serve as ethnic/political markers (Bowser
2000), but these differences go unnoticed by the untrained eye.
Although both Achuar and Quichua hunt using blowguns, only the
Achuar make blowguns, and the Quichua must get them directly or
indirectly from the Achuar. More Quichua adult men understand
and speak Spanish. Some of these men have spent time out of the
jungle working as laborers and two men brag about having done a
tour in the military during their youth. Some Achuar men have also
spent time working in oil company camps, and doing machete work
for plantations, but, by and large, Quichua men have had more
experience with outsiders and outside institutions. Achuar and

Quichua also self-identify themselves as such and are quick to draw this distinction. Every soccer game and volleyball match is played between the Achuar and the Quichua, although players are sometimes recruited across coalitional boundaries in order to even out the sides. The Achuar have a greater reputation as warriors and both sides recognize this (Patton 2000: 430). The Quichua state that the Achuar have trouble getting along with each other and the Quichua live more tranquil lives and are better at cooperating with each other.

Despite these differences, Achuar and Quichua in Conambo share much in common. Both are highly egalitarian. There are no headmen, and leadership is often situational and exercised primarily through example rather than from any position of authority. Both Achuar and Quichua are matrilocal. Men typically marry in from other communities. They hunt and eat the same animals using the same tools to acquire them. They both practice the same system of swidden horticultural. They grow the same varieties of plants in their gardens, and share the same system of usufruct-based land tenure. They share the same cosmology and many of the same myths, including myths of their origin. They also organize and cooperate in large and small cooperative labor exchanges according to the same system (*minga* in Quichua, *takát* in Achuar). Some *mingas* are community wide, such as helping to haul someone's freshly cut and carved canoe to the river or weeding the airstrip. Smaller *mingas* involving a few families are organized to help a household clear an area for a new garden or weed an existing one, haul small canoes, cut and clear trails, transport thatching for roofing a hut and logs for building a home, as well as to assist households in a number of other labor intensive jobs. The households that host a *minga* reciprocate those who provide labor for them by throwing a large party following the *minga* in which *chicha* (sweet manioc beer) flows freely and, if hunting was successful, all are well fed. Although people say that labor is fully reciprocated in the form of *chicha* and food, if someone has attended your *minga* there is an unspoken obligation to attend theirs if they have one within a reasonable period of time. This may be one reason that *mingas* tend to cluster in time. At times, months can go by without a *minga* and in one period in 1993 there were nineteen *mingas* in 21 days. These labor-sharing networks often reflect the political divide, but some families attend *mingas* hosted by Achuar and Quichua alike.

Meat, fish, garden products, and some gathered products such as turtle eggs and palm fruit are also shared between households. Food sharing networks also reflect the political divide but are generally, as with *mingas*, sub-factional; that is, smaller networks within the Achuar and Quichua factions (cf. Hames 2000). The sharing of meat is described in more detail subsequently.

Both Achuar and Quichua in Conambo share the same economic lifestyle and conditions because they live in the same isolated community. There are no roads to Conambo and no commercial trade via the Conambo River. The river below is closed at the border for military reasons, and starting about 2 days by canoe to the North the river is not navigable. There are no stores in Conambo or access to wage labor. There is radio contact with the missionaries and to a lesser degree with other jungle communities. The only reliable access to outside goods and services is by one of the six passenger airplanes operated by the Mission Aviation Fellowship based in Puyo, a 45-minute flight away. The cost of air transportation makes it prohibitive to market goods to or from Conambo. Individuals occasionally send out handicrafts, meat, or other jungle products to friends and kin who live in the city with the hopes that it will be reciprocated. The most common items shipped in to Conambo are shot and powder, hooks and line, soap, clothing, and medicine. No missionaries live in Conambo, but an elementary school, supported by Christian missionaries and the Department of Education, has been operating with two teachers in Conambo since soon after the community was founded in the mid-1970s.

In Conambo, the categories Achuar and Quichua are as much political as they are ethnic. People in Conambo explain that the Quichua live downriver from the center of the community, and that the Achuar live upriver from the center, but this generalization is based on political loyalties rather than ethnicity. Politics and ethnicity are malleable and fluid in Conambo and in the region as a whole. There is a great deal of intermarriage between Achuar and Quichua in Conambo. A number of households move in and out of the community, and others move their households across the political divide as their alliances shift. In 1993, two-thirds (eight of twelve) of the 'Quichua' coalition households were headed by an ethnically Achuar father or mother with mixed children (in one case, both household heads were ethnically Achuar), and one-fourth (three of twelve) of the 'Achuar' coalition's household heads were ethnically Quichua. Some individuals in Conambo identified themselves as either Achuar or Quichua depending on the context. Much of the mixing on the Quichua side was the result of political realignments following homicides. Genealogical data from Conambo indicate that in the recent past, 50 percent of men ended their lives as victims of homicide (Patton 2000: 424). Five families on the Quichua side have Achuar heritage, and realigned with the Quichua and intermarried with them following homicides that resulted from intra-Achuar feuding.

Between 1993 and 1998, when the Ultimatum Game was played, the population size of Conambo remained about the same, but divorces, migration, and relocations led to a reduction in the number of cross-over and mixed families, and a more ethnically homogeneous political divide. However, there remained a substantial degree of ethnic mixing on both the Achuar and Quichua side of the political divide. At the time the Ultimatum Game was played, one-fourth (four of sixteen) of the 'Achuar' households were ethnically mixed and about a third (three of ten) of the 'Quichua' households were mixed (see Figure 4.2). At the time the game was played, members of one Achuar household were in the process of politically realigning with the Quichua. A conflict arose between them and another Achuar household extensively over the contamination of a common source of clean drinking water. The realigning household was new to Conambo and had built a house upstream from an existing, well-established, household. They were accused of contaminating the stream, and tensions began to rise.

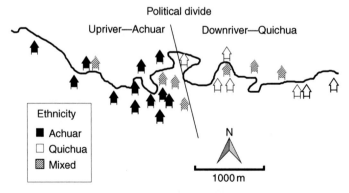

FIG. 4.2. Ethnic and political distribution of households in Conambo in 1998

Since conflicts in Conambo have the potential of escalating into violence and, potentially, homicide, it is typical for one of three things to happen in cases like this. They could leave the community. The male head of house could leave quickly, leaving his family, with the plan of returning after tempers have cooled. Or, if they have sufficient political ties with the opposing faction, they can stay within Conambo by joining the other faction. This last option usually involves building a new house across the political divide and moving. Political realignment has a number of advantages over the other options; an important one is that they can continue to harvest food from their existing gardens and not rely on the charity of others in a new community where they are less likely to have strong allies. During the time the Ultimatum Game was played, the realigning household was in the process of building a new home across and downriver on the Quichua side of the political divide.

The movements of people in and out of Conambo, and within the community, provide clear evidence as to the relative stability of the two coalitions. In the 5 years prior to playing the Ultimatum Game, the Achuar lost two and a half households (there were two divorces), and the Quichua coalition lost five households; four of these left to form their own community downriver. The Achuar gained four new households from outside of Conambo and one Quichua household realigned itself with the Achuar. During the same time, the Quichua gained only two households. One household left the Achuar coalition to join the Quichua. Of the twelve Achuar households in 1993, nine and a half (one women left Conambo after a divorce) remained in the Achuar coalition in 1998. Of the twelve Quichua households in 1993, only five remained with the Quichua coalition in 1998. During this time, the Achuar retained the vast majority of its members and had a net gain of four households. In contrast, the Quichua coalition was much less stable. They had a net loss of two households and a high degree of membership turnover. When the Ultimatum Game was played in Conambo, Quichua players were about half as likely to have their relationships within their coalition remain intact after 5 years, as compared with Achuar players.

The Achuar–Quichua coalitional divide largely defines the boundary of cooperation networks within Conambo. Both Achuar and Quichua cooperate in dealings with outsiders, but labor exchange networks, meat sharing, and the sharing of garden produce, as well as other reciprocal exchanges and 'gifts', are for the most part politically delimited.

Methods

Care was taken to follow the methods used by Henrich and Smith (Chapter 5, this volume) with the Machiguenga, but with one important exception. The game was implemented in such a way as to eliminate the opportunity for participants to talk with each other after details of the game were provided and prior to playing the game. The game was also designed in such a way as to minimize differences between individuals in terms of their understanding of money and symbolic representations of proportions.

All adult members of the community were invited to play a game for money. They were told that I was holding a *minga* in which participants' time would be compensated with money instead of *chicha* and food. Prior to this, people were asked what amount of money was worth a day's labor. The response was 20,000 *sucres* ($3.85). This was the amount of money they would expect to be paid if they were to fly out of the jungle and do machete work for a day at the tea plantation outside of Puyo. No one had access to this kind of wage labor in Conambo. I told people that they would receive 5,000 *sucres* for coming to play the game, and a chance to gain up to an additional 20,000 *sucres*. This was a very popular invitation and all fifty-eight adults in residence showed up on the day of the game. This included five individuals who were visiting from nearby communities. In addition to encouraging participation, the 5,000 *sucres* were offered so that no one would leave the game empty-handed and with ill feelings.

The morning of the game everyone gathered in one of the classrooms of the school. Each person entered the room, and his or her name was recorded on a card and placed in one of four piles, depending on sex and whether they lived up or downriver. Once everyone's name was recorded, I read the script used by Henrich in the Machiguenga study in Spanish and an assistant translated it into Quichua. A family member then gave one older Achuar woman who spoke only minimal Quichua the instructions in Achuar. After the instructions were given verbally, mock games were played for all participants to see, using various proposed divisions. At the front of the room was a table with a line drawn down the middle, and two chairs facing each other across the table on either side of the line. The chairs were empty and 20 coins, each worth 1,000 *sucres* were placed on the table in a pile in front of one chair. People were told that half of them would be proposers and half would be responders. The proposers would enter another room with a similar table in which the game would be played. Each proposer would be seated at the chair in front of the coins and would be asked to indicate the amount of their offer to the responder by placing a proportion of the coins across the line in front of the opposing empty chair. After the offer was made, the proposer would leave the room. Later, another participant would be asked to enter the room and sit in the responder's chair to see the division being offered, and then asked to accept or reject the offer. The two piles of coins on either side of the line were intended to provide an intuitive visual representation of the proposed division. Most adults in Conambo cannot read the denominations on monetary bills or calculate totals from coins of different denominations. It was made clear that accepting the offer meant that the responder would be able to keep the amount of money on their side of the line and that the anonymous proposer would be given the amount of money on the opposite side of the line. It was also made clear that refusing the offer meant that neither responder nor proposer would receive any proportion of the 20,000 *sucres*.

After the mock games were played, the four piles of cards on which participants' names were recorded were placed on top of each other and the cards were alternately dropped one by one into one of two boxes for all participants to see. The boxes were then shaken and people were asked to come forward when the card with his or her name was drawn from one of the boxes and read by an assistant. The first box contained the name of the proposers, although this was not revealed to the participants. When a person's name was called, that individual was asked to go to the one-room building in which the offers were made. Each proposer then handed me his or her card and was seated at the table to make an offer. Once the offer was made, the offer was recorded on the back of the card and the proposer was asked to report to a second assistant in a third room. The first assistant was then signaled and another name was called until the first box was empty and all of the offers made. The assistant then drew cards from the second box, and the responders reported to the second room and seated at the responder's chair. One of the proposer's cards was then chosen at random, and the responder's name was recorded on the proposer's card. The card was then flipped over and the proposer's offer was reconstructed on the table. The responder was asked to accept or reject the offer, was paid accordingly, and then given the 5,000 *sucres* for having participated. The responder was then asked the minimal offer that they would have accepted. The responder was then free to leave with his or her money. Once all the responders had been paid, the proposers were then asked to return to the room one by one to be paid and asked what his or her minimal acceptable offer would have been if he or she had been a responder. Throughout the game, the participants were asked not to speak to each other, and the assistants monitored the rooms to verify this.

Results

The mean offer from the twenty-nine proposers was 33.6 percent with a modal offer of 25 percent and a standard deviation of 19.5. Only two offers were rejected, a 20 and a 25 percent offer for a rejection rate of 6.9 percent. The mean minimal acceptable offer was 16.3 percent (14.7 percent for proposers and 17.9 percent for responders) and the mode for both proposers and responders was 5 percent, the lowest possible offer. In terms of mean offers, this places the people in Conambo closer to the Machiguenga than to the non-tribal societies. As with the Machiguenga, the distribution of offers in Conambo is bimodal with a secondary peak at 50 percent (Figure 4.3). The primary mode is relatively close to the Machiguenga and the secondary mode is consistent with offers from the non-tribal societies. There appear to be no sex differences in the amounts offered ($p = 0.791$ for independent samples t-test for equality of means; equal variance assumed, $p = 0.594$ for Levene's test for equality of variance, a multivariate regression with age and sex also yielded an insignificant correlation, $p = 0.300$). The fourteen women proposers had a mean offer of 34.6 percent and the fifteen men had a mean offer of 32.7 percent. Both had modal offers of 25 percent. There is a significant sex difference in minimal acceptable offers ($p = 0.013$ for independent samples t-test for equality of means; equal variance not assumed, $p < 0.001$ for

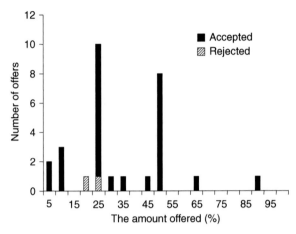

Fɪɢ. 4.3. Ultimatum Game offers, Conambo 1998

Levene's test for equality of variance). The mean minimal acceptable offer for women was 10.2 percent ($n = 29$), and for men the
mean minimal acceptable offer was 22.4 percent ($n = 29$).

COALITIONAL EFFECTS ON THE GAME

During the week following the playing of the Ultimatum Game in
Conambo, coalitional data were collected as part of an ongoing
longitudinal study of coalitional structures. In this section, these
coalitional data are used to examine coalitional differences in
people's performance in the game. Specifically, data concerning the
perceived strength of alliances between individuals within Conambo
are contrasted with the amounts offered in the Ultimatum Game.

Methods

A successive pile sort technique (see Weller and Romney 1988) was
used to estimate alliance strengths between the twenty-three male
household heads who were in residence at the time of the study.
Seventeen informants were shown photographs of each of the men
and asked to divide them into piles according to the criterion of who
would be most likely to maintain a coalition during a conflict.
Following a technique developed by Jim Boster (personal communication, see also Borgatti 1992*a*), informants were asked to

divide the photographs into as many piles or cliques as they liked. Then, informants were successively asked which of the piles were more easily aggregated until two piles were left. Then, returning to the original piles, informants were asked to start with the pile most easily divided (the clique with less cohesion), and to continue dividing piles until the informant felt that none of the remaining piles or cliques of men could be easily disassociated. Alliance strengths could be scored as the number of splitting events each pair of individuals survived before being divided into separate piles or the total number of divisions for those individuals who remained in the same pile at the end of each informant's successive pile sort task. Alliance strength scores for each dyadic pair of individuals were then normalized for each informant on a scale of zero to one, and then averaged across all informants using Anthropac 4.0 software (Borgatti 1992*b*). Each male head of household was then assigned an average alliance strength score by averaging the alliance strengths for his relationships with each of the other twenty-two male household heads in the sample. These male head of household's average alliance strengths were used to represent the average alliances between households. That is, other adult members of that household who were proposers in the game received the same average alliance strengths score as the male head of their household. Average alliance strengths were assigned for twenty of the twenty-nine proposers; of these, nine were women (five Quichua and four Achuar, one of the Quichua women was an adult daughter, and the rest were heads of households).

Results

There is a highly significant correlation (Pearson's $r = 0.565$, $p = 0.009$) between alliance strengths and offers in the ultimatum game (see Figure 4.4), such that proposers who have on average stronger alliances in the community make more generous offers than do proposers with weaker alliances. A hierarchical clustering of these alliance strength data was used to detect the coalitional boundary depicted in Figure 4.2 above.

There are highly significant differences in offers associated with the coalitional membership of the proposer (Figure 4.5). The fourteen upriver Achuar had a mean offer of 42.9 percent with a mode of 50 percent, and the twelve downriver Quichua had a mean

John Q. Patton

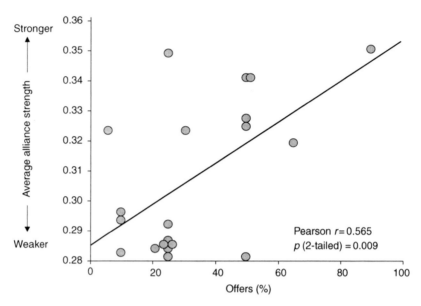

FIG. 4.4. Correlation between proposer's average alliance strengths and their offers

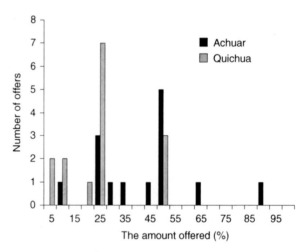

FIG. 4.5. Ultimatum Game offers by coalition

offer of 24.6 percent with a mode of 25 percent ($p = 0.007$ for independent samples t-test for equality of means; equal variance assumed, $p = 0.124$ for Levene's test for equality of variance). These data suggest that the Achuar play the game according to the logic of reciprocal fairness, while the Quichua play using a more rational economic logic, like the Machiguenga. Among the proposers, one individual was politically Achuar but ethnically Quichua (she is counted in the data above as an Achuar). She made an offer of 50 percent, consistent with other Achuar offers. None of the Quichua proposers were ethnically Achuar. In the sample of Quichua proposers, three were visiting from a community down-river. They have ties with Quichua households but are not members of the Conambo Quichua coalition, and they made offers of 5, 25, and 50 percent. These outsiders are not included in the *t*-test above. The relationship between average alliance strength and amounts offered appears to be a group effect rather than an individual effect (see Figure 4.6). The Achuar have on average stronger alliances than do the Quichua, and they on average make higher offers, but the relationship between stronger alliance strength and higher offers does not hold within the Achuar and Quichua coalitions.

Ethnic identity is also significantly associated with offers. The significance of the relationship between ethnic identity and offers has a 97 percent confidence ($p = 0.022$), slightly less than but comparable to that of coalitional membership (greater than

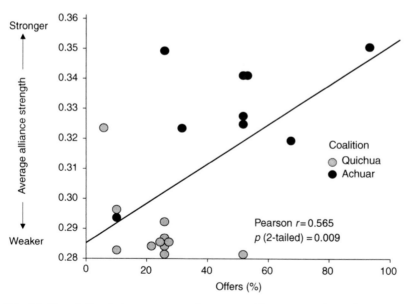

FIG. 4.6. Correlation between proposer's average alliance strengths and their offers by coalition

99 percent confidence), but given that there is only one proposer in the game who's ethnic identity does not correspond to her political identity, a definitive test to determine the relative importance of ethnic and political influences on offers is not possible with this sample.

No significant or near significant relationships were found between ultimatum game offers and sex, age, or social status either separately or in combination. Combining these variables with coalitional membership produced an insignificant model ($p = 0.130$), and ethnic identity in combination with these variables produced an even less significant model ($p = 0.317$).

There are coalitional differences in the minimal acceptable offer data. The minimal acceptable offer data set is twice as large (proposers and responders) as the data set for offers, and has a greater number of individuals whose ethnicity and coalitional membership do not correspond (four responders and one proposer). Coalitional independence in minimal acceptable offers is significant at the 98th percentile of confidence ($p = 0.016$ for independent samples t-test for equality of means; equal variance not assumed, $p = 0.004$ for Levene's test for equality of variance). The mean for the Achuar minimal acceptable offer was 22.9 percent ($n = 28$) and the mean for the Quichua was less than half that at 10.4 percent ($n = 25$). In contrast, dividing the minimal acceptable offer data into ethnic groups is done with lower confidence ($p = 0.083$ for independent samples t-test for equality of means; equal variance not assumed, $p = 0.033$ for Levene's test for equality of variance). The mean minimal acceptable offer for ethnic Achuar was 21.7 percent ($n = 26$), and the mean minimal acceptable offer for the Quichua is 12.4 percent ($n = 27$).

Considering coalitional membership and sex gives a range of mean minimal acceptable offers with Achuar men the highest (30.0 percent, $n = 14$), followed by Quichua men (16.3 percent, $n = 12$), then Achuar women (15.7 percent, $n = 14$), and finally Quichua women, who all said that they would have taken the minimal possible offer (5.0 percent, $n = 13$). The mean minimal acceptable offers for ethnic identity by sex was comparable, with women's mean minimal acceptable offers unchanged, but with a narrower range of mean minimal acceptable offers for the men (Achuar men 26.9 percent, $n = 13$; Quichua men 18.8 percent, $n = 16$; Achuar women 15.7 percent, $n = 14$; Quichua women 5.0

TABLE 4.1. Mean minimal acceptable offers by sex, coalition, and ethnic identity

Sex	Coalition		Ethnic	
	Achuar (%)	Quichua (%)	Achuar (%)	Quichua (%)
Men	30.0 ($n = 14$)	16.3 ($n = 12$)	26.9 ($n = 13$)	18.8 ($n = 16$)
Woman	15.7 ($n = 14$)	5.0 ($n = 13$)	15.7 ($n = 14$)	5.0 ($n = 15$)
Men and Women	22.9 ($n = 28$)	10.4 ($n = 25$)	21.1 ($n = 27$)	12.1 ($n = 31$)

percent, $n = 15$). See Table 4.1 for a summary of mean minimal acceptable offers by sex, coalition, and ethnic identity.

As stated above, there are few cultural and economic differences between Conambo Achuar (upriver coalition) and Quichua (downriver coalition) that would predict that they would perform differently in the Ultimatum Game. The differences that do exist would lead to an incorrect prediction. The Quichua are described as being more cooperative and as having more experience with markets and commerce. The expectation is that they would be more likely to play like the non-tribal sample—that is, invoke reciprocal fairness—yet they comprise the coalition whose members make less generous offers.

COALITIONAL DIFFERENCES IN MEAT-SHARING

The coalitional differences in Ultimatum Game offers and minimal acceptable offers are echoed in coalitional differences in cooperation indicated by patterns of meat-sharing. The alliance data from 1998 are consistent with data collected in 1993. The Achuar had on average stronger alliances and their alliances were more structured and predictable, than were Quichua alliances (Patton 1996). Meat-sharing data collected in 1993 also showed a marked coalitional difference, and provided evidence that men in Conambo were pursuing different strategies of cooperation depending on their status and coalitional affiliation.

Methods

In this section, data on men's status and the number of households to which they give meat are compared. To collect the status data in

1993, informants were shown photographs of the thirty-three adult men who were in residence, in sets of three, presented randomly, and asked to rank them in terms of their relative status (see Patton 2000 and 1996: 158–203 for a more detailed description of this data set and men's status in Conambo). Each man was given a score: two points for being ranked first in the triad (for being rank higher than each of the other two men), and one point for being ranked second. For this task forty-seven male and female informants (twenty-six Achuar and twenty-one Quichua) were consulted. The equivalent of ninety-nine dyadic comparisons were made by each informant for a total of 4,653 dyads, each representing a status judgment where one man is ranked higher than another man (each triad is equivalent to three dyads). Each of the thirty-three men appeared in 282 dyads and on average was compared 8.81 times with each of the other men. Of these thirty-three men, twenty-four were heads of households from which meat-sharing data were also collected.

For the meat-sharing task, representatives from twenty-four households were shown photographs of the male heads of households of the other twenty-three households and asked whether this man had ever given any meat to the representative's household. These twenty-four households were a complete sample of all of the extended family households in Conambo in 1993. Of these twenty-four household representatives, eleven were the senior man of the house and nine were the senior woman of the house. For the remaining four households where the senior husband or wife was unavailable at the time the task was performed, the next oldest adult in the extended household was consulted (two sons, one daughter, and one son-in-law). Once informants identified which men had given meat to their household, they were asked to rank-order these men in terms of who had given the most meat. These ranks were normalized for each household, with the man who gave the most often receiving a score of one, those who did not contribute a zero, and the others scaled in-between, according to their ranking.

Results

There is a highly significant relationship between a man's status and the number of households to which he gives meat (see Figure 4.7; $r = 0.568$, $p = 0.004$). There is no correlation between a man's status and the number of households from which he receives meat

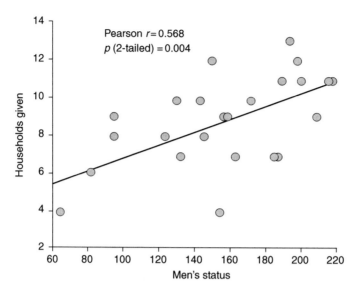

Fɪɢ. 4.7. The number of households a man gives to by his status

$(r = -0.025, p = 0.907)$. This asymmetry in household meat transfers indicates that the relationship between status and giving is not a
function of higher status men engaging in larger networks of
reciprocal relationships. Additionally, there is a highly significant
relationship between a man's status and his ranking as a meat-giver
averaged across households $(r = 0.533, p = 0.007)$. There is a marginally significant relationship $(r = 0.383, p = 0.065)$ between a
man's status and the ratio of the number of households to which he
gives divided by the number of households from which he receives.
This ratio is an index of generosity, with ratios above one indicating
that a man gives meat to more households than he receives meat
from. In summary, higher status men in Conambo gave to more
households than did lower status men, and of the households they
gave to, they gave more than did lower status men. Additionally,
the correlation between men's status and generosity was significant
at the 93rd percentile of certainty.

There are coalitional differences in the relationship between a
man's status and the number of households to which he gives meat.
There remains a significant relationship among men of the Achuar
coalition between status and the number of households to which he
gives meat (Figure 4.8; $r = 0.645, p = 0.013$), but not so for men of

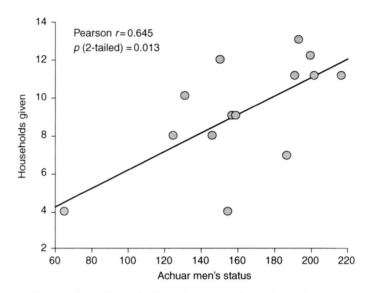

FIG. 4.8. The number of households Achuar men give to by their status

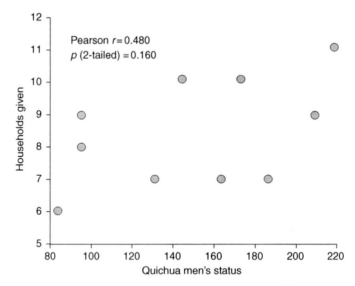

FIG. 4.9. The number of households Quichua men give to by their status

the Quichua coalition (Figure 4.9; $r = 0.480$, $p = 0.160$). Likewise, the relationship between a man's average rank as a meat-giver and his status remains significant for the Achuar ($r = 0.580$, $p = 0.030$), but not for the Quichua ($r = 0.467$, $p = 0.173$). Whereas there is a marginally significant relationship between a man's status and his ratio of giving to receiving in Conambo, this relationship is significant at the 98th percentile of certainty for the Achuar (Figure 4.10; $r = 0.612$, $p = 0.020$), but is not significant for men of the Quichua coalition (Figure 4.11; $r = 0.265$, $p = 0.460$). These correlations are tabulated in Table 4.2.

The relationship between a man's ratio of giving to receiving and status appears to be influenced more by politics than by ethnicity. The relationship of giving to receiving and status for ethnic Achuar is less significant ($r = 0.491$, $p = 0.054$, $n = 16$) than it is for coalitional Achuar. This relationship remains insignificant for ethnic Quichua ($r = 0.342$, $p = 0.407$, $n = 8$). This difference in confidence (93 percent verses 98 percent) results from the shifting of four men who were ethnic Achuar but coalitional Quichua, and two ethnic Quichua men who were members of the Achuar coalition. As with the Ultimatum Game data, patterns of cooperation in Conambo, as seen in their sharing of meat, show significant group differences that appear to be influenced by coalitional factors.

DISCUSSION AND CONCLUSIONS

The coalitional differences in performance in the Ultimatum Game and patterns in meat-sharing are striking. The meat-sharing data

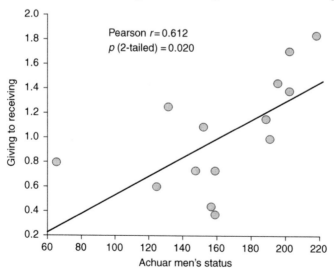

FIG. 4.10. Achuar men's ratio of giving to receiving by their status

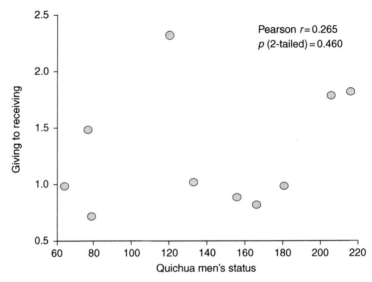

FIG. 4.11. Quichua men's ratio of giving to receiving by their status

TABLE 4.2. Correlations between men's status and meat giving by coalition

Meat giving	Men's status					
	All ($n = 24$)		Achuar ($n = 14$)		Quichua ($n = 10$)	
	r	p	r	p	r	p
Households given to	0.568	0.004**	0.645	0.013*	0.480	0.160
Households received from	−0.025	0.907	−0.077	0.795	−0.083	0.819
Average giving rank	0.533	0.007**	0.580	0.030*	0.467	0.173
Ratio of giving to receiving	0.383	0.065	0.612	0.020*	0.265	0.460

Note: All correlations (r) are Pearson's correlation coefficients. All measurements of significance (p) are two-tailed.
* Denotes significant correlations.
** Denotes highly significant correlations.

provide support to the notion that the coalitional differences in the experimental data reflect observable coalitional differences in patterns of cooperation in Conambo. However, the meat-sharing data do not support the notion that the Achuar as a group are more generous than the Quichua. Whereas high status Achuar men are generous as measured by their ratio of giving to receiving meat, this is balanced by ungenerous lower status Achuar men. Overall, of fourteen Achuar men (see Figure 4.10), seven gave generously (a ratio greater than one), six gave to fewer than they received, and one gave equitably (a ratio of one). Among the ten Quichua men (see Figure 4.11), four had giving to receiving ratios greater than one, three gave equitably, and three had ratios below one. None of the Quichua men gave to half as many households as they received from, but two Achuar men did. As a group, there appears to be little difference in overall generosity between Achuar and Quichua men. Certainly, given these meat-sharing data, it would be hard to make the case that Achuar men are more generous than Quichua men.

The difference in meat-sharing behavior between the Achuar and Quichua is not easily attributable to different norms of reciprocity; that is, it would be difficult to argue that the Achuar are culturally more generous and by contrast the Quichua are culturally stingy. This position does not correspond to the meat-sharing data, or to perceptions in Conambo as to the differences in the cooperative natures of Achuar and Quichua people. Rather, the differences in meat-sharing, offers in the Ultimatum Game, and minimal acceptable offers can be explained by reference to the same variable—coalitional strength and stability.

Whereas Achuar men may not be more generous overall, as compared with Quichua men, it appears that for some Achuar men it is worth the effort to provide gifts of meat as part of a political strategy (Patton and Bowser 2000). These high status Achuar men may be giving meat for the same reasons that lobbyists give resources to members of Congress; that is, to manage political risk by buying political loyalty. Such 'gift' giving only makes sense if one has trust that the political structures and the individuals within them will be around long enough to call in the favor. Lame-duck politicians get little attention from lobbyists because they are in the end rounds of a repeated cooperative game. Politically active Achuar men seem to have sufficient trust that their coalition will endure long enough to see a return to their investment, while Quichua men do not. Quichua men give just as much as Achuar men but they seem to be motivated by other factors such as kinship and reciprocity in kind (Patton and Bowser 2000).

The demographic data for Conambo indicate that the Achuar coalition is more stable and Achuar men are more likely to have enduring alliances. Coalitional stability is of primary concern in Conambo where the recent history of male homicide rates indicates the need to have strong alliances. Most people who leave Conambo do so to avoid conflicts, and the greater volatility in Quichua coalitional membership is one indication that Quichua households may not have the political support within Conambo to weather conflicts as compared with Achuar households. Avoidance of conflicts may also explain the low rejection rate in the Ultimatum Game. Only two offers were rejected (20 percent by a Quichua man, and 25 percent by an Achuar women). All of the 5 and 10 percent offers were accepted. The modal minimal acceptable offer for both responders and proposers was the smallest possible unit (5 percent). Compared with this, both Achuar and Quichua modal offers seem generous. Perhaps the people of Conambo are loss-averse, but another explanation is that refusing an offer would be seen as confrontational (see also Hill and Gurven, Chapter 13, this volume), equivalent to turning down someone's gift because it was not good enough. Such an act would be a declaration that you were dealt with unfairly and that you were mad enough to act spitefully. Such declarations may have serious consequences in tribal societies in which one's well-being is highly dependent on one's relationships with others, and less mediated by social institutions such as markets or formal legal systems which claim, and act to enforce, a monopoly on violence and revenge. Apart from possible retaliation, people who acquire a reputation for being confrontational may find that others will deal with them more cautiously and will be less likely to engage them in new social contracts. Reluctance to be confrontational may also provide an explanation for the sex and coalitional differences in the minimal acceptable offer data. Women may be more inclined to avoid confrontations than are men, and members of the weaker coalition (the Quichua) may also feel that they are less able to weather confrontations as compared with the Achuar, who have stronger and more stable alliances.

Among tribal peoples, political instability may come from many sources. Unequal access to outside goods and services, the transition to a market economy, acculturation, internal and external conflicts, and the inadequacy of western institutions to articulate with nonhierarchical political structures, among others, may contribute to the undermining of confidence that the traditional rules of reciprocity are still intact. Members of societies undergoing such transitions may find themselves between systems of reciprocity, or perceive that the new rules are not applied fairly. This may be the case with the Machiguenga, who played the Ultimatum Game. They recently made the transition to life in a settled community where some, but not all, have access to wage labor (Henrich 1997), and where some, but not all, may have made the transition to trust the new set of rules. This economic inequality may explain the low offers among the Machiguenga as well as the secondary mode at 50 percent. This unequal access to economic resources may have an impact on their perceptions as to whether or not the rules apply to them; that is, to their perception of the likelihood of recouping the cost of cooperation.

However, none of these economic factors explain the coalitional difference in how the people in Conambo played the Ultimatum Game or difference in the sharing of meat. Because they live in the same community, the Achuar and Quichua in Conambo have equal access to economic resources and are equally impacted by outside influences. Instead, I propose that the coalitional differences in the game are due to differences in coalitional stability that result from the internal dynamics of Conambo politics, and with recruitment and turnover problems associated with the need to maintain a balance of power. The Achuar do better in this regard than do the Quichua, and as a result have a stronger and more stable coalition.

Differences in coalitional stability must have a significant effect on perceptions of trust that if one pays the cost of cooperation today—that is, acts generously—that he or she will derive a benefit in the future. Said another way, coalitional instability undermines one's ability to condition future play, and discounts the benefits derived from investing in the creation and maintenance of a reputation as a fair player. In Conambo, maintenance of such a reputation may be more valuable for members of the Achuar coalition who are reasonably certain that their relationships will endure long enough for acts of altruism to be reciprocated. In contrast, members of the Quichua coalition may be less concerned with sending cues of selfishness, because their social contracts are less enduring and, as a result, their acts of altruism are more likely to go unreciprocated. Because of this, Achuar and Quichua may come to different conclusions as to what offers in the Ultimatum Game are fair, or at least acceptable, and differ in their need to provide cues that they are fair reciprocators.

I have argued above that the group differences in patterns of cooperation in Conambo are due more to political factors than to differences in enculturation. The bimodal distributions in the Machiguenga offers (Henrich and Smith, Chapter 5, this volume), as well as with the differences in small camps verses large camp Hadza (Marlow, Chapter 6, this volume), may also be the result of differences in political structures, since both of these studies used ethnically homogeneous populations and, in the case of the Hadza, people typically move back and forth between small and large camps. As with the Achuar and Quichua in Conambo, the Machiguenga and the Hadza may be of two minds as to what is an acceptable, if not fair, offer depending on their political context. It may be fruitful to explore the possibility that political variables may influence Ultimatum Game performance in other populations. Analyses of these data from Conambo indicate that differences in coalitional strength and stability may be an important factor influencing Ultimatum Game performance. Circumstantial evidence also indicates that politics is more important than ethnicity in the Ultimatum Game offers. Although only one proposer's ethnicity and coalitional membership are inconsistent, this ethic Quichua women married to an Achuar man and allied with the Achuar, made an offer that was equal to the Achuar mode (50 percent). The male head of the Achuar household in the process of defecting to the Quichua (described above) made the lowest offer among the Achuar (5 percent). The three outsiders who were proposers in the game, and who lacked a coalitional context in which to frame their decision, showed little consistency in their offers. Their offers equaled the Achuar mode (50 percent), the Quichua mode (25 percent) and the lowest possible offer (5 percent). Their offers ranged the full spectrum of the offers made by Conambo Quichua. This circumstantial evidence, combined with coalitional differences in Ultimatum Game offers, patterns in meat-sharing, and the minimal acceptable offer data indicate that at least in Conambo, politics do matter.

REFERENCES

Borgatti, S. (1992*a*). *Anthropac 4.0, Methods Guide*. Columbia: Analytic Technologies.
——(1992*b*). *Anthropac 4.0*. Columbia: Analytic Technologies.
Bowser, B. J. (2000). 'From pottery to politics: an ethnoarchaeological study of political factionalism, ethnicity, and women's domestic pottery in the Ecuadorian Amazon', *Journal of Archaeological Method and Theory*, 7, 219–48.
Fehr, E. and Henrich, J. (2003) 'Is strong reciprocity a maladaptation?', in P. Hammerstein (ed.), *Genetic and Cultural Evolution of Cooperation*, Cambridge, MA: MIT Press.
—— and Gächter, S. (1998). 'Reciprocity and economics. The economic implications of homo reciprocans', *European Economic Review*, 42, 845–59.
Hames, R. (2000). 'Reciprocal altruism in Yanomamö food exchange', in L. Cronk, N. Chagnon, and W. Irons (eds), *Adaptation and Human Behavior: An Anthropological Perspective*, New York: Aldine de Gruyter.
Harner, M. (1972). *The Jivaro: People of the Sacred Waterfalls*. Garden City, NY: Anchor Press/Doubleday.
Henrich, J. (1997). 'Market incorporation, agricultural change, and sustainability among the Machiguenga Indians of the Peruvian Amazon', *Human Ecology*, 25, 319–51.
——(2000). 'Does culture matter in economic behavior? Ultimatum game bargaining among the Machiguenga', *American Economic Review*, 90(4), 973–79.
Nowak, M. A., Page, K. M., and Sigmund, K. (2000). 'Fairness versus reason in the ultimatum game', *Science*, 289, 1773–5.
Patton, J. Q. (1996). Thoughtful Warriors: Status, Warriorship, and Alliance in the Ecuadorian Amazon. Ph.D. Dissertation, University of California, Santa Barbara.
——(2000). 'Reciprocal altruism and warfare: a Case from the Ecuadorian Amazon', in L. Cronk, N. Chagnon, and W. Irons (eds), *Adaptation and Human Behavior: An Anthropological Perspective*, New York: Aldine de Gruyter.
—— and Bowser, B. J. (2000). 'Hunting, Cooperation, and Political Strategies in the Ecuadorian Amazon'. Paper presented at the American Anthropological Association Meetings, San Francisco.
Paymal, M. and Sosa, C. (1993). *Amazon Worlds*. Quito, Ecuador: Sinchi Sacha Foundation.
Ross, J. B. (1984). 'Effects of contact on revenge hostilities among the Achuara Jivaro', in R. B. Ferguson (ed.), *Warfare, Culture, and Environment*, New York: Academic Press.

Sweet, D. G. (1969). The population of the upper Amazon valley, 17th and 18th Centuries. M.A. Thesis, University of Wisconsin, Madison.

Weller, S. and Romney, A. K. (1988). *Systematic Data Collection*. Newbury Park, CA: Sage Publications.

Whitten, N. (1976). *Sacha Runa: Ethnicity and Adaptation of Ecuadorian Jungle Quichua*. Chicago, IL: University of Illinois Press.

——(1981). 'Amazonia today at the base of the Andes: An ethnic interface in ecological, social, and ideological perspectives', in N. Whitten (ed.), *Cultural Transformation and Ethnicity in Modern Ecuador*, Chicago, IL: University of Illinois Press.

5

Comparative Experimental Evidence from Machiguenga, Mapuche, Huinca, and American Populations

Joseph Henrich and Natalie Smith

This chapter reports experimental results from bargaining and public goods experiments performed among the Machiguenga of the Peruvian Amazon, the Mapuche and Huinca of southern Chile, and with US control groups in Los Angeles and Ann Arbor (MI). We will emphasize three findings. First, results from both our ultimatum bargaining and Public Goods Games indicate much greater between-group variation than previous work has suggested (see the Introductory Chapter). Second, if individual economic decisions vary as a consequence of differences in individuals' circumstances, then variables such as wealth, household size, age, and sex should provide some explanatory power. However, individual-level economic and demographic variables do not account for much, if any, of the variation. Finally, despite the failure of individual-level variables to explain variation, our results do seem to reflect group-level differences in the economic life of these groups, as captured in numerous ethnographic accounts (including our own).

In this chapter, we begin with a brief ethno-historical sketch of the Machiguenga, Mapuche, and Huinca. Then, we sketch our Ultimatum Game methodologies, and present the results. Next, we describe the Public Goods Game methodologies, and present those results—we do this first for the Machiguenga/American comparison and then for the Mapuche/Huinca experiment. In presenting these results, we emphasize the results pertaining to our three major points. We will conclude with some theoretical and methodological points related to our findings.

ETHNOGRAPHIC SKETCHES

The Machiguenga

Traditionally, the Machiguenga lived in mobile single-family units and small extended-family hamlets scattered throughout the tropical forests of the southeastern Peruvian Amazon. They subsisted, and continue to subsist, on a combination of hunting, fishing, gathering and manioc-based, swidden horticulture (Johnson 1983). Economically independent at the family-level, this Arawakan-speaking people possess little social hierarchy or political complexity. Most sharing and exchange occurs within extended kin circles. Cooperation above the family level is almost unknown, except in a limited form during occasional communal fish poisonings (Baksh 1984; Johnson and Earle 1987).

During the last 30 years, missionaries, markets, and government-administered schools have sedentized and centralized most of the Machiguenga into a number of villages in a continual process of increasing market integration. As these demographic changes have strained local game and wild food resources, the Machiguenga have gradually intensified their reliance on horticultural products, especially manioc (a starchy root crop). Until recently, the Machiguenga faced few shortages, owing to their low population densities and their periodic resettlement in sparsely populated areas (moving every 4 years; Johnson 1989). In larger, settled communities, many Machiguenga face increasing shortages of good soil, fish, game, and palm roofing materials (Smith 2001*a*). Furthermore, in an effort to buy increasingly available western goods, many Machiguenga farmers have begun to produce cash crops (primarily coffee and cocoa), raise domesticated animals (e.g. chickens, ducks, and guinea pigs) and participate in limited wage labor (usually for logging or oil companies; Henrich 1997).

Although most Machiguenga now live in communities of about 300 people, they remain primarily a family-level society. This means that families can fully produce for their own needs (food, clothing, etc.) and do not rely on institutions or other families for their social or economic welfare—although there is a constant demand for market items such as machetes, salt, sugar, and steel axes. With the exception of recent trips to nearby towns (minimum 8-hour trip), anonymous transactions are almost unknown. When local bilingual schools (Machiguenga–Spanish) are not in session, and the incessant rains of the wet season make travel difficult, many families move away from the community to live in their distant gardens— often located two to three hours away from the village.

The Mapuche

Until the arrival of the Spanish in the mid-sixteenth century, the Mapuche lived much like the traditional Machiguenga. These semi-nomadic slash and burn horticulturalists organized themselves in economically independent single-family units or extended-family groupings, and subsisted on a mix of game, gathered foods and horticultural products (primarily potatoes, quinoa, and corn). Unlike the Machiguenga, however, the Mapuche 'Lonkos' (hereditary lineage leaders) were able to muster substantial numbers of fierce, stalwart warriors who thwarted Incan, Spanish, and Chilean efforts at conquest and pacification for more than 400 years.

Despite their struggle against European political conquest, the Mapuche gradually adopted cereal agriculture (primarily wheat and oats), ox-driven steel plows, three-field agriculture, and numerous Old World domesticates (horses, cows, chickens, pigs, and sheep). Since their permanent settlement in *reducciones* in the 1860s, the Mapuche have also been compelled to adopt sedentary living, private ownership of land, and higher levels of community integration (or at least the appearance of such). Only more recently have they begun to speak Spanish, construct European-style housing, and gained access to formal education. Expanding rural Mapuche populations are now experiencing intense land pressure and massive rural–urban migration. At the same time, Mapuche farmers have avoided agricultural innovation, intensification, and large-scale economic cooperation.

Today, families are highly independent, sedentary, subsistence-oriented agriculturalists. Households grow 1 or 2 ha of wheat (the primary source of calories), a few sacks of oats for the animals, and a small amount of vegetables and legumes for household consumption. The average family manages 6–8 ha, and owns two oxen, two cows, one horse, and two pigs. The sale of animals, lumber (fast growing species of pine and eucalyptus) and occasional/seasonal wage-labor generate some cash income. Individual families continue to engage in one-on-one reciprocal exchanges of labor, but larger-scale *mingacos*, in which many men perform cooperative work for a single family, have become increasingly rare—except in female headed households. Exchanges of goods (meat, animals, vegetables, etc.) between families and neighbors proceeds on a cash basis, although credit is extended to friends and relatives.

The Huinca

Inhabiting the small, rural towns around which Mapuche farmers live are non-Mapuche Chileans, or *Huinca* (the Mapuche term for non-Mapuches), who are of mixed European (primarily Spanish) descent, and of comparable economic status to the Mapuche. Most Huinca live in single or extended family households, are almost entirely dependent on the market, and work in their town as temporary wage laborers—although some have more permanent jobs in local businesses. Huinca households participate in larger, interdependent, social networks of exchange. Social ties and loyalty often hold sway over prices in deciding where to shop, or from whom to obtain services. We use the *Huinca* as a control group in the Mapuche Public Goods Game.

THE ULTIMATUM BARGAINING GAME

Although typical Ultimatum Game results consistently and substantially deviate from the predictions of game theory (under typical assumptions and standard preferences), the results are very robust. Experimental economists have systematically studied the influence of various factors on the game's results, including stake size[1] (Tompkinson and Bethwaite 1995; Fehr and Tougareva 1996; Hoffman, McCabe, and Smith 1996; Slonim and Roth 1998; Cameron 1999), degree of Anonymity (Forsythe *et al.* 1994;

---

[1] For example, Lisa Cameron's (1999) analysis of game data from Indonesia, where she was able to provide sums equivalent to approximately 3 months' salary for test subjects, strongly rejects the hypothesis that higher stakes move individuals closer to game-theoretic behavior. In fact, her data suggests that proposers generally move away from game-theoretical predictions and toward a 50–50 split; responders, consequently, accept these proportionately higher offers more frequently. Similarly, in Russia, Fehr and Tougareva (1996) used stakes involving 2–3 months' salary and found no differences in subjects behavior compared with low stakes games (also see Tompkinson and Bethwaite 1995; Hoffman, McCabe, and Smith 1996).

Bolton and Zwick 1995), context (Hoffman *et al.* 1994; Konow 1996), and 'culture' (Roth *et al.* 1991; Cameron 1999), but have found little or no effect on players' behavior. Readers unfamiliar with the Ultimatum Game should refer to Chapter 1 for summaries both of the relevant game theory and of previous experimental results. Most important for our purposes: the robustness of cross-national research led researchers to believe that people from all over the world behave quite similarly in the Ultimatum Game, and therefore possess similar notions of fairness and punishment. In studies from places as varied as Ljubljana, Pittsburgh, Tokyo (Roth *et al.* 1991), Yogyakarta (Cameron 1999), Tucson (Hoffman *et al.* 1994), and Los Angeles proposers make similar mean offers (40–50 percent of the total), and responders frequently reject low, 'inequitable' offers.

Ultimatum Game methodology

To deal with the particular challenges of performing experiments in the ethnographic settings of both the Mapuche and the Machiguenga, we had to modify the typical experimental procedures used in the Ultimatum Game. Among the Machiguenga, Henrich first gathered twelve men together between the ages of 18 and 30 under the auspices of 'playing a fun game for money'. He explained the game to the group in Spanish using a set script written with simple terminology like 'first person', to refer to the proposer, and 'second person', for the responder. After this, although the Machiguenga speak Spanish fairly well, a bilingual schoolteacher (a *mestizo* who teaches the Machiguenga) re-explained the game in the Machiguenga language (translating from the set script), and displayed the money that would be used to make payments. After this, each participant entered Henrich's house individually, where the teacher and Henrich explained the game a third time. A number of hypothetical, practice questions were administered to test the participant's comprehension of the game. Parts of the game were re-explained as necessary and often numerous examples were needed to make the game fully understood. After the individual confidently answered at least two hypothetical questions correctly, Henrich would submit the actual question with a pile of *soles* (the Peruvian currency) in view. The following day, after having successfully obtained twelve responses and paid out some money, randomly selected individuals were sought to play the game. Most people had already heard of the game and were eager to play. Henrich privately explained the game to each individual (usually in the participant's house) and ran through the same testing procedure as in the previous day. During this process several people were rejected because they, after 30+ minutes of explanation, could not understand the game—at least they could not answer the hypothetical questions. More details on this process and the sample can be found in Henrich (2000).

As a control experiment, Henrich repeated a nearly identical version of the Machiguenga Ultimatum Game with graduate students at the University of California, Los Angeles. This experiment sought to minimize differences in (1) stake size, (2) 'community closeness', (3) experimental procedures, (4) instructional details, and (5) the age of players, as well as controlling for some aspects of the experimenter himself. First, the Machiguenga's twenty-*soles* stake equals about 2.3 day's pay from the logging or oil companies that occasionally hire local labor. In order to match this amount, Henrich set the University of California, Los Angeles stake at $160, which is about 2.3 days pay for a graduate student working as a 'reader' ($9–$10 per hour after taxes). Second, because the Machiguenga were told that they were playing with an anonymous person *from their community*, which contains about seventy adults, the University of California, Los Angeles experiment was restricted to graduate students in the Department of Anthropology (also a community of about seventy adults), and the subjects were informed accordingly. Third, as with the Machiguenga, all University of California, Los Angeles players received instructions from the same script, and then further explanation was given informally using a series of examples. Each subject then had to answer hypothetical test questions before actually playing the game. Fourth, in both cases the same written instructions were used (translated into English at University of California, Los Angeles), as well as the same pattern of examples and test questions. Fifth, the average age of Machiguenga and University of California, Los Angeles subjects was about the same (26.3 and 25.7, respectively). Finally, Henrich was the experimenter in both cases, and was personally known (to varying degrees) by most of the University of California, Los Angeles and Machiguenga subjects.

Among the Mapuche, Henrich again repeated the procedure used among the Machiguenga as closely as possible. However, four differences deserve note. First, unlike with the Machiguenga, Henrich manipulated thirty 100-*peso* coins (the stakes were 3000 Chilean *pesos*) to demonstrate the game and to pose the test questions—Machiguenga examples were only verbal or occasionally sketched on paper. This was done with the hope of facilitating instruction. Second, Mapuche players were told that they would be paired with another Mapuche in the region, but not with a neighbor. Third, the stakes were somewhat lower in this game: 3000 *pesos* equals about 1 day's pay in local wage labor (remember, stake size has little or no effect in previous work). Fourth, the average age of Mapuche players was 38, a decade or so older than the Machiguenga and University of California, Los Angeles participants (we show in the next section that age does not affect the offers).

ULTIMATUM GAME RESULTS

Our Ultimatum Game results show much greater cross-group variation than previous experimental work, and the size of this effect is substantially larger than that created by existing manipulations of context, stake size, within-population subject selection (e.g. whether the players majored in Economics or not), and anonymity. Table 5.1 summarizes ultimatum game data for seven different groups: University of California, Los Angeles graduate students, University of Pittsburgh undergraduates, Hebrew University students (Jerusalem), University of Arizona students (Tucson), Gadjah Mada University students (Yogyakarta, Java, Indonesia), the Mapuche, and the Machiguenga. In comparing industrial, market contexts, like Los Angeles, Tucson, Pittsburgh, and even Yogyakarta,[2] we observe little or no difference. However, as we hop from Los Angeles to Jerusalem, to the Mapuche, and to the Machiguenga (see Table 5.1), we see the mean offer plummet from 48 to 36 to 34 percent and finally to 26 percent, respectively. In terms of modal proposer offers, these groups all have a single dominant mode at 50 percent, except for Yogyakarta, the Machiguenga, and the Mapuche. Yogyakarta has a mode at 40 percent with a strong

---

[2] Note that Table 5.1 shows that when overall distributional characteristics are taken into account (using the Epps-Singleton test), Yogyakarta is actually significantly different from Pittsburgh. Cameron (1999) uses only the Mann–Whitney test and shows that the means cannot be distinguished statistically.

TABLE 5.1. Summary of cross-cultural Ultimatum Game data and statistical tests

Place	Los Angeles	Machiguenga	Mapuche	Yogyakarta[a] (high stakes)	Yogyakarta[b]	Tucson[c]	Pittsburgh[d]	Jerusalem[e]
No. pairs	15	21	31	37	94	24	27	30
Stake size	$160	$160	$60	$80–120	$10–15	$10	$10	$10
Mean	0.48	0.26	0.34	0.44	0.44	0.44	0.45	0.36
Mode	0.50	0.15	0.50/0.33	0.50	0.40	0.50	0.50	0.50
SD	0.065	0.14	0.18	0.11	0.17	0.072	0.096	0.16
Rejection freq.	0	0.048	0.065	0.081	0.19	0.083	0.22	0.33
Rej < 20 %	0/0	1/10 = 0.1	2/12 = 0.17	0/0	9/15 = 0.6	—	0/1	5/7 = 0.71
EST p (LA)[d]	—	—	0.0037	0.081	0.0000	—	0.089	0.010
MW p (LA)	—	2.64E-5	0.02	0.053	0.032	—	0.11	0.001
EST p (Mach)[d]	0.0000	—	0.130	0.0000	0.0000	—	0.0000	0.001
MW p (Mach)[e]	2.64E-5	—	0.087	1.22E-5	3.64E-5	—	3.06E-5	0.049
EST p (Mapuche)[d]	0.0037	0.130	—	0.003	0.0067	—	0.014	0.192
MW p (Mapuche)[e]	0.02	0.087	—	0.029	0.023	—	0.041	0.913

[a] Pittsburgh and Jerusalem data are from round 1 games in Roth et al. (1991). Roth et al. used the round 10 data (the last round) for inter-study comparison. Using either round 1 or round 10 to compare with a single-shot game generates analytical ambiguities. In round 10 players may have modified their strategy through learning, while in round 1 players know it's a repeated game (but not repeated with the same person), so they may also make strategic adjustments compared with a single-shot game.

[b] The Yogyakarta data comes from Cameron (1999)—the data was extracted from bar charts and the 'errors' were omitted in the re-analysis. The 'high stakes' data is from a second round game, after having played the low stakes ($10–$15) game. This may explain the decrease in the standard deviation from the low stakes game.

[c] The 'Tucson' data is from Hoffman et al. (1994).

[d] 'EST p' gives the p-value from the Epps-Singleton non-parametric test for Los Angeles ('LA'), the Machiguenga ('Mach'), and Pittsburgh ('Pitt') compared against each of the other populations.

[e] 'MWp' gives the p-value for the Mann–Whitney non-parametric test (corrected for ties and continuity) for the Machiguenga compared with each of the other populations.

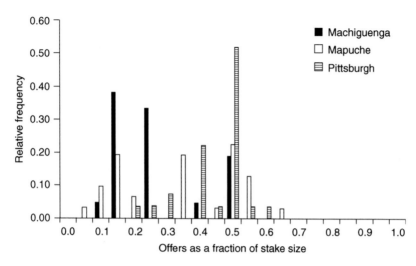

FIG. 5.1. Distribution of offers in the Ultimatum Game with Machiguenga ($n = 31$) and Pittsburgh ($n = 27$)

secondary mode at 50 percent, while the Mapuche have a weak mode at 50 percent and a strong secondary mode at 33 percent (with the two modes differing by only a single individual). The Machiguenga have a primary mode at 15 percent, and a secondary mode at 25 percent. The variances in proposer offers within groups also suggest an interesting difference between groups. In Los Angeles, Pittsburgh, and Tucson, the variance in offers is quite small compared with what happens outside the United States, where the variance in offers doubles and triples.[3] Americans (and Europeans) seem to share more agreement about what the 'proper' behavior is in the Ultimatum Game context than the other groups.

Figure 5.1, which compares the Ultimatum Game offer distributions for Machiguenga, Mapuche, and Pittsburgh, shows that the multi-modal offer distributions of the two small-scale societies are quite different from those found in places like Pittsburgh (which is a typical US result). While the Machiguenga distribution is dominated by modes at 15 and 25 percent, the Mapuche are widely scattered from 5 to 65 percent with peaks at 15, 33, and 50 percent. In contrast, Pittsburgh shows a single dominant mode at 50 percent, and no offers below 20 percent. The figure also highlights the fact

---

[3] This increase in the variance also applies to Roth *et al.*'s (1991) Tokyo data.

that means and modes do not tell us much about Ultimatum Game distributions.

On the receiving end, responders from industrial societies often reject offers below 20 percent (see 'Rej < 20 percent' in Table 5.1), although these offers are quite rare. For example, proposers in both Los Angeles and Pittsburgh made zero and one offers below 20 percent, respectively, while Mapuches, Machiguengas, and Israelis made numerous low offers: ten of twenty-one Machiguenga offers, ten of thirty-one Mapuche offers, and seven of thirty Israeli offers were below 20 percent. Unlike Israelis, however, Machiguenga and Mapuche responders almost always accept offers less than 20 percent. The Machiguenga and Mapuche rejection rates for offers less than 20 percent are significantly lower (all $p < 0.012$) than the rates found in Jerusalem and Yogyakarta, which are the only places with enough offers below 20 percent to make this analysis possible. If we had larger samples in Los Angeles and Pittsburgh, the rejection rates for low offers might be even higher than those in Jerusalem and Yogyakarta, and thus even more different from the Machiguenga and Mapuche. The overall rejection rates (rather than the rate for offers less than 20 percent) for the Machiguenga (0.048) and the Mapuche (0.065) were also significantly smaller than Pittsburgh (0.22), Jerusalem (0.33), and Yogyakarta (0.19). See Table 5.2. This difference is especially provocative because responders in Pittsburgh, Jerusalem, and Yogyakarta faced higher average offers, so we might expect lower, not higher, rejection rates.

It's worth noting that our University of California, Los Angeles control data does look slightly different from the typical US results. University of California, Los Angeles subjects have a slightly higher mean offer and a smaller variance (the mode of 50 percent entirely dominates the University of California, Los Angeles offers) than typically occurs in US Ultimatum Game experiments. However, both of these differences (the mean and variance) tend in directions

TABLE 5.2. Binomial *p*-values for rejection rates

Group	Jerusalem	Indonesia	Pittsburgh
Machiguenga	0.0023	0.071	0.0375
Mapuche	0.00052	0.049	0.044

opposite to those demonstrated by the Machiguenga and Mapuche data relative to the typical results. Therefore, the particular methodology/stakes used in the University of California, Los Angeles experiment may explain the variation from other US results, but cannot be used to account for the differences found between University of California, Los Angeles and the Machiguenga, and Mapuche. Also note, the pattern of differences between the University of California, Los Angeles data and typical US data is consistent with the effect created by increasing the stakes shown in previous experimental studies—more 'fair' offers and less variance in offers. For example, Burks *et al.* (under review) performed high stakes ($100) Ultimatum Game among employees at a large publishing company (mean age = 38) in Kansas City and got results (Ultimatum Game offer mean = 46.5 percent, standard deviation = 0.098) indistinguishable from our Anthropology graduate students.

It is also possible that Anthropology graduate students represent a self-selected and biased portion of the US student population, which tends to exhibit a greater sense of social responsibility and concern for economic equality than the average American student. Consequently, proposers make more 'fair' offers, and responders quite willingly reject 'unfair' offers (at least according to post-game interviews). So then, in the same way that Economics students tend to make somewhat lower than average offers (Carter and Irons 1991), perhaps Anthropology graduate students tend to make higher than average offers.

Does 'strategic understanding' and 'mathematical ability' matter?

To get some handle on how individual differences in 'strategic understanding' and 'mathematical ability' affect people's decisions, Henrich ranked Mapuche players with 1s, 2s, and 3s according to both how well they understood the strategic nature of the game (with 3 being the highest and 1 being the lowest), and how well they were able to do the mathematical calculations.[4] Very few of the

---

[4] For strategic understanding, a rank of '3' meant a player's postgame interview indicated that they fully understood the strategic nature of the game, and could express it. Players received a '2' if their answers to postgame questions about the strategic nature of the game were somewhat fuzzy, but still captured the essential conflict. Players were assigned '1's when players failed to reveal any understanding of the game's strategic conflict. For mathematical ability, '3's were assigned to players who could do the

individuals receiving a 1 for mathematical ability occur in the dataset because they were often unable to complete the game. For both mathematical ability and strategic understanding, the game behavior of players receiving '3s' cannot be distinguished from those receiving '2's (using Epps-Singleton, $p = 0.78$ and 0.81, respectively). There were too few '1's to analyze, and '1's were removed from our analyses. The regressions below further illustrate the lack of effect of these measures.

Can individual-level variables explain Ultimatum Game offers?

A substantial amount of theoretical work on human behavior predicts that, in making decisions that carry non-trivial economic consequences, much of the variation should be explained by individual-level differences in economic and demographic circumstances. Our games among the Machiguenga and Mapuche were high stakes games relative to people's earning abilities, their cash-on-hand, and previous experimental work. Consequently, one might expect variables such as age, wealth, sex, household size, and risk preference to account for a significant portion of the variation. However, our analyses indicate that such individual-level variables do *not* account for any substantial portion of the variation.

Table 5.3 analyzes the predictive capability of ten different variables on Mapuche Ultimatum Game offers using a series of linear regression models. These independent variables are Animal Wealth, Land Wealth, Household Size, Head-of-Household, Age, Sex, Risk Preference, Wage Labor, Strategic Understanding, and Mathematical Ability. Animal Wealth is the total market value of an individual's livestock—sheep, pigs, horses, cows, and oxen—based on the most recent price reports from local farmers. Land Wealth is the number of hectares owned by the player's household. Animal Wealth can fairly easily be converted to cash, but Land Wealth cannot, as Mapuche can only sell their land to other Mapuches, and Mapuche buyers are extremely hard to find.[5] Household Size is the total number of individuals living in the player's household. Head-of-Household is a dummy variable in

---

subtraction easily. Players received a rank of '2' if they had problems doing the math and answered the test questions by manipulating stacks of coins and counting them. Players receiving '1's had serious difficulties with both subtraction and counting.

[5] It's difficult to even assign a *peso*-value to Mapuche-owned land, and no Mapuche has any idea of what the 'going price' is for a hectare of land.

TABLE 5.3. Multivariate linear regression models for Mapuche Ultimatum Game data

Variable	Bivariate[a]	Model 1[b]	Model 2	Model 3	Model 4	Model 5	Model 6	Model 7	Model 8	Model 9
Constants	—	(0.003)	(0.18)	(0.17)	(0.27)	(0.27)	(0.12)	(0.72)	(0.017)	(0.60)
Animal wealth (n = 30)[c]	0.051	0.056	0.055	0.026	0.54	0.019	0.09	0.12	—	—
	(0.80)	(0.80)	(0.81)	(0.91)	(0.88)	(0.96)	(0.73)	(0.62)	—	—
Land wealth[d] (n = 33)	0.011	−0.24	−0.028	−0.019	0.013	0.024	0.01	−0.009	—	—
	(0.96)	(0.92)	(0.90)	(0.93)	(0.97)	(0.94)	(0.97)	(0.97)	—	—
Household size (n = 31)	−0.051	—	−0.050	−0.050	0.009	—	−0.025	−0.022	—	—
	(0.78)	—	(0.82)	(0.86)	(0.98)	—	(0.93)	(0.092)	—	—
Head of household[e] (n = 35)	0.14	—	—	0.17	—	—	—	—	—	—
	(0.42)	—	—	(0.56)	—	—	—	—	—	—
Age (n = 36)	0.19	—	—	—	0.17	0.21	0.18	—	0.22	—
	(0.28)	—	—	—	(0.66)	(0.57)	(0.51)	—	(0.44)	—
Sex (n = 36)[f]	−0.25	—	—	—	−0.26	−0.26	−0.29	—	−0.25	—
	(0.15)	—	—	—	(0.45)	(0.45)	(0.25)	—	(0.36)	—
Risk preference (n = 17)[g]	0.043	—	—	—	—	−0.10	—	—	0.11	0.012
	(0.88)	—	—	—	—	(0.77)	—	—	(0.69)	(0.97)
Wage labor[h] (n = 30)	−0.045	—	—	—	—	—	0.11	—	—	—
	(0.82)	—	—	—	—	—	(0.69)	—	—	—

(Table continued on next page)

TABLE 5.3. *Continued*

Variable	Bivariate[a]	Model 1[b]	Model 2	Model 3	Model 4	Model 5	Model 6	Model 7	Model 8	Model 9
Strategic understanding[i] (n = 36)	−0.17 (0.66)	—	—	—	—	—	—	0.031 (0.94)	—	−0.003 (0.99)
Math ability[j] (n = 36)	0.22 (0.22)	—	—	—	—	—	—	0.27 (0.50)	—	0.21 (0.62)
R^2 (adjusted)	—	−0.09	−0.14	−0.17	−0.401	−0.40	−0.19	−0.19	−0.099	−0.17

[a] These are simple linear regression coefficients with constants (constants and their significance are not shown). Beneath these, in parentheses, is the p-value.

[b] Except in the row labeled 'constants', each box contains the standardized regression coefficient and its p-value (based on the t-statistic) in parentheses. The row 'constants' give the p-value for the constant included in each regression model.

[c] Animal wealth was calculated using the average market value of each kind of livestock—oxen, cows, sheep, horse, and pigs—at the time of the game.

[d] Land wealth is the number of hectares of land owned by a subject's household. By law, Mapuche cannot sell land to non-Mapuche, so no active market exists for land. For this reason, we've not combined land and animal wealth into a single aggregate measure.

[e] Head of household is a dummy variable code 1, head; 0, not the head. A Head of household is the primary economic decision-maker for the household.

[f] Sex is a dummy variable: 1, male; 0, female.

[g] Risk preference was measured using an indifference point calculated using a series of binary lottery choices involving substantial sums, see text.

[h] Wage labor was incorporated as a dummy variable: 1, experience in wage labor; 0, no experience.

[i] Strategic understanding was assessed through postgame questions about the interaction. Henrich assigned subjects scores on a 3-point scale, see text.

[j] Mathematical ability was assessed through the pregame testing and examples with values of 1–3 assigned to each subject based on his ability (see text). For the regression, ability rankings were converted into 0's and 1's. Subjects capable of doing all the mathematics received a '1'. Subjects who needed to move the coins around and count them in order to answer test questions received '0's. Subjects who could not count were removed from the analysis.

which 'one' indicates the player is the primary economic decision-maker in his or her household. Risk Preference was measured several months prior to the Ultimatum Game using a series of binary lottery choices to titrate out each person's indifference point. These lotteries involved substantial financial incentives of the same magnitude as the Ultimatum Game stakes (Henrich and McElreath 2002). Wage Labor is also a dummy variable in which 'one' indicates that the individual has (at some point) participated in Wage Labor, while 'zero' indicates he has not. 'Strategic Understanding' and 'Mathematical Ability' were explained in the preceding section. We hope sex and age are self-explanatory.

The single message from Table 5.3 is that none of these variables matter very much. Looking at the 'bivariate' column, we see that nothing is significant. Models 1 through 3 indicate that the variables Land Wealth, Animal Wealth, Household Size, and Head-of-Household do not provide any substantial predictive power. Adding for Age and Sex in Models 4 does not improve matters. Model 5 controls for Age, Sex and Risk Preference, but still the wealth variables remain inert. Adding Wage Labor (and removing Risk Preference), also fails to exhume anything in Model 6. Model 7, which adds controls for Strategic Understanding and Mathematical Ability to Model 2, lacks any predictive significance. In analyses not summarized in this table, we also looked at how Head-of-Household might interact with Land Wealth, Animal Wealth, and Household Size, thinking that perhaps only Heads-of-Households might consider their household's wealth and size in making decisions. However, these efforts revealed nothing of significance. Similarly, models examining wealth per household member (i.e. Animal Wealth/Household Size and Land Wealth/Household Size), instead of absolute wealth, also came up empty. Using adjusted R^2 values, none of our bivariate or multivariate models explain any of the variation in Ultimatum Game offers.[6]

Interestingly, analyses of our experimentally derived Risk Preference measure revealed no relationship with Ultimatum Game offers. In addition to the bivariate analysis, Models 8 and 9 attempted to control first for age and sex, and alternatively for Strategic Understanding and Mathematical Ability. None of these efforts unearthed any connection between Risk Preference and

---

[6] $R_{adj} = R^2 - (p(1 - R^2)/n - p - 1)$ where p is the number of independent variables and n is the sample size.

TABLE 5.4. Multivariate regression analyses for the Machiguenga Ultimatum Game data. The dependent variable is Ultimatum Game offer

Variable	Bivariate[a]	Model 1[b]	Model 2	Model 3
Constant	—	(0.014)	(0.63)	(0.76)
Cash crop land[c] ($n = 19$)	0.48	0.52	0.43	—
	(0.021)	(0.034)	(0.19)	
Wage labor[d] ($n = 21$)	0.11	0.21	0.11	—
	(0.31)	(0.37)	(0.72)	
Age ($n = 21$)	0.25	—	0.18	0.39
	(0.14)		(0.60)	(0.14)
Sex[e] ($n = 21$)	0.22	—	0.13	0.36
	(0.35)		(0.71)	(0.17)
Sex*Crash Cropping Land	0.51	—	—	—
($n = 19$)	(0.027)			
R^2 (adjusted)	—	0.18	0.072	0.068

[a] These are correlation coefficients. The value in parentheses is one-tailed *p*-value.

[b] Except in row 'constants', each box contains the standardized regression coefficient and its *p*-value (based on the *t*-statistic) in parentheses. The row 'constants' give the *p*-value for the constant included in each regression model.

[c] This is the amount of land the player's household has allocated to cash cropping (as opposed to subsistence cropping).

[d] Wage labor was incorporated as a dummy variable: 1, experience in wage labor; 0, no experience.

Ultimatum Game offers. Multivariate analyses examining Risk Preference as the dependent variable (with a much larger sample) also fail to show significant predictive powers for Land Wealth, Animal Wealth, Wage Labor, Age, Sex, and Head-of-Household (Henrich and McElreath 2002).

For the Machiguenga, Table 5.4 summarizes our regression analyses using the variables Cash Cropping Land, Wage Labor, age, and sex. Cash Cropping Land is the amount of land an individual's household devotes to producing cash crops. It provides an indirect measure of an individual's market participation and his experience in the local cash economy. As with the Mapuche, Wage Labor indicates participation (Wage Labor = 1) versus non-participation (Wage Labor = 0) in occasional wage labor. Bivariate analyses of these four variables suggest that only Cash Cropping

Land has any significant predictive value. Cash Cropping Land remains significant in Model 1, after controlling for Wage Labor. Models 2 and 3, which further control for Age and Sex, show nothing significant. Because only men do the cash cropping, we also analyzed a simple linear regression model with Cash Cropping Land and a constant. The standardized β for Cash Cropping Land equals 0.46 ($p = 0.08$; $n = 15$).

The importance of Cash Cropping Land may reflect a tendency for individuals with more cash to offer more in the Ultimatum Game. However, we believe it captures an individual's greater exposure to the larger Peruvian society. Cash croppers also tend to speak better Spanish, participate more in exchange with non-Machiguenga, have more experience with Protestant missionaries and have spent more time in local Peruvian towns. Consequently, we hypothesize that this greater degree of contact outside the Machiguenga social sphere makes these individuals more likely to have acquired different norms of fairness. Postgame interviews further suggest that these Machiguenga have acquired some ideas about 'what's fair' from non-Machiguenga.

The lack of predictive capability from our independent variables probably does not result from noise introduced during our data collection. We believe our measures are generally better than the self-report data found in many social science datasets, outside of Anthropology. Our measures of both animal wealth and household size involved both interviews and direct observation. For example, in most cases the number of cows a person reported owning was verified by actually counting his cows, and further inquiries were made into any discrepancies between interviews and observation. Other data, like wage labor participation, was cross-checked in three ways: (1) we repeated the same questions several months apart; (2) a local informant re-asked many of the same questions in our absence; and (3) we often cross-checked data with other family members—that is, we asked wives and adult children (living at home) about their husbands and fathers, or vice versa. Any discrepancies provoked further inquiry. Finally, unlike census takers or annoying phone callers, we were familiar visitors and friends to many of these households.[7]

---

[7] As explained above, we attempted to deal with the potential problem of 'familiarity' between the subjects and the experimenter in the University of California, Los Angeles control experiment.

Acquiring data of this quality has an important cost. Both the Mapuche and Machiguenga samples are rather small for regression analyses, so the lack of significant results merely means that these variables probably are not *powerful* predictors. Larger samples may reveal that they are weak predictors. However, in the final chapter of this volume we'll show that such variables are rarely powerful predictors of game behavior, even using larger samples and many different groups.

Comparison of postgame interviews for the Machiguenga,
Mapuche, and University of California, Los Angeles students

Discussions, postgame interviews, and observations of body language gleaned from the Machiguenga, Mapuche, and Americans during these experiments provide some further explanatory insights into the differences between them. Machiguenga had difficulty articulating why they were willing to accept low offers, but several individuals made it clear that they would always accept any money regardless of how much the proposer was getting. Rather than viewing themselves as being taken advantage of by the proposer, Machiguengas seemed to feel it was just bad luck that they were responders, and not proposers. In contrast, Mapuche responders expressed some frustration at low offers, but despite long, pensive reflection and clearly ambivalent feelings (they wanted to reject), most Mapuche finally accepted even very low offers—except for the two rejecters. Mapuche farmers felt that low offers were unfair and the proposer should have offered more, but they were not willing to take nothing in order to punish proposers.

In comparison to these two groups, American students claimed they would reject 'unfair' offers (usually below 25 percent), and a few claimed they would reject any offer below 50 percent. Correspondingly, some University of California, Los Angeles proposers, when asked why they offered 50 percent, said they were thinking of offering less, and thought that most people would accept less, but figured there were some people out there who might reject an offer below 50 percent. Proposers said that they wanted to be sure that they would get at least $80 (half of the $160 stake), rather than proposing less and risk getting nothing.

These three groups also differ in their views of fairness. The few Machiguenga who offered 50 percent, when asked why, said that 50/50 was 'fair'. When asked if they thought their fellow Machiguengas would accept less, they said 'yes, for sure'. Many University of California, Los Angeles proposers, particularly those who seemed to know exactly what they were going to offer immediately (rather than pondering over it for 5 minutes like many other University of California, Los Angeles proposers), said they offered 50 percent 'to be fair'. When asked how much they thought their fellow responders would have accepted (had they offered less), they seemed uncertain, and said things like, 'it depends on the person' or 'I don't know'.

Contrastingly, Mapuche proposers seem to be entirely driven by a fear of punishment, and not at all by notions of fairness or equity, when compared with Machiguenga and American students. Mapuche proposers, especially those offering 50 percent and above, expressed concern that someone out there might spitefully reject anything but a generous offer. Those Mapuche offering lower amounts felt that some few might reject, but that most people would not, and they were willing to risk it. Like the Machiguenga, the Mapuche are unaccustomed to verbally justifying their actions, so getting detailed responses was difficult and sometimes impossible. However, of the eleven proposers who successfully responded to the postgame questions about why they offered what they offered, ten indicated that a fear of rejection guided their offer and only one indicated that fairness guided his decision. This differs from University of California, Los Angeles where 60 percent suggested that fairness considerations influenced their decision and about 53 percent suggested that a fear of rejection played a part (one-third said both were important). Even among the Machiguenga, four proposers (19 percent) indicated the importance of fairness, compared with only one Mapuche. Further, unlike University of California, Los Angeles and Machiguenga proposers, who never offered greater than 50 percent of the total, four Mapuches (16 percent) made offers greater than 50 percent of the total. These Mapuche expressed a sense of fear that someone out there might reject an offer of 50 percent or less, but if they offered more than 50 percent, acceptance would be assured. Contrastingly, during postgame discussions, two University of California, Los Angeles students mentioned that they would not consider making an offer greater than 50 percent, as that would be unfair to themselves. Compared with the Mapuche and Machiguenga, Americans seem obsessed with fairness—which includes punishing people who act unfairly.

PUBLIC GOODS GAME

Public goods experiments are designed to investigate how people behave when facing a conflict between individual and group benefits (see Camerer and Fehr, Chapter 3, this volume). They have been run with a wide range of structural variations with researchers exploring variables such as group size, initial endowments, rates of return, basis for dividing money among players, etc. With the exception of modifications involving communication between players and punishment, behavior in the first round of experiments is fairly consistent (even when players know future rounds are coming): average contributions to the group consistently fall between 40 and 60 percent of the maximum possible contribution (Camerer and Fehr, Chapter 3, this volume; Davis and Holt 1993; Ledyard 1995). This behavior, derived from research in industrial, urban settings with university students, clearly conflicts with the game theoretical prediction (under standard preferences) of zero contribution to the group investment. Consequently, because of the robustness of round one behavior, and its substantial deviation from game theoretic predictions, we sought to explore the cross-cultural replicability of these results.[8] In order to do this, we conducted a Common-Pool Resource games with Machiguengas and American university students, and a Voluntary Contributions game with the Mapuche and Huinca.[9] We first explore the methods and results of the Common-Pool Resources games and then discuss the Voluntary Contributions game.

Common-Pool Resource game methodology: the Machiguenga

Among the Machiguenga, each experimental round was played with four individuals above the age of 16 (average age $= 20.3$), in groups of either all males or all females. Participants and administrators sat

---

[8] We focus on results from the first round of experiments because learning processes influence behavior in the subsequent rounds, with contributions to the public market decreasing substantially in later rounds. However, we are concerned with the norms that govern people's economic decisions, not the strategies that they can learn by playing repeated rounds of the game. We want to know what people bring to the game.

[9] In a Common-Pool Resources game, the endowment goes to the group investment and players decide how much to withdraw. In a Voluntary Contributions game, the endowment goes to the individual players and each person decides how much to contribute to the group. The payoffs for the two games are symmetrical, although there may be an endowment effect (Brewer and Kramer 1986).

in a circle around a pile of twenty *soles* ($1 equals 2.4 *soles*). The participants were read the game instructions in Spanish, in which they were told that they could withdraw any amount between zero and five *soles* from the pile. Any money they withdrew was theirs to keep, and whatever money was left in the pile after all players had made their withdrawals would be increased by 50 percent and distributed equally among all the players. In order for the game to be played anonymously and simultaneously, money was not literally taken from the pile. Instead, each player wrote down on a piece of paper how many *soles* he wanted. Smith performed all subsequent calculations and then paid the players. After reading the rules to the players, Smith performed an extensive series of examples to both teach the rules of the game, and to test players' comprehension—as well as to evaluate their ability to perform the mathematical calculations. We do not believe that the examples and testing led to a 'learning effect' because the examples made evident the payoff outcomes of various scenarios, but there was no strategic learning since players could not obtain information about how other people would play. In addition, the concept of the game was so foreign to the players that they needed this training to achieve the level of comprehension necessary to participate in the game.

The game was played in two rounds, (1) private/anonymous and (2) public/non-anonymous, although players were not initially told there would be a second round. In the private round, each player wrote on a slip of paper her name, age, and the amount of money that she wanted to withdraw from the pile. The paper was then handed to the game administrator and payoffs were calculated. Payoffs were distributed in envelopes so that the players would not know how much the other members of the group received. In the public round, players again wrote down their name, age, and the amount to withdraw, after which they handed these papers to the experimenter. This time, however, before calculating and distributing the payoffs, each player had to announce to the group the amount that he/she withdrew. The players were told before the round began that they would be making this announcement to the group and that payoffs would be distributed without envelopes so that all the players could see how much each person received. The reason for the public round was to determine if public approval and fear of punishment/social repercussions motivated players' decisions.

Justification of game structure

We designed our Common-Pool Resources game in this way for three reasons. First, money was placed in a communal pile rather than distributed as an endowment to each player in order to better simulate the communal resources situation under investigation. We made cash an existing public resource from which people made personal withdrawals—just as natural resources are harvested. Second, the payoff structure was designed to be as simple as possible in order to increase game comprehension. Rather than making the rate of return dependent on the amount of money left in the pot (as is done is some Common-Pool Resources games), the rate of increase was fixed at 50 percent and all players received an equal return from the pot. Structuring the payoffs in this manner polarizes the optimal strategies for maximizing group versus individual benefits—a group maximizer should withdraw nothing from the pot and the individual maximizer should withdraw the full amount (five *soles*). This setup is much simpler than games in which determining the optimal level involves withdrawing a portion of the total amount (for examples of experiments with complex maximizing strategies, see Ostrom, Gardner, and Walker 1994). Third, we used higher stakes than have been used in other experiments. Each player earned approximately half a day's wage in each round (there were two rounds). We chose to use high stakes so that the players would take the experiment seriously. With a significant amount of money on the line, players should be more concerned with actual monetary outcomes, and less concerned with what they perceive the experimenters to expect or desire as an outcome.

Common-Pool Resource game: control experiment in US

In order to control for the effects of our game structure, and any experimenter effect, on the results, we replicated our experiment with undergraduates at the University of Michigan and the University of California, Los Angeles. Our results from the University of California, Los Angeles and University of Michigan experiments fell within the usual cooperation range of 40–60 percent typically found in public goods experiments conducted with students in developed countries, and that our two student populations were indistinguishable from each other.

To perform this control experiment at University of Michigan, Smith recruited subjects from two large, introductory Economics classes.[10] Students were told that they would earn an average of $20–$30 for approximately 45 minutes of their time. We expected this monetary incentive to create sufficient interest in the experiment that we would be able to gather all the necessary subjects (forty) from these two classes (each of which had approximately 200 students). However, this was not the case, and Smith recruited the remainder of the subjects by randomly approaching students on campus. All University of California, Los Angeles subjects were recruited by an e-mail that was sent out to students randomly selected from a class list of a large, lower division, undergraduate course in biological Anthropology. To maintain methodological uniformity between the Machiguenga and the university students, the following steps were taken.

1. As with the Machiguenga, both Smith and Henrich were present during all of the experimental rounds with Smith leading the experiment and Henrich interjecting to emphasize and clarify certain points.
2. The communal pot consisted of $80, with each subject able to withdraw a maximum of $20. With these stakes, subjects earned approximately one-half a day's wages, based on an hourly rate of $7/h (a standard after-tax undergraduate wage). This is roughly equivalent to the stake size for the Machiguenga.
3. Since the Machiguenga could withdraw between zero and five soles, which gave six possible withdrawal amounts (and the inability to withdraw exactly half), the university students were restricted to withdrawals in $4 increments. This created a withdrawal structure that paralleled that confronted by the Machiguenga.
4. Prior to making withdrawal decisions, Smith demonstrated several examples to illustrate the rules of the game and the results of different strategies. As with the Machiguenga, each subject was tested for comprehension before the game was played.

---

[10] As these classes were introductory level and the experiment was conducted within the first month of the semester, students were from a variety of majors, and had very little economic training. This avoided students with any knowledge of game theory and increased the diversity of different majors—and thus minimized the non-randomness created by and self-selection into particular disciplines (as was found by Marwell and Ames 1981; Carter and Irons 1991).

5. As with the Machiguenga, the university students were not allowed to discuss their withdrawal decisions or strategies with the group. Withdrawals were marked on a slip of paper, folded, and handed back to Smith. Payoffs were given out in envelopes.

Overall, the control experiment was performed with forty subjects at the University of Michigan and twenty-four subjects at University of California, Los Angeles. The University of California, Los Angeles methodology varied slightly from the Michigan format described above in that Henrich was not present during the experiment, subjects were not restricted to $4 increments ($1 increments were allowed), and a surprise public round was conducted in addition to the private round (as with the Machiguenga). A comparison of the Michigan and University of California, Los Angeles experiments shows that they are nearly identical, and are statistically indistinguishable ($p = 0.99$, Epps-Singleton non-parametric test). Consequently, we combined the two samples for our analysis (hereafter termed the 'American control'); however, comparing only the Michigan sample to the Machiguenga does not significantly change the analyses or our conclusions.

Common-Pool Resource game results

Unlike results from typical one-shot Public Goods Game and our control experiments, in which people tend to exhibit weak free riding, the Machiguenga are strong free riders, withdrawing an average of 77 percent from the communal money. In comparison, subjects in the American control experiment withdrew an average of 57 percent. Figure 5.2 shows the distribution of withdrawals in the anonymous rounds of the Machiguenga and American control experiments. The results of our control experiment closely resemble the typical results found in other public goods experiments (Ledyard 1995, Chapter 1, this volume; Fehr and Gächter 1998). It is important to note the bi-modal distribution from the American control, which has peaks at full free riding (withdraw 100 percent) and full cooperation (withdraw 0 percent). This may indicate the presence of two possible strategies or ways of interpreting the game in the population. Although complete information about distributions is typically missing from published sources, Fischbacher, Gächter, and Fehr (1999) and Croson (1999) also found bi-modal

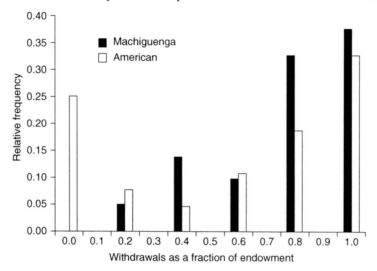

FIG. 5.2. Distribution of withdrawals in the Common-Pool Resources game with Machiguenga ($n = 21$) and Americans ($n = 64$) (stake size = five *soles*)

distributions with peaks at the two extremes. This leads us to believe that our bi-modal distribution may be a common characteristic of university student populations. In contrast, the uni-modal distribution of the Machiguenga (with the mode at 100 percent) is consistent with a relatively homogenous strategy of self-interest. The key difference between the American and Machiguenga results is the frequency of players who fully cooperate (withdraw zero). While both populations have many free riders, the Americans also have a contingency that fully cooperates and it is these players who produce the greater variance in the American sample, otherwise the distributions are quite similar.[11]

To explore the effect of public knowledge on individuals' decisions in our Common-Pool Resources game, we played a surprise, non-anonymous, second round in which players had to announce their withdrawal to the group and payoffs were distributed publicly. The results from the anonymous and the public rounds are nearly identical, with mean withdrawals of 77 and 80 percent for the

---

[11] Ledyard (1995) suggests that the 40–60 average contribution in round one of Voluntary Contributions public goods experiments could be a result of people being uncertain about what to do and consequently picking near the middle. Our control distribution indicates this is clearly not the case, as most people withdrew either 0% or 100%—which may be the case with most Public Goods games. Although the mean ends up in the middle, few people actually withdrew amounts near the middle.

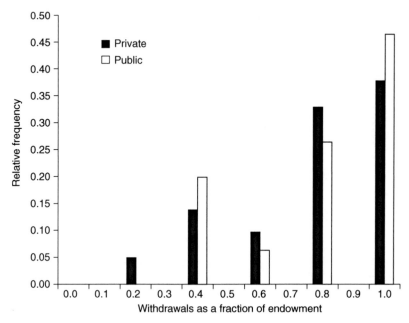

F<small>IG</small>. 5.3. Distribution of withdrawals in the Machiguenga Common-Pool Resources game in Private condition ($n = 21$) and Public condition ($n = 15$) (stake size = five *soles*)

private and public rounds, respectively, and a mode of 100 percent in both rounds. Figure 5.3 compares Machiguenga behavior in the public and private rounds. While an opportunity to punish was not built into the game itself, the public knowledge of game conduct could lead to punishment outside of the context of the game (such as gossip and social ostracism). However, the invariant behavior between the two rounds suggests that public knowledge about one's actions does not lead to an increase in group-oriented behavior. This finding supports two interpretations. First, the Machiguenga lack any shared rules about equity among group members, so acting selfishly evokes no punishment because no behavioral rules were violated. Second, the Machiguenga seem to lack any general taste for third-party punishment, so even if shared rules about equity were broken, violators need not fear repercussions, and thus have no reason to act less selfishly. Ethnographic evidence suggests that both explanations contribute to the observed results in the experiment (Baksh 1984; Johnson 2000; Smith 2001*a*).

We played the public round of the Common-Pool Resources game with the University of California, Los Angeles control and found a similar result—public knowledge of conduct in the experiment did not lead to increased levels of cooperation.[12] However, unlike in the Machiguenga experiment, the subjects were strangers so the possibility of punishment outside of the context of the game was negligible. Our results show that public knowledge without social familiarity does not affect people's behavior, but we don't know if cooperation would in fact have increased had the players known each other. We do know that for the Machiguenga public knowledge and social familiarity did not affect game conduct.

Evidence from Gächter and Fehr (1999) suggests that in some groups, individuals act less selfishly when there is social familiarity and an opportunity for social approval (i.e. public knowledge of behavior). In a multi-round version of our Common-Pool Resources game, Gächter and Fehr found that a combination of these two conditions significantly increased cooperation, but that neither social familiarity nor opportunities for social approval (public knowledge) *alone* had significant effects. Our University of California, Los Angeles result is consistent with their conclusions—social approval of strangers had no effect on cooperation, although we do not know what would have happened if the subjects knew each other. Interestingly, Gächter and Fehr's effect appears to be culturally variable, as the Machiguenga, who have both strong social familiarity and were provided an opportunity for social approval, did not increase cooperation, and field research with an ethnic community in Michigan (the Chaldeans) also reveals a lack of effect from strong social familiarity and punishment on cooperation levels[13] (Smith 2001*b*). Furthermore, other experiments suggest that in some cultures, public knowledge can induce cooperation even in the absence of social familiarity. In a Public Goods experiment comparing Canadian, mainland Chinese and Hong Kong students, low anonymity conditions led Asian students, especially the Chinese,

---

[12] Our preliminary analysis suggests that the public manipulation may have opposing effects on males and females that cancel out any overall effect. We intend to investigate further.

[13] Members of a volunteer organization, all of whom come from the same community and have extensive relationships outside of the context of the organization, make commitments to participate in group projects but frequently fail to follow through even though the rest of the group knows they broke their promise and they are scolded in front of the group by the heads of the organization.

to behave very cooperatively while having no effect on Canadians (Kachelmeier and Shehata 1997). The effects of public knowledge and familiarity appear to be highly variable and very culturally sensitive.

Comparison of postgame interviews for the Machiguenga and American students

As mentioned earlier, Machiguenga say little during debriefing because they lack the cultural training to produce *post-hoc* rationalizations of their behavioral choices. The most frequent response to the question of why a subject withdrew the amount that he did was that it was the amount he wanted to withdraw. The three men with the most contact with outsiders explained that they each had withdrawn the maximum amount of money because they had hoped that the other members of the group would withdraw little, thus increasing their own returns. The clarity of their answers indicated two important things. First, the men were motivated by self-interest. And second, that they understood the strategic component of the game.

In contrast to the Machiguenga, the American university subjects had plenty to say after the experiment, and are excellent at generating *post-hoc* justifications for their behavior. Smith interviewed each subject privately about the reasons for his decisions, what he had expected the other members of the group to do, and his reactions to what the other members actually did. Although the variation in behavior was high among the subjects, their reactions to the experiment were quite similar. They expressed concern with greed and selfishness, with 38 percent of subjects using at least one of these words during their debriefing. The nature of their concern varied—low withdrawers said they didn't want to appear or feel greedy/selfish, and high withdrawers recognized their behavior as being greedy/selfish but were willing to live with this negative image because of the financial gains. Interestingly, concepts of greed and selfishness came up more frequently with subjects who had withdrawn more than 50 percent, which may reflect underlying guilt about acting self-interestedly. One subject, with respect to her withdrawal of $20 (maximum withdrawal allowed), said that she felt 'bad, greedy... but I got over it really quick'. Another subject commented that he felt so guilty about withdrawing $20 in the private round that he kept his head down and avoided making eye contact with the other members of the group. In contrast to the subjects who felt greedy but took large amounts, other subjects were sufficiently motivated to avoid feeling bad/greedy about themselves that they did withdraw zero, or near zero, in both rounds. One such subject succinctly stated, 'I just didn't feel good about taking a whole $20.' It is interesting that *regardless* of what people did in the game, most players shared a belief that withdrawing a large amount reflected negatively on one's personality. This seems to reflect a shared belief that cooperative, group beneficial behavior is valued.

Of the subjects who withdrew less than 50 percent of the maximum possible withdrawal, 39 percent explicitly expressed negative feelings, such as anger, toward the other members of the group. A male who withdrew $0 in both rounds said that he was 'a little ticked' at the players who took more than $0, while another subject scornfully said that by the end of the experiment he realized that 'it was an issue of doing things for yourself ... you can note the subtle resentment in my voice'. Anger was directed toward players who withdrew large amounts, but since the withdrawals were anonymous, the subjects were left with a non-directed feeling of anger or disappointment. In some cases, the subjects told Smith who they thought withdrew the large amounts, although in all but one of six cases their guesses were incorrect. More than the 39 percent appeared to be angry that some people took large amounts, but since they denied having negative feelings when Smith asked them, we did not count them. Despite the anger and disappointment of low withdrawers, 42 percent said that they would continue to take the same low amount again if there was another round with a different group, in hopes that the present group was an aberration from the norm, and that most people would take low withdrawals.

According to the interviews, the primary indicator of what a subject will do is what the subject thinks the rest of the group will do. In other words, people expected their behavior to match others (Orbell and Dawes 1991; Yamagishi and Yamagishi 1994; Dawes, McTavish, and Shaklee 1977).[14] This expectation was highest

---

[14] Our finding that people are most likely to cooperate when they think others will also (and vice versa) is not restricted to the domain of experimental games. Weiner and Doescher (1991) found that utility customers are more likely to install regulating devices on air conditioners when they think that others will also install the devices.

among people who withdrew more than 50 percent: 88 percent of these subjects expected others to withdraw high amounts. In contrast, only 12 percent of the people who expected others to withdraw high amounts had withdrawn less than half for themselves. Similarly, 64 percent of the people who expected others to withdraw low amounts had withdrawn less than half for themselves. This is consistent with findings of conditional cooperation in other public goods experiments (Croson 1999; Fischbacher, Gächter, and Fehr 1999).

Of the subjects who changed the amount of their withdrawal from the private round to the public round (44 percent changed their withdrawal), everyone who *decreased* her withdrawal had taken between 75 and 100 percent of the maximum in the private round and everyone who *increased* her withdrawal had taken between 0 and 25 percent of the maximum in the private round—people appear to be adjusting their behavior toward the mean (this has been observed in repeated Public Goods Games; Fehr and Gächter 2000).

According to the players' statements, a decline in the amount withdrawn was strongly affected by a concern for one's reputation. In the postgame interviews, subjects made statements such as: 'I didn't care how much money I made, I was just concerned with what others thought' (from $20 to $5); 'I didn't want to seem so wrong in front of other people' (from $15 to $10); and '(I thought that) everyone would go lower because it was public and that people would be embarrassed to take more and thought of as money hungry' (from $15 to $10). It seems that many subjects had an idea of what amount was 'right' or 'fair', and that by taking this amount they would appear to be a good person. While this amount was always less than $20, indicating that a positive value is placed on benefiting the group, most people did not think that it was necessary to withdraw $0 in order to protect their reputation. Of the four subjects who increased their withdrawals in the public round, three had taken $0 in the private round. These participants explained that the reason for their increased withdrawal was that they felt they had been taken advantage of in the first round (now it was their turn to make some money), and because they wanted to *punish* the group for having withdrawn high amounts in the first round. It appears that the motivation to get even with defectors outweighed either their concern for their reputation, or their ideals of working for the good of the group.

Voluntary Contributions game: the Mapuche and Huinca

Among a mixed group of Mapuche farmers and Huincan townspeople (non-Mapuche Chileans), we used a contributions version of
a Public Goods Game to examine how cooperation and defection
varied between these groups. The game had the following structure:
(1) initial endowments were given directly to players; (2) the communal money was doubled after all contributions were made
(increased by 100 percent); (3) all rounds were private (player–
player anonymity); and (4) games were played with five players. To
generate five-person groups, we sampled from an intermixed group
of male Huinca and Mapuche students, ages 17–22, at a small
agricultural secondary school in the rural town of Chol-Chol. The
initial endowment of 1000 *pesos* was about 40 percent of a day's
pay.[15]

Figure 5.4 shows the distribution of contribution levels for the
Huinca and Mapuche. Despite the small samples, the distribution
and statistical tests suggest some differences may exist between the
cultural groups. The Huinca contributed an average of 58 percent,
with a modal contribution of 50 percent, while the Mapuche contributed an average of only 33 percent with a mode of 10 percent.
A dramatic difference between the groups occurs at the ends of the
contribution spectrum. A substantial contingency of Huinca
cooperated strongly, with 25 percent of the subjects contributing
90–100 percent of their endowment. In contrast, only 8 percent of
the Mapuche contributed in this range—in fact, this 8 percent
of Mapuche were the only ones to contribute anything above
60 percent. At the other end of the spectrum, non-cooperation,
more than 40 percent of Mapuche contributed 10 percent, while

---

[15] Although an experiment identical to the Machiguenga would have facilitated
further comparisons with the Machiguenga and the American control, we altered the
game for several reasons. The *contributions* format, unlike the common pool resource
format, allowed us to test for experimenter anonymity bias. That is, we tested for any
effect that may arise from the experimenters' knowledge of players' behavior. To do
this, we ran several rounds of the experiment with a double-blind in which players were
left alone to contribute anonymously to the communal pot. Second, our experience with
administering the Ultimatum Game with the Mapuche made us suspect that explaining
the Public Goods Game to the Mapuche would probably be more difficult than
explaining it to the Machiguenga (meaning it would be extremely difficult to get them to
understand). Consequently, we decided to change from an increase of 50% to an
increase of 100% (increasing by 50% turns out to be much more difficult to communicate than simply doubling something). Third, time and money prevented us from
further testing public versus private contributions.

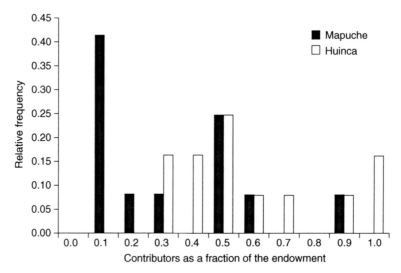

F<small>IG</small>. 5.4. Distribution of contributions in the Voluntary Contributions game with
the Mapuche ($n = 12$) and Huinca ($n = 12$) player (stake size $= 1000$ *pesos*)

no Huinca contributed less than 30 percent. The distributions are
different at $p = 0.09$ (Epps-Singleton non-parametric test).

In both the Machiguenga and the Mapuche/Huinca games the
participants all knew each other well and expected to interact again in
the future, unlike most western public goods experiments. This
suggests that Machiguenga, Mapuche, and Huinca should be more
willing to contribute to the group (in anticipation of future interactions) than students at a large university who have, at most, only
ephemeral associations with their classmates. Despite this, we found
that university students behaved more cooperatively in their experiment than the Machiguenga or the Mapuche. However, the Huinca
were high cooperators, as would be expected from their social
familiarity and on-going interactions. The puzzle, then, is why do the
American subjects cooperate when they lack close relationships with
the other players, and why do the Mapuche and the Machiguenga
cooperate so little given the nature of their relationships with their
co-subjects? Other experiments have demonstrated that expectation
of future interactions can increase cooperation. In Fehr and Gächter
(2000), subjects contributed approximately 60 percent when future
interaction was anticipated (the Huinca contributed 58 percent), but
since we have found that this is not always the case, we propose that

this expectation only effects cooperation when it is coupled with beliefs and norms about when to cooperate, and in what kinds of situations.

In a subsequent experiment, Henrich administered a simplified, four-person Voluntary Contributions game, to a subject pool drawn from the general Mapuche population around Chol-Chol. This sample of twenty-eight individuals was 64 percent male, with a mean age of 35 (SD 13.5). To make the game more tractable for uneducated Mapuche farmers, players faced only two options, 'contribute' or 'don't contribute'. Games were described within the context of contributing to a community project, and all the players at any particular session were from the same community. Each player received 1000 *pesos*, and was given an opportunity to secretly contribute these 1000 *pesos* to the group project or to keep the full 1000 *pesos* for himself. Contributions were doubled and distributed equally among all players.

Exactly half of the twenty-eight subjects contributed to the public good, yielding a mean contribution of 0.50. Logistic regression analyses using age, sex, community (where they live), fluency in Mapudungun (the Mapuche language), ethnic ancestry (*mestizo* versus *Mapuche*), animal wealth, and animal wealth per household member, land wealth, land wealth per household member, household size, and average monthly income show no predictive power. The only robust predictor, and the best overall model (plus a constant), was an individual's stated beliefs about how many of the other people in his four-person group he believed would contribute, $\beta = 2.46$ ($p = 0.03$). This means that believing one additional person will contribute increases in Mapuche's probability of cooperating 11.7 times. Interestingly, these guesses generally over estimated the number who would contribute. On-average, Mapuche guessed that 70 percent of players would cooperate, but only 50 percent did.

ETHNOGRAPHIC DATA SUPPORTS GAME RESULTS

The Machiguenga's behavior in both the public goods and Ultimatum Game is not surprising to those familiar with the Machiguenga culture and lifeways. The Machiguenga are individualistic, independent, and not given to taking orders. Although they have begun to live in villages, they remain largely a family-level society. Social sanctions and punishment are rare in Machiguenga life (Baksh 1984; Henrich 2000; Johnson 2000; Smith 2001a). Machiguenga are usually unaware of what others in their own community are doing (Smith 2001a), because they make little effort to monitor one another—which illustrates their lack of interest in punishing, since punishing requires monitoring in order to detect norm-breakers/cheaters. Disagreements and disputes cause families to disperse into the forest. Consequently, Machiguenga players probably did not feel a threat of punishment in the games, nor would they be expected to act for the benefit of the group, since there is little social pressure to cooperate or make equitable distributions (i.e. withdraw less from the pot in the Public Goods Game, or offer more in the Ultimatum Game).

Ethnographic work provides numerous example of the lack of community-oriented interests. Community work projects and cooperative gardening ventures typically flop, as many people refuse to contribute at all, or help for a while and leave on a whim (Baksh 1984). Democratically elected community leaders, after three decades of striving to 'build community', remain largely powerless and ineffective. During our time in one community, we frequently witnessed the village community president blowing a horn to call people to a meeting, but usually no one responded to the call. And when it came to build a new schoolhouse, the men largely avoided the task, even when the community president and construction leaders pleaded for assistance.

One situation in which the community members cooperate to some degree is in *barbasco* fishing. In this type of fishing, a section of the stream is dammed and *barbasco* roots are squeezed into the water to release a poison, which stuns the fish. The stunned fish float to the surface, as people frantically scramble to collect as many fish as possible. This endeavor requires the coordinated efforts of many people to properly dam the river and release the poison at the correct time. However, even in this group project, we observe no concept of fairness or equity as each family tries to acquire as many fish as possible. There is no redistribution of fish between families so that all participants receive similar quantities of fish; instead, families compete in fish collection, and the amount of fish that a family acquires can be highly disproportionate to the family's effort in the damming and poisoning. Even when the Machiguenga are working together, they lack any sense of unity, and families tend to behave individualistically. Johnson observed a disastrous *barbasco* effort in which the people releasing the poison did not wait for the signal from the dammers, and consequently the poison entered the water before the damming was completed. Interestingly, even when the fish are unevenly distributed between families, or when the rashness of a few causes failure for the group, people do not yell or punish, nor appear to feel great resentment. These situations are merely part of their way of life (Johnson 2000).

Together with the experimental data, this ethnographic description supports the idea that the Machiguenga have little or no expectations of favorable treatment from anonymous persons, no sense of group fairness, and thus no reason to punish. That is, there's no expectation of 'fairness' to violate or get punished for violating. This suggests that the presence of some kind of norm is critical for cooperation, punishment, and equity in bargaining.

The Mapuche results in both the Ultimatum Game and Public Goods Game are also consistent with field observations and ethnographic data. Like many small-scale sedentary agriculturalists, the Mapuche often view bad luck, negative events, discomfort, and suffering as resulting from witchcraft enacted by unknown malevolent neighbors. A bad harvest, the deaths of several cows, or an illness will probably be attributed to witchcraft coming from another Mapuche who suffered an accidental injury or social embarrassment months or even years in the past. Envy is considered dangerous and can produce bad luck for the envied. To deal with illness attributed to malevolent magic and envy, these impoverished farmers will travel several hours by oxcart, and wait several more hours for treatment by shamanistic healers, or *Machis*, who supposedly possess the power to identify the transgressor, and defeat the malevolent magic. These healers are paid substantial sums of money for their services (relative to the finances of farmers), and continue to prosper despite more conveniently located, biomedical health services that are provided free by the Chilean government and local Christian organizations.[16] Out of the hundreds of Mapuche Henrich spoke with, not one could identify a particular witch, although most were quite certain that witches are out there. Further, nobody admitted to practicing malevolent magic, and all

---

[16] This prominence of these healers is not isolated to Mapuche. Non-Mapuche Chileans from all levels of the social strata, as well as foreigners, travel great distances to consult with famous Machis.

said it was a bad idea—not because it was morally wrong, but because bad magic generates a cycle of dreadful retributions. A belief that people will be punished for norm violations and interpersonal transgressions seems to be a strong part of Mapuche heritage, even though the punishments they fear come through magic and supernatural agency.

Relations between neighboring households are frequently distrustful, jealous, and contentious. Gossip abounds. Individual households do interact in small, local socioeconomic exchange networks, based on kinship and friendships, which operate with great trust and reciprocity. Households in these networks frequently extend credit, share, and cooperate. However, nearest neighbors and many other households within the same community may not be part of the same network. Consequently, families keep secrets from one another because they fear that jealously will provoke supernatural attacks or bad luck. During Henrich's time with the Mapuche, he was often asked by his various hosts to keep the amount he paid for assistance, lodging, etc., secret, in order to avoid the envy of others. He was also frequently asked by neighbors how much he paid his benefactors. In accordance with the Ultimatum Game data, many Mapuche have a clear *belief* that there are people out there willing to punish inequities (out of jealous, spite, or revenge), even at a cost to themselves, which explains the high offers. Responders, on the other hand, did not feel any obligation to actively punish inequities, and seemed motivated to 'accept' by pecuniary payoffs.

Observations of Mapuche life also fit the Public Goods Game results. Mapuche households are largely independent, and almost all cooperative activities (except for occasional harvest festivals, or *Ngillatuns*) occur repeatedly among two or three friends, or kinsmen. Even the once prominent agricultural work-parties (*Mingacos*, Faron 1968) that households hosted during planting and harvesting have all but vanished, except in female-headed households. Mapuche communities elect 'presidents' who are encouraged by development organizations and agricultural extensions agents to organize public work projects to build irrigation systems, community storage facilities, stables, public buildings, and agricultural terraces, as well as to buy community-owned farming equipment. However, despite the general recognition by most farmers that such projects are often good ideas, neither these elected leaders, nor visiting Chilean government agents, can get people to participate.

The big exception to the typical lack of cooperation and group-level organization is the Mapuche's religious harvest festivals (*Ngillatuns*). In these rituals, communities host hundreds of visitors from surrounding communities in 3 days of dancing, meat-eating, and drinking. These festivals are led by the community's *Lonko*, who acquires his power and position through his bloodline, the endowment of custom, and the general support of his fellows. Households from the host community supply all the labor (erecting altars and temporary housing), materials, meat, and wine. Substantial proportions of livestock are expended for food and sold for ready cash. Failure to participate sufficiently in the *Ngillatun* certainly results in social sanctions and gossip. Folks believe that failure to fulfill the requirements of the *Ngillatun* will result in bad luck—involving bad harvests and the deaths of animals. If asked, most people can provide cases in which they themselves or others experienced the negative consequences of such failures. The only community members who won't participate are usually the devout Christians whose social network ties them closely to local churches. Interestingly, in contrast to the *Ngillatun*, failure to participate in public works projects will not generate supernatural retribution or social sanctions, even though people believe these projects to be important. In comparison with *Lonkos*, elected Mapuche leaders lack the sanction of tradition or the strength of supernatural forces. From this perspective, experimental games—at least in their standard format—are extremely unlikely to cue the *Nguillatun*-related cooperative behavior because the games are administered by outsiders (who is associated with community projects) not *Lonkos*, there is no ritualized context (singing, symbols, etc.) and cash is the contribution rather than labor, certain food, and livestock.

CONCLUSION

In this paper, we have made three observations. First, our experiments reveal substantial differences in how people from different places behave in simple bargaining and Public Goods Game. This variation was previously missed because experimenters focused on industrial, urban, market societies rather than tapping into the broader spectrum of human cultural diversity. The magnitude of the between-group effect we have revealed is substantially larger than variables typically manipulated by experimenters, such as stakes size, anonymity, number of players (in Public Goods Games), marginal return rates (in Public Goods Games), etc.

Second, individual-level differences in economic and demographic variables account for little of the variation within these groups. Such findings suggest to us that average differences between groups (in something like wealth) probably do not explain the large differences between groups. The Huinca and Mapuche Public Goods samples, for example, are quite similar both demographically and economically, yet they contribute significantly different amounts in the Public Goods Game. Similarly, although the Mapuche behave more like university students in their experimental behavior, it is not possible to argue that the Mapuche behave more like university students because they are substantially richer or more educated than the Machiguenga. The Machiguenga learned the games more quickly than the Mapuche, and have more education on-average. Mapuche proposers actually behave most like Israeli proposers—although responders from these two groups behave quite differently.

Third, the behavioral patterns observed in both the Public Goods Game and Ultimatum Game experiments reflect the pattern of daily life for the Mapuche, Huinca, and Machiguenga—that is, the results are not some strange experimental artifact. As we explained, despite pressure from elected leaders and a general recognition that group-level activities would be beneficial, Machiguenga and Mapuche rarely sustain cooperation or punish non-cooperators, except in very specific and culturally prescribed circumstances— such as the Mapuche's harvest festival.

In order to exist, modern, industrial, urban centers must have developed norms (behaviors and expectations) to deal effectively with anonymous transactions, and allow people to cooperate in a wide variety of contexts. Market societies are filled with opportunities to 'cheat', such that, if most people took advantage of these loopholes, our systems would rapidly crumble. We think these systems persist because people share sets of re-enforcing norms about how to behave in different contexts, what is 'fair' in different contexts, and what to punish. Tipping in highway diners persists in the United States because waiters and customers share a belief that tipping is the right thing to do, and that non-tippers should be socially sanctioned. In other places, such as the Kingdom of Tonga, waiters believe that tipping is an insult, and will forcefully admonish presumptuous foreigners who leave a tip at the end of the meal.

People do lots of things because they have acquired the belief that it is the right thing to do, or because they fear social sanctions, supernatural retribution, and ostracism. The point is, large-scale, market-based societies could not function without well-coordinated norms for dealing with anonymous, one-shot, monetary interactions.[17] However, there's no reason to expect other societies, where anonymous monetary transactions are recent and rare, to share such norms.

Both ethnographic and experimental evidence suggest that whether an action is considered 'right', 'fair', or 'proper', or whether it deserves punishment, may depend on context-specific rules that vary among human groups. For example, in the late 1970s the oil crisis led to long lines at the gasoline pump in the United States. Line-jumpers, who attempted to cut the line, were quickly punished by those waiting—shouting matches and fistfights were not uncommon. Frank (1994) and Fehr and Gächter (2000) use this example to illustrate that people are not willing to passively accept free riders in public goods situations.[18] Now move to Peru. In airports and many other places, Peruvians do not form well-ordered waiting lines; instead, they form chaotic balls of humanity in which each person tries to get served next. During one instance, after patiently waiting while others went ahead, Henrich's Chilean traveling companion had had enough, and began yelling and scolding the Peruvians for their 'rude' behavior. People looked at her for a second, but quickly turned away and promptly returned to their efforts at being the next one served. Henrich and his companion were finally compelled, much to their dismay and displeasure, to adopt the common strategy.

This example demonstrates that orderly lines first require that most people have the idea that forming such a line is the proper mode of conduct, *and* that some minimum number of people have the idea that they should punish deviant line-jumpers. Whether people cooperate and punish seems to depend on the existence of context-specific rules, which vary substantially among groups.

---

[17] The evolution of such norms due to competition among culturally variable groups may be an important part of the explanation of the gradual evolution of social and economic complexity over the last 10,000 years or so (Henrich and Boyd 2001; Henrich, forthcoming).

[18] Waiting in line is a public good because it minimizes the waiting time for the group, but the best individual strategy if everyone is waiting in line is to cut the line and get served first. If no one waits in line, the place is chaos.

Our devotion to waiting quietly in line—one kind of public goods problem—doesn't help us solve other kinds of public goods problems, like driving small, fuel-efficient automobiles to reduce air pollution. If people acquire their rules for how to behave in different social circumstances through experience and/or cultural transmission in specific social groups, then the behavior we observe in experimental games depends on how particular game structures or experimental presentation connects to the diverse sets of rules in people's heads. If a game strongly cues one particular set of rules in the minds of people from one particular group, we should observe uni-modal distributions with little variation (as we do in the Ultimatum Game in the United States). If the game structure weakly cues two or more sets of rules, then we will observe multi-modal distributions with large variances (as we do in Mapuche Ultimatum Game and the American Public Goods Game). If we are correct about this, then re-structuring the contextual set-up of the Ultimatum Game and Public Goods Game to cue the rules of behavior for *Ngillatuns* (for Mapuche) or waiting in line (for Americans) should increase cooperation and punishment among these group. Using fairly weak contextual cues, it has already been shown that Americans and Japanese will vary their contributions depending on the context of a situation. Pillutla and Chen (1999) used two versions of a Public Goods Game: one dressed up as a joint investment and the other as a contribution to a social event. As you might guess, players contributed significantly more to the social event (an average contribution of 39 percent) than to the investment (32 percent) despite the fact that the two versions have the same payoff structure. Similarly, Hayashi *et al.* (1999) show that simple framing differences strongly affect rates of cooperation in a two-person prisoner's dilemma, and that the emergence of these effects depends entirely on whether one is from Japan or the United States.

From our perspective, the central questions of future research should be: why do fairness, cooperation, and punishment vary among groups? What processes can produce behavioral variation among groups, while diminishing the relevance of individual differences within groups? How context-specific are fairness, cooperation, and punishment? That is, do brains contain a multiplicity of different sets of culturally transmitted rules/models about how to behave, with different contexts cueing different models/rules? Are there innate social grammars (e.g. Fiske 1991) for acquiring contextually specific rules and cues about fairness, cooperation, and punishment? And, why are some rules or cues for cooperation and punishment homogeneous across large geographical areas with many sub-populations (in the United States and Europe), while other cooperative norms vary between populations living close together and in similar environments (as seems to be the case in many small-scale societies; e.g. Gurven, Chapter 7, this volume; Marlow, Chapter 6, this volume; Patton, Chapter 4, this volume)?

REFERENCES

Baksh, M. G. (1984). Cultural Ecology and Change of the Machiguenga Indians of the Peruvian Amazon. Unpublished doctoral dissertation, University of California at Los Angeles.

Bolton, G. E. and Zwick, R. (1995). 'Anonymity versus punishment in ultimatum bargaining', *Games and Economic Behavior*, *10*(1), 95–121.

Brewer, M. B. and Kramer, R. M. (1986). 'Choice behavior in social dilemmas: Effects of social identity, group size, and decision framing', *Journal of Personality and Social Psychology*, *3*, 543–9.

Burks, S., Carpenter, G., Carpenter, J., and Verhoogen, E. (2001). 'High Stakes Bargaining with Non-Students', Working paper, Middlebury College, Middlebury UT.

Cameron, L. (1999). 'Raising the stakes in the ultimatum game: Experimental evidence from Indonesia', *Economic Inquiry*, *37*(1), 47–59.

Carter, J. and Irons, M. (1991). 'Are economists different, and if so, why?', *Journal of Economic Perspectives*, *5* (Spring), 171–7.

Croson, R. (1999). 'The disjunction effect and reason-based choice in games', *Organizational Behavior and Human Decision Processes*, *80*(2), 118–33.

Davis, D. D. and Holt, C. A. (1993). *Experimental Economics*. Princeton, NJ: Princeton University Press.

Dawes, R., McTavish, J., and Shaklee, H. (1977). 'Behavior, communication, and assumptions about other people's behavior in a commons dilemma situation', *Journal of Personality and Social Psychology*, *35*, 1–11.

Faron, L. C. (1968). *The Mapuche Indians of Chile*. Prospect Heights, IL: Waveland Press.

Fehr, E. and Gächter, S. (1998). 'Reciprocity and economic: The economic implications of *Homo reciprocans*', *European Economic Review*, *42*(3–5), 845–59.

—— and Gächter, S. (2000). 'Cooperation and punishment in public goods experiments', *American Economic Review*, *90*(4), 980–95.

Fehr, E. and Tougareva, E. (1996). 'Do high monetary stakes remove reciprocal fairness: evidence from Russia'. http://www.iew.unizh.ch/grp/fehr/wp-fehr.html.

Fischbacher, U., Gächter, S., and Fehr, E. (1999). *Anomalous behavior in public goods experiments: how much and why? A comment.* Zurich: University of Zurich, Institute for Empirical Research in Economics.

Fiske, A. (1991). *Structures of Social Life.* New York: Free Press.

Forsythe, R., Horowitz, J., Savin, N., and Sefton, M. (1994). 'Fairness in simple bargaining experiments', *Games and Economic Behavior, 6,* 347–69.

Frank, R. (1994). *Microeconomics and Behavior.* New York: McGraw Hill.

Gächter, S. and Fehr, E. (1999). 'Collective action as a social exchange', *Journal of Economic Behavior and Organization, 39*(4), 341–69.

Hayashi, N., Ostrom, E., Walker, J., and Yamagishi, T. (1999). 'Reciprocity, trust, and the sense of control', *Rationality and Society, 11*(1), 27–46.

Henrich, J. (1997). 'Market incorporation, agricultural change and sustainability among the Machiguenga Indians of the Peruvian Amazon', *Human Ecology, 25*(2), 319–51.

—— (2000). 'Does culture matter in economic behavior: Ultimatum game bargaining among the Machiguenga', *American Economic Review, 90*(4), 973–80.

—— and Boyd, R. (2001). 'Why people punish defectors: Conformist transmission stabilizes costly enforcement of norms in cooperative dilemmas', *Journal of Theoretical Biology, 208,* 79–89.

—— and McElreath, R. (2002). 'Are peasants risk averse decision-makers?', *Current Anthropology, 43*(1), 172–181.

——. 'Cultural Group Selection, coevolutionary processes and large-scale cooperation', *Journal of Economic Behavior and Organization* (forthcoming).

Hoffman, E., McCabe, K. A., and Smith, V. L. (1996). 'On expectations and the monetary stakes in ultimatum games', *International Journal of Game Theory, 25*(3), 289–301.

—— Shachat, K., and Smith, V. (1994). 'Preferences, property rights, and anonymity in bargaining games', *Game and Economic Behavior, 7,* 346–80.

Johnson, A. (1983). 'Machiguenga Gardens', in R. Hames and W. Vickers (eds), *Adaptive Responses of Native Amazonians* (pp. 29–63). New York: Academic Press.

—— (1989). 'How the Machiguenga manage resources: Conservation or Exploitation of Nature?', in D. A. Posey and W. Balée (eds), *Resource Management in Amazonia: Indigenous and Folk Strategies* (Vol. 7), Bronx, New York: The New York Botanical Garden.

—— (2000). *The Matsigenka of the Peruvian Amazon: A Psychoecological Study.* Stanford, CA: Stanford University Press.

—— and Earle, T. (1987). *The Evolution of Human Societies: From Foraging Group to Agrarian State*. Stanford, CA: Stanford University Press.

Kachelmeier, S. and Shehata, M. (1997). 'Internal auditing and voluntary cooperation in firms: a cross-cultural experiment', *The Accounting Review*, *72*(3), 407–31.

Konow, J. (1996). 'A positive theory of economic fairness', *Journal of Economic Behavior & Organization*, *31*, 13–35.

Ledyard, J. O. (1995). 'Public goods: A survey of experimental research', *The Handbook of Experimental Economics* (pp. 111–94). Princeton, NJ: Princeton University Press.

Marwall, G. and Ames, R. E. (1981) 'Economists free ride, does anyone else?', *Journal of Public Economics*, *15*, 295–310.

Orbell, J. and Dawes, R. (1991). 'A cognitive "miser" theory of cooperator's advantage', *American Political Science Review*, *85*(2), 515–28.

Ostrom, E., Gardner, R., and Walker, J. (1994). *Rules, Games and Common-Pool Resource Problems*. Ann Arbor, MI: University of Michigan Press.

Pillutla, M. M. and Chen, X.-P. (1999). 'Social norms and cooperation in social dilemmas: The effects of context and feedback', *Organizational Behavior and Human Decision Processes*, *78*(2), 81–103.

Roth, A. E., Prasnikar, V., Okuno-Fujiwara, M., and Zamir, S. (1991). 'Bargaining and market behavior in Jerusalem, Ljubljana, Pittburgh and Tokyo: An experimental study', *American Economic Review*, *81*(5), 1068–95.

Slonim, R. and Roth, A. E. (1998). 'Learning in high stakes ultimatum games: An experiment in the Slovak Republic', *Econometrica*, *66*(3), 569–96.

Smith, N. (2001*a*). 'Are indigenous people conservationists? Preliminary results from the Machiguenga of the Peruvian Amazon', *Rationality and Society*, *13*, 429–61.

——(2001*b*). Ethnicity, Reciprocity, Reputation and Punishment: An ethnoexperimental study of cooperation among the Chaldeans and Hmong of Detroit, Michigan. Unpublished doctoral dissertation, University of California, Los Angeles.

Tompkinson, P. and Bethwaite, J. (1995). 'The ultimatum game—raising the stakes', *Journal of Economic Behavior and Organization*, *27*(3), 439–51.

Wiener, J. L. and Doescher, T. A. (1991). 'A framework for promoting cooperation', *Journal of Marketing*, *55*, 38–47.

Yamagishi, T. and Yamagishi, M. (1994). 'Trust and commitment in the United States and Japan', *Motivation Emotion*, *18*(2), 129–166.

6

Dictators and Ultimatums in an Egalitarian Society of Hunter–Gatherers: The Hadza of Tanzania

Frank Marlowe

INTRODUCTION

Game theory and the empirical results of game experiments provide insight into human behavior, especially cooperative behavior. It has often been suggested that the foundation for much human cooperation is the widespread food sharing observed among hunter–gatherers (Isaac 1978; Cosmides and Tooby 1992; McGrew and Feistner 1992; Boehm 1999). To investigate this proposition, I enlisted one of the few remaining societies of active hunter–gatherers, the Hadza of Tanzania, to play two related games, the Ultimatum Game (UG) and the Dictator Game (DG) (see box below for an explanation of these games).

Box: The Ultimatum Game, Dictator Game, and Standard Economic Theory

In the Ultimatum Game, a proposer is asked to divide a sum of money with a responder. If the responder accepts the proposer's offer the money is so divided, but if the responder rejects the offer, both players get nothing. The Ultimatum Game elicits the proposer's propensity to hoard or share and the responder's propensity to accept or punish. The Dictator Game is played exactly like the Ultimatum Game except that the responder does not get to reject offers. The Ultimatum Game reveals how people behave when there are potential costs, whereas the Dictator Game reveals how willing people are to share without such costs, thus revealing more about internalized norms of fairness. Proposers' offers in the Dictator Game, therefore, help explain their offers in the Ultimatum Game.

Thanks to the Hadza for always being so tolerant. Thanks to the Tanzanian government (COSTECH) for permission to conduct research, the Hanbygotts for assistance, and the MacArthur Foundation for funding.

(*Continued*)

According to Standard Economic Theory, responders in the Ultimatum Game should accept any offer above zero, since something is better than nothing. Proposers should therefore, offer the smallest non-zero amount allowed by the game protocol. Yet experiments in complex societies show that proposers tend to offer much more than this; the modal offer is usually 50 percent (Camerer 2003). Such high offers seem irrational, unless responders often reject offers above zero. And they do; offers of 20 percent usually have about a 50 percent chance of being rejected (Camerer 2003). This makes the responders the irrational ones.

How hunter–gatherers play these games is interesting for several reasons. First, if we think there is a universal psychology mediating sharing and cooperation, then it likely evolved in the context of hunting and gathering, and we'd expect to see hunter–gatherers exhibit something closer to the baseline predisposition than would people in the evolutionarily novel environments of complex societies. Second, hunter–gatherers should be little influenced by markets that regulate exchange. Third, the ethnographic literature on hunter–gatherers is replete with accounts of a strong sharing ethic and widespread sharing of food, especially big-game meat (Hadza—Woodburn 1998; Hawkes, O'Connell, and Blurton Jones 2001; Ju/'hoansi—Wiessner 1982; Lee 1984; Aka—Bahuchet 1990; Kitanishi 1998; Inuit—Smith 1985; Ache—Kaplan and Hill 1985; Murngin and Wik-mungkan—Peterson 1993).

Among foragers, much food sharing occurs within the household and is nepotistic, but certain foods are also shared outside the family. Sometimes one type of food is traded for another type, but most sharing does not meet the criterion of simultaneous, not-in-kind trade. Occasionally, people will forage together and share both the work and the food, which could be an example of by-product mutualism. Among many foragers like the Hadza, however, a man will forage alone and bring game or honey back to camp to share, which is clearly not a case of by-product mutualism.

Evolutionary anthropologists have focused on three other explanations for widespread food sharing. (1) Tolerated scrounging proposes that individuals relinquish shares of food when the marginal value of those shares falls below the cost of defending them

(Blurton-Jones 1984, 1987). (2) Delayed reciprocity proposes that individuals are predisposed to share their food with others so that others will give them food later on and minimize their risk of going without food on any given day (Kaplan and Hill 1985). (3) Costly signaling proposes that individuals gain mating or other advantages by freely giving food away because such generosity is an honest signal of their phenotypic quality when resources are difficult to acquire (Bird 1999; Hawkes and Bliege Bird 2002). Costly signaling has more to do with what motivates the forager to work, while tolerated scrounging and delayed reciprocity attempt to explain the pattern of food distribution.

Food transfers should be fairly evenly balanced (at least in terms of value) if reciprocity is important while they need not be with tolerated scrounging. Presuming the games elicit the same behavior as food sharing, we might predict people should be more generous givers in the games if food sharing is motivated by reciprocity or costly signaling than if it is motivated by tolerated scrounging. That is, if people are primed to give to signal their generosity, or to build cooperative partnerships, we might anticipate fair (equal) offers in the games (for a more detailed discussion of predictions based on food sharing hypotheses see (Marlowe n.d.)). I will return to the issue of whether the games do elicit the same behavior as food sharing in the discussion section.

Given that responders are able (and may be willing) to punish in the Ultimatum Game, we should expect higher offers in the Ultimatum Game than the Dictator Game. If a proposer can offer between 0 and 100 percent in increments of 10 percent, the rational offer (assuming standard preferences) would be 0 percent in the Dictator Game and 10 percent in the Ultimatum Game. However, if people often reject offers of 10 percent in the Ultimatum Game, it is rational to offer enough to avoid rejection—with an acceptable degree of risk. But what is an acceptable degree of risk? And why should people reject offers of 10 percent, and why should the likelihood of rejection vary? These also are questions to which I return in the discussion section.

STUDY POPULATION

The Hadza are nomadic hunter–gatherers who live near Lake Eyasi in northern Tanzania and number about 1000 (Blurton-Jones *et al.* 1992), 300–400 of whom are full-time foragers. The other Hadza are part-time foragers and part-time laborers for farmers, or depend on tourist money or handouts from missionaries. The area is savanna-woodland receiving 300–600 mm of rain, almost all of which falls between November and May. Most Hadza camps are located in rocky hills where there are permanent water holes and a variety of game animals.

The Hadza have probably been in the area for a very long time. Stone artifacts, found in rock shelters show a continuous occupation over many thousands of years (Mabulla 1996). There have been other ethnic groups in the area for a long time as well. The Cushitic-speaking Iraqw have been farming in the highlands for at least 2,000–3,000 years (Sutton 1989). The Nilotic-speaking Datoga pastoralists and the Bantu-speaking Isanzu agro-pastoralists have been in the area for over 100 years (Newman 1995). Although there is a record of interaction with these other groups over the past century, consisting mainly of Hadza trading meat and honey for tobacco, iron, and beads, a high degree of Hadza autonomy has been maintained. This is reflected in the fact that the Hadza language, which is not at all related to any of the languages of their neighbors, is still spoken by all Hadza as their first language.

Virtually all Hadza today speak Swahili as a second language and many also know a third or fourth language. From the time they are about four or five, most Hadza children understand Swahili, only a handful of the oldest women have some difficulty. All other adults are fluent in Swahili even though women have fewer interactions with outsiders and leave the bush less often than men.

The Hadza are one of the most egalitarian societies in the ethnographic literature (Woodburn 1982). Adults are dominant over children and males over females, but even in this respect the differences are slight. There are no chiefs, no big men, no official titles or roles, no specialists of any kind. Very good hunters are usually more highly esteemed but even this is subtle. Occasionally some man who has a connection with missionaries or a government official may try to tell others what to do, but since no one likes to be bossed around, they simply get up and move to another camp or start a new camp when someone gets bossy. Being nomadic and lacking ownership of property means everyone is free to 'vote with their feet'.

Camp composition is flexible and camp population and location may change with the seasons or for a host of other reasons. Camps are referred to either by a place name or by the name of some man who is usually an older man who has long been married to a woman in the camp. Such a woman often has her parents or her sisters living with her, so the core of a camp is usually a group of related females. However, like most things in Hadza society, post-marital residence is quite flexible and depends on circumstances since descent is bilateral and kin are treated equally on mother's and father's side.

The Hadza I work with are full-time foragers who practice no agriculture. In 1995–96 only about 7 percent of calories consumed across five camps came from food gained through trade with their agro-pastoralist neighbors or missionaries and some camps were virtually 100 percent dependent upon foraging (Marlowe 2002). Women use simple digging sticks to dig for underground storage organs, or tubers, on an almost daily basis, while they gather berries seasonally, and collect baobab fruit when it falls to the ground. They usually go foraging in groups of 3–6 women. When they are digging for tubers, they often help each other lever boulders up out of the way and sometimes help each other dig up the same tuber.

Men do not do as much cooperative foraging as women. They carry their bows and arrows with them wherever they go and will shoot at most any mammal or bird, usually going alone on forays. During the late-dry season, however, men will go hunting at night, waiting at the few permanent waterholes to ambush game that must come to drink. Because other predators like lions and leopards use the same strategy, night hunting is very dangerous and they always do this in pairs. Men also help each other track game once it has been hit if the hunter returns to camp before beginning to track. Men also use axes to break into beehives for wild honey and this they also usually do alone but sometimes go in pairs and sometimes go with their wives. Men also get baobab and berries but do not take them back to camp as frequently as women do.

About one-third of the food in the diet is consumed while out foraging, while the rest is taken back to camp where it is shared to varying degrees within the household and with other households. The most widely shared foods are big game. When a man kills a gazelle, he may bring the whole animal back to camp where it is divided up fairly equally among the households, especially if there are only a few households. When a man kills a giraffe, he cuts off as much meat as he can carry back to camp and then others go to the kill site to cut off their own shares. In addition to meat, honey is often shared widely with people outside the household. Even items like the tubers women dig and the berries people pick are sometimes shared back in camp with others who are not members of the forager's household.

Hadza men also scavenge from other predators, mostly lions, leopards, hyenas, and wild dogs, running them off their kills. Sometimes, the meat they scavenge is many days old and completely rotten and covered with maggots. They cook it and eat it and get stomachaches but value it nonetheless. The Hadza also dry meat to preserve it. One Hadza man kept dried meat hidden in the luggage rack of the Land Rover and ate from it for almost a month as we traveled from camp to camp. Rarely, however, do the Hadza bother to dry meat because it gets shared and eaten up so quickly.

Some Hadza live in or near a village and have some interaction with markets and money. Most of the Hadza I work with, however, live in the bush and have little such interaction. For example, many people in 1995 refused money, preferring gifts instead. This was especially true of women who rarely get to a village where they can use money. But change is coming rapidly, mainly in the form of tourism. By 1998, almost all Hadza, even in remote bush camps, were occasionally visited by tourists who paid money to see them. For this reason, many Hadza now prefer money to gifts.

METHODS

I used 2000 Tanzania shillings ($3.08 at 1998 exchange rate) as the stakes in each game. Tanzania's per capita GDP equals $650 (1995 est.), which means a day's wage equals $1.78 (for a 7-day work-week). Thus, the stakes were 1.69 day's wage. These figures are skewed by the influence of Dar es Salaam; the wages in the area where the Hadza live would be much lower. Although we were asked to use one day's wage, I used 2000 shillings because it meant there would be ten easy units of 200 shilling bills. Wages have no meaning to the Hadza anyway, since only a very few have ever performed wage labor. A day's wage in the US is $78.36 (per capita GDP = $28,600, 1997) for a 7-day week. That means the stakes were 1/26th of a day's wage in the United States but in Tanzanian purchasing power equivalent to $132—perhaps twice that much in Hadzaland.

I conducted the games in Swahili and played with one subject at a time inside a Land Rover with money laid out in front of us. The Hadza language only has words for numbers up to four, beyond that Swahili words have been borrowed. Because the Hadza are not very familiar with money or numbers I used the bills as a visual aid. I explained that I would talk about ten bills of money rather than 2000 shillings, which made it easier for them to add and subtract. For example, instead of having to calculate that 400 from 2000 left 1600 shillings, they could count the bills to see that two from ten left eight bills.

The game procedure was explained to each subject individually by reading a standard text in Swahili and providing further clarification when necessary. Next, I gave the subject a hypothetical offer and asked what the payoffs to the two players would be if the offer were accepted and if the offer were rejected. I repeated the trials until the subject appeared to understand and got the correct answers to four scenarios. The subject's comprehension was scored from one to three (three being highest) by the number of trials it took to get correct answers. Once a subject passed the tests, I told him or her that the real game was beginning. If in the role of player one (proposer), the subject was asked to make an offer. If assigned the role of player two (responder), the subject was told what the offer had been and asked whether he or she accepted or rejected the offer.

Deciding who would play and in which role is tricky in a nomadic population, where people come and go so frequently. I tried to assign roles randomly while also insuring everyone would have a partner in the same camp. First, I estimated the number of people who would play in each camp, roughly the number of resident adults. The first few to play were proposers. Thereafter, I decided the exact number of players who would be responders to those first few offers. In whatever order they arrived, responders were sequentially matched with the previous offers. After all offers had been responded to, the next few players were assigned the role of proposers again, and so on, repeating the process. This meant those waiting to play did not know which role they were going to be assigned and it meant my assignment of roles was not influenced by the identity of the players.

After playing, I asked subjects why they offered the amount they did or why they accepted or rejected an offer. I also asked responders what offer was the minimum they would have accepted.

I paid everyone before leaving each camp. This meant that all players (with only two exceptions) were matched against others in the same camp. This was the only way to insure that all would receive their payoffs since it is not easy to find everyone a second time after leaving a camp. Some people might have been able to figure out who their partner had been by the time all had played if they asked who had made particular offers. The chances of that would be greater the smaller the camp, but I saw no sign that anyone ever knew who their partner had been, and I believe the subjects had complete confidence in the anonymity of the games.

The Dictator Game

I only played the Dictator Game with people once I had finished playing the Ultimatum Game in a camp. In the Dictator Game, I used beads instead of money. This accomplished three things. First, it meant I was not flooding the Hadza with quite so much money, a problem since it quickly goes to the neighboring agro-pastoralists who make and sell alcohol to the Hadza. Second, it allowed me to assess if there was any difference in subjects' understanding when bills with 200 written on them, were replaced by more familiar beads. Since beads did not seem to make it noticeably easier, I think it is legitimate to extrapolate from one game to the other. Third, even though the rules of the two games were carefully explained to subjects, using a different currency helped to further distinguish the games in people's minds.

I filled transparent plastic tubes with beads and laid ten tubes down in front of the subject. I used the ten units (tubes) as a visual aid in the trials to make subtraction easier for players. This amount of beads was worth roughly the same to the Hadza as was the 2000 shillings. Because different people prefer different colors of beads, I let the subjects choose which color or combination of colors to use.

RESULTS

The Ultimatum Game

I played with most adults in five different camps ranging in population from 16 to 134. Eight people played in camps where they were visiting, rather than living. There were fifty-five pairs of players, fifty-five males (twenty-seven proposers, twenty-eight responders)

Frank Marlowe

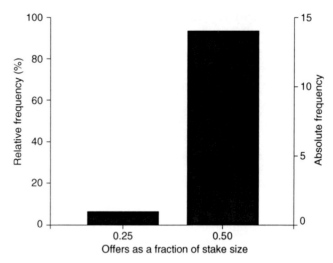

FIG. 6.1. University of California, Los Angles Ultimatum Game offers
Note: Mode = 0.5, mean = 0.48, SD = 0.065, $n = 15$, no rejections.

and fifty-five females (twenty-eight proposers, twenty-seven responders), with a mean age of 37.2 years (17–70, SD = 14.4). In stark contrast to the strong modal offer of 0.5 of the stakes (50 percent) typical of complex societies, as represented by Los Angeles (Figure 6.1), the Hadza modal offer was 0.2 (20 percent) (mean = 0.33, SD = 0.17, $n = 55$) (Figure 6.2).

In complex societies, where there are only a few low offers, the mode is usually higher than the mean, while the opposite is true of the Hadza and Machiguenga (Henrich 2000). The mode, especially a pronounced one, is the more meaningful statistic if one is interested in group norms and cross-cultural variation. Next to the Machiguenga, the Hadza modal offer was the lowest of all small-scale societies so far tested (Figure 6.3), but note that eight of the fifteen small-scale societies (53.3 percent) in this volume had modal offers below 0.5 (50 percent).

There were thirteen rejections among the Hadza. Not surprisingly, rejections were negatively correlated with offers ($r = -0.485$, $p = 0.000$, $n = 55$). The rejection rate was 24 percent and the mean offer rejected was 18 percent (range 0–40 percent) (Figure 6.4). This contrasts with the Machiguenga where there was only one rejection. Thus, while the Hadza mean and modal offers were very low like the

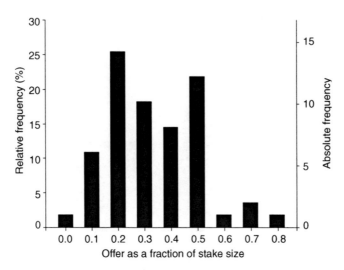

Fig. 6.2. Hadza Ultimatum Game offers

Note: Mode = 0.20, mean = 0.33, SD = 0.17, 13 rejections.

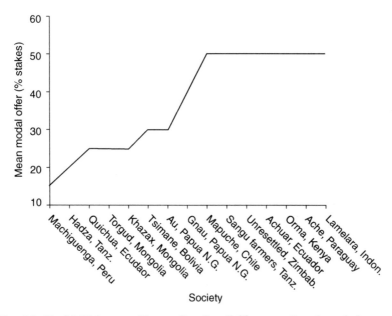

Fig. 6.3. Modal Ultimatum Game offers for all fifteen small-scale societies

Note: Mode = 37%, mean = 39%, SD = 13%.

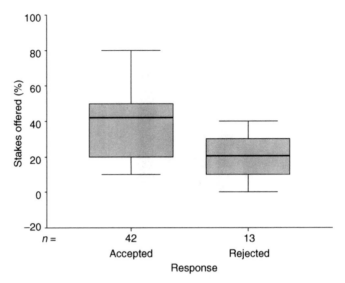

Fig. 6.4. Hadza Ultimatum Game rejections by offer
Note: Rejection rate = 24%, mean rejected offer = 18%.

Machiguenga, the rejection rate was not low. Consequently, Hadza earnings overall were low (mean = 38.1 percent, range = 0–90 percent, SD = 27.5, n = 110). The maximum overall earnings possible is 50 percent per person, which would be the case when there were no rejections and group benefit was being maximized.

There were no significant differences in mean offer for males or females (but see below), nor was there any age effect on offers or rejections. There was no effect on offers or rejections due to the number of siblings (but see below) or the number of children one had. Comprehension came close to having a significant effect on offers. There were only three subjects who did not understand well, and nine with an intermediate score, the remaining ninety-eight were scored high on comprehension. Although not significant, those who understood better tended to make higher offers. One might think savvy people would figure out that it is irrational to reject offers above zero and so make low offers. On the other hand, since there were some rejections of offers of 30 percent and even one of 40 percent, savvy people may have had a better understanding of Hadza psychology.

In a multiple linear regression analysis of age, gender, comprehension, number of siblings, number of children, and camp population, the only significant predictor of offers was camp population (Table 6.1). Offers were higher in larger camps ($\beta = 0.475$, $p = 0.000$, $df = 48$) (Figure 6.5). Entering comprehension only makes the association between offer and population stronger, showing that the effect was not an artifact of greater comprehension in larger

TABLE 6.1. Ultimatum Game and Dictator Game multiple regression results

Variables	Ultimatum		Dictator	
	β	p	β	p
Age	− 0.097	0.562	− 0.017	0.926
Gender	− 0.174	0.199	− 0.203	0.153
Comprehension	0.277	0.067		
Number of siblings	0.010	0.943	− 0.196	0.162
Number of children	− 0.077	0.634	0.040	0.824
Camp population	0.475	0.000	0.544	0.000
Equation	$R^2 = 0.283$	$df = 48$	$R^2 = 0.396$	$df = 34$

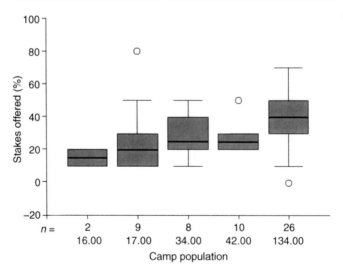

FIG. 6.5. Hadza Ultimatum Game offers by population

Note: $\beta = 0.475$, $p = 0.000$, $df = 48$.

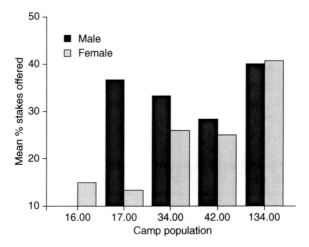

FIG. 6.6. Hadza Ultimatum Game offers by gender by population

Note: Males: $\beta = 0.200$, $p = 0.347$, $df = 21$; females: $\beta = 0.628$, $p = 0.000$, $df = 22$.

camps (in fact, there was no correlation between comprehension and camp population).

Offers by males were not significantly different across camps ($\beta = 0.200$, $p = 0.347$, $df = 21$), and the population effect came mainly from females ($\beta = 0.628$, $p = 0.000$, $df = 22$) (Figure 6.6). When males and females were analyzed separately, the greater the comprehension, the higher were the offers made by females ($\beta = 0.360$, $p = 0.019$, $df = 22$), but not the offers made by males ($\beta = -0.063$, $p = 0.803$, $df = 21$). In addition, unlike males, females who had more siblings made lower offers ($\beta = -0.377$, $p = 0.013$, $df = 22$).

Because offers were lower in small camps we might expect the overall earnings of proposers and responders to be lower in small camps since overall earnings will drop as the rejection rate increases. However, because there was a slight tendency to accept lower offers in smaller camps, there was no correlation between population and overall earnings ($r = 0.097$, $p = 0.316$, $n = 55$). I found no correlation between population and what responders said was the minimum offer they would have accepted ($r = 0.078$, $p = 0.645$, $n = 37$), but perhaps proposers judged responders well since they got away with offering less in small camps. Still, there was no correlation between proposers' earnings and population ($r = -0.073$, $p = 0.596$, $n = 55$) but since responders were faced with lower offers

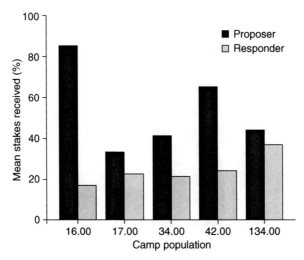

FIG. 6.7. Hadza Ultimatum Game earnings by role and population

Note: Proposers: $r = -0.073$, $p = 0.596$, $n = 55$; responders: $r = 0.348$, $p = 0.009$, $n = 55$.

in smaller camps, and to some extent accepted them, responders' earnings were correlated with population ($r = 0.348$, $p = 0.009$, $n = 55$) (Figure 6.7). Proposers earned 18 percent more than responders (47 percent versus 29 percent), a significant difference ($t = 3.61$, $p = 0.000$, $df = 98.2$, unequal variances).

When the one largest camp (which is much larger than all other camps), is excluded, Hadza offers are much lower (mode $= 0.20$, mean $= 0.27$, SD $= 0.16$, $n = 29$) (Figure 6.8), and virtually indistinguishable from the Machiguenga offers (mean $= 0.26$, $n = 21$). The mode is still 0.20 versus 0.15 for the Machiguenga but 0.15 was not an allowed offer for the Hadza. This similarity is interesting because the Machiguenga have typically lived in very small family groups much more similar in population to that of smaller Hadza camps. Given that the largest Hadza camp is unusually large and a fairly recent development, smaller camps are probably more reflective of Hadza norms.

When only the largest camp is considered, Hadza offers are not that different from complex societies (Hadza mode $= 0.50$, mean $= 0.40$, SD $= 0.17$, $n = 26$) (Figure 6.9). This is also interesting because the Ache of Paraguay, who were strict hunter–gatherers until the 1970s, gave high offers, and they now live in a mission

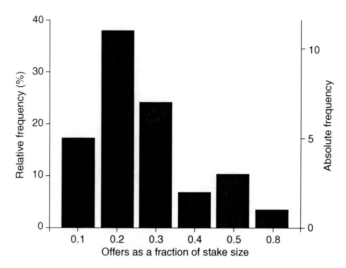

FIG. 6.8. Hadza Ultimatum Game offers in the four smallest camps
Note: Mode = 0.2, mean = 0.27, SD = 0.16, *n* = 29.

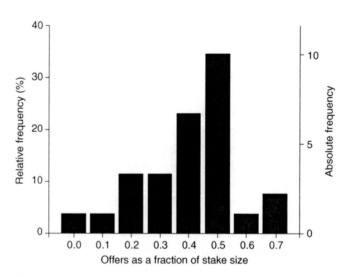

FIG. 6.9. Hadza Ultimatum Game offers in the one largest camp
Note: Mode = 0.5, mean = 0.4, SD = 0.17, *n* = 26.

settlement with a large enough population that we would expect such high offers, even by Hadza standards.

When offers of only 20 percent or less are considered, there was a higher probability of rejection in the largest camp, four of five versus five of sixteen in all the smaller camps combined (Mann–Whitney $U = 20.5$, $p = 0.061$, $n = 21$) (Figure 6.10). This suggests there may have been a higher likelihood of rejecting low offers in larger camps and that proposers were making rational offers.

It is interesting that of all the societies we tested, the Hadza came closest to making income-maximizing offers (IMO) (see Chapter 1). Using Income-Maximizing Offers to calculate a value of risk proneness or avoidance where $r = 1$ means subjects were risk neutral, we see that most societies were extremely risk avoiding and made offers far higher than needed to avoid rejection (Figure 6.11). Even the low offers of the Machiguenga were too high. On the other hand, Hadza proposers were almost risk neutral ($r = 0.94$) (Henrich *et al.*, Chapter 2, this volume), and it paid off for most of them. Although making low offers was risky because Hadza responders were quite willing to reject, 47.3 percent of proposers nonetheless earned over 50 percent of the stakes (Figure 6.12).

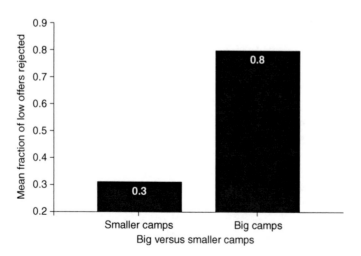

Fɪɢ. 6.10. Hadza rejections of Ultimatum Game offers of $\leq 20\%$, big versus smaller camps

Note: Rejection of offers of 0, 0.1, and 0.2 (5/16 versus 4/5); Mann–Whitney $U = 20.5$, $p = 0.061$, $n = 21$.

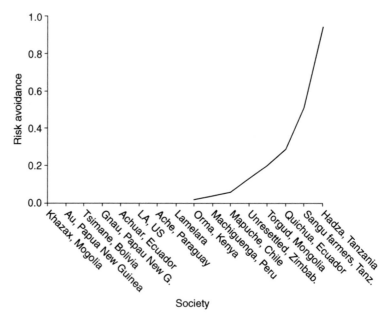

FIG. 6.11. Ultimatum Game risk avoidance in sixteen societies (0 = risk avoiding, 1.0 = risk neutral)

Note: Risk aversion: 0.02–0.94, hada = 0.94, big = 0.3, smaller = 1.0.

Percent paid

		Frequency	Percent	Valid percent	Cumulative percent
Valid	90.00	1	1.8	1.8	1.8
	80.00	11	20.0	20.0	21.8
	70.00	6	10.9	10.9	32.7
	60.00	8	14.5	14.5	47.3
	50.00	12	21.8	21.8	69.1
	40.00	1	1.8	1.8	70.9
	30.00	2	3.6	3.6	74.5
	20.00	1	1.8	1.8	76.4
	00.00	13	23.6	23.6	100.0
	Total	55	100.0	100.0	

FIG. 6.12. Payoffs to Hadza Ultimatum Game proposers (47.3% earned ≥ 60% of the stakes)

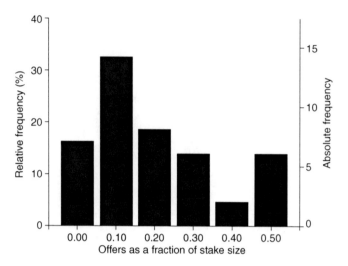

FIG. 6.13. Hadza Dictator Game offers

Note: Mode = 0.1, mean = 0.2, SD = 0.16, *n* = 43.

The Dictator Game

In the Dictator Game, there were forty-three pairs. Among the proposers, twenty-two were male, twenty-one were female, and mean age was 36.6 (17–68, SD = 15.7). In complex societies, the modal offer in the Dictator Game is between 0.31–0.50, with a mean of 0.15–0.25 (Camerer 2003). The modal offer for the Hadza was 0.10 (mean = 20 percent, SD = 16.2, $n = 43$) (Figure 6.13). Again the Hadza mode was less than the mean, the opposite of complex societies.

In a multiple linear regression analysis of age, gender, number of siblings, number of children, and camp population, the only significant predictor of offers was again camp population ($\beta = 0.544$, $p = 0.000$, $df = 34$) (Table 6.1) (Figure 6.14). The effect of gender was almost significant ($t = 1.76$, $p = 0.088$, $df = 35.1$, unequal variances), with females offering less. In the Dictator Game (unlike the Ultimatum Game), the population effect came mainly from males ($\beta = 0.630$, $p = 0.007$, $df = 16$), rather than females ($\beta = 0.343$, $p = 0.209$, $df = 14$) (Figure 6.15). However, this gender difference is probably an artifact of the sample distribution since there were no female dictators in the largest camp.

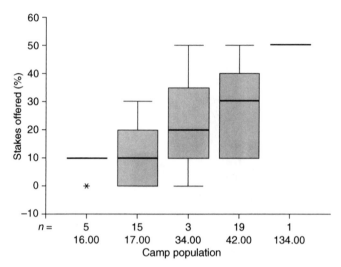

FIG. 6.14. Hadza Dictator Game offers by population

Note: $\beta = 0.544$, $p = 0.000$, $df = 34$.

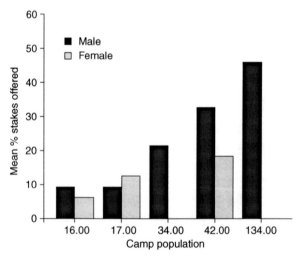

FIG. 6.15. Hadza Dictator Game offers by population by gender

Note: Males: $\beta = 0.630$, $p = 0.007$, $df = 16$; females: $\beta = 0.343$, $p = 0.209$, $df = 14$.

Finally, only eighteen subjects were proposers in both the Ultimatum Game and Dictator Game. Their offers are almost significantly correlated ($r = 0.450$, $p = 0.061$, $n = 18$). Even though it was the behavior of women overall that was more similar in the two games, in relation to the variable of camp population, it was men's offers in the two games that were more positively related.

DISCUSSION

The Hadza modal offer of 0.10 in the Dictator Game is presumably the extent to which the Hadza are compelled by their own strong sense of fairness to share with others. The modal offer of 0.20 in the Ultimatum Game represents an extra 0.10 due to the threat of rejection. Those who gave 0.5 usually said it was the only fair offer. Those who gave less were quick to pull any old rationalization out of thin air. For example, one said he offered his partner little, 'because he is my good comrade', and another said, 'because my partner is younger than me'. On the other hand, the person who offered 0.8 said they did so, 'because it is in my heart to help a friend'.

The Hadza made lower offers in both the Ultimatum Game and Dictator Game than is typical of complex societies. This result is especially interesting given the Hadza can only be described as extremely egalitarian, with a strong sharing ethic. They daily share food, as well as many other items. Americans, on the other hand, usually do not share food on a daily basis with anyone outside the household. We too have a strong sense of fairness that dictates that we share equally—when we do share. But sharing simply does not happen nearly so often in the United States, where privacy and private property are paramount. For the Hadza, living in the open, with no privacy, sharing is a constant, inescapable fact of life. I suggest the difference between the Hadza Ultimatum Game mode of 0.20 and the US Ultimatum Game mode of 0.50 must be related to this never-ending sharing among the Hadza. Perhaps the more frequently one must share, the more weary one grows of it, and the more one looks for any opportunity to escape it.

This same response might also explain why Hadza offers were lower in smaller camps. I have observed that food is more frequently shared outside the household in smaller camps, where everyone usually eats together because there may only be three households and there is absolutely no privacy. Not only have I seen more frequent sharing, I have also seen a wider range of food types being shared. In small camps, for example, even berries, which everyone can pick for him or herself, are often shared outside the household. Large camps, where there may be twenty households, are usually broken up into clusters of two or three huts and function somewhat like several small camps. However, there is one important difference. At times, everyone in a large camp is congregated in one spot. This means someone returning to camp can sneak into a hut without his or her food being seen, especially after dark. People in large camps often do just this, asking me to discreetly weigh their food inside to keep others from seeing. In a small camp it is impossible to sneak anything in. Of course, it is also more difficult for any free rider to go unnoticed in a small camp so it may be easier to make reciprocity work.

People may tend to behave more generously when they find themselves in a large camp since the modal Ultimatum Game offer in the largest camp was 0.50 while it was 0.10–0.20 in all other camps. This may partially explain why large camps even exist. Earnings for responders were higher in large camps, and a similar benefit in real life could be the incentive to move to a large camp. Camp population is an important factor in Hadza life. There is much more bickering in larger camps, as the Hadza so often note. I also found that men provide less direct care to children in larger camps, spending more time with other men instead (Marlowe 1999). Considering that when the largest Hadza camp is excluded, Hadza and Machiguenga offers were equivalent, perhaps overall Machiguenga offers were lower because work–eat groups are smaller, also suggesting group size may be an important factor driving offers.

Originally, I expected offers might be higher in small camps where I had seen more sharing. I also thought stinginess might be greater in large camps because with more possible dyads it would be more difficult for anyone to figure out who their partner was, which would insure greater Anonymity and less concern about one's stinginess being discovered. The opposite was true, which suggests to me there may be a greater fear of punishment in larger camps.

Hadza say people who do not share are bad people and that they will move away from them. Punishment comes in the form of gossip and exile. Among the Hadza's neighbors punishment often comes in the form of accusations of witchcraft. The Hadza do not practice witchcraft but occasionally, if they are upset with another Hadza, the suggestion is made that he has learned witchcraft from neighboring tribes. Being accused of stinginess by several people in a large group would be more dangerous than being accused by one or two people in a small group. There is probably more hoarding by everyone in large camps because it is easier to hide food, and I suspect people are more apt to accuse others of stinginess to try to force them to share in large camps; hence, the greater degree of bickering.

Hadza might have offered more in larger camps because they were advertising their generosity. If we assume the game triggers the food sharing context, then even though there was Anonymity, the Hadza may have been responding to population just as they would if the currency was food and there were no Anonymity. Where there are more benefits to be had, more potential mates, for example, we should expect to see more advertisement. We might expect that men stand to gain more than women do from advertising their generosity in larger camps because of a greater potential variation in reproductive success as a function of prestige, but in fact the population effect came mainly from females, at least in the Ultimatum Game. Because the number of free riders should rise with population (Boyd and Richerson 1988), reciprocity predicts people should give higher offers in small groups, contrary to the Hadza results. Nonetheless, reciprocity and costly signaling might explain why Dictator Game offers were 10 percent, rather than 0 percent as tolerated scrounging would predict for a perfectly defendable currency.

But how well do these games reflect the behavior involved in food sharing? Money introduced as a windfall might seem different from food that is earned by foraging. However, much food is actually obtained through secondary transfers from someone other than the producer. Such transfers are not unlike a windfall of money to be divided up. There is, however, one important difference between money and many kinds of food: money can more easily be hidden. When a resource can be hidden there is no cost of defending it, so tolerated scrounging predicts the resource will be hoarded.

The Hadza exhibit a high degree of sharing of items they cannot hide like large game, but less sharing of items that can be hidden. Money and beads, which can be hidden, generally do not get shared much. Beads, however, are a durable rather than consumable item and can thus be loaned out and returned, perhaps causing them to be treated differently. Tobacco can be hidden but cannot be smoked in camp without being detected and it is very widely shared when smoked. In fact, I chose not to use tobacco in the games for this very reason; there is little motivation to maximize one's income if it cannot be kept.

For the Ultimatum Game proposer who wants to maximize his or her earnings, the crucial question is, 'What is the probability my partner will reject offer X?' To maximize earnings, proposers must risk a higher probability of rejection. How risk-avoiding individuals are should vary with circumstances that determine the utility of a particular resource. If a risk-avoiding strategy guarantees a steady supply of food, for example, but only at a level below that required for survival, a risk-prone strategy will be selected for (Krebs and Davies 1993).

The Ultimatum Game has nothing to do with risk for the responder, but in real life with repeated interactions, there is a chance that spitefully and angrily rejecting low offers now will force others to give larger shares in the future. The all-or-nothing nature of the responder's decision in the Ultimatum Game does not translate well to Hadza reality. For example, when food is shared among the Hadza, rather than simply accepting whatever initial offer is made, people normally hold out a hand, encouraging the giver to keep giving until the giver finally draws the line.

The most puzzling thing about the Ultimatum Game to rational theorists is why responders would reject any offer above zero. However, the logic that, 'something is better than nothing', evaluates resources only in terms of absolute gains. In many contexts, people appear to assess their welfare in relative, rather than absolute terms. For example, a person may get angry if he or she is the only one who does not get a raise even though they get no less money than they did before.

In many situations it is probably adaptive to assess welfare relatively since Darwinian fitness is relative. Spite makes sense if the endgame is relative success. People may use a conditional strategy to evaluate their welfare in relative or absolute terms depending on the circumstances. When the benefit of an absolute gain would ultimately add less to one's fitness than preventing another from gaining the upper hand, people may behave in a way that only appears to be spiteful but is actually rational. Perhaps this explains the seemingly spiteful, but ultimately rational, behavior of responders in the Ultimatum Game. And given the tendency for responders to reject low offers, the high offers of proposers are also not irrational, at least when, like Hadza offers, they are not exceedingly high.

CONCLUSION

Food sharing is often attributed to a lack of storage ability among foragers. If meat is going to rot and be worthless, why not give it away. This explanation simply will not suffice for the two reasons described earlier: (1) Hadza eat very rotten meat, and (2) they know how to dry and preserve meat. It also does not explain the widespread sharing of honey, which does not spoil. Assuming that playing for money in these games does tell us something about what motivates food sharing, we can draw some tentative conclusions. Tolerated scrounging predicts that people should give 0 percent in the Dictator Game if they can hide their winnings. Instead, the Hadza most often gave 10 percent, suggesting sharing is not completely due to tolerated scrounging.

On the other hand, even though they are egalitarian with a strong sharing ethic, the Hadza were not reluctant to hoard. They were also not reluctant to punish others for hoarding. In evolutionary perspective, such a seeming contradiction makes perfect sense. People should try to keep as much as possible for themselves and their family, while demanding as much as possible from others, as tolerated scrounging predicts. But one thing must be made clear. The Hadza are very generous. Just because those of us working with them have described their sharing as tolerated scrounging or demand sharing does not mean it is rife with grumbling. Tolerated scrounging does not mean the Hadza steal food. On the contrary, the Hadza do not steal anything at all, except from other species. Most food is simply not classified as private property, so it cannot be stolen. Once seen, food must be shared. At first glance, one would think all this sharing is motivated by altruism. But as generous as it appears, we know that the persistent demand to share can wear one out. We get worn out and so do the Hadza, which one observes only after being there a while and being privy to it.

I suggest the Hadza results are explained by a combination of a greater fear of punishment in larger camps (even when there is Anonymity), and a greater desire to escape from constant sharing in smaller camps. In addition to tolerated scrounging, reciprocity and costly signaling are supported by the results to some extent and I suspect all three are involved. Hadza sharing is ubiquitous because there is no status differentiation and no privacy, which means that others can demand shares. Private property and privacy in complex societies allow us to escape from such demand sharing.

REFERENCES

Bahuchet, S. (1990). 'Food sharing among the Pygmies of Central Africa', *African Study Monographs*, *11*(1), 27–53.

Bird, R. (1999). 'Cooperation and conflict: The behavioral ecology of the sexual division of labor', *Evolutionary Anthropology*, *8*(2), 65–75.

Blurton-Jones, N. G. (1984). 'Selfish origin for human food sharing: Tolerated theft', *Ethology and Sociobiology*, *5*, 1–3.

——(1987). 'Tolerated theft: Suggestions about the ecology and evolution of sharing, hoarding, and scrounging', *Social Science Information*, *26*, 31–54.

——O'Connell, J., Hawkes, K., Kamuzora, C. L., and Smith, L. C. (1992). 'Demography of the Hadza, an increasing and high density population of savanna foragers', *American Journal of Physical Anthropology*, *89*, 159–81.

Boehm, C. (1999). *Hierarchy in the Forest: The Evolution of Egalitarian Behavior*. Cambridge, MA: Harvard University Press.

Boyd, R. and Richerson, P. J. (1988). 'The evolution of reciprocity in sizeable groups', *Journal of Theoretical Biology*, *132*, 337–56.

Camerer, C. F. (2003). *Behavioral Game Theory: Experiments in Strategic Interaction*, Princeton: Princeton University Press.

Cosmides, L. and Tooby, J. (1992). 'Cognitive adaptation for social exchange', in J. Barkow, L. Cosmides, and J. Tooby (eds), *The Adapted Mind*, Oxford: Oxford University Press, pp. 163–228.

Hawkes, K. and Bliege Bird, R. (2002). 'Showing off, handicap signaling, and the evolution of men's work', *Evolutionary Anthropology*, *11*, 58–67.

——O'Connell, J., and Blurton Jones, N. G. (2001). 'Hadza meat sharing', *Evolution and Human Behavior*, *22*, 113–42.

Henrich, J. (2000). 'Does culture matter in economic behavior? Ultimatum game bargaining among the Machiguenga Indians of the Peruvian Amazon', *American Economic Review*, *90*, 973–9.

Isaac, G. (1978). 'The food-sharing behavior of protohuman hominids', *Scientific American*, *238*, 90–108.

Kaplan, H. and Hill, K. (1985). 'Food sharing among Ache foragers: Tests of explanatory hypotheses', *Current Anthropology*, *26*(2), 223–46.

Kitanishi, K. (1998). 'Food sharing among the Aka hunter–gatherers in northeastern Congo', *African Studies Monographs*, *25*, 3–32.

Krebs, J. R. and Davies, N. B. (1993). *An Introduction to Behavioural Ecology*. Oxford: Blackwell.

Lee, R. B. (1984). *The Dobe !Kung*. New York: Holt Rinehart and Winston.

Mabulla, A. Z. P. (1996). Middle and Later Stone Age Land-Use and Lithic Technology in the Eyasi Basin, Tanzania. Unpublished Ph.D., University of Florida.

Marlowe, F. (1999). 'Male care and mating effort among Hadza foragers', *Behavioral Ecology and Sociobiology*, *46*, 57–64.

——(2002). 'Why the Hadza are still hunter–gatherers', in S. Kent (ed.), *Ethnicity, Hunter–Gatherers, and the 'Other': Association or Assimilation in Africa*, Washington: Smithsonian Institution Press, pp. 247–75.

——. (n.d.) What explains Hadza food sharing?

McGrew, W. C. and Feistner, T. C. (1992). 'Two nonhuman primate models for the evolution of human food sharing: Chimpanzees and Callitrichids', in J. H. Barkow, L. Cosmides, and J. Tooby (eds), *The Adapted Mind*, Oxford: Oxford University Press.

Newman, J. L. (1995). *The Peopling of Africa: A Geographic Interpretation*. New Haven, CT: Yale University Press.

Peterson, N. (1993). 'Demand sharing: Reciprocity and the pressure for generosity among foragers', *American Anthropologist*, *95*, 860–74.

Smith, E. A. (1985). 'Inuit foraging groups: Some simple models incorporating conflicts of interest, relatedness, and central-place sharing', *Ethology and Sociobiology*, *6*, 27–47.

Sutton, J. E. G. (1989). 'Toward a history of cultivating the fields', *Azania*, *21*, 27–48.

Wiessner, P. (1982). 'Risk, reciprocity and social influences on !Kung San economies', in L. Eleanor and R. B. Lee (eds), *Politics and History in Band Society*, Cambridge: Cambridge University Press, pp. 61–81.

Woodburn, J. (1982). 'Egalitarian societies', *Man*, *17*(3), 431–51.

——(1998). 'Sharing is not a form of exchange: An analysis of property-sharing in immediate-return hunter–gatherer societies', in C. M. Hann (ed.), *Property Relations: Renewing the Anthropological Tradition*, Cambridge: Cambridge University Press, pp. 48–63.

7

Does Market Exposure Affect Economic Game Behavior?

The Ultimatum Game and the Public Goods Game among the Tsimane' of Bolivia

Michael Gurven

INTRODUCTION

This chapter attempts to expand the cross-cultural literature on economic games by focusing on the game behavior of the Tsimane', a group of Bolivian forager–horticulturalists. One salient feature that has been proposed as a possible explanation for cross-cultural differences in game behavior is the degree of market exposure and acculturation (Henrich 2000; Henrich *et al.*, Chapter 2, this volume). This study therefore attempts to answer two questions: (1) Does Tsimane' game behavior differ from the standard results found among westernized, market-oriented, and industrialized populations? (2) Does differential exposure to competitive markets and an acculturated environment affect norms of fairness and game behavior across Tsimane' villages, or does a common Tsimane' identity and culture overshadow any differences due to acculturation?

Cross-cultural results

In one of the first cross-cultural comparisons in Ultimatum Game behavior, Roth *et al.* (1991) discovered only minor differences

This research was funded by a grant from the MacArthur Foundation Network on Economic Environments and the Evolution of Individual Preferences and Social Norms, a National Science Foundation Graduate Fellowship, and a University of New Mexico Student Resource Allocation Committee grant. Special thanks to Ricardo Godoy and his research team for their generous hospitality and logistic assistance during my visits in San Borja. I would also like to thank the Gran Consejo Tsimane' for their endorsement of my research, and of course the Tsimane' of Puerto Mendez, La Pampita, Cachuela, Catumare, and Ocuña, for their kindness and support. I also would like to thank Sam Bowles, Herb Gintis, and Hillard Kaplan for their helpful editorial comments.

in the distributions of offers and acceptances between student populations in Pittsburgh, Tokyo, Ljubljana, and Jerusalem. Although the four countries differ in cultural heritage (and hence cultural norms that may affect social and economic behavior), they are all examples of student populations living in industrialized nations with a long history of westernized market economies. Similarities in game behavior across the four countries suggest that the overwhelming market influence dominates any cross-cultural notions of fairness or norms of exchange, so that the sample was 'cross-cultural' only in a very limited sense. Henrich's (2000) finding of low offers and few rejections in the Ultimatum Game, and low contributions in the Public Goods Game among the Machiguenga, suggests that the cultural trajectory associated with a traditional, nonmarket oriented subsistence economy can lead to vastly different outcomes, thus calling into question the assumption that departures from game-theoretic predicted behavior are the result of a pan-human cognitive architecture (cf. Hoffman, McCabe, and Smith 1998).

The Tsimane' represent an interesting test case for exploring cross-cultural differences for two reasons. First, they are a self-sufficient forager–horticulturalist group very similar to the Machiguenga (see below). We might therefore expect to find similar patterns in Ultimatum Game and Public Goods Game behavior, which would then add more weight to the Machiguenga results. Second, Tsimane' villages vary significantly in the degree to which they are exposed to markets, wage labor, and Bolivian national society. For the most part (but see below), these differences in exposure are captured by the distance of various villages to the urban center, San Borja. The Tsimane' case allows us to test whether market association and acculturation are partly responsible for the game behavior found in the West.

Predictions

Expectations of game behavior are typically based on notions of short-term income-maximization, strategic play, fairness, reciprocity, altruism, or cultural norms. Precise predictions of game behavior in both Ultimatum Game and Public Goods Game have only been made with game theory, assuming that individuals selfishly act as if to maximize the amount of money they can expect to receive. While it is recognized that the variance in responses deviating from these predictions can be due to a combination of strategic behavior, 'warm-glow' giving, a desire to punish unfairness, or partial adherence to behavioral norms, it is as yet unclear the extent to which exposure to markets and frequent dyadic interactions with strangers also account for cross-cultural differences in game behavior.[1]

Given the current state of knowledge of Ultimatum Game and Public Goods Game behavior, we are in a position to make several predictions regarding game behavior among the Tsimane':

Income-maximization

> A1. All offers should be small (e.g. 1 B), and all positive offers should be accepted in the Ultimatum Game.
>
> A2. All players should contribute nothing to the common pot in the Public Goods Game.

Universal 'fairness' (market-oriented norms)

> B1. In the Ultimatum Game, all offers should hover around the 'fair' or 'strategic' offer of 50 percent and small offers (typically less than 25 percent) should be rejected.
>
> B2. Contributions to the common pot in the Public Goods Game should range between 40 and 60 percent.

Market exposure versus culture-specific norms

> C1. More acculturated Tsimane' living closer to San Borja should display Ultimatum Game and Public Goods Game similar to predictions B1 and B2, if long-term exposure to money-oriented markets leads to cultural norms that produce those behaviors.
>
> C2. Less acculturated Tsimane' living farther away from San Borja should display Ultimatum Game and Public Goods Game significantly different than B1 and B2, as well as C1 (although it is unclear whether we need expect A1 and A2).
>
> C3. If cultural norms of fairness common to all Tsimane' are a more powerful influence on fairness equilibria than exposure to competitive markets, wage labor, and urban living, then

---

[1] Variation in game behavior can also be due to differences in stable personality traits, risk preferences, or pre-existing wealth among individual players.

we might not expect any differences in the pattern of offers and rejections in the Ultimatum Game, or in public good contributions in the Public Goods Game across villages.

The Tsimane'

The Tsimane' are an Amazonian forager–horticulturalist group inhabiting a vast area of lowland forests and savannas east of the Andes. Their territory is located between the villages of San Borja and San Ignacio de Mojos in the Ballivián province of the Beni department of Bolivia. There are currently about fifty Tsimane' villages settled along the banks of the Maniqui River, and about thirty other villages dispersed along the headwaters of the Cuvirene, Yacuma, Apere, Matos, and Sécure rivers. Estimates of total population size range from 5,967 (Primer Censo Indígena Rural de Ticssas Bajas, Bolivia: LaPaz: Instituto Nacional de Estadistica, 1996) to about 7,130 (VAIPO 1998) over a total area of 1.35 million ha (CIDDEBENI 1990), giving an overall population density of about 0.5 individuals per square kilometer.

Like other Amazonian rain forest indigenous groups, the Tsimane' subsist by practicing shifting swidden horticulture, fishing, hunting, and gathering wild forest products. The chief cultigen staple is the plaintain (*pe're*), while sweet manioc (*oyi*) is used only for processing into the beer (*shucdye*) that plays an important role in Tsimane' social life (Ellis 1996). Other important cultivated foods include corn (*tana*), rice (*arrosh*), papaya (*pofi*), and sweet potato (*ka'i*). Solitary and group fishing are important subsistence activities, particularly during the dry season months from May to October. The Tsimane' fish with hooks (purchased in San Borja or from upstream merchants), bow and arrow (sometimes in conjunction with *chito* or *washi*, the two most commonly used forms of barbasco poison), and occasionally with nets, if available. The Tsimane' mainly hunt with the use of rifles or shotguns, sometimes with the use of tracking dogs, and with machetes. However, the use of bow and arrow is not uncommon, especially when ammunition is not available.

A 1997 census of forty-five Tsimane' villages along the Maniqui River (PRODESIB 1997) (representing about 70 percent of the entire Tsimane' population) reveals a mean village size of ninety-three individuals (median = 75, SD = 75, range = 8–374), with 42 percent of all villages containing less than fifty individuals,

20 percent between 50 and 100, 25 percent between 100 and 150, and 13 percent greater than 150 individuals. The majority of Tsimane' villages are therefore still small-scale, where direct interactions with most group members on a daily basis is fairly common.

Although the Tsimane' were exposed to Jesuit missionaries in the late seventeenth century, they were never successfully settled in missions. New mission posts in several different villages only began in the 1950s, with an increasing influence of missionaries and other outsiders on the Tsimane' lifeway (Chicchón 1992). The greatest influence of the twenty year-old New Tribes Mission was to create a system of bilingual schools with trained Tsimane' teachers and an elected village chief (*corregidor*) in each of the villages downstream from the Catholic mission, Fátima. Indeed, three of the four villages with over 200 individuals contain either a Catholic Redemptorist or Evangelical New Tribes mission.

Tsimane' villages are typically composed of dispersed clusters of several kin related households (Riester 1978, 1993). The household is the basic economic unit for food production and consumption because each household has its own fields (*quijjodye*). Meat, fish, and cooked stew are often pooled among households within a cluster, although it is not uncommon for portions to be distributed to other nearby unrelated households, especially when large amounts are harvested. While the distribution of raw foods is restricted relative to that of many foragers, requests of cooked foodstuffs are not uncommon, and are rarely denied. Furthermore, high levels of visiting and sharing among members of different households are associated with s*hucdye* beer consumption. Huge vats of fermented manioc, corn, or plantains act always attract visitors from other household clusters and even other villages.

Study population   An attempt was made to choose villages of similar population sizes that were either in close or distant geographical proximity to San Borja. Thus, study villages were chosen based on only two characteristics: distance to San Borja (close and far away) and population size (40–70). The five study villages were Puerto Mendez, La Pampita, Ocuña, Catumare, and Cachuela. The first two were within several hours bus-ride of the main town, San Borja (population ~ 13,000). The latter three were further away, requiring several days' journey upstream (up to about 6 days) in a dugout canoe. Table 7.1 lists the distance to San Borja (in km), the number

TABLE 7.1. Village demographics

| Distance Rank | Village | Distance to San Borja (km) | Observed | | | | Sampled | | % sampled |
			Number of individuals	Number of nuclear families	Number of houses		Number of players	Number of eligible players	
1	Puerto Mendez	6	77	16	10		34	40	85
2	La Pampita	7	71	14	13		31	35	89
3	Cachuela	58	49	8	8		21	21	100
4	Catumare	85	41	8	6		20	22	91
5	Ocuna	93	65	14	9		31	33	94

TABLE 7.2. Ultimatum Game and Public Goods Game sample sizes

Village	Ultimatum Game		Public Goods Game
	Proposer	Responder	
Puerto Mendez	17	17	34
La Pampita	16	15	31
Ocuna	16	15	31
Catumare	10	10	18
Cachuela	11	10	20
	70	67	134

of individuals reported to live in the village, the observed village size, complete sample size for the games, and percent of available adults (aged fifteen and up) who participated in the games. Table 7.2 gives the sample sizes for both proposers and responders in the Ultimatum Game and for all players in the Public Goods Game.

Market exposure and acculturation

In testing the effect of market exposure on game behavior, we must realize that geographical distance to the main town, San Borja, is only an approximate measure of overall market exposure. Furthermore, 'market exposure' is hardly synonymous with 'acculturation' and 'modernization'. Although there are some overlaps between the concepts, it is not entirely clear how these should independently influence the direction of game behavior. Among the Tsimane', migration between villages several times over one's lifespan is not infrequent, nor are extended visitations to nearby and distant villages by young men in search of wives, by newly wed couples shifting residences, or by kin. Also, while downstream villagers visit San Borja far more frequently than do distant upstream villagers (Table 7.3), merchants (*comerciantes*) often travel upstream, trading various items from San Borja (e.g. machetes, steel pots, cans of sardines, medicines) for roofing panels constructed from leaves of the *jatata* palm. Loggers have also maintained a presence in the area, especially in the upper Maniqui, where there remains much primary forest. Thus, familiarity with outsider exchange may not vary as much as one would expect by simply using distance to San Borja as a proxy variable of market exposure.

Table 7.3. Acculturation descriptors by village and sex

Village	n	Sex	Spanish	SE	Number of visits to San Borja	SE	Number of times hunted	SE	Number of times fished	SE	Number of years in education	SE	Number of days worked	SE
Puerto Mendez	34	All	2.79	0.14	2.32	0.34	0.73	0.25	5.64	1.41	2.71	0.50	18.42	8.16
La Pampita	31	All	3.06	0.13	2.37	0.25	3.87	1.33	11.80	1.89	2.19	0.52	25.30	8.54
Near san Borja	65	All	2.92	0.10	2.34	0.22	2.22	0.67	8.57	1.22	2.46	0.36	21.80	5.87
Cachuela	21	All	1.81	0.21	0.33	0.13	3.19	1.47	8.57	1.74	1.24	0.45	0.00	0.00
Catumare	20	All	1.30	0.11	0.50	0.18	2.90	1.36	7.20	1.50	0.00	0.00	0.00	0.00
Ocuna	31	All	1.68	0.14	0.19	0.10	0.77	0.49	7.30	1.53	0.34	0.16	6.61	2.53
Far away	72	All	1.61	0.09	0.32	0.08	2.07	0.61	7.65	0.92	0.51	0.16	2.85	1.15
Puerto Mendez	15	Male	3.13	0.19	2.93	0.50	1.36	0.44	9.21	2.59	3.47	0.79	32.21	15.45
La Pampita	17	Male	3.35	0.17	2.56	0.34	6.94	2.22	15.94	2.60	3.17	0.89	46.06	14.21
Near San Borja	32	Male	3.25	0.13	2.74	0.30	4.33	1.29	12.80	1.91	3.31	0.59	39.60	10.36
Cachuela	12	Male	2.42	0.26	0.58	0.19	5.58	2.39	10.50	2.19	1.68	0.73	0.00	0.00
Catumare	10	Male	1.60	0.16	0.60	0.27	5.80	2.43	10.90	1.93	0.00	0.00	0.00	0.00
Ocuna	14	Male	2.36	0.17	0.43	0.20	1.71	1.05	10.64	2.57	0.61	0.34	10.36	4.70
Far away	36	Male	2.17	0.13	0.53	0.12	4.14	1.13	10.67	1.31	0.79	0.29	4.03	1.98
Puerto Mendez	19	Female	2.53	0.17	1.84	0.45	0.26	0.26	3.00	1.28	2.11	0.62	7.06	7.06
La Pampita	14	Female	2.71	0.16	2.14	0.36	0.36	0.36	7.07	2.23	1.07	0.25	1.57	1.07
Near San Borja	33	Women	2.61	0.12	1.97	0.30	0.30	0.21	4.73	1.23	1.67	0.38	4.58	3.88
Cachuela	9	Female	1.00	0.00	0.00	0.00	0.00	0.00	6.00	2.73	0.67	0.33	0.00	0.00
Catumare	10	Female	1.00	0.00	0.40	0.27	0.00	0.00	3.50	1.63	0.00	0.00	0.00	0.00
Ocuna	17	Female	1.12	0.08	0.00	0.00	0.00	0.00	4.38	1.51	0.12	0.08	3.53	2.42
Far away	36	Women	1.06	0.04	0.11	0.08	0.00	0.00	4.54	1.07	0.22	0.10	1.67	1.16

To address these complications, several questions were asked that decompose various elements of market exposure and acculturation. In particular, (a) level of spanish ability, (b) frequency of visitations to San Borja in the past month, (c) frequency of hunting and fishing trips in the past month, (d) number of years of formal education, and (e) number of days of wage labor outside the village in the past year were examined. Examination of the effects of each of these variables on game behavior in the Ultimatum Game and Public Goods Game relaxes the assumption that all individuals in the three upstream villages are 'isolated' or that all individuals in the two downstream villages are all 'acculturated'. Furthermore, the effects of demographic variables such as sex and age on game behavior across villages were explored, because if different age and sex classes behave differently, and if villages vary in their age and sex composition, then differences across villages could be an artifact of demography.

METHODS

The games

Instructions for the Ultimatum Game and Public Goods Game were adapted from those used by Henrich (2000) for the Machiguenga, and are given in Appendices A–C of this chapter. The standard procedure used in all five villages was first to gather all individuals over age fifteen in one location. This location was the school in the three villages that had schools (Puerto Mendez, La Pampita, Cachuela), in a temporary shelter along the beach at Ocuña, and in an empty house in Catumare. After everyone had arrived, the instructions for the Ultimatum Game were read first in Spanish, then translated into Tsimane' with the help of a translator. In the villages with schools, bilingual teachers were used as translators, while in Ocuña and Catumare, a translator from the mission village of Fátima was used to facilitate understanding of the games to the villagers. The instructions were read again in both languages, and the details summarized in both Spanish and Tsimane'. Several hypothetical questions were asked of numerous individuals in an attempt to test understanding of the rules of the games. The answers were explained to all in the group, and more questions were asked until it seemed apparent that all individuals understood the rules of the game. Special attention was given to younger and older individuals, who appeared to have greater difficulty in understanding how to play. Before beginning play, I re-emphasized the anonymity of their decisions. The Ultimatum Game was then played, and a similar procedure was then employed for the Public Goods Game.

In each game, individuals entered a separate area (i.e. the school, an abandoned house on the beach, or an empty house) one by one until all available individuals had played each game. During play, I was the only other individual exposed to the decisions of the players. Assistance from translators was used only if I felt a player still did not understand the rules of the game. For the Ultimatum Game, I told each individual whether they were the 'first person' (proposer) or the 'second person' (responder), then read the script given in Appendix B. After the 'first person' gave an offer, they were told the consequences of their choice (e.g. you offered 4 Bs, so if the second player accepts, you receive 16 and the other person receives 4; if the second player does not accept, neither of you receive anything) to insure further that their choice was based on a proper understanding of the game. The 'second person' was also told the consequence of their decision to accept or reject the offer in a similar manner.

Although the Public Goods Game was played after the Ultimatum Game, villagers were not aware that another game would follow the first one. The rules of the Public Goods Game were easy to understand, but the consequences of specific game behavior were not. To clarify the implications of specific game behavior in the Public Goods Game, I demonstrated through example the consequences of three group scenarios: (a) all contribute everything to the common pot; (b) all contribute nothing to the common pot; and (c) three players contribute everything while the fourth player contributes nothing. During actual play of the game, little interaction between myself and the players was required. Each player entered the separate area, and was given an envelope containing fifteen pieces of paper. During the instructions, the players were told that each piece of paper represented 1 B.[2] Players then decided how

---

[2] Paper was used in the envelopes instead of actual boliviano coins because it would have been impossible to obtain sufficient quantities of 1 Bs coins for play. Finding change for even 10 Bs bills (<$2) was often difficult in the town of San Borja.

many pieces of paper to take with them, and how many to leave in the envelope, which represented the 'common pot'.

Total time for explaining the instructions and for play in each game totaled about 2 hours. After the games were played, I calculated the returns for each player, and paid each individual (or each nuclear family the combined total for its members since change was a rare commodity) the appropriate amounts they earned. Each player was also given a participation fee of 5 Bs. The stakes for the Ultimatum Game were set at 20 Bs, and for the Public Goods Game at 15 Bs ($1 = 5.8 Bs at time of study). These were based on current average daily wages obtained from Tsimane' during household interviews (mean = 16.5 Bs, SD = 4.4, $n = 41$) and on a larger sample of average wages in 1998 for Tsimane', Yuracare, Mojeño, and Chiquitano inhabiting the Maniqui and Isiboro-Secure region (mean = 12 Bs, SD = 12.5, $n = 376 - R$. Godoy, personal communication). The maximum possible earnings from the Ultimatum Game and Public Goods Game, respectively, are 20 Bs (offer nothing and this offer is accepted) and 37.5 Bs (self contributes nothing to public good while others contribute everything). Minimum earnings are zero in the Ultimatum Game (be offered nothing, or having an offer rejected) and 7.5 in the Public Goods Game (self contributes everything to public good whereas others contribute nothing).

Household interviews

Interviews were also conducted with the help of a translator several days prior to playing the games. These were done to obtain demographic and socioeconomic information on all potential players. For all adult household members, I recorded their name, sex, age, place of birth, number of children (and their sex and ages), the number of times they visited San Borja in the past month (and the purpose of their visits), the number of times they went hunting or fishing in the past month,[3] and the number of days they worked for wages outside the village in the past year (and their average daily wage). I also ranked their Spanish ability on a four point scale (4 = fluent speaking and can read and write, 3 = fluent speaking only, 2 = speaks little, 1 = speaks none). Table 7.3 gives the means and standard errors for these measures for the combined samples,

---

[3] Most fishing and hunting trips are single-day trips, and usually occur once per day.

'distant' and 'close' to San Borja, for all individuals, only males, and only females, and presents the same information organized by village. As expected, individuals from Puerto Mendez and La Pampita are more fluent in Spanish, visit San Borja more frequently, have more years of formal education, and work more days outside the village than those from Ocuña, Catumare, and Cachuelita.

RESULTS

All Tsimane'

Figures 7.1 and 7.2 give the distributions of offers made in the Ultimatum Game ($n = 70$ pairs) and contributions made in the Public Goods Game ($n = 134$), respectively. The mean and median offer in the Ultimatum Game was 37 percent (7.5 Bs), with a primary mode at 50 percent (10 Bs) and secondary modes at 30 percent (6 Bs) and 25 percent (5 Bs). While the Tsimane' distribution of offers differs from several western university samples (Epps-Singleton test, Pittsburgh—$CF = 12.99$, $p = 0.01$; Jerusalem—$CF = 12.92$, $p = 0.01$: data from Roth *et al.* 1991), it also differs from that reported for the Machiguenga ($CF = 15.70$, $p < 0.01$: Henrich 2000). Significant differences are most likely due to the presence of multiple modes among the Tsimane'. Indeed, offers cluster around 25, 30, 40, and 50 percent. Thus, offers in the Ultimatum Game are lower than those typically reported in western university populations (and with significantly higher variance, including the presence of hyper-fair offers), but higher than those found among the Machiguenga.

Mean contribution in the Public Goods Game was 54 percent (8.1 Bs), with a median of 60 percent (9 Bs) and a mode of 67 percent (10 Bs). The distribution of contributions for the Tsimane' is significantly different from that found among a combined American sample of twenty-four University of California, Los Angeles students and forty University of Michigan students ($CF = 100.59$, $p < 0.0001$) and that found among the Machiguenga ($CF = 31.00$, $p < 0.0001$) (data from Henrich and Smith Chapter 5, this volume). Roughly one third of Henrich's Machiguenga and US samples contributed nothing to the public good and about a fifth gave between 60–80 percent, compared to 5 percent contributing nothing, and three-fifths giving between 60–80 percent among the

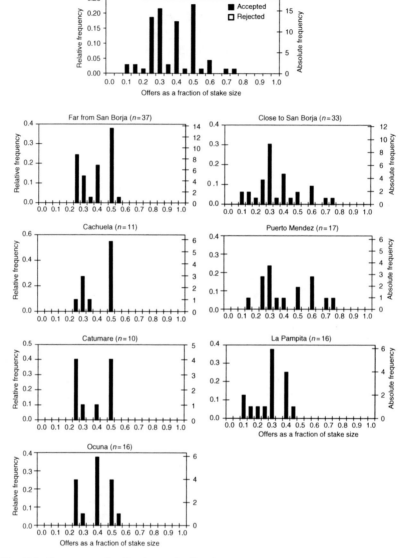

FIG. 7.1. Frequency distributions of offers in Ultimatum Game (stake size $S = 20$ Bs)

Tsimane'. Thus, contributions in the Public Goods Game are slightly higher than those typically reported in western populations (with again more variance in contributions), and significantly higher than those reported for the Machiguenga.

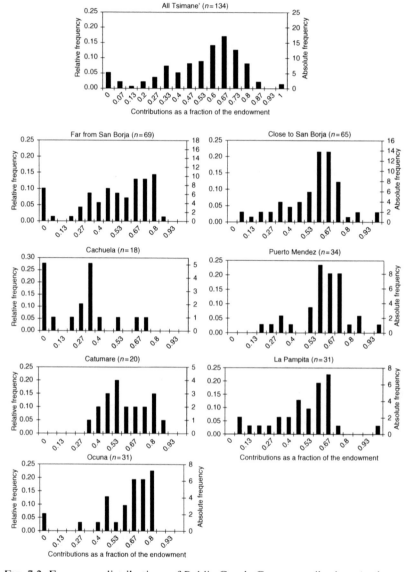

FIG. 7.2. Frequency distributions of Public Goods Game contributions (endowment e = 15 Bs)

By market context

Figures 7.3 and 7.4 give the distributions of offers and contributions for the clustered samples, 'distant' and 'close'. While means for the two sets of distributions in both games are not statistically different at the typical levels of 5 or 10 percent (Figures 7.1 and 7.2), the overall shapes of the distributions for the Ultimatum Game are different at the 6 percent level (CF $= 9.07$, $p < 0.06$). The median in the 'distant' sample is 10 percent greater (and the mode 20 percent greater) than that in the 'close' sample. The result that offers tend to be larger in the distant sample is in the opposite direction predicted if more intensive affiliation with money-oriented markets correlates with standard western notions of fairness (C1 and C2). Indeed, there were no offers less than 25 percent or greater than 55 percent

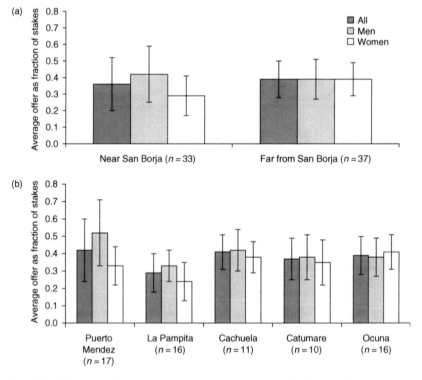

FIG. 7.3. Ultimatum Game results by market context and village (offers by proposers in Ultimatum Game)

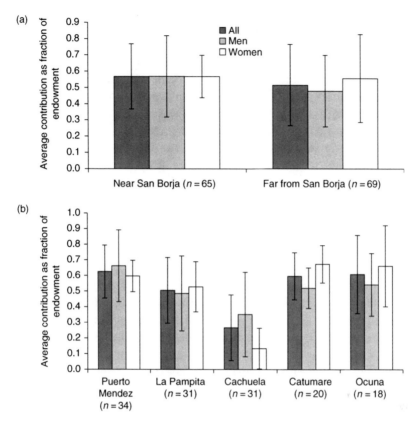

FIG. 7.4. Public goods contribution in Public Goods Game by, (a) distance to San Borja and (b) village (Contribution to common pot)

in the distant sample, compared with 15 percent offering both less than 25 percent and more than 55 percent in the close sample.

In the Public Goods Game, there was no statistically significant difference in means or in the distributions of contributions between the distant and close samples (Epps-Singleton, $CF = 3.73$, $p = 0.44$). Although the distributions were not statistically different, two distinguishing features are noteworthy. First, 10 percent of all contributions in the distant sample were zero, while there were no zero contributions in the close sample (Figure 7.4). Second, there was a clear mode of 60–67 percent in the close sample, while contributions in the distant sample were more uniformly distributed across the range of 33–75 percent (Figure 7.4).

By village

If distance to San Borja has a significant effect on Ultimatum Game offers, then any pair of two downstream or upstream villages should display similar distributions, and any pairwise comparison between up- and downstream villages should be significantly different. However, analysis of pairwise comparisons across villages is not consistent with this conclusion. Of the ten possible village comparisons, only four give results consistent (i.e. distant and close villages are significantly different, distant and distant, or close and close, are not) with the notion that distance from the city affects game behavior. In particular, Puerto Mendez is significantly different from La Pampita (the two close villages, CF $= 8.99$, $p = 0.06$), Ocuña is significantly different from Cachuela (two distant villages, CF $= 9.58$, $p < 0.05$), Puerto Mendez is similar to Ocuña, Catumare, and Cachuela ($p = 0.19$, $p = 0.68$, $p = 0.23$, respectively), and La Pampita is similar to Ocuña (CF $= 7.41$, $p = 0.12$). It therefore appears that although distance to San Borja produces an overall statistical difference in the distribution of Ultimatum Game offers, this difference is unlikely an effect of distance to San Borja.

A pairwise village comparison in the Public Goods Game reveals again that of the ten possible village comparisons, only four yield results consistent with the distance effect on game behavior. Again, the two close villages were significantly different (CF $= 10.30$, $p = 0.04$). Additionally, Cachuelita is significantly different from every other village (Puerto Mendez, Ocuña, and Catumare— $p < 0.0001$, La Pampita—$p = 0.02$), and is responsible for two-thirds of the statistically significantly different comparisons! Again, distance to San Borja is not an important predictor of Public Goods Game behavior across villages.

By acculturation variables

Although distance to San Borja was not a very significant predictor of game behavior in either game, we now explore the possibility that differential exposure within villages, as measured by Spanish-speaking ability, visitations to San Borja, work history, and formal education, might account for the effect of market exposure on fairness norms, and thus economic game behavior.

Individuals of different Spanish-speaking ability, as measured on a four-point qualitative scale, differ relatively little in their

Ultimatum Game or Public Goods Game behavior (Figure 7.5). However, those ranked as most fluent with the ability to read and write (also those most likely educated outside the village) offered significantly more money in the Ultimatum Game (45 percent) than those of lesser ability (37 percent) ($p < 0.05$). There are no consistent directional effects of Spanish-speaking ability, which suggests that perhaps any significant pairwise comparisons may be due to confounding factors.

There are also no statistically significant directional effects for visitations to San Borja in the month prior to interview for offers made in the Ultimatum Game (Figure 7.6(a)—$p = 0.87$) or contributions in the Public Goods Game (Figure 7.6(b)—$p = 0.38$). Similarly, the number of years of formal education and the number

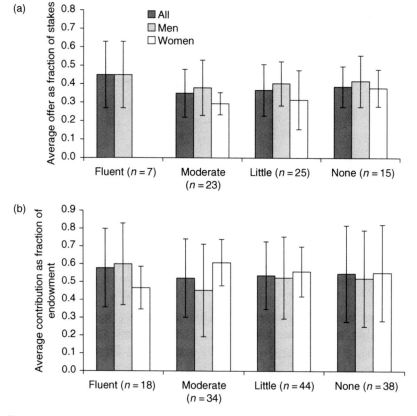

FIG. 7.5. Spanish-speaking ability and (a) Ultimatum Game, and (b) Public Goods Game behavior

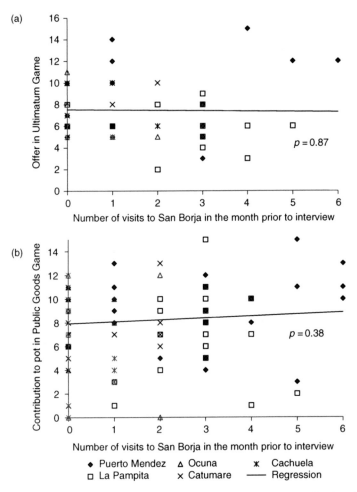

FIG. 7.6. Visits to San Borja and (a) Ultimatum Game, and (b) Public Goods Game behavior

of days worked outside the village as a wage laborer both had negligible effects on Ultimatum Game offers (Figure 7.7(a)— $p = 0.68$, Figure 7.8(a)—$p = 0.49$) and Public Goods Game contributions (Figure 7.7(b)—$p = 0.80$, Figure 7.8(b)—$p = 0.31$).

By age and sex

If age and sex produce significant differences in game behavior due to either differential costs and/or benefits to cooperation or perhaps

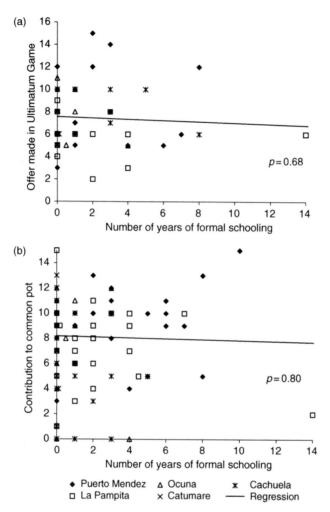

FIG. 7.7. Formal education and (a) Ultimatum Game, and (b) Public Goods Game behavior

an effect of differential learning, and if villages differ significantly in their age and sex profiles, then differences between villages might only be an artifact of demographic differences. Although men offered an average of 7 percent more money than women, there were no statistically significant differences between the distributions of offers ($CF = 6.29$, $p = 0.18$). Age also has little overall impact on Ultimatum Game offers or Public Goods Game contributions.

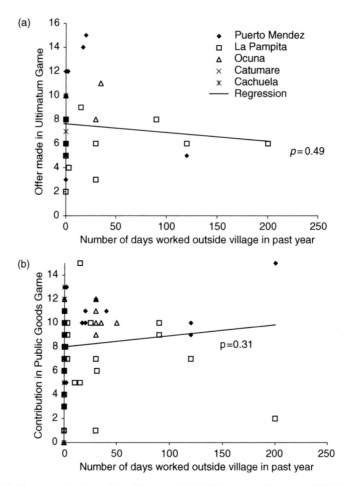

FIG. 7.8. Days worked outside village and (a) Ultimatum Game, and (b) Public Goods Game behavior

The only observed significant difference is that middle-aged women (age 40–55) contribute about 12 percent more money to the public good than their older or younger counterparts. See Figure 7.9.

Regression summary

A series of regressions designed to examine the relative contributions of village membership, demographic variables, and acculturation are presented in Table 7.4. For the Ultimatum Game, village membership accounted for 13 percent of the variance in offer

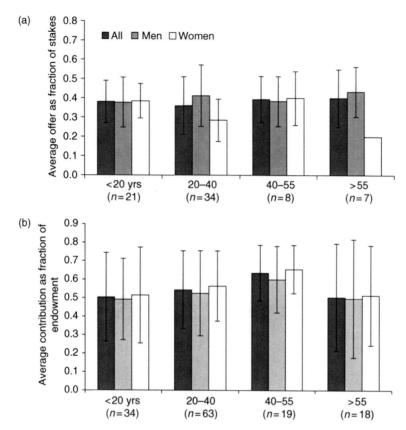

FIG. 7.9. Age and sex for (a) Ultimatum Game, and (b) Public Goods Game behavior

responses and is thus the strongest predictor of Ultimatum Game offers. Indeed, the distribution of offers at La Pampita is responsible for much of this village effect (see above section). Ranked distance to San Borja is uninformative ($p = 0.84$, analysis not shown), as was evident from casual inspection of the distribution of offers in Figure 7.3. The sum total effect of all the acculturation variables accounts for 10 percent of the variance in offers. When all the variables are examined simultaneously (column 4), only village, sex, Spanish ability, and education are statistically significant. While holding other variables constant, males offered about 10 percent more than females, the most fluent offered about 18 percent more than the less fluent, and those with the highest level of formal

TABLE 7.4. Multiple regression of demographic and market variables on Ultimatum Game and Public Goods Game

Predictor	p estimate for Ultimatum Game (% offer)				p estimate for Public Goods Game (% contribution)			
Village								
Puerto Mendez	0	0		0	0	0		0
La Pampita	-11.70***	-13.46***		-17.23***	-12.01**	-11.81**		-15.38**
Cachuela	-0.86	-2.72		-10.19	-35.88***	-35.53***		-38.24***
Catumare	-4.76	-6.20		-16.65*	-2.88	-2.60		-7.56
Ocuna	-2.70	-2.77		-10.13^	-1.69	-1.57		-5.98
Age		-0.05		-0.04		0.03		-0.04
Sex (1 = male)		7.04		10.42*		-1.65		-1.41
Spanish								
None			0	0			0	0
Little			-1.21*	-9.08*			-2.69	-2.15
Speaks			0.78*	-6.09*			-4.17	-2.51
Literate			19.34*	8.70			2.42	6.51
Visit SB			-0.42	-0.04			1.74	0.17
Education			-1.26	-1.89^			-1.71	-1.99
Wage labor			-0.05	0.02			0.10	0.09
R^2	0.13	0.20	0.10	0.35	0.27	0.27	0.03	0.31
p-value	0.06	0.02	0.40	0.02	0.0001	0.0001	0.64	0.0001
Intercept	41.76***	36.95***	58.49***	59.72***	62.55***	62.13***	57.16***	76.03***

Note: ^ = p-value < 0.10, * = p < 0.05, ** = p < 0.01, *** = p < 0.001. The parameter estimates of 0 refer to the baseline value (Puerto Mendez, no spanish knowledge) in a series of dummy variables for village and spanish ability.

education (about 8 years) offered about 14 percent less than those with no formal education. Thus, the Spanish result is consistent and the education result inconsistent with the notion that accultura tion produces results more similar to those found in western populations.

In the Public Goods Game, the only significant predictor, which alone accounts for 27 percent of the variance in contributions, is village membership. Both Cachuela and La Pampita are responsible for the bulk of differences across villages (see above). As in the Ultimatum Game, ranked distance to San Borja is a poor predictor of contributions ($p = 0.87$, analysis not shown), and all variables related to acculturation or market exposure are statistically insig-nificant at the typical levels of significance.

SUMMARY

The important results of this chapter are summarized below:

1. Offers in the Ultimatum Game tend to be lower than those found among western populations and higher than those reported for the Machiguenga, while contributions in the Public Goods Game tend to be higher than those reported for the Machiguenga, but within the range found among western populations. There is also a high level of variation in Ultimatum Game offers and Public Goods Game contribu-tions by Tsimane' in comparison to standard western results.
2. There are few differences in Ultimatum Game or Public Goods Game behavior that can be attributed to market exposure or acculturation, and the few differences that exist do not support the notion that exposure to modern markets produces game behavior similar to that found in the west:
   (i) Distance to San Borja is a poor predictor of game behavior (and perhaps of market exposure).
   (ii) The number of visits to San Borja, years of formal educa-tion, and days in wage labor outside the village, have only a small composite effect on Ultimatum Game behavior and negligible effects on Public Goods Game behavior.
3. The strongest predictor of both individual Ultimatum Game and Public Goods Game behavior is village membership.

DISCUSSION

Several important questions are raised by the current research: (1) Has the methodology adequately captured the effects of market exposure and acculturation? (2) What specific aspects of western populations are responsible for norms that emphasize fairness and punishment? (3) Why do not individuals in several traditional populations ever reject unfair offers in the Ultimatum Game? (4) Why do the Tsimane' offer low in the Ultimatum Game, but contribute high in the Public Goods Game? (5) Why are there differences in game behavior across villages? (6) How can we begin to understand the observed cross-cultural variation in Ultimatum Game and Public Goods Game behavior?

Methodology and acculturation

Although Tsimane' villages vary considerably in their exposure to San Borja and money-based, competitive labor markets, it is possible that only minimal levels of exposure are necessary to adopt norms of fairness similar to those purported to exist for western populations. Therefore, the level of acculturation might not vary as much as suggested by the differences in the acculturation measures or distances to San Borja. Furthermore, as mentioned in a previous section, families often migrate between villages, and indeed, 33 percent of all adults in the distant, upstream villages were originally from downstream villages, and could therefore be responsible for sharing experiences (and transmitting western-like values) to other villagers.[4] Another possibility is that although downstream villages are more acculturated, they are still not intensely involved in the market economy and competitive labor markets of San Borja. Indeed, individuals in downstream villages continue to obtain the majority of their subsistence from cultivation, fishing, and hunting.[5] In San Borja, visiting Tsimane' are regarded as low status by Bolivian nationals, and often complain about being swindled during economic transactions with nationals. Although I cannot rule out the possibility that these confounders eliminate any true effect of

---

[4] Individuals moving upstream may not be a random sample from the downstream population, and may therefore self-select into the upstream sample.

[5] Another self-selection problem is that individuals in the downstream villages that are heavily involved in the market were unlikely to be present during my brief study period, and are therefore not included in the sample.

acculturation on game behavior, it seems more likely that Tsimane' social relations and cultural norms (see below) are a more salient influence on economic behavior than differential market exposure.[6]

Cultural norms

It has been suggested that norms of fairness can partly explain observed Ultimatum Game behavior in western populations (Roth *et al.* 1991; Camerer and Thaler 1995), and that propensities for reciprocity can lead to moderate levels of allocations to the public good even in one-shot versions of the Public Goods Game (Dawes and Thaler 1988). The fact that kindergarteners accept minimal offers about 70 percent of the time, third and fourth graders 40 percent of the time, and adults < 10 percent of the time, implies that any fairness-based norms or cooperative strategies are learned or condition dependent (Murnighan and Saxon 1994). If the gradual learning of norms results from interactions and socialization specific to modern western economies (rather than from rules-of-thumb derived from an evolved psychology tending towards reciprocity), we must ask which aspects of modern environments are responsible for evolving these learned norms. Is it exposure to money-based exchanges? The emphasis on free-market competition? An industrialized, service-oriented economy? Frequent interactions with large numbers of strangers?

Although the emphasis on money exchanges for all commodities is a relatively recent innovation in human cultures, trade has existed for tens if not hundreds of millenia, and is therefore not a unique feature to modern populations. When the Ultimatum Game is framed in a competitive market context of buying and selling, offers are lower and tend to be accepted (Roth *et al.* 1991; Schotter, Weiss, and Zapter 1996). Although immersed in these market-based competitive environments on a daily basis, individuals in bilateral bargaining situations without the market framing often reach cooperative outcomes.

The rule, 'cooperate unless information otherwise indicates you are being taken advantage of, in which case you should defect', is consistent with increasing frequencies of defection in repeated

---

[6] Since all games were played in the villages, the village social context alone might account for similarities in game behavior despite differences in market exposure. It would be interesting to see if games played by Tsimane' in San Borja give results significantly different from those played in the village.

rounds of the Public Goods Game (Ledyard 1995), and the observation that low offers made by a computer are accepted more often than low offers made by humans in the Ultimatum Game (i.e. intentions matter) (Blount 1995). Furthermore, cooperative outcomes are even reached among groups of strangers that interact only once, suggesting that Axelrod and Hamilton's 'shadow of the future' (discount rate) may not be a critical component to explaining commonplace cooperation (but see below). Although membership in large groups is often viewed as an obstacle to stabilizing cooperation, and of generating significant contributions to the public good, assortative interactions can generate cooperative outcomes (Boyd and Richerson 1988). Future work should therefore focus on which aspects of modern economies should generate cultural norms different than those found in traditional societies.

Even though populations may consist of different proportions of obligate cooperators and defectors, institutions can affect cooperative outcomes by structuring the costs people pay and the potential benefits they can receive (Fehr and Gächter 2000). Institutions that promote harsh punishment to those caught defecting may be an important condition responsible for high levels of cooperation, no matter the composition of cooperators or defectors in the population (Fehr and Schmidt 1999). It appears that no such institutions exist among the Tsimane'. As mentioned above, village chiefs, schools, and town meetings are recent innovations; chiefs and teachers, however, hold little authority, and act mainly as village representatives for dealing with outsiders. This leads us to the third question.

No rejections of offers

Why do the Tsimane', Machiguenga, Ache, and Achuar players accept low offers in the Ultimatum Game? Moreover, if it is known that low offers would be accepted, why don't all individuals offer low? An obvious first answer to these questions is that the one-shot nature of the games did not capture learning effects (especially if players' daily experiences depart greatly from the artificial conditions of the games), and that if these groups played repeated rounds of the Ultimatum Game, their behavior might quickly resemble the game-theoretic predictions (or those of western populations). This possibility is observed in repeated rounds of the Public Goods

Game in western populations, but not in repeated rounds of the Ultimatum Game. Yet in the Public Goods Game, the first round of a new game played with different players does not see the high levels of defection found in the last round of the previous game. Contributions start high again, even though the players have 'learned' the game. These results suggest that even one-shot games still require explanation. One-shot games might reflect norms of behavior (especially if there is confusion as to how to play the game) that may only be 'extinguished' after repeated rounds and a deeper understanding of the true costs and benefits of the games. However, these norms might be difficult to extinguish even when players fully understand the rules and consequences of the games and know that they cannot connect specific actions with other individuals. The players are members of small communities who may continue to interact for much of their lives, and any event that greatly irritates or angers others might disrupt social partnerships, which if difficult to obtain, might constitute an opportunity cost to rejecting offers. From this perspective, the real costs of rejecting low offers may be much higher than simply losing the monetary offer.

Similarly, members of small traditional communities may be unfamiliar with strictly dyadic interactions, irrespective of the larger context of the public sphere. Frequent interaction in the public sphere might favor other ways of punishing individuals, such as public humiliation, damaging of reputations, negative gossip, and joking. Although public confrontations are uncommon among the Tsimane', grievances are commonly made known during extensive beer drinking events (when people lose their shyness, or *tsicadye'*) (Ellis 1996).

Another possibility is that 'groupish' behavior might lead these groups to accept any positive offer from a fellow group member, thereby giving the large remainder to another group member rather than to an outsider (the experimenter). While not explicitly requiring individuals to be altruistic towards group members, economic behavior based on in-group–out-group predilections at least requires a greater aversion to having money go to the experimenter. This may be particularly true if group members suspect that the same money is worth more to themselves than to the experimenter.[7]

---

[7] In this sense, accepting any positive offer maximizes the total amount of money flowing from the experimenter to the community. This is, in essence, a contribution to the public good, and is consistent with the observed Public Goods Game results.

This possibility could be investigated by allowing any failure to coordinate to result in money being given either to an outsider (e.g. a Bolivian national) or to another Tsimane' (or perhaps the Gran Consejo Tsimane', the centralized organization representing all Tsimane'). Interestingly, Gil-White's results (Chapter 9, this volume) show that individuals offer less to other in-groupers, and more to out-group members.

Still another possibility is that if many Tsimane' wish to offer low (or can at least understand why others might offer low), and if they understand that being a proposer or responder is a random decision, responders might not have any reason to reject low offers that they themselves would have made had they been named as proposers. This argument requires a lack of spite and desire to punish, which is inconsistent with observed western behavior, but consistent with the common observation, typified by one player's postgame comments, 'I just want the money . . . it doesn't matter how much the other person gets'—these comments are remarkably similar to those made by the very similar Machiguenga (Henrich 2000; Henrich and Smith Chapter 5, this volume). In such a scenario, punishing the proposer by rejecting his or her offer is a costly act for the responder, more so perhaps than for the groups of university students in the west. Although the stakes were set at roughly one day's wage labor, wage labor opportunities for the Tsimane' are few, thereby perhaps inflating the perceived value of even small offers.

No relationship between Ultimatum Game and Public Goods Game results?

Figure 7.10 shows no relationship between game behavior in the Ultimatum Game and Public Goods Game by the same individuals ($p = 0.22$). However, if we separate individuals by sex, males show a slight relationship between their Ultimatum Game and Public Goods Game behavior (slope $= 0.16$, $p = 0.07$), while females show none (slope $= 0.02$, $p = 0.83$). If economic games capture real-life preferences, then how can no relationship exist between Ultimatum Game offers and Public Goods Game contributions made by the same individuals? There are several possibilities for this pattern. One potential boost in cooperation in the Public Goods Game could have come from communication that occurred among the crowd of

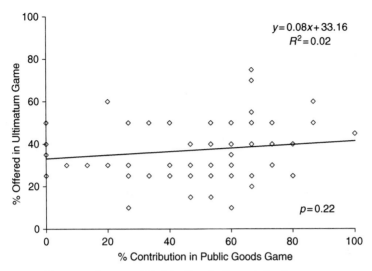

Fig. 7.10. Ultimatum Game and Public Goods Game behavior

players waiting to play, or from an understanding that doubling the sum of money in the common pot greatly increases individual payoffs. Although the translator attempted to insure a lack of coordination-like discussion, this possibility cannot be ruled out, despite my emphasis to each player that their responses were confidential. Even pregame discussion unrelated to the game has been shown to lead to higher levels of cooperation in the Public Goods Game (Ledyard 1995), more so than in the Ultimatum Game. Another interpretation is that if the Tsimane' are risk prone, they might be more willing to sacrifice personal gain to win the big gamble of the doubled pot of money in the Public Goods Game, just as they might be more willing to offer a small amount in the Ultimatum Game and hope that the responder (rightly so) will accept. Given that males have been described as more risk prone than females cross-culturally across a wide spectrum of behaviors (Daly and Wilson 1988), it is surprising that Tsimane' males offered slightly more in the Ultimatum Game than did females, but there were no sex differences in public goods contributions.

Two anecdotes that mimic the flavor and results of the games are relevant to include in this section because they support the argument that common experience might be an important influence on game behavior. As an analogy to the Ultimatum Game, merchants frequently travel upriver to the distant villages to trade various goods from San Borja for *jatata* roofing panels (collected and constructed by Tsimane'), which they later sell in San Borja and sometimes export to other areas of Bolivia at much higher prices. It takes 1 day to collect enough *jatata* to build about ten roofing panels, often requiring harvesters to carry heavy loads several hours distance back to the village, where it takes another day to construct the panels. The exchange rates imposed upon the Tsimane' by the merchants for different demanded goods are quite poor (e.g. five panels for 1 kg of sugar, twenty panels for a shirt, etc.). In essence, the merchants give the offer (i.e. the price), and the Tsimane' almost invariably accept the offer and make the trade. They acknowledge that prices are 'unfair' because the same goods are much cheaper if bought in San Borja, but then also acknowledge that merchants travel long distances to transport the goods (and hence are justified in charging higher prices). Still, others believe that the prices are so high only because the merchants know that the Tsimane' have few other means of obtaining the desired goods.

Analogous to the decision in the Public Goods Game in the upstream villages, individuals can choose between two main production options on any given day. They can collect *jatata* and/or construct roofing panels (which will be converted to goods that will be consumed or used almost exclusively by family members) or they can hunt or fish, where the spoils are typically shared outside the family (resembling a public good). Some Tsimane' spend much of their productive time involved in the *jatata* trade, often to the chagrin of others, who never see any returns from their labor. Most individuals involved in *jatata* work, however, harvest *jatata* in small groups on some days, and then engage in cooperative fishing or hunting together on other days.

Differences across villages

Why are there differences in Ultimatum Game and Public Goods Game behavior among the five villages? The most anomalous intervillage differences in the Ultimatum Game include hyper-fair offers in Puerto Mendez and the abundance of low offers in La Pampita (Figure 7.1, Table 7.4). In the Public Goods Game, members of Cachuela either contributed nothing to the common pot, or relatively little (Figure 7.2, Table 7.4). As mentioned above, pairwise differences across villages are not easily explained by single variables such as distance to San Borja, or other acculturation measures. There are several possible interpretations of these results. First, small sample sizes for each village, or unexpected differences in protocol, may have produced spurious differences where none exist. While it is also possible that pregame communication may have caused different focal responses, there were no clear ordering effects of ultimatum offers or public goods contributions in any village.

If observed differences in game behavior are real, the most fascinating possibility to consider is that different villages can arrive at different game equilibria through some combination of local social interaction and learning processes. The same theory that should explain cross-cultural variability in norms that influence cooperative (and hence game) behavior, should also apply here for explaining cross-village variability. The presence of cross-village variability also cautions us when attempting to explain game results by fitting just-so anecdotal stories that capture key cultural traits or behaviors. Cachuela, for example, which saw relatively low public goods contributions, was a small village with the houses all within sight of each other, and where food sharing, production, and household visitations were more intensive than in other villages.

Understanding cross-cultural variation

What additional insight can these results add to our current understanding of cooperation in humans? Despite the variation in Ultimatum Game and Public Goods Game behavior, the robust cross-cultural result is that strict self-interest predictions are wrong in all societies where they have been tested. As mentioned in the introduction, revisions to neoclassical theory have included social utility modifications of normal utility functions (Bolton 1991), incorporation of fairness equilibria (Rabin 1993), invocations of an evolved psychology based on reciprocity (Hoffman, McCabe, and Smith 1998) or strong reciprocity (Bowles and Gintis 1998; Fehr and Schmidt 1999), and culturally transmitted social norms (Henrich 2000). The only revision that addresses the pattern of low offers (or very high offers) and high acceptances in the Ultimatum Game is the notion of differential cultural norms. However, we have little understanding of why certain norms have evolved in some societies and not in others, or what the relationship might be between these norms and an evolved psychology based on reciprocity. Henrich (2000) suggests that because Machiguenga live in economically independent household clusters, as do the Tsimane', they need not be concerned about what others think of their choices, nor be concerned with the relative amounts that others receive. While this may be true, perhaps the same could be said about Americans, who are perceived and modeled as being very concerned about relative payoffs.

It is interesting to realize that Ultimatum Game and Public Goods Game results obtained so far in traditional populations, where daily cooperation is often viewed as a crucial component of subsistence strategies, are far closer to the self-interest predictions than those found in the western world. It is therefore somewhat tricky to link observed behavior in games such as the Ultimatum Game or Public Goods Game and the kinds of cooperation that typically occur within populations. Unless the costs and benefits over time are similar for two acts requiring cooperation, or if some individuals truly act out of nonegoistic or even 'warm-glow' altruism, we should not expect consistency in behavior. For example, groups that have no problem engaging in cooperative fishing or hunting often find it difficult to obtain levels of cooperation necessary for successful long-term outcomes of many conservation projects (also see Henrich and Smith Chapter 5, this volume).

There is little doubt that humans everywhere have worked out cultural ways of attaining gains from cooperative ventures, and that these cultural methods might require some universals of human cognitive machinery, including abilities to detect and punish cheaters (Cosmides 1989; Bolton and Zwick 1995; Bowles and Gintis 1998). Because cooperation is usually costly in terms of time, energy, or other resources, there are strong incentives to control free riding in cooperative ventures. However, most economic experiments, including the Ultimatum Game and Public Goods Game performed here, are costly only in the sense that part of the potential gains go to other individuals. The endowment of the games represents a 'windfall'—a large sum obtained without any cost. It is unclear whether rules of thumb or cultural norms designed to direct costly acts of cooperation apply for cooperative acts that are relatively costless. Deciding how much of a windfall should go to others might more accurately require an economics of etiquette or manners (Camerer and Thaler 1995).

The idea that cultural norms can explain cross-cultural variation in game behavior is an attractive one, and can surely benefit from further investigation. For example, the observation that individuals playing the Dictator Game offer smaller amounts the greater the perceived social distance between players (Hoffman, McCabe, and Smith 1996) is related to the above discussion on 'groupishness', but whether this is a common cultural norm or a part of an evolved human nature is debatable. Ultimately, we may discover that, although propensities for reciprocity exist as an important feature of human cognition, differences in actual behavior can be best explained as a combination of differences in rule-of-thumb norms based on long-term cultural experiences, as well as different weightings of short-term monetary and long-term social costs and benefits. It is true that players may not be conditional reciprocators if they cooperate in one-shot games, where the shadow of the future is narrow, but as discussed earlier, they may indeed be conditional reciprocaters if the perceived shadow of the future goes beyond the context of the games, extending to long-term mutual coexistence within their community. Whenever long-term consequences of short-term selfish behavior are sufficiently negative or uncertain, a successful rule-of-thumb might be to cooperate. Thus this rule-of-thumb might apply to interactions with in-group members, consistent with the above statements regarding groupishness effects on cooperative impulses. Future work focusing on repeated rounds, learning (or perhaps unlearning of cultural norms for the duration of the experiments), reputational effects, and groupishness might reveal that cross-cultural variation in game behavior is smaller than indicated by first glance at one-shot games.

APPENDIX A: THE ULTIMATUM GAME (EL JUEGO ULTIMATUM)

(Adapted from Henrich 2000)
Este juego está jugado en pares de individuos. Hay dos personas en cada par, una primera y una segunda persona. Voy a decir Ud. Si Ud. es el primer o la segunda persona del par. Cada persona en el par no sabe el nombre de la otra persona (son desconocidos). Yo proveo una suma de 20 bolivianos a cada par. La primera persona tiene que decidir como él quiere dividir la suma de plata. Esta

persona tiene que ofrecer una porción de la suma (desde 0 a 20) a la segunda persona (quien es desconocido).

Entonces, más tarde, yo se la dirá la oferta a la segunda persona (el nombre de la primera persona quedará desconocido). La segunda persona tiene que decidir si él o ella quiere aceptar o rechazar la oferta de la primera persona. Si la segunda persona acepta la oferta, la segunda persona recibe la oferta en pesos reales, y la primera persona recibe el resto (20 menos la oferta de la primera persona) en bolivianos. Sin embargo, si la segunda persona rechaza la oferta, ambos personas reciben nada (0 bolivianos)—la primera persona recibe cero pesos y la segunda persona recibe cero pesos.

La primera persona puede ofrecer a la segunda persona (en bolivianos):

0	1	2	3	4	5	6	7	8	9	10
	11	12	13	14	15	16	17	18	19	20

La segunda persona puede: aceptar o rechazar

Se Recuerda

1. No hay constestas correctos o incorrectos; escoga lo que usted prefiere. Nadie va a saber vos repuesta.
2. La plata es real y viene desde La fundación 'MacArthur' en los Estados Unidos.
3. Todos los participantes reciben 5 bolivianos por su participación en este juego.

APPENDIX B: ULTIMATUM GAME

To first player (Proposer):

Mi nash taschety muntyi. Juñucsi buty ma'je codaqui mi jaquivej muntyi? (You are the first player. How much do you want to offer to a second person?)

Jaquivej muntyi maje, mi ra so'me ___ Bs jedyeya mu ra so'me ___ Bs. (If the second player accepts, you will receive ___ Bs and he/she will receive ___ Bs.)

Jaquivej muntyi jam maje, mi jam ra so'me querecha jedyeya mu jam ra so'me querecha chimedye.

(If the second player does not accept, you will not receive any money and he/she will not receive any money, also).

To second player (Responder):

Mi nash jaquivej muntyi. Mis nash mo'ya yutacdye ___ Bs.
(You are the second person. The offer to you is ___ Bs.)

Are ma'je mi, are jam ma'je mi?
(Do you want the offer, or do you not want the offer?)

Ma'je mi, mi ra so'me ___ Bs, jedyeya yucsi muntyi ra so'me ___ Bs.
(If you accept, you will receive ___ Bs and the other person will receive ___ Bs.)

Jam ma'je mi, mi jam ra so'me querecha jedyeya yucsi muntyi jam ra so'me querecha chimedye.
(If you don't accept, you will not receive any money, and the other person will not receive any money, either).

APPENDIX C: PUBLIC GOODS GAME (EL JUEGO CONTRIBUCIONES)

(Adapted from Henrich 2000)
En este juego 4 personas juegan juntos. Al principio del juego, cada persona recibe 15 papeles. Cada papel significa un boliviano. Entonces cada persona tiene una oportunidad contribuir, en secreto, una porcion de su 15 bolivianos a la caja comunal (entra el cuarto y pon tu contribución *en la caja*, pon el resto en tu bolsillo). Cada persona puede contribuir entre 0 y 15 bolivianos a la caja comual (incluyendo 0 y 15). Depues de los contribuciones a la caja comual, la suma de plata en la caja comual se estará duplicado y estará distribuido *igualmente* entre las 4 personas.

Cuánto usted quiere contribuir a la caja comunal:

0	4	8	12
1	5	9	13
2	6	10	14
3	7	11	15

Se Recuerda

1. No hay constestas correctos o incorrectos; escoga lo que usted prefiere.
2. La plata es real y viene desde La fundación 'MacArthur' en Estados Unidos.
3. Los otras jugadores no van a saber cuanto plata usted recibe en total.

REFERENCES

Blount, S. (1995). 'When social outcomes aren't this: the effect of causal attributions on preferences', *Organizational Behavior and Human Decision Processes* 63(2), 131–44.

Bolton, G. (1991). 'A comparative model of bargaining: Theory and evidence', *American Economic Review*, *81*, 1096–1136.

Bowles, S. and Gintis, H. (2004). 'The evolution of cooperation in heterogenous populations', *Theoretical Population Biology*.

Boyd, R. and Richerson, P. J. (1988). 'The evolution of reciprocity in sizeable groups', *Journal of Theoretical Biology*, *132*, 337–56.

Camerer, C. and Thaler, R. (1995). 'Anomalies: Ultimatums, dictators, and manners', *Journal of Economic Perspectives*, *9*, 209–19.

Chicchón, A. (1992). Chimane Resource Use and Market Involvement in the Beni Biosphere Reserve, Bolivia. Ph.D. Dissertation. University of Florida.

CIDDEBENI (1990). *Diagnóstico socio-económico del bosque de chimanes: el problema de la territorialidad de los pueblos indígenas*. Trinidad: CIDDEBENI.

Cosmides, L. (1989). 'The logic of social exchange: Has natural selection shaped low humans reason? Studies with the Watson Selection Task', *Cognition 31*, 187–276.

Daly, M. and Wilson, M. (1988). *Homicide*. New York: Aldine de Gruyter, Inc.

Dawes, R. M. and Thaler, R. (1988). 'Anomalies: Cooperation', *Journal of Economic Perspectives* 2(3), 187–97.

Ellis, R. (1996). A Taste for Movement: An Exploration of the Social Ethics of the Tsimane of Lowland Bolivia. Ph.D. Thesis, University of St. Andrews, Scotland.

Fehr, E. and Gächter, S. (2000). 'Cooperation and punishment', *American Economic Review* 90(4), 980–94.

—— and Schmidt, K. M. (1999). 'A theory of fairness, competition, and cooperation', *Quarterly Journal of Economics*, *114*, 817–68.

Forsythe, R., Horowitz, J. L., Savin, N. E., and Sefton, M. (1994). 'Fairness in simple bargaining experiments', *Games and Economic Behavior*, 6, 347–69.

Henrich, J. (2000). 'Does culture matter in economic behavior? Ultimatum game bargaining among the Machiguenga of the Peruvian Amazon', *American Economic Review*, 90(4).

—— McCabe, K. (1996). 'Social distance and other-regarding behavior in dictator games', *American Economic Review*, 653–60.

—— —— (1998). 'Behavioral foundations of reciprocity: experimental economics and evolutionary psychology', *Economic Inquiry*, 36, 335–52.

—— Shachat, K., and Smith, V. (1994). 'Preferences, property rights, and anonymity in bargaining games', *Games and Economic Behavior*, 7, 346–80.

Ledyard, J. O. (1995). 'Public goods: A survey of experimental research', in John H. Kagel and Alvin E. Roth (eds), *Handbook of Experimental Economics*, Princeton, NJ: Princeton University Press.

Murnighan, J. K. and Saxon, M. S. (1994). *Ultimatum Bargaining by Children and Adults*. University of British Columbia, Working paper.

Proyectro de Desarrollo Sostenible de los Pueblos Indigenas del Beni (PRODESIB). (1997). *Diagnostico rural participativo sobre la situacion legal de comunidades del territorio indigena Chimanes*. San Borja, Beni, Bolivia.

Rabin, M. (1993). 'Incorporating fairness into game theory', *American Economic Review*, 83, 1281–302.

Riester, J. (1978). *Canción y producción en la vida de un pueblo indígena: los chimane del oriente boliviano*. La Paz: Editorial Los Amigos del Libro.

—— (1993). *Universo mítico de los chimane*. La Paz: Pueblos Indígenas de Bolivia.

Roth, A. E., Prasnikar, V., Okuno-Fujiwara, M., and Zamir, S. (1991). 'Bargaining and market behavior in Jerusalem, Ljubljana, Pittsburgh, and Tokyo: An experimental study', *American Economic Review*, 81, 1068–95.

Schotter, A., Weiss, A., and Zapater, I. (1996). 'Fairness and survival in ultimatum and dictatorship games', *Journal of Economic Behavior and Organization*, 31, 37–56.

Vice-Ministerio de Asuntos Indigenas y Pueblos Originarios (VAIPO). (1998). *Pueblos indigenas y originarios de Bolivia*. Trinidad.

8

Market Integration, Reciprocity, and Fairness in Rural Papua New Guinea

Results from a Two-Village Ultimatum Game Experiment

David P. Tracer

> As one digs deeper into the national character of the Americans, one sees that they have sought the value of everything in this world only in the answer to this single question: how much money will it bring in?
>
> de Tocqueville, 1831 (in de Tocqueville *et al.* 1985)

What French political commentator and statesman Alexis de Tocqueville regarded in his 1831 letter to be a fundamental character trait of Americans, many contemporary economists and evolutionarily oriented students of human behavior now regard as a basic part of the *human* behavioral repertoire. According to most economists, human behaviors are designed to maximize utility, the usefulness or satisfaction provided to an individual by some preferred good, activity, or balance thereof. In modern industrialized societies, where access to individuals' preferred goods and activities is facilitated largely through monetary transactions, individuals in these societies might be expected to behave as self-interested money maximizers. For social and behavioral scientists guided by the logic and expectations of evolutionary theory, behavior is designed to maximize *fitness*, which can be defined alternately as the propensity of an individual to survive and reproduce in a particular environment (Mills and Beatty 1984; Smith and Winterhalder 1992) or an individuals' proportional contribution of alleles or genotypes to succeeding generations (Price 1996). Among females, fitness maximization is achieved by gaining access to and consumption of the resources necessary to sustain the energetically costly physiological states of pregnancy and lactation (Daly and Wilson 1983; Tracer 1996). For males, it is achieved by maximizing mating opportunities, but in higher primate species such as chimpanzees (Stanford

1996) and humans (Kaplan and Hill 1985), access to females has itself been demonstrated on numerous occasions to be a function of male resource holdings. For both evolutionarily oriented behavioral scientists and many economists then, humans are expected to act as self-interested resource maximizers in the service of utility and fitness maximization, respectively. The view of humans as rational, self-interested utility maximizers has sometimes been referred to in the economics literature as the '*Homo oeconomicus*' model (Fehr and Gächter 1998).

Although the predictions of the social sciences for human behavior have often been clear enough, there has been less agreement about what methods might best be used to profitably test them. Economists, sociologists, and anthropologists have historically studied human behavior in a 'natural' milieu. For economists, this has meant studying human behavior in markets (Davis and Holt 1993); for sociologists and anthropologists human behavior has been studied by conducting survey or ethnographic research among societies or cultural groups. Moreover, individuals in these disciplines have historically shunned the use of experimental manipulation of their subjects due in part to concerns about the applicability of such results to real world situations. Recently, however, economists have with increasing frequency employed experimental tools that aim to measure such behavioral propensities as risk aversion, altruism, selfishness, and reciprocity in ways that are minimally invasive (Camerer 2003). They may also shed light on individuals' propensities to be risk averse, altruistic, selfish, and trusting in situations that are more controlled than 'real world' situations. Presumably the results of such experiments give insight into players' endogenous working models of these behaviors in the absence of multiple, complicating, and varying social factors, though, certainly, variables such as the players' gender, ethnicity, and socioeconomic status, as well as effects created by the researchers themselves may still affect the results.

One of the simplest games among those employed by experimental economists is the ultimatum game (for a detailed description of the game see Camerer and Fehr, Chapter 3, this volume). The results of the Ultimatum Game performed in the industrialized cities of Pittsburgh (USA), Tokyo (Japan), Ljubljana (the former Yugoslavia), and Jerusalem (Israel) deviated significantly from the expectation that humans should behave as self-interested maximizers (Roth *et al.* 1991). In contrast to the results obtained in relatively industrialized settings, Henrich (2000) conducted a one-shot Ultimatum Game among twenty-one pairs of Machiguenga swidden horticulturalists in the Peruvian Amazon and obtained results that more nearly approached the equilibrium predictions of game theory. The contrast between Henrich's results and those of Roth *et al.* (1991) have indicated the possibility that culture and/or ecology may play a profound role in determining the course of reciprocity, bargaining, and social interactions in general. The populations studied by Roth *et al.* occupy a cultural–ecological niche that is evolutionarily novel in many salient respects including its degree of monetarization, literacy, extensive extralocal governmental structure, and probable shift from extensive extended kin networks to a focus on nuclear family structure. The Machiguenga by contrast, while certainly not unaffected by cultural diffusion from outside sources, likely live more nearly in an environment approximating that inhabited by the human species for much of its evolutionary history than do the populations of Pittsburgh, Tokyo, Ljubljana, or Jerusalem. Moreover, this is precisely true with regard to those domains just mentioned—degree of monetarization, literacy, extralocal government structure, and kin networks. It is just possible, therefore, that the tendency to act as rational, self-regarding utility maximizers, as predicted by the *Homo oeconomicus* model, might be more evident among less monetarized and westernized populations than among individuals living in the radically novel environments of the urban industrialized world.

In order to test the proposition that performance in bargaining experiments is significantly affected by degree of monetarization, Market Integration, and relative westernization, a one-shot Ultimatum Game was conducted during the months of June and July 1998 in two villages in a rural region of Papua New Guinea. Although the villages, Anguganak and Bogasip, are located in close proximity to one another and are relatively homogeneous culturally, as is demonstrated below, they are distinguished by their average degree of exposure to and integration in a cash-based economy, as well as their degree of education. In the sections that follow, I present an ethnographic account of the two villages followed by a description of the experimental methods employed, results, and a discussion of the implications of the results for understanding factors that may affect participants' decisions in bargaining experiments.

ANGUGANAK AND BOGASIP: AN ETHNOGRAPHIC ACCOUNT

The physical environment

New Guinea, the world's second largest island, is situated in the Pacific Ocean just a few degrees north of the continent of Australia. The island is composed of two nearly equal-sized political entities. Its western half, once under Dutch administrative control, became a province of Indonesia in 1963 called 'Irian Jaya' (and more recently, 'West Papua'). The eastern half of the island, once composed of two distinct German- and British-administered areas, the Territory of New Guinea and the Territory of Papua, passed into Australian administrative control and then achieved independence in 1975 becoming the independent nation of Papua New Guinea.

The two villages that participated in this study, Anguaganak and Bogasip, are situated at approximately 3° 30' south of the Equator in Sandaun Province, the northwestern-most of Papua New Guinea's nineteen provinces. The villages are located in the southern foothills of the Torricelli Mountains, a rugged range located only 50 or so kilometers inland from the north coast. The villages of Anguganak and Bogasip are located on the tops of cleared mudstone ridges at an altitude of about 700 meters.

The climate of the study area is extremely hot, wet, and humid and supports a luxuriant lowland rainforest vegetation consisting of hardwoods and palms with a variety of mosses, trailing lianas, and orchids abounding throughout the understory. The lowest regions of the Torricelli range act as drainage beds for the upland areas and contain numerous standing freshwater pools and swamps. These areas are home to dense stands of sago palm (*Metroxylon* sp.) from which the primary dietary staple of the local population is derived. At the highest elevations in the Torricelli Mountains, the lowland rainforest is replaced by lower montane forest. At all elevations, an abundance of mammalian, avian, reptilian, and amphibian wildlife is supported.

The sociocultural environment

Papua New Guinea is the most linguistically diverse country in
the world. Current estimates are that Papua New Guinea is home
to more than 800 distinct languages, and although the villages
that participated in this study, Anguganak and Bogasip, are
located only about 1.5 kilometers from one another, they speak
two different languages; Au and Gnau, respectively. Though
many Gnau speakers tend to understand Au and vice-versa, few
individuals are fully conversant in both languages. The villagers
of Anguganak and Bogasip, like most other Papua New Guineas,
are also conversant in Neo-Melanesian (*Tok Pisin*), the *lingua
franca* of Papua New Guinea, and the language that was
employed predominantly in carrying out this study.

    Like many villages in the area, Anguganak and Bogasip are built
atop cleared mudstone bluffs. Each village is not a single entity, but
rather, is composed of hamlets located within a 15–20 minute trek
from one another and connected by bush roads. Bogasip is composed of two main hamlets plus a scattering of solitary dwellings on
the fringes of the hamlets. Anguganak is composed of four main
hamlets plus additional fringe habitation sites. Traditionally, all
hamlets contain a central men's spirit house in which all men and
most boys (beginning at about the age of 10 or 11) sleep and individual women's houses occupied by village women, their daughters,
and immature sons. Hamlets also contain smaller men's meeting
houses. Women are prohibited from entering either the men's
spirit or meeting houses. All of these structures are constructed with
walls of sago palm midribs, posts of tree fern and bamboo, and a
thatch of sago palm leaves lashed together with rattan. As opportunities for engaging in the cash economy and wage income have
entered the area, some individuals have begun to build houses using
corrugated metal sheeting in place of a sago thatch and the presence
or absence of metal roofs in the villages has essentially become a
locally recognized marker of socioeconomic differentials. At the time
of this study, roughly 20 percent of the houses in Anguganak village
had corrugated metal roofs. Houses in Bogasip had exclusively
thatched roofs.

    The spatial layout of Au and Gnau villages and, in particular, the
separation of male from female dwellings and core areas, is reflective also of general male and female social relationships. Men try to

maintain a distance from women and believe that spending too much time around women and, especially, engaging in sexual activity, saps their energy, leads to illness, and diminishes their hunting ability. Women are regarded as particularly dangerous to men during menstruation and immediately after childbirth (Lewis 1975, 1980). Despite the distinctive separation between men and women, polygynous marriage is allowed, though uncommon. For both monogamously and polygynously married men, it is considered shameful to have more than four children with any one wife. Residence is patrilineal and virilocal.

The people of Anguganak and Bogasip subsist by practicing a mixture of foraging and horticulture. Their principle dietary staple is starch extracted from semi-wild stands of sago palm. The starch is most often mixed with boiling water and consumed as a gelatinous pudding, but it is also sometimes eaten, particularly by those in mourning, in a dry roasted form. Sago starch is generally consumed with a stew of leaves boiled in coconut cream. The leaves are derived from foraging as well as from gardens and if available, the stew will also contain meat or insect larvae derived from hunting and collecting, respectively. Organized daytime hunts for large game (pigs and cassowaries) as well as night hunts for nocturnal mammalian prey are conducted solely by men, while women act as opportunistic hunters, procuring animals encountered by chance during their daily foraging rounds. Meat hunted by men is distributed between the hunter's family and his extended kin, however, both the Au and Gnau have a strict taboo against hunters consuming any part of their own kill. This taboo is part of a larger prohibition against 'consuming one's own body' that extends into many areas of everyday life. In the domain of hunting, because animals are shot with arrows that have been carried by the hunter next to his body, it is believed that some of the hunter's sweat and bodily 'dirt' is injected into the animal when it is shot. The hunter is thus prohibited from consuming the animal as it contains 'his own body', and is instead required to distribute it to others.

In addition to hunting, the Au and Gnau also practice pig husbandry. Pigs are an important source of wealth and prestige and are only killed infrequently for ceremonial occasions. When killed, a pig may not be consumed by members of the family that raised it, since it was likely given food premasticated for it by its owners. It thus falls under the taboo of 'consuming one's own body'. Women observe a brief mourning period when their pigs are killed.

The Au and Gnau also make small gardens averaging 1/10 ha from which they derive their secondary staples, roots, and tubers such as taro, yams, and sweet potatoes, as well as bananas, papaya, pandanus, pitpit (*Saccharum edule*), squash, and beans. The gardens also yield stimulants, most notably tobacco and betel nut, which are smoked and chewed habitually by most adults. A wide variety of other wild fruits and nuts are procured from foraging in the rainforest. More recently, the people of the region have begun cash cropping cocoa, which grows quite well in the hot, humid climate.

There are no chiefs in either Au or Gnau society and neither does there exist in these societies a true 'big man complex' as has been described in other Melanesian populations (Sillitoe 1998). Au and Gnau males can acquire prestige as they age through personal charisma and oratory skills, fierceness in interactions with members of other villages (when appropriate), and especially, success in pig hunting. Men frequently hang the mandibles of wild pigs that they have shot outside their houses to advertise hunting success and this advertisement does bring them prestige, but it is by no means a foregone conclusion that such individuals can coerce other individuals, particularly those outside of their clan or lineage, to do anything they do not wish to. Important village decisions are commonly debated in the evenings around a fire in the men's meeting houses, and while the words of the best orators, warriors, and hunters are given special consideration and weight, final decisions on important matters are negotiated among all present. Another basis upon which certain individual's views may be accorded special weight has to do with what is locally referred to as the individual's 'story'. In local lore, Anguganak and Bogasip were originally settled by immigrants from other areas fleeing warfare and/or sorcery. In each village, there is a hierarchy of lineages that is based upon their order of arrival. The views of persons belonging to earlier arriving lineages tend to have 'preferred' status (though again these individuals are far from being able to completely dictate decisions to others in the village).

One element common to both Au and Gnau society that is undoubtedly relevant to the current study on bargaining, reciprocity, and fairness is their elaborate system of exchange relationships. Some of these relationships are obligatory and quite standardized with regard to who gives what to whom, while others are to some degree optional and less standardized. Many of these exchange relationships are described by Lewis (1975) in his ethnography of the Gnau. Although an ethnography of the Au has not been published, field work among the Au by the author over the last 12 years has revealed identical patterns of exchange, obligation, and indebtedness.

Some of the most well-defined exchanges and ones that occasion a succession of later exchanges are those centered around marriage. Although it is preferred that a man marry his father's father's mother's brother's son's son's daughter (roughly akin to a three-generation removed cross-cousin), in fact many marriages do not follow this pattern but are decided by the prospective groom in concert with his prospective wife's father and brothers. Occasionally, individuals now decide for themselves whom they will marry, but these are still considered by most Au and Gnau to be 'wrong' marriages. Once a marriage is agreed upon, a bride price is set, which is usually paid in installments by the groom with help primarily from his agnates, and to a lesser extent his matrilateral relatives and unrelated hamlet co-residents (Lewis 1975). Before the bride price is fully paid, the bride periodically visits the groom's hamlet and works in food production with his mother for short (1–2 week) spans of time. When it is fully paid, there is a 'sending ceremony', in which the bride's hamlet formally sends her with gifts of food and betel nut to her husband's hamlet. With this ceremony full rights over the woman are transferred to her husband signified in part by individuals in her natal hamlet smearing their faces with mud and observing a brief mourning period. Dissolution of unions is quite common prior to full payment of bride price and it is also not uncommon for unions to break up after full payment of the bride price but before the couple has produced their first child. In the latter case, the bride price is usually refunded. If the marriage is successful and a child is produced, only then is the bride price distributed among the male relatives in her natal village (i.e. her father, father's brothers, and her brothers). Subsequent events that occasion additional payments by a husband to his wife's male kin (especially her eldest brother, or in some cases, the brother who precedes her in birth order) include the birth of his first child, the child's first consumption of meat (which must be provided by the child's maternal uncle), the child reaching puberty and undergoing initiation, the death of his wife, and the death of his first son.

Apart from formal exchange obligations between individuals and their maternal and paternal relatives, the Au and Gnau place a premium on generosity. If a co-resident of one's hamlet (and sometimes even a non-co-resident) makes a request of him or her to give the co-resident some item, it is incumbent upon that person to give the item requested. Items requested may be food, clothing, household goods, string bags, tools, or money. In Anguganak, for example, the Au request *aoto mas* (give me betel nut) is one of the most frequently heard utterances and, if the individual indeed has betel nut to give, the request must be honored. Similarly, *aoto taanik* (give me [your] string bag), *aoto hrina* (give me [your] knife), and *aoto sak nan* (give me pig meat) while less commonly heard, must also be honored. An individual who refuses to honor a request but is known to possess the item requested is shunned in the community and may not have his own requests honored, especially if he is a repeat offender. For this reason, many Au and Gnau prefer to be discreet about what they may or may not have in their possession. Nocturnal hunters, for example, who commonly hunt alone, will often sneak into the hamlet before sunrise and hide whatever quarry they may have obtained. In addition to one who does not honor requests, an individual who makes too many requests may also be shunned, talked about scathingly, or more importantly, retaliated against by having a rapid series of requests made of him. The option of making requests and having them honored is considered by the Au and Gnau to be a right, but one that must not be abused.

Individuals may also at times display generosity by giving out unsolicited items, such as meat, to others. Although the items were not requested, their acceptance does inherently bind the two individuals in a reciprocal relationship with one another. It is understood by both that a debt has been incurred and that at some future time it will be repaid either with or without a specific request being made to do so. Unsolicited offers are thus sometimes refused if the person offered the item does not wish to become indebted.

Market integration

Anguganak and Bogasip were specifically chosen for the one-shot Ultimatum Game because, despite their proximity and relative cultural homogeneity, these villages display some of the largest

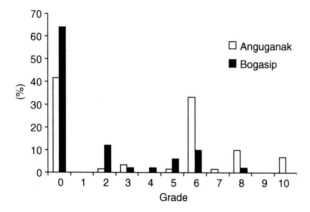

FIG. 8.1. Highest grade completed among participants at Anguganak and Bogasip ($n = 110$)

differences seen in the area in degree of Market Integration, education, and acculturation. As noted earlier, many houses at Anguganak use corrugated metal sheets for roofing, while no houses at Bogasip do. In addition, the number of years of schooling varies significantly between the two villages. Among the sixty participants from the village of Anguganak, number of years of schooling ranged from 0 to 10 with a mean of 3.8, while among the fifty participants at Bogasip number of years of schooling ranged from 0 to 8 with a mean of 1.5 ($p < 0.0001$). The distribution of the number of years of schooling completed in each of the villages is shown in Figure 8.1. At Bogasip, 64 percent of the sample had no schooling whatsoever, while at Anguganak only 42 percent of the sample had no schooling and a full 33 percent had completed 6 years of education. The average number of gardens devoted solely to the cash cropping of cocoa also varied slightly though not significantly between the two villages with a mean of 3.8 gardens per household at Anguganak and 3.3 gardens per household at Bogasip. Perhaps more interestingly however, when a subsample of households in each village was asked to recall the amount of money brought in to the household in the past month as a result of the cash cropping of cocoa, Anguganak household incomes ranged from 0 to 135 *kina* (K) with a mean of 38.5 K, while Bogasip incomes ranged from 0 to 14 K with a mean of 7.3 K. The difference is almost certainly due to the fact that Bogasip villagers were selling wet cocoa beans, while Anguganak had constructed a fermentary for smoking the wet beans, and sold predominantly dry cocoa which fetches a much higher price. In fact, many Bogasip villagers reported having sold their wet beans to Anguganak, who in turn smoked them and resold them at a higher price.

Differences in the degree of Market Integration and education also lead to obvious differences in the nutritional status of individuals in the two villages. Concurrent with this study the author in concert with several graduate students carried out a nutritional survey among mothers in eight villages including Anguganak and Bogasip. A roster of six standard anthropometric measurements including weight (kg), mid-upper arm circumference (cm), maximum calf circumference (cm), and skinfolds (mm) measured at the triceps, subscapula, and medial calf were taken among a sample of sixteen Anguganak and fifteen Bogasip women. The results are presented in Table 8.1. The table shows that weight, mid-upper arm circumference, maximum calf circumference, and medial calf skinfold thicknesses are all significantly higher at Anguganak (Au) compared with Bogasip (Gnau). These results are concordant with previous studies demonstrating that significant differences in indices of nutritional status including anthropometric measures (Tracer 1996), hemoglobin levels (Tracer 1997), birth weight, and growth and development of children (Tracer *et al.* 1998) among six different

TABLE 8.1. Anthropometric characteristics of Anguganak ($n = 16$) and Bogasip ($n = 15$) women

Variable	Anguganak	Bogasip
	Mean (SD)	Mean (SD)
Weight (kg)	48.47 (5.49)	43.77 (5.04)*
Triceps skinfold (mm)	5.86 (1.26)	4.97 (1.76)
Subscapular skinfold (mm)	8.65 (1.78)	9.15 (3.02)
Medial calf skinfold (mm)	4.68 (1.44)	2.72 (0.73)***
Mid upper arm circumference (cm)	23.58 (1.51)	22.09 (1.95)*
Maximum calf circumference (cm)	31.41 (1.89)	29.46 (1.51)**

Note: Difference between Anguganak and Bogasip tested using two-tailed *t*-test:
*$p < 0.05$.
**$p < 0.01$.
***$p < 0.001$.

language groups in the Torricelli foothills are indicative of differences in degree of Market Integration and participation in the local cash economy.

EXPERIMENTAL METHODS AND MATERIALS

A one-shot Ultimatum Game was conducted over the course of 1 week in June 1998 in the village of Anguganak, and over a 2-day period in July 1998 in the village of Bogasip. In order to set the stakes for the game, a brief survey of wage levels among skilled and unskilled workers in the area was conducted. The main unit of currency in Papua New Guinea is the *kina* (K). Wages ranged from highs of K270 per fortnight among 'professional' workers such as local health center workers and community school teachers, to mid-level wages of K100 per fortnight among skilled mission station workers (office workers, Church Education Secretary), K50 per fortnight among unskilled mission station workers (grass cutters), and K1–2 per fortnight among villagers selling food items at the mission station market. It was decided to set the stakes of the game at a middle per-day level among all workers, that is, at K10, but for most village dwellers (only a tiny fraction of whom engage in any wage labor (Wage Labor) at all) this is a rather large sum of money. In the field season during which the experiment was conducted, K10 could purchase one small bush knife, five 'D' batteries, three large tins of mackerel, 3–1 kg bags of rice, 4–1 kg bags of iodized salt, or 3–1 kg bags of sugar. All of these are highly desired commodities. Apart from the stakes of the game, participants were also paid a fixed sum of K3 for participating.

The people, particularly women, of both Anguganak and Bogasip are quite accustomed to participating in research conducted by the author. Most of this research, however, has been oriented around assessments of disease, nutritional status, and child growth and development. Participation in all past research, as is the case here, has always been fully voluntary. However, research among the Au and Gnau has never before involved any monetary compensation to the participants.

In order to recruit volunteers, a meeting was set up in a central location in each of the villages. At the meeting, it was announced that a new project that differed from those conducted in the past would be carried out. It was explained that participation was completely voluntary, that participants would be compensated with the sum of K3, and that only married adult individuals could participate. To prevent the possibility of collusion, the details of the experiment were not explained at the meeting, but participants were told that the research did not involve any invasive procedures (as some had in the past), participants would be assured of anonymity, and the work entailed the possibility that participants could garner an additional K0–K10 over and above the K3 compensation fee.

At Anguganak, the experiment was performed over the course of 1 week in a variety of locations as individuals willing to participate were encountered throughout three village hamlets. In Bogasip, the experiment was performed over the course of 2 days. The author was located in a small covered meeting area in the village and individuals came one at a time to participate. In both villages, a standard script was used to explain the rules of the game (see Appendix A). Because the author speaks Au but not Gnau, the rules of the game were presented in both villages in Neo-Melanesian (*Tok Pisin*). The Neo-Melanesian script was translated back into English by an educated Papua New Guinea national employed at the Anguganak Christian Centre, a local mission station. From this translation, the author was satisfied that the rules of the game were presented correctly and as intended and that they should be readily intelligible to most speakers of Neo-Melanesian.

After reading the script to proposers, a period of testing followed where each proposer was presented with a standardized roster of offer amounts and asked how much he/she and the responder would receive if the responder accepted or refused the offer. Responders were also tested by presenting them with the same roster of offer amounts and asking them how much they and the offerers would receive if they accepted or refused each offer. The testing often revealed lapses in participants' understanding of the experiment's rules. Indeed, on many occasions the script supplemented by additional explanation was presented twice and in several instances three times. In roughly six cases, individuals were incapable of understanding the rules of the game and were excluded from participating, though they were still paid K3. In general, the greatest amount of confusion about and (re)explanation of the experiment's rules seemed to occur among the most elderly participants. Upon satisfactorily completing testing in the experiment, each participant was given a short survey in which they were asked to report their age (if known), the size of their sibship and birth order, number of children, number of gardens devoted to growing food, number of gardens devoted to cash cropping, whether their house had a thatch or sheet metal roof, whether they had ever been employed for wage income, and their highest grade completed in school.

The final sample consisted of 110 individuals; thirty pairs of participants at Anguganak and twenty-five pairs of participants at Bogasip. Although I had hoped to obtain an equal number of participants at each of the villages, the experiment at Bogasip was ended early after a woman carrying a knife announced that the experiment was 'the work of Satan'. Villagers reported that this woman was imbued with the 'holy spirit' and given to bouts of prophecy. Strangely, this woman later in the day actually participated in the experiment, saying that her husband had convinced her to participate. Still, that afternoon, the knife-toting woman continued to linger around the periphery of the area where the experiment was being carried out, raising concerns among the author and the graduate students accompanying him about their safety.

Following participation in the experiment, individuals were instructed not to discuss the particulars of the experiment, though they could indicate that they were paid K3 for participating and that the experiment included the possibility that they might receive more. At Anguganak, the first thirty participants and at Bogasip the first twenty-five participants were all assigned the role of 'proposer', while the second thirty and twenty-five individuals at each village, respectively, were assigned the role of 'responder'. Responders in each village were paired with proposers from the same village, but completely at random with respect to offer amount, gender, and age.

RESULTS

The sample of participants at Anguganak ($n = 60$) was 52 percent male and 48 percent female, while the Bogasip sample ($n = 50$) was 54 percent male and 46 percent female. Ages in the Anguganak sample ranged from 19 to 72 years with a mean of 38.8. Ages in the Bogasip sample ranged from 18 to 69 years with a mean of 35.9. The difference in mean age between the villages was not significant.

Figure 8.2 shows the distribution of offers in the one-shot ultimatum experiment as well as rejection and acceptance rates in Anguganak and Bogasip combined ($n = 55$ offers). There were no

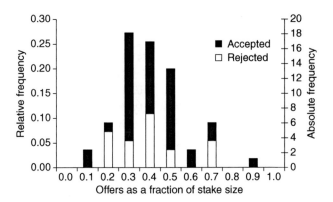

FIG. 8.2. Distribution of accepted and rejected offers at Anguganak and Bogasip combined ($n = 55$)

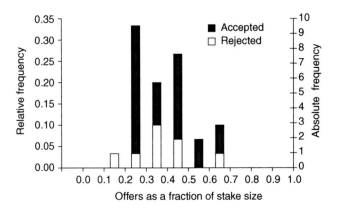

FIG. 8.3. Distribution of accepted and rejected offers at Anguganak ($n = 30$)

offers of K0, K8, or K10 and the modal offer, totaling 27.3 percent of all offers, was K3 or 30 percent of the stakes. The mean offer was 40.7 percent. The overall rejection rate for all offers was an astonishingly high 32.8 percent. This included rejection of: 80 percent of offers of K2 (four of five), 20 percent of offers of K3 (three of fifteen), 42.9 percent of offers of K4 (six of fourteen), 18.2 percent of offers of K5 (two of eleven), and most intriguingly, 60 percent of offers of K7 (three of five).

Figure 8.3 shows the distribution of offers as well as rejection and acceptance rates in Anguganak ($n = 30$ offers). There were no offers made either below K2 or above K7 in this village, and the modal offer, totaling 33.3 percent of all offers, was K3 or 30 percent of the stakes. The overall rejection rate at Anguganak was 26.6 percent.

Figure 8.4 shows the distribution of offers as well as rejection and acceptance rates in Bogasip ($n = 25$ offers). There were no offers of K0, K6, K8, or K10 made, and the modal offer, totaling 32 percent of all offers, was K4 or 40 percent of the stakes. The overall rejection rate at Bogasip was almost 15 percent higher than that at Anguganak at 40.0 percent. An Eps-Singleton test comparing the distribution of offers at Anguganak and Bogasip was not, however, significant ($p = 0.23$).

Figure 8.5 shows a pairwise comparison of acceptance rates for Anguganak and Bogasip at each level for which at least two or more

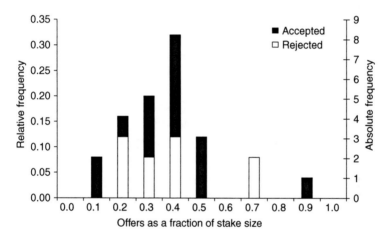

FIG. 8.4. Distribution of accepted and rejected offers at Bogasip ($n = 25$)

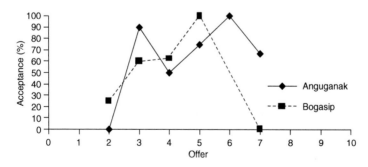

FIG. 8.5. Pairwise comparison of acceptance rates at Anguganak and Bogasip

offers was made. At most offer levels, Bogasip shows a tendency to have higher acceptance rates than Anguganak. Both villages show a sharp decline in acceptance of offers above K5, though the decline is more pronounced for Bogasip.

Although there were no houses with sheet metal roofing at Bogasip, of the thirty participants at Anguganak designated to be 'proposers', twenty-six lived in a dwelling with thatched roofing and four lived in a dwelling with sheet metal roofing. Although the sample sizes are small, the modal offer among individuals living in each type of dwelling at Anguganak was explored in order to lend insight into possible effects of socioeconomic status on the level of offers. Among those twenty-six individuals living in thatched dwellings, the modal offer was K3, while among those four individuals living in dwellings with sheet metal roofing, the modal offer was K5.

The relationship of offer amounts and acceptance and rejection rates with gender was also explored. As illustrated in Figure 8.6, there was more than one modal offer among both males and females. The modes for males were at K4 and K5, while those for females were at K3 and K4. Despite the higher male modes, however, the distribution of male offers tended to be skewed toward lower offers while that of females tended to be skewed toward higher offers. As a result, the mean offer among female proposers was higher, K4.4, while among male proposers it was K3.9. The difference in offer distributions by gender did not, however, reach the level of statistical significance (Eps-Singleton Test, $p = 0.21$).

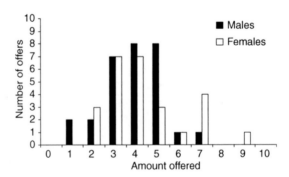

FIG. 8.6. Distribution of offers by gender in Anguganak and Bogasip combined ($n = 55$)

Figure 8.7 shows a pairwise comparison of offer acceptance rates for males and females for each level at which two or more offers were made. From the graph it appears that male responders are much more likely than female responders to accept both high and low offers (i.e. above K5 and below K3). At mid-level offers of K3–K5, male and female acceptance rates appear to be roughly equal.

The number of gardens devoted to the cash cropping of cocoa among the sample of proposers ($n = 52$; three missing cases) ranged from zero to ten with a mean of 3.6. Although the average monthly income generated from cash cropping is probably a better measure of involvement in the cash economy than is number of gardens (especially since as noted above, some individuals sell predominantly wet beans while others sell the much more valuable dried beans), these data were difficult to obtain and are also likely to suffer from significant recall bias. For this reason, the distribution of offers, and the modal offer among those having fewer than ($n = 29$) and equal to or more than ($n = 23$), the mean number of cocoa gardens was explored. These distributions are shown in Figure 8.8. The figure shows that the distribution of offers among those having four or more cocoa gardens appears roughly normal, with a mode of K4. The distribution of offers among proposers having fewer than four cocoa gardens is right-skewed, with a mode at K3. The modal offers among individuals that reported a history of Wage Labor versus those who were exclusively subsistence forager-horticulturalists followed a similar pattern. The modal offer among those with a history of wage employment was K4, while the modal offer among those never employed was K3.

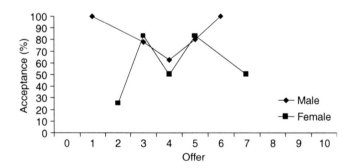

Fɪɢ. 8.7. Pairwise comparison of acceptance rates by gender

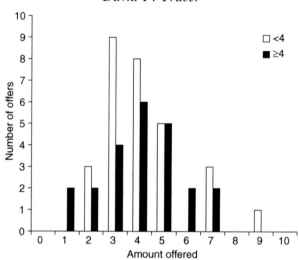

FIG. 8.8. Distribution of offers by number of cocoa gardens (mean $= 3.6$)

Number of children living in the proposer's household varied in the sample from zero to nine with a mean of 3.6. Like number of cocoa gardens and history of wage employment, it is possible that number of children might also be a proxy for socioeconomic status with those having more children being of higher than average status. Therefore, an examination of offers among individuals having fewer than the mean number of children (i.e. <4) versus those with four or more children in the household was conducted. Individuals having four or more children ($n = 25$) exhibited a modal offer of K3 with a mean of 3.8 while those with fewer than four children ($n = 30$) had a modal offer of K4 with a mean of 4.4. This pattern, of those having more children actually offering less, may suggest that rather than being indicative of greater wealth, having more children might actually tax family resources more and lead to a greater economization of those resources (i.e. a tendency toward thriftiness). For this reason, an examination of the rejection rate of low offers (K1–K3) was examined in these groups with the expectation that individuals with above average numbers of children and taxed family resources might be willing to accept low offers more frequently than those with fewer than average numbers of children. In fact, however, individuals with higher than average numbers of children rejected offers of K1–K3 37.5 percent of the time (six of sixteen) while individuals with fewer than average numbers

TABLE 8.2. Regression analysis of the effect of proposer's sex, age, number of children, number of food gardens, number of cocoa gardens, work history, and highest grade completed on offer amounts at Anguganak (Au)

Variable	Standardized coefficient	Significant values
Sex	−0.259	0.225
Age	−0.225	0.472
No. of children	−0.119	0.670
No. of food gardens	0.458	0.038
No. of cocoa gardens	−0.172	0.414
Ever worked?	−0.044	0.823
Education	0.113	0.625

TABLE 8.3. Regression analysis of the effect of proposer's sex, age, number of children, number of food gardens, number of cocoa gardens, and highest grade completed on offer amounts at Bogasip (Gnau)

Variable	Standardized coefficient	Significant values
Sex	0.268	0.352
Age	−0.120	0.704
No. of children	0.012	0.972
No. of food gardens	−0.051	0.861
No. of cocoa gardens	−0.128	0.635
Education	0.138	0.650

of children rejected these low offers only 14.3 percent of the time (one of seven).

Tables 8.2 and 8.3 show the results of multiple linear regressions of proposers' sex, age, number of children, number of food gardens, number of cocoa gardens, work history,[1] and highest grade completed on the amount offered at Anguganak and Bogasip, respectively. These analyses show that offer amounts are directly correlated with number of food gardens (standardized $\beta = 0.458$; $p = 0.038$) at Anguganak but not at Bogasip. None of the other variables, however, are significantly associated with offer amounts

[1] Work history is a dichotomous variable denoting whether the individual ever worked for a wage. This variable is not included in the regression analysis at Bogasip since none of the individuals in that village reported working for wages.

in either of the two villages. Finally, a logistic regression examining factors that might predict offer rejection including sex, age, number of children, number of food and cocoa gardens, educational attainment and work history did not yield any significant results.

DISCUSSION

The level of offers seen in the combined Anguganak and Bogasip ultimatum experiment falls between those obtained among western industrialized populations and the Machiguenga horticulturalists of Peru. Roth *et al.* (1991) reported modal offers in Pittsburgh, the former Yugoslavia, and Israel of 50 percent of the stakes. Mean offers in these countries ranged from a low of 37 percent of the stakes in Israel to 47 percent of the stakes in Pittsburgh. By contrast, Henrich found a modal offer of 15 percent and a mean offer of 26 percent among the Machiguenga. Anguganak and Bogasip showed a modal offer just above that of the Machiguenga, 30 percent, but the distribution of offers was such that the mean offer, almost 41 percent, was closer to that seen in the other westernized countries studied by Roth *et al.* As discussed earlier, the Au and Gnau have both an elaborate system of formal exchange obligations and place a very high premium on generosity and fulfilling requests. In fact, the obligation to fulfill requests often results in individuals being quite secretive about what they possess. It is likely that the high virtue placed upon generosity in these societies played a role in generating the relatively high mean offer seen in this experiment.

It has been hypothesized that differences observed in the modal and mean offers between the populations studied by Roth *et al.* and the Machiguenga might have been due in large part to differences in degree of monetarization and Market Integration (Henrich 2000); that is, individuals conform more to the *Homo oeconomicus* model of utility maximization in less monetarized contexts. For this reason, the results obtained from the Ultimatum Game at Anguganak, a village with a longer history of Market Integration and cash cropping and relatively high socioeconomic status, were compared with those from Bogasip, a more typical, less acculturated Torricelli village. Taken at face value, the modal offer of 30 percent at Anguganak and 40 percent at Bogasip would seem to run contra to the hypothesis that individuals act as self-interested utility maximizers in less acculturated or monetarized contexts. However, the distribution of offers in the two villages does lend at least some support to the hypothesis. The distribution of offers at Anguganak yielded a mean offer of 43 percent, similar to that seen among the Pittsburgh, Yugoslav, and Japanese samples studied by Roth *et al.*, while the Bogasip distribution showed a proportionately higher frequency of low offers and yielded a mean offer of 38 percent. The difference between the villages does not, however, reach the level of statistical significance, and it should be kept in mind that while Anguganak does have a greater level of Market Integration and western acculturation than Bogasip, Anguganak still resembles Bogasip more closely in these measures than it does any of the industrialized nations studied by Roth *et al.*

The relationship between a roster of additional indices of wealth and Market Integration and offer amounts were also examined. Provisional support for the hypothesis that greater Market Integration yields higher offers was seen in the comparison of modal offers among those living in thatched ($n = 26$) versus metal-roofed ($n = 4$) dwellings at Anguganak. Metal roofs are indices of greater wealth compared with thatched roofs. Although admittedly the sample sizes are quite small, individuals living in metal-roofed dwellings had higher modal offers (50 percent) than their more traditional counterparts (30 percent). Individuals with higher than average numbers of cocoa gardens and those with a history of Wage Labor also displayed higher modal offers than those with fewer gardens or no history of wage employment, again offering some support for a positive relationship between Market Integration and degree of deviation from the *Homo oeconomicus* model. The results of an analysis between number of children and offer sizes was less conclusive. Individuals with higher than the average number of children tended to offer less than those with fewer children. It is uncertain, however, whether having higher numbers of children is indicative of greater wealth or whether it actually results in family resources being taxed to a greater degree. My own experience with populations in the area indicates that the former tends to be true among polygynously married men while the latter is more true among those who are monogamous. All males in this study were in monogamous marriages. Finally, multiple regression analyses of influences on offer amounts in each of the two villages revealed that, at Anguganak, individuals with more resources as measured by their having greater numbers of gardens devoted to food (but not cash crops) tended to offer significantly more than those with fewer food gardens. However, this relationship was not seen at Bogasip.

In 1998, Eckel and Grossman reported the results of a double-anonymous dictator experiment indicating that women had a tendency to be more generous and less 'individually oriented' than men. Gender-specific results of the Ultimatum Game at Anguganak and Bogasip showed that the distribution of offers by women was skewed toward higher offers while that of men was skewed toward lower offers. Men were also more likely than women to accept both low ($<K3$) and high (>5) offers. These results offer at least some corroboration, however tentative, of Eckel and Grossman's findings.

By far one of the most interesting and unique findings in this study was the very high rate of rejection of offers by responders. In both villages combined, the overall rejection rate was almost 33 percent with the highest rate of rejection seen in response to both the lowest and highest offers (80 and 60 percent, respectively). Rejection was also much more common at Bogasip, with 40 percent of all offers rejected compared with Anguganak, whose 27 percent rejection rate was closer to that of western industrialized nations. For comparison, rejection rates varied between 19 and 27 percent in the four developed nations studied by Roth *et al.* (1991).

There are a number of possibilities that could account for the very high rate of rejection seen at Anguganak and Bogasip. It is possible that there was a researcher effect—in particular, that individuals were reluctant to take money from the researcher. There are, however, several reasons that this explanation is unlikely. First, in no instance did any participant display any reluctance whatsoever to take the K3 payment offered to them for participating. Second, individuals were told that the money was not the researcher's but was a pool of money from America earmarked specifically for the project. Third, individuals have never before displayed a reluctance to make requests of the principal researcher for either money or goods, though they have always repaid such 'debts' by eventually giving the researcher unsolicited goods in return, mostly bush foods. Fourth, if the tendency to reject offers was due to a reluctance to take money from the researcher, one might expect the tendency to be stronger at Anguganak, the village at which the researcher has lived over the past 11 years than at Bogasip. In fact, however, Bogasip villagers rejected offers at a much higher frequency than the villagers from Anguganak.

Rather than a 'researcher effect', it is much more likely that the high rejection rate is an outcome of beliefs and values about generosity and the necessity of repaying debts that players brought into the game from their daily lives, coupled with a lack of exposure to 'impersonal transactions'. As noted earlier, both the Au and Gnau at times display generosity by giving out unsolicited gifts to others and although these gifts were not explicitly requested, their acceptance does inherently bind the two individuals in a reciprocal relationship. It becomes understood by both the gift-giver and its acceptor that a debt has been incurred and that at some future time it must be repaid. Unsolicited offers are thus sometimes refused, especially if the potential acceptor does not wish to become indebted and bound in a reciprocal relationship with the giver. It is also worth noting that all transactions in Au daily life are 'personal' and conducted in a face-to-face fashion. Anonymity and 'impersonal transactions' of the kind employed here in the economic experiments are foreign to the Au and Gnau. Thus even though both proposers and responders were assured that their identities would be safeguarded, players inescapably bought the understandings, beliefs, expectations, and values that they apply to daily life into the experiment. Among these was a fear of indebtedness to proposers for their generosity. When individuals rejected offers, they commonly said such things as 'I can take the K3 I received from you, I can't take money from someone in the village'. When offered sums above K5, they often seemed genuinely afraid, and on several occasions responders remarked 'no, that's too much'. Thus, individuals seemed to react to the game using the same frames of reference and values that they apply to exchange interactions outside the game.

In sum, the data presented here suggest that variability in the level of Market Integration among populations tested may have an influence on the results of bargaining experiments. Even within this one remote region of Papua New Guinea, there was a small but direct relationship between indices of Market Integration/familiarity with the cash economy, and the degree of deviation from the predictions of the *Homo oeconomicus* model of economic behavior. The results seem to have been equally influenced by local beliefs about reciprocity and generosity. Participants seemed to bring the cultural beliefs that they use to navigate through their daily lives into the game. In particular, beliefs and values related to reciprocity and indebtedness coupled with an unfamiliarity with 'impersonal transactions' may have played a profound role in influencing them to reject offers (especially relatively high ones) to guard against incurring reciprocal obligations.

APPENDIX A: STANDARDIZED SCRIPTS

Individuals participating in the experiment were initially given their K3 participation fee and told:

Dispela tripela kina, ol i 'tok tenkyu' bilong yu helpim mi long mekim dispela samting. Dispela K3 em i bilong yu, mi no inap kisim bek gen. Kisim na putim long sampela hap na lus tingting long em olgeta. Nau bai yumi lukluk long dispela tenpela kina.

These three kina, they are a 'thank you' for you helping me do this research (literally, 'thing'). These three kina are yours (to keep), I cannot take them back again. Take them and put them away in some (safe) place, and forget about (literally, 'clear your mind of') them completely. Now we shall focus on these ten kina.

Individuals' attention was then focused on a cloth upon which ten K1 coins were laid out in a row. The following script was then recited:

Pastaim mi makim tupela manmeri bilong wokim dispela wok wantaim. Tasol wan wan bilong dispela tupela mi bin makim, em I no inap save husat narapela. Nambawan em i no inap save husat nambatu manmeri na narapela tu em I no inap save husat tru dispela nabawan manmeri. Na behain tu em I bai stap olsem, taim dispela wok I pinis, mi no inap tokaut husat poroman bilong narapela, no kolim nem bilong husat I bin mekim dispela wok.

Orait, mi givim dispela tenpela kina long yu na em I bilong yu nau. Mi no giaman, em I tru tru. Na em I no mani bilong mi, no ken wari long kisim dispela mani. Orait, dispela tenpela kina em I bilong yu nau, yu ken salim sampela bilong en I go long nambatu manmeri mi bin makim long wokim dispela samting wantaim yu. Em I laik bilong yu: yu ken salim K0 na holim K10 bilong yu yet, yu ken salim K1 na holim K9 yu yet, yu ken salim K2 na holim K8 ... yu ken salim K10 olgeta na holim K0 bilong yu yet. Yu tingting liklik na klostu bai mi askim yu hamas bilong dispela tenpela kina yu laik holim bilong yu yet na hamas bai yu salim I go long nambatu manmeri.

Orait, taim yu tokim mi hamas yu laik holim na hamas bai yu salim, behain bai mi go long nambatu manmeri na tokim em olsem: mi givim pinis tenpela kina I go long narapela manmeri bilong ples (tasol mi no inap tokim em husat manmeri tru no kolim nem bilong yu). Na nau em I kina bilong en. Na mi tokim em olsem em I ken givim long yu (tasol mi no kolim nem bilong yu, mi tokim em 'narapela manmeri' tasol) hamas kina em I gat laik, nogat olgeta I go inap olgeta tenpela, na em bai holim olgeta arapela kina bilong em yet. Na bai mi tokim em: dispela nambawan manmeri tokim mi long givim yu—kina, na em yet laik holim—kina. Na bai mi askim nambatu manmeri olsem: yu laik kisim dispela kina o nogat? Sapos em I tok 'orait,' bai mi givim em hamas kina yu bin makim long givim long en, na bai mi kam bek long yu na givim yu olgeta arapela bilong dispela tenpela kina. Tasol, sapos em I tok 'nogat,' em bai kisim nogat olgeta na yu tu bai kisim nogat olgeta.

First I have marked pairs of people to carry out this research (literally, 'work') together. But each member of the pair that I have marked cannot know who is the other. The first cannot know who is the other and the other too cannot know who is the first person. And later too, it will remain thus. When this work is finished, I will not announce who was partnered with another nor announce the names of those that participated in this work.

Ok, (pointing to the kina) I give you these ten kina and they are now yours. This is not a lie, it is really true. And it is not my money, don't worry about taking it. Ok, these ten kina that are yours now, you can give (literally, 'send') some of them to the second person that I have marked to do this work (literally, 'thing') with you. It is your decision (literally, 'desire'): you can send 0 and keep (literally, 'hold') 10 for yourself, you can send 1 and keep 9 for yourself, you can send 2 and keep 8 for yourself . . . you can send 10 and keep 0 for yourself. You think a bit and shortly I will ask you how many of these ten kina you will hold for yourself and how many you will send to the second person.

Ok, when you tell me how many you want to keep and how many you will send, after a bit I will go to the second person and speak to him/her thusly: I gave ten kina to another person of this village (but I will not say which person or utter your name). And now these kina are his/hers. And I told him/her that he/she can give to you (but I did not utter your name, I told him just 'the other person') however much he/she desired, from nothing whatsoever up to all ten, and he/she will keep all the remaining kina for him/herself. And then I will say to him/her: this first person told me to offer (literally, 'give') you—kina, and he/she desired to keep—kina for him/herself. And then I shall ask the second person: do you want to accept these kina or not? If he/she says 'ok,' I will give to him/her the amount of kina you marked for giving to him/her, and I will return to you and give to you the remainder of this ten kina. But, if he or she says 'no,' he/she will be given nothing at all and you too will receive nothing at all.

Individuals designated to be 'proposers' in the ultimatum experiment were read the entire script, while those designated as 'responders' were read the relevant section of the third paragraph. A cloth with 10 one kina coins lined up was also placed in front of the recipients, and when the section 'this first person told me to offer you . . . , and he/she desired to keep . . .' was read, the lineup of ten kina was divided such that the offered amount was pushed slightly to one side of the cloth and the kept amount to the other side. Following the script reading, individuals were given an opportunity to ask questions and clarify any 'rules' that were unclear to them.

REFERENCES

Camerer, C. (2003). Behavioral Game Theory: Experiments in Strategic Interaction. Princetion, NJ: Princeton University Press.

Daly, M. and Wilson, M. (1983). *Sex, Evolution, and Behavior*, 2nd edn. Belmont, CA: Wadsworth Publishing Company.

Davis, D. D. and Holt, C. A. (1993). *Experimental Economics*. Princeton, NJ: Princeton University Press.

de Tocqueville, A., Boesche, R., and Toupin, J. (1985). *Selected Letters on Politics and Society*. Berkeley, CA: University of California Press.

Eckel, C. C. and Grossman, P. J. (1998). 'Are women less selfish than men?: Evidence from dictator experiments', *Economic Journal, 108*, 726–36.

Fehr, E. and Gächter, S. (1998). 'Reciprocity and economics: The economic implications of *Homo Reciprocans*', *European Economic Review, 42*, 845–59.

Henrich, J. (2000). 'Does culture matter in economic behavior?: Ultimatum game bargaining among the Machiguenga Indians of the Peruvian Amazon', *American Economic Review* 90(4).

Kaplan, H. and Hill, K. (1985). 'Hunting ability and reproductive success among male Ache foragers', *Current Anthropology, 26*, 223–45.

Lewis, G. (1975). *Knowledge of Illness in a Sepik Society: A Study of the Gnau, New Guinea*. New Jersey: The Athlone Press.

—— (1980). *Day of Shining Red: An Essay on Understanding Ritual*. Cambridge: Cambridge University Press.

Mills, S. and Beatty, J. (1984). 'The propensity interpretation of fitness', in E. Sober (ed.), *Conceptual Issues in Biology*, Cambridge, MA: MIT Press, pp. 34–57.

Price, P. W. (1996). *Biological Evolution*. New York: Saunders.

Roth, A.E., Prasnikar, V., Okuno-Fujiwara, M., and Zamir, S. (1991). 'Bargaining and market behavior in Jerusalem, Ljubljana, Pittsburgh, and Tokyo: An experimental study', *American Economic Review, 81*, 1068–95.

Sillitoe, P. (1998). *An Introduction to the Anthropology of Melanesia: Culture and Tradition*. Cambridge: Cambridge University Press.

Smith, E. A. and Winterhalder, B. (1992). 'Natural selection and decision-making: Some fundamental principles', in E. A. Smith and B. Winterhalder (eds), *Evolutionary Ecology and Human Behavior*, New York: Aldine de Gruyter, pp. 25–60.

Stanford, C. B. (1996). 'The hunting ecology of wild chimpanzees: Implications for the evolutionary ecology of Pliocene hominids', *American Anthropologist*, 98, 96–113.

Tracer, D. P. (1996). 'Lactation, nutrition, and postpartum amenorrhea in lowland Papua New Guinea', *Human Biology*, 68, 277–92.

—— (1997). 'Reproductive and socio-economic correlates of maternal haemoglobin levels in a rural area of Papua New Guinea', *Tropical Medicine and International Health*, 2, 513–18.

—— Sturt, R. J., Sturt, A., and Braithwaite, L. (1998). 'Two decade trends in birth weight and early childhood growth in Papua New Guinea', *American Journal of Human Biology*, 10, 483–93.

9

Ultimatum Game with an Ethnicity Manipulation

Results from Khovdiin Bulgan Sum, Mongolia

Francisco J. Gil-White

INTRODUCTION

This chapter reports two Ultimatum Game experiments conducted with Mongols and Kazakhs in Western Mongolia. The first was an exploratory experiment, and the second is the full-fledged study, with the ethnicity manipulation. This manipulation consists of having proposers and responders be of either the same or different ethnicity.

As with the other studies reported in this volume, one important question is: how will people from a small, nonindustrialized society—in this case a traditional pastoral–nomadic culture—largely disconnected from modern capitalism and state structures, perform in the Ultimatum Game? If culture has an important effect on economic reasoning and decision-making, then perhaps the rather narrow range of variation obtained from Ultimatum Games conducted in the west (and heavily westernized settings) has been a product of western culture, rather than some more general underlying human nature.

The results on this question are paradoxical. Responders were very reluctant to punish low offers, but proposers were nevertheless very careful not to offend them, and made offers well above the empirically ascertained Income-Maximizing Offer. I will argue that this result, though paradoxical, is consistent with a parallel paradox that Torguuds experience in their daily lives: people are very afraid of reputation loss, but there are no tangible consequences for those perceived to be 'bad people'.

Another important question guiding this research was to investigate whether the behavior of proposers and responders was affected in any way by having the opposing player be a member of a different ethnic group. This result ought to be taken seriously in the context of explanations that have been offered for intergroup discrimination. For clarity of organization, I discuss the major relevant theories—Social Identity Theory, and Realistic Conflict Theory—in the discussion. But I presage here the most important point: it does not appear likely that these theories can easily account for the results found, and so perhaps we should revisit the assumptions that have justified explaining in-group favoritism in ecologically valid groups (such as ethnies) in terms of the above theories, which relied on experimental setups that may be much too exotic.

LIFE AND ECONOMY IN BULGAN SUM

This section places the present research in economic context. If the cultural/economic environment affects people's ideas of fairness, and the calculation of costs and benefits, then to understand Ultimatum Game performance differences in different localities we need a competent grasp of the economic framework and standard-of-living conditions affecting our respondents.

Ethnogeography

Bulgan Sum is a district in the province of Khovd, Republic of Mongolia. The fieldsite lies against the international border with China, across which is the Chinese province of Xinjiang. The district 'center', Bulgan, is a town that serves as a focal point for the nomadic pastoralists that roam the district, and it is also their legitimate point of contact with state structures. The district is divided into *bag* (or 'brigades'), two of which comprise the town itself, while the rest carve up the nomads roughly along ethnic and clan lines. The *bag* are territorial units, in a sense, but the different lands which constitute the 'territory' of a *bag* need not be contiguous, as some of the nomads, and in particular the Bangyaxan clan, with whom I worked, migrate quite far to their summer pastures. In the process, they traverse territory belonging to other clans. The chiefs of the nomadic *bag*, who are invariably nomads themselves, are members of the relevant communities by descent and upbringing (which communities elect them), and migrate together with the rest. So the *bag* is in this sense a mobile *social* unit, whose minimal administration (in addition to the *bag* chief there is a forestry chief and a vet—all nomads) travels with it. Nevertheless, the *bag* chief is a member of the state structure, a government functionary, though at the lowest level, and he answers directly to the elected bosses in the district center.

Torguud Mongols and Kazakhs comprise the two main ethnies in Bulgan. Both Torguuds and Kazakhs are represented among the town dwellers in the district center, and among the nomads who roam beyond it. There are about 5,000 inhabitants in town, employed in government, petty trade, artisanship, and small-time horticulture and farming. Many are unemployed. Beyond town is the desert-steppe, where another 5,000 people eke out a living as nomads.

During the fall, winter, and spring months, the nomads are not too far from town, though some are much farther than others. Members of the Torguud Bangyaxan clan, with whom I worked primarily, herd their animals to the west of town, in one of the two large floodplains of the Bulgan river, a glacial river that descends from the Altai into the Gobi. A few herders (15 percent at most) are true nomads, migrating throughout the winter season in the low hill-country or in the sands of the true desert. However, even these have a 'winter' property, a plot of land to which they own title with full property rights, which is sometimes equipped with a small bunker used for storage, and always with a corral to protect the animals from winter conditions and to store fodder collected in late August/September. These titled pieces of land are very small and, apart from these, the wilderness is ownerless. Most herders spend the winter in the floodplain and do not migrate during this time. In the summer months all nomads move to high ground, in the Altai Mountains, changing their location constantly as they judge the need for better pastures (they may make as many as ten migrations in a 4-month period). The high ground to which the Bangyaxan clan moves in the summer is very green, high-altitude forest-steppe, crisscrossed by innumerable glacial rivers and streams. Although there are a few Kazakh families in what is essentially Bangyaxan territory, on the whole Torguuds and Kazakhs are territorially segregated—the Kazakh herding to the *East* of Bulgan. Even Torguud and Kazakh town-dwellers live in separate parts of town, separated by a no-man's land about a kilometer wide.

The town center is a collection of dilapidated and decrepit buildings, of which the largest (and most well maintained) is the school. Except for two small, four-storey apartment buildings, the school, the hospital, and all buildings are one-storey. The other buildings in the town center are mostly small shops and the administrative buildings of the town government. Some live in small mud houses, and a few others in wooden houses left behind by the military when they used to quarter themselves in Bulgan. Many others live in *ger* (yurts), just like the nomads.

In the summer, the main feature of the town is dust—dust everywhere. I hear that there used to be plenty of trees, but illegal cutting for firewood has left the town with the appearance and feel of a ghost town. There are no paved roads anywhere, as indeed there aren't in most of Mongolia. Even the airstrip is nothing more than a convenient stretch of flat, dusty, and gravelly ground to the north of town. The result of all this is that the frequent west-to-east windstorms (which mercifully are absent during the winter) make life in town very uncomfortable, as they kick up awesome sandstorms that make outside activities impossible whenever they rage. Much of town-dweller small talk revolves around the miseries of dust and sand. Vicious Central Asian mosquitoes occupy much conversation as well. Add to that the considerable summer heat of the Gobi desert, the stench and discomfort of the latrines, and it does not make for a very pleasant summer in town.

In the floodplains of the Bulgan river, life is considerably more pleasant, for the abundant grass that grows there holds down the dust and sand. Mosquitoes are even more plentiful than in town, but then the nomads are not there for most of the summer, moving to the highland pastures that are cool, beautiful, and free of dust and mosquitoes. There is no need for latrines in such under-populated surroundings, and everything smells wonderful. It is small wonder that the herders disdain town life. The cost is in distance to the services located in town, such as they are.

The unforgiving winter is hardly much better for town-dwellers. The mosquitoes and sandstorms leave, but snow and bitter cold take their place. Even here, they don't have much of a comparative advantage with the nomads because the nomad winter *ger* is almost as cozy as a town bunker (*baishang*). However, the nomads do have to labor outside significant amounts of time, whereas town-dwellers can afford to be inside for the most part.

Brief history

For much of the twentieth century, Mongolia was a communist country under the direct influence and tutelage of the Soviet Union, stepping in as a 'protector' state to guarantee Mongolia's borders from the encroachments and claims of the Chinese, and later from Japanese imperialism during Second World War. Early on, the Bolshevik revolution spilled into Mongolia, and later Mongolia's own 'people's revolution' was engineered by Soviet agents and their puppets on a stunned populace. The excesses of this time were many, including wholesale persecution and slaughter of dissidents, especially members of the feudal Lamaist clergy.

In time, a command economy was instituted where everybody, nomad or town-dweller, was a government employee, but unlike the nomadic peoples of the Soviet Union, Mongolian herders were by-and-large not forcibly sedentized. Rather, the herders were organized to herd animals for the collectives, called *negdel*, which owned the animals and paid them wages. The government distributed medals and bonuses to good workers but effort and talent were not really an avenue to riches. Jobs, pensions, and health care were subsidized and guaranteed, and most services were delivered through the *negdel*. The subsidies for these services were paid mostly by large Soviet outlays rather than broad-based taxation, which generated very little revenue.

After the democratic revolution in 1990 the command economy collapsed with the disappearance of Soviet subsidies. Livestock was redistributed and the economy privatized. Initially, a few herders tried of their own free will to reorganize in voluntary collectives called *xorshoo*, but after only 2 or 3 years, even these experiments were abandoned for full privatization. This of course means that for 8 years prior to the completion of this study, Mongolians experienced the connection between work and wealth/security which is characteristic of societies with private property. The herders have readapted remarkably fast, rebuilding kin- and reciprocity-based patterns of association that existed prior to the revolution to substitute for (now absent) state services (Szynkiewicz 1993). Nevertheless, many are understandably nostalgic for the subsidized command economy.

Cash economy, development, and market penetration

This section examines the degree to which this site is different from more industrialized settings. It is important to know the extent to which people in Bulgan use cash (since the experiments involve cash), the degree to which they participate in markets, and the degree to which they have access to services typical of a developed country. The prices of different things, and in particular of hired labor, are also examined.

These days, the country folk in Bulgan Sum do not earn wages and the town folk do—that is, those who still have a job. In town unemployment is supposedly rampant but, except for government jobs, those with an occupation employ themselves, so real unemployment statistics are hard to come by. Since during communism nomads earned cash wages, the economy may have become *less* of a cash economy than it was before. The state has also receded from view considerably; most noticeably for the nomads, in the provisioning of basic services such as health care.

Among nomads, cash is used but many (perhaps most) transactions are barter (as indeed are many transactions even in town). Cash is used primarily on several yearly trips that nomad women make across the nearby Chinese border to get clothes, flour, and other things. Among themselves, the nomads trade almost nothing, for trade efficiencies are few when everybody has virtually the same way of life. There are two prominent exceptions: Kazakhs tend not to breed as many horses as Mongols, from whom they buy them. The same appears to be true for camels. On the other hand, Kazakhs make horseshoes and knives, which Torguuds buy.

Many townsfolk earn wages or freelance honoraria, and most petty commerce transactions are for cash. On the whole, however, there is a great deal of friend-to-friend quid-pro-quo, and kin-based altruism/reciprocity involving no cash. Some of the most important exchanges of this sort occur between the nomads and townsfolk.

Food   The food economy is largely cashless. Important items in the diet such as *aaruul* (cheese curds) and butter are obtained by townsfolk from herders as gifts or as part of loose and informal reciprocal exchanges. Most townsfolk own livestock which is herded by herder relatives or friends in exchange for housing their children during the school year. In addition townsfolk keep cows or goats for milk, or else they make do with low-prestige *khar tsai* (black tea) rather than *süütei tsai* ('tea with milk' the traditional beverage of Mongols, which contains about $\frac{1}{3}$ milk). Some townsfolk plant a few horticultural products such as cabbage and potatoes. Some nomads and townsfolk plant a little rye, but they buy wheat-flour for cash either in Bulgan Sum, or else the cheaper (and lower quality) flour from China. A 25 kg sack of wheat-flour cost T6,000 ($\approx$\$7.50) in 1998.

Other items bought for cash include salt (wildly abundant in the Gobi and brought to town by industrious people with a vehicle) and tea. The latter is the most omnipresent item in the Mongolian diet. Everybody pays cash for this, and it comes either from Russia (high quality) or from China (low quality). It is considered an expensive item and is sold in bricks of pressed stems and throwaway leaves that typically are not sold in other parts of the world. One brick of tea sells for T1,500 (about \$2) and it lasts a family of five for about a month and a half. There are also incidental items such as vodka, fruit, candy, cookies, hydrolized protein, chili sauce, sugar, etc.; but none of these are consumed in great quantities, except for vodka, sugar, and candies.

Services   A *tandig jolooch* ('a driver you know'), will give you a free ride or merely take gas money if you don't go far. When my friend Baajaa and I drove to the floodplain once in his truck, we transported three people's belongings, but he didn't charge *any* of them for his services, and took gas money from only two because the other one was very poor. Baajaa was going in that direction anyway, and this appears to be the norm: drivers do favors to people who are going their way. There is no regular public transportation, and for long trips one must hire a driver outright. In town people simply walk unspeakable distances, or stay put.

Every week, a small plane from Ulaanbaatar stops first in the provincial capital of Khovd and then lands in the airstrip to the north of town. The reliably awful windstorms may cause delays of a few days, or outright cancellations. The round trip from Ulaanbaatar was, in 1997, a subsidized \$50 for Mongolians and \$350 for the foreigner anthropologist. The alternative is to brave 1,500 km of dirt roads for 3–4 days (including night-time driving) in good weather.

About forty families have a phone—out of about 500 that live in the perimeter to which phone lines reach (for some of these, the phones no longer work). There is only one public phone in town, at the phone company headquarters, and one must pay cash to use it. I made use of it several times, and at worst never saw more than ten or twelve people waiting (often just one or two). Most people have no use for the phone or find it too expensive. They may send letters instead, although this will be expensive too—T220 (about 22 cents) to Ulaanbaatar. Just sending 4–6 letters will eat up a day's wages for a hired hand (see below).

These days the diesel to run the electricity plant is no longer subsidized by Russia and must be bought from the Chinese just across the border. It is too expensive. To fill up Baajaa's truck's tank, for example, requires all of US$25, or about three weeks' salary for a hired hand (see below). The town can afford to run its new Japanese plant only for 4 hours a day, and only in the winter, when electricity is absolutely indispensable given the short duration of sunlight at this latitude.

Fresh water comes from wells, easily dug since the water table is only a few feet below the surface. Human feces are disposed of in latrines. The nomads, on the other hand, get their water either from wells or from streams, and practice open-air fecalism. The one service that surprisingly—and thankfully—does exist is garbage collection. The trash is deposited on the sands, downwind, to the east of town.

There is a bank in town which apparently is used by very few people and does nothing more than provide safe-keeping and petty lending, much like a frontier bank in the old American West.

Clothing   A prominent item in the cash economy. Nomads buy material for cash and the women confection and tailor their *dels* (long coats). They also make felt 'socks' for their winter boots. Aside from this, however, everybody wears western-style clothing brought from either China (much of it cheap surplus dumping) or Ulaanbaatar and which is sold for cash—for example, a pair of boots T20,000 ($\approx$\$25), a pair of socks T300, a shirt T1,500, and a pair of pants T1,500, at 1998 prices and exchange rates.

Industry   There is really no primary production of any sort in Bulgan Sum except for the products of nomads and farmers. The only real middleman economy, however, is for products produced elsewhere, such as clothing, fruits, candy, school supplies, etc. It is not a large economy, but it is the largest sector in town by far (perhaps forty tiny stores in town, all of them virtually identical in size and merchandize). There are also people who buy skins and fur from the nomads and sell them elsewhere. In addition there is a very small secondary processing industry that turns grain into flour for local consumption, and another which minimally processes livestock entrails for sending to China where real value is added by turning them into such things as hats which are then sold back to the nomads. I have seen this tripe 'industry'. It is a sorry-looking bunker about the size of three typical *baishang* (two-room adobe winter-dwelling) put together, and supposedly employs all of ten people. I suspect the flour 'industry' supports the same. That is the extent of industry in Bulgan.

Labor for hire   Every once in a while somebody needs an *ajilchin* [hired worker], even among the nomads, and this is perhaps the best measure of how much money, in relative terms, my subjects were playing for in the Ultimatum experiments. Consider that the stake was T8,000, equivalent to about $10 at the time of the experiments.

Ariüngerel (a Torguud nomad) one day hired another herder to do some work for him in exchange for a small goat that he reckons goes for T3,000 to T4,000. The worker never delivered and Ariüngerel complained loudly to his sympathetic sister-in-law and her children. He expected to get 3 or 4 days labor, or else the man should give him back an equivalent goat. On a separate occasion (much later) I learned from him that for a *full*-grown goat (valued at T8,000) the *ajilchin* would work for eight days. So his answers on two separate occasions are consistent, and indicate a daily wage rate of T1,000. In this reckoning, and comparing it to the US minimum wage, people are playing for the equivalent of $400. This is obviously a distortion because the price of labor relative to the prices of other things is almost certainly cheaper here than in the United States. It nevertheless indicates that people are playing for definitely nontrivial sums: a week's worth of your labor is a week's worth, in Bulgan Sum and in the United States. For a comparison estimate, I asked Kairatpic (a Kazakh nomad), and he told me that a hired hand would get T1,500 daily, and this is not too far away from Ariüngerel's estimate.

My friend Baatarcüren has the most beautiful *baishang* that I have seen among Torguud nomads. It is so well finished one could almost mistake it for a Kazakh *baishang*, which are much nicer given that

Kazakhs have a stronger tradition of living in houses, whereas Torguud nomads typically only build bunkers for storage, spending the winters in their *gers*. It is a two room 7×4 meter cabin made out of wood (but not logs), built by Aavda, who finished carpentry school. Baatarcüren provided him with all of the materials but helped not at all with construction. It took Aavda 5 days to complete it, and he was working from 8:00 AM to 8:00 PM. Baatarcüren gave him T20,000 for the job. This means that Aavda was getting T4,000 per day. That seems like an awfully high wage-rate. These high wages may be explained by the fact that carpenters are rare (in Bulgan Sum there are no more than four). Baatarcüren tells me that they are invariably very well-respected people—Ariüngerel's *ajilchin*, on the other hand, had been hired to do unskilled labor. Besides, Aavda was working 12 hour days, which is unusual. A driver from Bulgan Sum who came to Baatarcüren's looking for his lost cows (a common occurrence), told me that the norm is for a hired hand to work 8 hour days, with a daily wage adjusted for the heaviness of the task but never higher than T3,000 and, on average, T1,500. In light of all this evidence I settle on a conservative estimated daily wage rate of T1,500 which may be inflated given the incentive to do this with the rich foreigner. My hired assistants for the experiments all got paid higher than this: a daily T1,600 and, after the devaluation, T2,000, but always the equivalent of $2. They seemed to think that they were being paid handsomely.

THE EXPERIMENTS

Study 1

The first study unintentionally ended up as an exploratory one, for its data were inconclusive due to unforeseen problems with the methodology. Nevertheless, the data are very suggestive, and a review of the evidence obtained, and the lessons learned from it, help increase the confidence for the results in study 2. It was conducted exclusively with Torguud nomads from the Bangyaxan clan, while in their high-altitude summer pastures. Thus, this is a simple Ultimatum Game experiment except for the idiosyncrasies of this field site and its methodological requirements.

Methods   The study population consists of forty adults ranging in ages from eighteen to fifty-six. There were twenty proposers (twelve men and eight women), and twenty responders (nine men and eleven women).

The clan veterinarian, Boldoo, is an intelligent 30-year-old nomad with higher, technical education, and familiar with the notion of an experiment and its methodological requirements. Moreover, he could see why it was interesting. He was hired as an assistant. At the time of this experiment, my Mongolian was not enough for conversational fluency, but it didn't prevent communication or explanation. Boldoo corrected the Mongolian in the draft of my explanations and was instructed to intervene only if, after failing to communicate a particular point, I asked him to do so. This way I could have the highest degree of control over what was said, especially since my Mongolian was adequate for me to almost always understand Boldoo's interventions.

The dispersed manner in which steppe-nomads live made it impossible to gather all participants for the experiment, so the experimental protocol unfolded as follows:

1. Twenty responders were recruited, but the game was not explained to them.
2. For every responder, a Polaroid was obtained.
3. Twenty proposers were recruited and the game was explained to them.
4. Each proposer, after having the game explained to him/her, made a proposal, having been advised that the responder was a person among the twenty photographs I presented, but whose precise identity I could not reveal, as everybody would play anonymously.
5. Following the offer, a Polaroid was taken of every proposer.
6. Responders were assigned randomly to proposers.
7. Another trip was made to each responder's tent.
8. The game was explained to each responder, and the offer made by the proposer was demonstrated, pointing out that the proposer was among the twenty people in the photographs presented (this time, of proposers), but this person's identity would remain anonymous. If the responder accepted the offer, the offered money was immediately apportioned to her/him.
9. A final trip was made to each proposer's tent. The responder's response was conveyed, and any money due was apportioned.

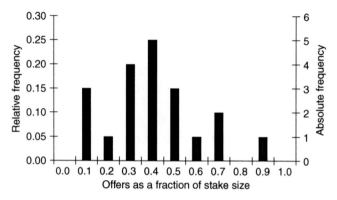

FIG. 9.1. Distribution of offers in Study 1

Appendix A has the details of the methodological protocol for the explanations used during proposer recruitment (the explanations to the responder were essentially identical, with a few obvious modifications necessary to make it specific to responders). I was always left alone in the *ger* with the proposer/responder when witnessing their choices, when revealing how much money was due to them and making the payments, and during cross-examinations (Figure 9.1). Each one was assured of confidentiality, and I explained that they could not even be identified by name in my charts for everybody was getting a number.

Proposers were disqualified if they failed repeatedly to understand the experiment, as evidenced by incorrect responses to iterated quizzes after re-explanations. Only one proposer was disqualified in this manner. Unfortunately, initial smugness over the ease with which the experiment would be understood resulted in the following serious methodological flaw: no disqualifying procedure was employed for the responders, as these had the experiment explained to them *after* they had been recruited, and after the proposers had made their offers. This shortcoming cost me two data-points, because two of my responders proved incapable of comprehending the logic of the experiment, and I couldn't use their responses.

After apportioning any money due, I cross-examined participants to examine their reasoning. In particular, I sought answers to the following questions: (1) what was the punishing threshold that they anticipated, and was this answer consistent with their reasoning in the experiment, and with their offers?; (2) what is the lowest amount that the proposers themselves would have accepted, had they been responders?; (3) for those responders who had rejected the offers made to them, why had they?; and finally (4) for those responders who had accepted the offers made to them, was there a level at which they would consider the offer too miserly to be accepted?

Results and discussion   There is no difference between males and females (male mean $= 0.43$, female mean $= 0.46$; CF $= 4.6$, $p = 0.33$). The mode (0.40) and mean (0.44) of this distribution are not too surprising from what we know of experiments carried out in developed settings (see Camerer and Fehr, Chapter 3, this volume). However, the variation seems rather wild, especially considering that it includes four data points (0.20 of the total) above the 50/50 line, including a very high outlier at 0.90, and also a rather largish spike at 0.10. This was surprising.

There was only one rejection, and it went to a 0.10 offer. This too was surprising, especially given that fully six offers were for 0.30 or less, and that even this lonely rejection may not be real. It was given by Boldoo's father, Shavia. Under cross-examination, Shavia told me that he had rejected the offer because he thought it was 'ugly', and he wanted the proposer to take a loss. This reply pleased my prejudices, but as we departed, an amused Boldoo relayed to me that when his father had stepped out of the *ger* he had told Boldoo that his real reason for refusing the offer was that he could not accept money from a poor student like myself. This charming generosity, from a man whose entire property I could have bought with a little bit of credit card debt, was entirely in character for the late and sorely missed Shavia (he died in 1999)—a wonderful host, father, husband, and friend. I went back and confirmed Boldoo's statement with Shavia, and explained that the money was the university's and it did not affect me whether he took it or not. Had he understood—he informed me when queried—he would have rejected the offer anyway. But I must be skeptical because Boldoo—who had discovered that this is what I wanted to hear—was whispering the answer in his father's ear.

There were other confusions. I undertook a second round of cross-examinations, and the sum total of these investigations yielded even greater uncertainty over the proper interpretation of the experiment, as it became obvious that many participants had not understood the point of it all. Some of this information came to me serendipitously. For example, Galcnii Mönxbat's offer of T7,500 (only one T500 increment below giving everything away) seemed ridiculously high to me. His brother Anxbat (who had gone before him, and assisted Boldoo and myself in the role-playing part of the explanations), Boldoo, and myself, were all satisfied that he had understood the object of the game. In the cross-examination, I again was not able to uncover evidence that he had misunderstood. The day after, as Boldoo and I relaxed in Mönxbat's *ger*, the two of them chatted. Boldoo let out a big laugh and then told me that Mönxbat had not understood the game after all. Mönxbat, he explained, thought he was supposed to get the responder to agree to the partition, but did not realize that real money was involved and that he could make real money in the experiment. He thought the money aspect of it was hypothetical and had been very surprised when I brought him back his winnings. Thus, he naturally had offered T7,500 (0.93) because he reasoned that nobody in his right mind would disagree to such a partition. Had he understood, he said, he would have offered half. His wife, Oyungerel, had misunderstood the experiment in exactly the same way (though her offer was in fact 0.50). At least three other people made the same mistake.

Again, this was initially very surprising. My explanation protocol was careful, stepwise, gently paced, and heavily demonstrative. Moreover, it included a test to see whether participants had understood. Thus, it was at first bewildering and discouraging to find in the second round of cross-examinations that several participants still had not understood (even though they had passed my test). My methods, careful as they were, could not anticipate the great cultural gulf separating me from my respondents, for I could not have imagined some of the hypotheses they made concerning the object of the game. Nor could I have anticipated some of their scruples given that some incorrectly believed the money to be mine.

The cross-examination of the responders added to my growing skepticism. Most responders did not seem to have a punishing threshold, and, when they did, it was extremely low. It was not consistent with proposer behavior that responders would accept any offer, and neither was the strong reluctance I found in responders to characterize low offers as punishable or particularly miserly. These data from the responders quite directly contradicted what the proposers said they would have done had they been responders themselves. Most proposers indicated that they would have punished low offers (though what they thought was a punishable offer was not always the offer immediately below the one they themselves made).

All of this led me to doubt that responders had truly understood the experiment. I hypothesized that, despite my precautions, they might not have understood that the proposer was *required* to make an offer in order to play the game. If so, they might have regarded any offer as a gift, and missed the point of the game, which lies in the power of the responder, and the respect or disrespect for this power implied in the proposer's offer. A corollary hypothesis was that the logic of the game might be easier to grasp for those who are socialized into the proposer role, and this might explain the discrepancy between responder behavior and the answers proposers gave as hypothetical responders. Study 2 was designed with an eye to improving the methodology in light of all of the misunderstandings, to resolve these troubling theoretical questions, and to test for possible ethnicity effects in Ultimatum Game decisions.

Study 2

As originally intended, Study 1 would provide an in-group baseline (in Study 1 all of the participants are Torguud Mongols) against which to compare the results in Study 2, where Mongols and Kazakhs would be playing against each other. In this manner I would test for an ethnicity effect. However, because of the problems listed above, I was not confident that I could interpret Study 1. Thus, I redesigned Study 2 so that I could simultaneously fix the methodological problems in Study 1, *and* obtain both in-group and intergroup performance data.

Methods   The study population consists of forty adults, ages 20–50. They were not nomads but town-dwellers (except for a few nomads among the Kazakh). Half of them are Torguud and half Kazakh. Of the twenty Torguuds, ten are proposers and ten responders, and likewise for the Kazakhs. The ratio of males to females per ethnie per role, in both cases, is 60/40. Each proposer made two offers, one to a Kazakh responder, and one to a Torguud responder, anonymously. Each responder thus had to make two decisions, one for the offer a Kazakh made, and one for the offer a

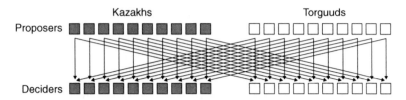

FIG. 9.2. Structure of offers and responses

Torguud made. Figure 9.2 illustrates the two offers every proposer must make, as well as the two decisions facing every responder. Proposers and responders were assigned at random.

The following steps summarize the experimental protocol.

1. Twenty responders (ten from each ethnie) were recruited and the game was explained to them. They were tested, and those who failed were disqualified.
2. For every responder, a Polaroid was obtained.
3. As in step 1 for the proposers.
4. Each proposer, after having the game explained to him/her, and passing the test, made a proposal. Each proposer was told that the responder was among those portrayed in ten photographs which I presented, but whose precise identity I could not reveal, as everybody would play anonymously.
5. Following the offer, I explained that there was a second responder with whom the proposer would play. I was very careful to point out that this was a completely new game, played with a fresh batch of T8,000 *tögrög*. A new batch of ten photographs was presented (half of the participants made an in-group offer first, and the other half made an out-group offer first).
6. Following the second offer, a Polaroid was taken of every proposer.
7. Responders were assigned randomly to proposers.
8. Another trip was made to each responder's dwelling.
9. The object of the game was quickly reviewed. The offer made by the proposer was explained, pointing out that the proposer was among the ten people in the photographs presented (this time, of proposers), but this person's identity would remain anonymous. If the responder accepted the offer, the offered money was immediately apportioned to her/him.

10. A final trip was made to each proposer's tent. The responders' responses were conveyed, and any money due was apportioned.

For the Polaroids I always insisted on ethnic headwear. This is more predictive for the Kazakhs, as no Torguud wears the Kazakh *kapesh*, but some young Kazakhs sometimes wear the commercially bought hats that the Torguuds favor. However, the ethnic manipulations worked every time—every single participant was aware that one set of photos consisted of exclusively Torguud individuals, whereas the other consisted of exclusively Kazakh individuals.

The new recruitment procedure included the one used earlier *in full* (Appendix A), including the test contained therein, followed by a new, second test, which tried to search exhaustively for any of the likely misunderstandings (Appendix B). Every potential participant had to pass the new test before being admitted into the experiment. The earlier protocol was incorporated with only two differences: (1) I now used two assistants, so that I could play myself in the explanatory pantomime and preempt confusion; (2) no participant was paid merely for participating. This latter change was due to the considerable unease and consequent distraction (not to mention extra time devoted to explaining experimental custom in the United States) caused by their bewilderment at my trying to pay them for agreeing to humor me while I asked them some questions—with which they might make money to boot! It was obvious that their bewilderment occupied their minds considerably and interfered with their comprehension of the explanations surrounding the object of the game (e.g. they were often confused about whether they could keep the participation payment, or whether it was part of the money for play). The effort to treat these participants with no less respect and consideration than is due to Western subjects is laudable, but this must include sensitivity to the cultural situation. If importing a given cultural value of ours to the field distracts and unsettles the participants, in addition to imperiling the experiment, its wisdom in the field setting ought to be reconsidered.

In Study 1, I found little evidence of a punishing threshold, whether in performance or in answers to hypothetical questions. In order to test whether this had been a problem of comprehension or a true populational attribute, I used the following procedure when presenting the offer to the responder:

1. On my chart (which only I can see) I pretend to search for the line that corresponds to this person's anonymous proposer.
2. I pretend to find it and I demonstrate for the responder the lowest possible offer, saying 'This is the offer that the proposer made. Do you accept or reject?'
3. After the responder gives the answer, I write it down in my chart, and, as I do, I pretend to notice that I made a mistake, claiming to have read a different line which corresponds to somebody else's proposer.
4. I then demonstrate the real proposal, and record the responder's answer. Naturally, any money due to them came from how they responded to the real offer.

In this manner I obtained very good data for reactions to the lowest possible offers. Half of all responders saw the out-group offer first, whereas the other half saw the in-group offer first. The fake offer was always presented as coming from whichever proposer came first. My only defense for thus breaking with the conventional norms of experimental economics is that I was neither knowledgeable enough nor creative enough, at the time, to come up with the titration method, where subjects commit themselves in advance—before seeing the offer—to the quantities that they will either accept or reject. Faced with the decision of keeping to the norms or coming back without having answered the question as to whether responders were likely or not to punish low offers, I opted for breaking the norms.

Results The considerable extra work involved (not least because the test led to many disqualifications, which multiplied the number of times the exhausting explanatory routine had to be repeated) seems to have paid off. Out of twenty proposers, thirteen showed an 'excellent' performance in the test, which means they understood all the smallest nuances (e.g. guessed right the first time whose money they were playing with and so forth), even though these were not overly emphasized in my explanatory routine. Another five got a 'pass', which means they made one or two mistakes, but not on the basics, and had no trouble understanding the right answers when I explained them. Only two people were passed with some reservations. The numbers for responders are virtually identical.

TABLE 9.1. Torguud and Kazakh offers in Study 2

	By Torguuds	By Kazakhs	CF	p
In-group offer mean	0.350	0.356	2.63	0.62
Out-group offer mean	0.418	0.431	6.08	0.19

TABLE 9.2. Comparing Study 1 and Study 2[a] offers

	Study 1	Study 2	CF	p
Mean	0.44	0.35	8.27	0.08

[a] The Study 2 sample is of the combined Kazakh and Torguud *in-group* offers.

Is the increased confidence in participant comprehension reflected in corresponding changes in the data? It is for the distribution of offers. Table 9.1 shows the means of Torguud offers to an in-group and an out-group responder, and the corresponding Kazakh means (each sample $n = 10$), with the Epps-Singleton test results comparing the Torguud and Kazakh distributions.

Since the Torguud and Kazakh offers do not appear statistically different, I group the combined in-group offers and compare them to the offers in Study 1 to see if the new methodology has affected the results. (see Table 9.2 for the statistical test, and Figures 9.1 and 9.3 for visual comparisons of the distributions).

Compared to offers in Study 1 (see Figure 9.1), the offers are lower. This makes sense given the kinds of misunderstandings that resulted in Study 1: that the money was not for real, that the object of the game was just to get the responder to agree, that the money was mine, etc. When the game is properly understood as one where real money can be made, and where making money will not harm the researcher economically, people who wish to make money will tend to make smaller offers. In this second study there was only one offer above 0.5, and it was only marginally so (0.56), whereas in the first study there were four such offers, including one at 0.9. This is a big part of the difference.

The Epps-Singleton test adds weight to the conclusion that the distributions are different, as shown in Table 9.2.

The result falls short of the conventional threshold for statistical significance concerning the apparent difference between the two distributions, but we have data in excess of the statistical test. We have systematic interview and fortuitous ethnographic data concerning people's misunderstandings in Study 1 (and these data *under*estimate the potential misunderstandings). We also have a thorough test and rigorous disqualification procedure in Study 2 that rules out such misunderstandings there. Moreover, the idea that the distributions would be different in the direction found makes intuitive sense if the methodology was indeed successful at removing such misunderstandings.

Next, does facing an in-group or an out-group responder affect the size of the offers? First, I group together the out-group offers (Torguud *and* Kazakh) as I did above for the in-group offers. Comparing the distributions in Figures 9.3 and 9.4 shows them to be different (see Table 9.3). The effect is perhaps better appreciated in Figure 9.5.

TABLE 9.3. Offers to in-group versus to out-group responder; paired *t*-Test

	In-group	Out-group	*t*	*p*
Offer mean	0.35	0.425	− 2.88	0.01

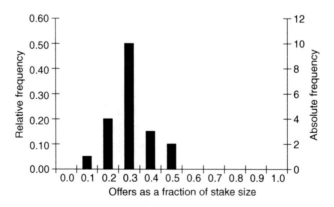

FIG. 9.3. Combined Kazakh and Torguud *in-group* offers in Study 2

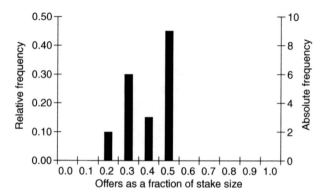

FIG. 9.4. Combined Kazakh and Torguud *out-group* offers in Study 2

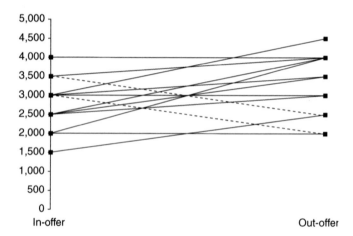

FIG. 9.5. Individual in-/out-group offers

Only two people gave an in-group offer higher than their out-group offer. Everybody else either stayed the same, or gave a higher offer to the out-group responder (some lines overlap exactly, so the total number of apparent lines is less than twenty).

Every responder faced one fake offer (and then two real ones). Half of all responders thought the fake offer came from an in-group, and the other half from an out-group, member. Table 9.4 summarizes their responses.

TABLE 9.4. Responder responses to fake, T500
(lowest possible) offers

	Accept	Reject
In-group offers ($n = 10$)	7	3
Out-group offers ($n = 10$)	7	3

TABLE 9.5. The three responders who rejected
real offers (A = accept; R = reject)

Responder	In-group offer	Out-group offer
1	0.375 (R)	0.25 (A)
2	0.313 (A)	0.375 (R)
3	0.50 (A)	0.375 (R)

Responders seem oblivious to whether the low offer is from an
in-group or an out-group proposer, and a strong majority does not
think that an offer which is T500, or 0.063 of the total T8,000 stake,
deserves punishment. The real offers, naturally, were accepted at a
higher rate (three rejections out of twenty real offers). The behavior
of the three rejecting responders is summarized in Table 9.5.

Responder 1 rejected an in-group offer but accepted a *lower* out-
group offer. Responder 2 by contrast rejected an out-group offer,
but accepted a lower in-group offer. Responder 3 rejected the low
offer and took the high one. So one responder's behavior (3) yields
no information about group bias, and the other two cancel each
other out. In summary, the data from rejections yielded no evidence
of group favoritism, whether in-group or out-group. But the failure
again to find evidence of in-group favoritism must be noted.

One thing does emerge very clearly from the rejection data. In
Study 1, it seemed to me counterintuitive and skewed that responders should accept anything at all in light of the fact that the offers
were, relative to this reluctance to punish, high. I speculated that
this might be due to methodological errors in Study 1 that caused
responder lack of comprehension (even though I was not able to
uncover this clearly in my interviews). Now I believe that this

strange result is real: responders will take practically anything. Despite this, the offers, even in Study 2, are relatively high.

General discussion

Why does not responder behavior predict proposer behavior?   It is puzzling that the offers of proposers are so high when the punishing threshold is so low. Mine is not an isolated result. Except for perhaps the Machiguenga (Henrich 2000), the results we have for simple societies suggest that people are, for the most part, not making Income-Maximizing Offers (see Henrich *et al.*, Chapter 2, this volume). This could be because people have a stronger preference for avoiding losses than they do for maximizing income (in the sense of Prospect Theory). Or it could be because, although people wish to maximize income, they have a poor estimate of where the punishing threshold is. If there is a bias to assume that this threshold is higher than it actually is, offers will seem large relative to empirically determined rejection rates.

At least for the present case, this second hypothesis receives some support from the cross-examination data in the first experiment.[1] I queried proposers, immediately after they had made their offers, on what they thought was the punishing threshold for the anonymous responder. This I did with role-playing and demonstration, as I had not yet truly mastered the use of counterfactuals. For every proposer, I would demonstrate the lowest possible offer (T500) on the ground with actual bills and would say, 'What do you think the responder thinks? If you make this offer, do you think the responder will accept?' If they said no, I would raise the demonstration offer by T500, and ask again—and so on until they said this was an offer the responder would be inclined to accept. Most proposers said that rejections would happen all the way up to and including the offer right below the one they had actually made. In this sense the proposers were consistent even though the individual estimates of punishing thresholds (and corresponding offers) varied. When I used a similar routine to find out what these proposers would have done as responders, the typical answer was that they would have punished offers below the one they had made.

---

[1] The protocol in Study 2 was so tiresome that I did away with the very thorough cross-examinations I had used in Study 1, so I do not have this kind of data for Study 2.

There are two puzzles here. The first is that the proposers over-estimate the rejection rate. The second is that they predict that they themselves would punish at the rate that they predict others will, even though this is almost certainly not true (given that people were assigned to proposer and responder roles at random). I examine each puzzle in turn.

The tendency in proposers to overestimate the rejection rate—that is, to overestimate the negative consequences of their 'bad' behavior, can be reconciled with the ethnographic data. These data revealed that people were quite neurotic about their reputations and feared greatly the possibility of being perceived as a 'bad person'. Moreover, they appeared hyperaware (at least by my standards) of the presumed or real moral qualities of individuals, and very prone to speaking of them in moralistic and essentialist terms—for example, *sain khün* or 'good person'; *muu khün* or 'bad person'; *tsagaan khün* or 'a person without any malice or guile' (lit. 'white person'). I remarked about this to my friend Tsoloo, who grew up in Bulgan Sum as a nomad but has lived in the capital city for a few years. Full of surprise that I understood this, he exclaimed that people in Bulgan Sum were indeed quite concerned that they be not thought of as *muu khün*.

Despite all this, nothing at all seems to befall those with a bad reputation. The data for this comes from people's introspections, when I ask them what the likely social consequences will be to someone with the reputation for being a 'bad person'. To this question people consistently drew a blank, no matter how hard I tried to tease it out of them. I began collecting such interview data early on, as part of a general interest in social punishment, and did not realize its relevance to the experiments until they were concluded.

What I found is that people claim they will not change their behavior towards 'bad people' in any way, even when I suggest mild forms of social punishment such as visiting 'bad people' less. And I found reluctance to punish even when I asked about admittedly serious transgressions, such as free riding on the work of others in one's *khot ail*. People certainly do gossip, but more significant punishments (of the kind that require the punisher to incur some tangible costs to him or herself) are apparently not typically mobilized against social offenders.

My ethnographic observations are consistent with this, and I illustrate with a dramatic anecdote. X, an elderly man who lived

close by to my first host, H1, was early on described by the latter as
a very bad person. This was supposedly a family shortcoming. I was
assured by H1 that this was his general reputation in the community. I later heard other people refer to X in negative terms. In the
end it became clear that such an opinion of him is not universal but
it is also not limited to my initial host's family—although, to be
sure, I never heard an accusation worse than 'he gossips a lot' and
to my way of judging the attribution even of this mild failing was
gratuitous.

Despite my inherited suspicions I came to have great affection for
X, and found him one of the nicer and most decent people I met
during my ethnographic stay.[2] The circumstances under which
I came to do so are telling. X had been to my host's *ger* several times
in order to invite me for a stay at his. This is a local custom: a
person may be honored by being hosted and feted for a few days.
The host brings one of his own horses to the home of the guest, and
they both ride back to the host's *ger*. This happened to me countless
times as people wanted their photographs taken. Every time X came
by to suggest this, my hostess made excuses for me or deflected the
invitation. But X persisted and let her know that he was killing a
goat for me. At this point my hostess insisted that I must go. I myself
was not keen to go given that he was supposed to be such a bad
person. But my hostess was adamant, and explained that if I didn't
go, X would blame her and people would think she was a bad
person. In other words, despite her strong dislike for X, and despite
his supposedly bad name, any perception that my hostess was dis-
respecting him would have affected her reputation negatively, or so
she thought, and this was intolerable.

In his capacity as guest at other people's *ger*, X was not treated
with less respect than was due to a man of his age. *Shimiin arkhi* (a
home-distilled spirit from cow and goat milk that the nomads drink)
must always be served when the host wishes to honor a guest, and

---

[2] I think X is disliked not because of moral failings, of which I have no evidence—all
to the contrary. Rather, I think he is disliked because X is, quite simply, very *weird*. He
has a strange, high-pitched, loud, theatrical laugh which has a knack for exploding
often and in all sorts of situations where other people see nothing funny, resulting in
much awkwardness. In addition, X constantly breaks many other small norms of
propriety. One particularly extreme transgression is his habit for slapping himself and
other people on various parts of the body when he has a fit of laughter. This is common
in other cultures and intensifies the shared experience of humor, but among the generally reserved Torguuds, *nobody* else does this.

for elderly guests it is *de rigeur*. *Shimiin arkhi* was always brought out when X visited H1. And H1 invited X to the inauguration of H1's younger brother's *ger* (a ceremony which anticipates the younger brother's impending marriage), and was treated with great respect.

So this anecdote suggests that Torguuds are worried so much about being perceived as a 'bad person' that they dare not transgress even those with a bad reputation. This statement nicely contains the paradox: if the idea of punishing even those who are considered 'bad' makes the potential punisher worry that this punishing behavior will give him or her a 'bad name', then violators will not be punished. But if they are not, then why should anybody fret so much about getting a bad reputation when this carries no tangible costs?

Town-dwellers seem no more likely than nomads to punish others for social offenses. My friend Baajaa, a town-dweller, is typical. Asked what would be the social cost to a person whom all recognize as a *muu khün*, he replied almost automatically: 'no cost whatever'. So I tried with an example:

'Okay', I said, 'Suppose that there is this person whom everybody says is a *muu khün*. You are driving your truck and you pass by this person, who signals to you that he is going your way and needs a ride. Do you stop and give him a ride?'

'If he hasn't done anything to me personally, then yes, I will. If he has done something to me, then I won't.'

As Baajaa suggests, if punishment is forthcoming it is only after specific offenses and only from those directly offended. The structure of the experiment is interesting, in this respect. A responder cannot affect future proposer behavior with respect to that dyad specifically, because the game is played once, and anonymously. The responder also knows that the proposer does not know the responder's identity, so 'bad' proposer behavior may be interpreted as an offense against the social order, rather than the responder's person, as in the case of real-life offenses against third-parties. From this perspective, the ethnographic observations predict that there will be no responder punishment, and, as seen above, there almost wasn't any.

Proposer behavior also seems to match the ethnographic observations. Proposers fret about their behavior in the experiment even though responder punishment is not forthcoming, and in real life people worry much about behaviors that will bring them a bad reputation, even though no tangible costs appear to follow. One interpretation of this is that the same mechanisms which make proposers worry about their reputations in their ordinary lives also operate in the experimental situation. However, there is one discrepancy: in the experiment, proposers *did* actually think there would be tangible costs to 'bad' behavior (i.e. they believed responders would irrationally punish low offers), whereas in my open-ended interviews people routinely explained to me that there were no real costs to those with a bad reputation.

I believe that this discrepancy, though it appears rather sharp, is in fact illusory. It may result from the fact that when I interview people about everyday social punishments, they are asked to reason about hypothetical third-parties, rather than their own behavior. In the experiment, on the other hand, they are reasoning about the consequences of their own imminent behavior, and there may well be a psychological bias to exaggerate the possible negative consequences of one's own imminent and immoral behavior beyond what the empirical data of one's experience supports. Why? Perhaps because such a mechanism adaptively keeps people from the costs of social reactions on the tail of a distribution of reactions, which tail they typically will not have seen (but should avoid). When thinking of *other* people, however, the problem is not strategic but empirical, and the bias may not operate. This hypothesis explains why people are worried about their own reputations even though they judge the bad reputations of others to carry no costs, and it also explains why responders did not share the erroneous intuitions of proposers: responders were not thinking of their own impending behavior, just reacting to somebody else's.

A wrinkle remains: why did proposers say that *they themselves* would have punished low offers? It is quite possible that this is a *post facto* rationalization of the trepidation they feel when making the offer. Having told me explicitly that they think responders will punish certain amounts in order to explain their trepidation in making an offer, they hypothesize their own behavior as responders in such a way as to keep their rationalizations consistent. There is evidence that much explicit moral reasoning is a *post facto* effort to render one's behavior plausible, rather than causally determinative of moral behavior (Haidt, Koller, and Dias 1993; Haidt 2001), and this could be a case in point. This hypothesis has the additional virtue that it explains why the intuitions of proposers and responders were different: responders, by and large, did not think there was such a thing as a punishable offer.

Although the above may help establish a continuity between the ethnographic and experimental data, and therefore add plausibility to the hypothesis that participants frame the experimental situation with the same paradox that rules their behavior in the world, it still does not explain the paradox. We may state the problem as two questions: first, why is so little social punishment leveled against third parties who are perceived to be 'bad'?; and second, why do my informants worry so much about their moral reputations when tangible punishment is so seldom forthcoming? I'll tackle each question in turn.

Why is so little social punishment leveled against third parties who are perceived to be 'bad'?   It is possible that the ecology of nomadic pastoralism explains the paucity of social punishment. Within reasonable costs, punishment in the context of reciprocal interactions can give a clear benefit to the punisher in that it socializes the 'cheater' not to offend the punisher, motivating improved behavior in that particular dyad. But third-party punishment (i.e. for generalized offenses against the social order, rather than against one's individual person) is a public good, and for this reason is susceptible to free-rider effects. However, third-party punishment may give a net benefit to the punisher when it can be witnessed by other members of society, who are the beneficiaries of one's punishment, and who therefore can attest to one's moral rectitude as evidenced by one's exertions to enforce the moral order. In other words, by punishing those who offend third parties, the punisher emits a signal that she is morally upright and therefore a good partner for risky reciprocal interactions subject to cheating temptations. If others then prefer this punisher in all sorts of reciprocal games, such benefits may overcompensate the costs incurred in punishing.

If this is the logic of third-party punishment, then one would expect that as the signal strength of punishment weakens, one should see less punishment, because when other people are not on hand to witness one's acts of social punishment, severing or imperiling one's reciprocal ties to a person may be too expensive to perform if that person has not offended against oneself. In such an environment, a norm holding social punishment *itself* as against the moral order may be favored.

This interpretation receives support from the fact that the behavior of Kazakhs and Torguuds, whether proposers or responders, is statistically indistinguishable. Although Kazakhs and Torguuds are different ethnies with many important contrasts in their interactional norms (Gil-White 2003), they should be very similar in this domain of behavior if it is indeed strongly determined, as hypothesized, by the ecological adaptation. And Torguuds and Kazakhs earn their living in almost exactly the same manner, with a very dispersed lifestyle consisting of relatively isolated family units (Mongolia has the lowest density of any country in the world).

Also supporting this ecological hypothesis is the fact that the other herder groups in the sample, Orma and Sangu, with comparably sized offers, had essentially identical rejection rates, respectively, 0.04 and 0.05; Torguuds had a rejection rate (for the *real* offers) of 0.05, and Kazakhs of 0.10. The Achuar, Mapuche, Tsimané, Quichua, and Machiguenga, although they are not pastoralists, share with the pastoralist groups a relatively low-density arrangement with individual households living in considerable isolation from each other. The Quichua and Machiguenga have mean offers that are too low for the comparison of rejection rates with the herders to be meaningful. But this comparison can be made with the other three, and these rejection rates are 0.14 (Achuar), 0.07 (Mapuche), and 0.0 (Tsimané). By contrast, groups with denser lifestyles and comparable mean offers showed higher rejection rates. The difference between Sangu farmers (0.25) and herders (0.05), is significant, because what distinguishes them here is the spatial arrangement, not so much their cosmology, which they largely share, being members of the same ethnie (see Henrich *et al.*, Chapter 2, this volume, for the complete data set). By contrast, as we saw, Kazakhs and Torguuds, who are members of different ethnies, but have an almost identical spatial arrangement, have very similar (and predictably low) rejection rates.

Although it is true that Torguud town-dwellers have a denser lifestyle (but not really the Kazakhs who, even as 'town'-dwellers, live very dispersed), they did not punish. It is true that the norms in town and among nomads (though differently nuanced) are largely the same because many factors contribute to the bidirectional flow of norms. First, nomads and town-dwellers are each other's kin, and there are many reciprocal ties between nomads and town-dwellers. Second, migration in livelihood goes both ways: many children of nomads become townsfolk and some townsfolk take up pastoralism. Third, even the children of town-dwellers spend the summers in the highlands assisting their herder relatives in order to escape the mosquitoes in the floodplains. Fourth, nomads are considered experts in tradition so that even though there is a tendency for the townsfolk to relax some norms, there is nevertheless a gravitational pull towards the nomads' standards, which are considered more genuine. But these arguments are not entirely persuasive because Sangu herders and farmers have different rejection rates even though they are members of the same ethnie. I believe the best answer is that the signal value of punishment is not much better in town than it is among the nomads. Interaction in town is far from intense. People mostly keep to themselves and immediate neighbors do not really share much community life unless they are relatives. Town life in fact feels oppressively desolate and ghost-townish, and the town itself is quite spread out, with considerable spacing between dwellings in some of its sections.

The signaling interpretation of the logic of third-party punishment I am defending here is similar to Smith and Bliege-Bird's (2000) account of the provision of public goods following from the benefits of signaling one's quality. In their explanation, public goods are produced if they require qualities that are costly to fake, and if advertising those qualities brings net benefits to the producer of public goods. Moralistic punishment is a public good, but it advertises nothing if it is not observed, which requires a relatively dense way of life. What I have suggested above is that with a sufficiently dense lifestyle, such punishment advertises 'commitment to the moral order', and this results in benefits to the punisher because s/he will then be preferred in reciprocal interactions due to the lower interaction risk this person is understood to represent. To make this work, however, moralistic punishment should be an *index* for the moral person, and a costly signal for would-be fakers (i.e. hypocrisy should be difficult). The solution to this requirement is at hand if it is the case that abiding by the moral order is a matter of emotional 'commitment' (see Hirschleifer 1987; Frank 1988). That is, if it is one's deep, non-negotiable, and non-calculating emotional commitment to the social norms that *causes* one to punish violations of it directed against third-parties, then one expects that the same emotional commitment makes violations by the same punisher unlikely. A 'faker' who lacks the emotional commitment, however, will find it difficult to incur the costs of punishment given that this requires an irrational short-term decision to incur considerable costs to provide a public good.

This signaling/ecological hypothesis may help explain the absence of any—even mild—punishment by third parties in Bulgan Sum. But a puzzle remains: why should there be a bias to exaggerate the costs to one's own bad behavior—as suggested above—even when one lives in a low-density herding society where 'bad people' are not punished?

Here is one possible answer. Given entry into adaptive zones where the signal value of punishment is low (e.g. low-density nomadic herding), then, as suggested earlier, a norm that 'punishing is bad' will be favored and become part of the moral order, because those who punished when nobody was around to see it would quickly learn that the costs of this behavior were larger than its benefits. But if entry into this kind of adaptive zone is recent and populations that occupy it are less common than more dense societies, and if they are not reproductively isolated from those in which the signal value of punishment is high, then evolution by natural selection has not been able to remove an innate tendency to develop an emotional commitment to the moral order that was selected for in denser social arrangements that are much older. Khazanov's (1994) well-founded argument that nomadic herding is very recent because it depends on nearby agricultural societies for its success lends support to this idea.

In conclusion, if the proximate psychological mechanisms that provide individuals with an emotional commitment to the moral order include a fear for one's reputation (because in the environments of history, punishment for 'bad people' has been common, and a fear for one's reputation adaptively prevents such punishment), this may lead to rationalizations about the costs to *one's own* 'bad' behavior that exaggerate the perceived costs beyond what is typically observed when *other* individuals are 'bad'.

My explanations are not exactly elegant, but they are not wholly implausible. Human historical processes, both genetic and cultural (to say nothing of their dual-inheritance interactions; Boyd and Richerson 1985), will produce eddies and whorls; elegance is not always what one sees in the data, so perhaps the best explanations will not always be terribly elegant either.

Why no in-group favoritism? Proposers made larger offers to *out-group* ethnics, and responders were not more likely to punish the fake, low, putative 'out-group' offers (or, for that matter, the real offers). These results are in conflict with the expectations of Social Identity Theory and Realistic Conflict Theory, so I revisit the relevant arguments in the context of this result.

Social Identity Theory (and its more recent offspring, self-categorization theory) posit that there is a generalized bias to favor one's in-group, regardless of how the in-group is construed, because one's self-esteem is partly a result of a positive evaluation of those groups in which one is a member (Tajfel and Turner 1979; Turner *et al.* 1987). This theory began as an attempt to explain a whole collection of results obtained with so-called 'minimal groups'. Such groups are formed by arbitrary criteria (e.g. by flipping a coin) and, at the extreme, they have no ecological validity (even to the point of enforcing complete anonymity between members). It was found that even such 'minimal' groups can promote an in-group favoritism bias in evaluations of, and in the allocation of positive rewards to, in-group and out-group members (the original and classic study is Tajfel 1970; see Tajfel 1982; Diehl 1990 for reviews). Social Identity Theory claims that self-esteem rises upon performing discriminatory behaviors with an in-group favoritism bias, and the preferential allocation of benefits to in-group members is performed in order to achieve that rise in self-esteem.

The problems with this research are coextensive with its strengths. Establishing that discriminatory behavior can take place between any kind of social categories seems important, but any real significance is contingent on allowing for broader interpretations. If what motivates the behavioral bias with minimal groups in the lab is very weak (as suggested by the very weak effect typically obtained), then perhaps it will get swamped by other biases in the context of more realistic group contrasts and situations. In such a case, we have no more than an interesting exotic result, relevant only to the exotic experimental context of minimal groups. Thus, the purported importance of the minimal group literature rests on the claim that here is evidence for a general in-group favoritism bias applicable to any and all intergroup contrasts, and therefore helpful for understanding all sorts of intergroup conflict, such as ethnic conflict. Such claims have indeed been made (Tajfel and Turner 1979). But such a powerful 'ingroup favoritism' bias predicts that in the Ultimatum

Game there will be a bias to favor the in-group responder, who will get higher offers than the out-group responder. This prediction is not incompatible with proposers who wish to make money, it merely says that proposers have a bias making them more reluctant to profit at the expense of the in-group rather than the out-group responder.

Consider first that the Ultimatum Game with an ethnicity manipulation forces the proposer to explicitly consider costs and benefits to self (the larger the share for the responder, the smaller the remainder is for the proposer), something that is absent in the minimal group experiments. That this might be important is suggested by the classical minimal group experiments themselves. The in-group favoritism differential is typically quite small, suggesting that perhaps a larger difference would make the allocator feel bad for having been too unfair to the minimal out-group member. If in-group enhancement were the only consideration, then surely participants would be choosing to maximize the difference in favor of the in-group. Dramatic evidence that allocators indeed weigh costs and benefits to their sense of 'fairness' comes from a study by Mummendey *et al.* (1992), where participants were found to be scrupulously fair in their allocation of a high-pitched blast of noise, which happens to be a sizable negative reward when compared to the symbolic points or almost worthless rewards typically used in minimal-group experiments. Thus, if people want to be 'fair,' a consideration of sizeable costs and benefits, which the design of the present experiment forces, may be partly responsible for erasing an abstract 'ingroup bias', if indeed such a thing exists.

But the 'ingroup bias' was not here merely erased. The effect goes in the *opposite* direction, and this requires explanation. The apparent mystery is compounded by the fact that these are ecologically valid groups, drenched in reality in a way that the minimal group paradigm explicitly tries to avoid. Intuitively, one would expect an in-group bias detectable in the context of minimal groups to grow as reality is added to the group contrast, but the opposite happened.

Realistic Conflict Theory explicitly tries to explain the behavior of realistic groups when they find themselves in conflict. This theory 'argues that groups become prejudiced toward one another because they are in conflict over real, tangible, material resources' (Sabini 1995: 104). Such prejudice in turn motivates discrimination with in-group favoritism for both positive and negative rewards. The *locus classicus* of Realistic Conflict Theory is the famous Robber's Cave experiment (Sherif *et al.* 1961) where it was found that pitting two teams of adolescents (the teams were formed at random) in different zero-sum contests increased hostility between them, and led to in-group cooperation for intergroup competition. The converse was also shown: giving them a common goal that could only be solved through cooperation reduced hostility and even caused friendly intergroup relations toward the end. From the perspective of this theory, I should have found in-group favoritism greater than the meager differentials found in minimal group experiments. After all, a resource is explicitly at stake.

There are two important differences between the groups in the Robber's Cave experiment, and the groups in the present Ultimatum Game: (1) in Robber's Cave the groups are formed at random and have a shallow history; in the present study the groups coming into the experiment are anything but random and they have a very long history; (2) in Robber's Cave realistic conflict was experimentally manipulated, and the conflict, created as it was by the rewards at stake, was immediately palpable and structurally clear; in the present experiment, realistic conflict must be inferred from the ethnographic situation and is less directly palpable and structurally clear. The first point makes Robber's Cave a less good case for realistic conflict than the present study, and the second point a better one.

Do these considerations cancel out exactly? It is impossible to say. What *can* be said is that the present study has groups for which a *sense* of realistic conflict is plausible. The district of Bulgan Sum is composed primarily of Torguud Mongols and Kazakhs. It would be remarkable if Torguud Mongols, living as they are in a state calling itself Mongolia, with an overwhelming majority of ethnic Mongols, did not have at least a vague proprietary feeling about the territory—especially considering that right next door is a state calling itself Kazakhstan where ethnic Kazakhs—at least until recently—could automatically get a passport if they so wished. Moreover, Kazakhs are expanding faster than Mongols because they reproduce more than twice as fast and migrate away only about a third as much as Torguuds do, or less. Again, it would be remarkable if Mongols didn't at least vaguely perceive this as a form of 'invasion'. Where the Mongols are 'proprietary', the Kazakhs could be expected to be 'defensive' about the very same issues. Moreover, in the 1940s there was much raiding and killing going on by bands of outlaws that were eventually driven back behind the Chinese border. The outlaws were of Kazakh ethnicity (followers of a charismatic bandit by the name of Osman). Some of my ethnographic observations suggest that this historical episode does not aid interethnic trust on the part of the Mongols, and neither does the fact that the land across the neighboring Chinese border is populated by Kazakhs. It is certainly true that interethnic relations are on the surface quite friendly, if for the most part distant, and it is not difficult to find positive stereotypes of the Kazakh among the Mongols (as hardworking, responsible, etc.; of course, these could have a double-edge, because it is precisely by doing well that the Kazakhs will take over the territory). Positive stereotypes of Mongols are much harder to find among the Kazakh. What I am arguing for is no more than a vague sense by local actors that the groups are in conflict, even if in a weak and diffuse sense.

From the point of view of Realistic Conflict Theory, this *could* lead to an out-group favoritism bias in proposers. If the perception of conflict makes responders more likely to reject out-group offers, *and proposers anticipate this*, then they might make higher offers to the out-group responder. However, to do so would not be an in-group favoritism strategy for the proposers. So this explanation has the proposers caring more about making money than favoring the in-group, but not the responders. It is not a straightforward prediction from Realistic Conflict Theory, and neither does it seem plausible. Besides, the behavior of responders showed no such bias so the anticipation of proposers would have to be imagined rather than empirically based (though, admittedly, this is far from impossible, in principle).

The way to maximize satisfaction of an in-group favoritism bias, in the absence of competing biases, would be for proposers to try to offend out-group responders but make fair offers to the in-group responders. Every proposer should reason that low offers to the out-group and fair or hyper-fair offers to the in-group will result in either: (1) low gains for the out-group with large gains for the in-group; or (2) zero gain for the out-group with moderate gains for the in-group. Responders should reason that any offer from an in-group proposer should be taken but that any offer from an out-group proposer should be rejected. Adding a preference for money will weaken the size of these effects but should not tilt them in the opposite direction. However, the observed effects are in the opposite direction.

Thus, neither theory just considered can easily account for the fact that out-group responders get larger offers. This should be troubling to Social Categorization Theory and Realistic Conflict Theory, given that the present experiment has ecologically valid groups and presents players with cost/benefit decisions more like those they encounter in the real world. The result obtained here suggests that the experimental evidence on which Social Categorization Theory relies is indeed exotic, and that more work is needed to fill out Realistic Conflict Theory.

What can account for the out-group bias found in my experiment? One possible answer is that ethnies are norm-groups (see Barth 1969) and in human cognition they are *naturalized* norm-groups, where the differences in normative behavior are believed to follow from what is imagined to be an inherent nature (Gil-White 1999, 2001*a, b*, 2002*a*, 2003). Thus, a Torguud proposer, say, may reason that she has a pretty good guess of how low she can go before a Torguud responder punishes, and that an offer only slightly above that can be made with little risk of rejection. However, the punishing threshold of a Kazakh responder—underlain as it is by a foreign 'nature'—is something they feel less equipped to guess. These considerations, plus the reasonable assumption that participants follow a return-maximizing strategy within the framework of assumptions they make about the world, may lead proposers to 'play it safe'. If they have no way to judge where the out-group punishing threshold is, they may take what they believe is the in-group punishing threshold as an anchor, and either offer at that level, or a little higher.

There is no opportunity for this sort of calculation in minimal group experiments because: (1) there is no conflict between favoring oneself versus the other player (by contrast, in this Ultimatum Game the opportunity cost of a bad strategy was large because the money at play was about a week's salary); and (2) group norms are irrelevant. In the Robber's Cave experiment, a conflict between individual and group benefit does exist, but in point of fact there was very little free riding there. The difference in the Ultimatum Game may be that the game is played anonymously, and so the lack of monitoring strengthens selfish motives. This consideration suggests that Realistic Conflict Theory and the hypothesis just offered are not necessarily in conflict. It may be simultaneously true that ethnic groups are perceived as naturalized norm groups, and that realistic conflict will promote discriminatory in-group altruism when there is good monitoring.

Not every participant was articulate under cross-examination about why the out-group had received a better offer. But from those who were, I obtained two main categories of responses, which I paraphrase and stylize: (1) 'I know my coethnics. I know how low I can go without getting a rejection. Them [outgroup members] I don't really know, so I play it safe'; and (2) 'I don't want to foster any misunderstanding between the groups.' Another plausible reason for giving higher offers to the out-group is an anticipation that out-group members will be likely to punish low offers *coming from an out-group member*. However, nobody gave such an explanation. The two main categories of introspections are not necessarily mutually exclusive. Take, for example, the player who made the only *hyper*-fair offer in Study 2. This was a very polite and agreeable Kazakh man, and his hyper-fair offer went to the out-group responder (0.56). After I suggested that he had made such a 'nice' offer because he wanted to make sure the responder accepted and he got his money, he replied: 'That, in the first place. But, in the second place, I don't want to hurt people's feelings.' I do not doubt his sincerity, but his coethnics have feelings too, and he only offered 0.38 to the in-group responder. The fact that 'people's feelings' are more carefully respected when they belong to an out-group member speaks volumes about the plausible instrumentality of such considerations: players want, first and foremost, to make money, but they err on the side of safety when they feel insecure about the location of the punishing threshold. If ethnic groups are norm groups, and our psychology has evolved to deal with this (Gil-White 1999, 2001*a*, 2003) then a feeling of insecurity about the location of the punishing threshold is more likely with the out-group responder.

This, of course, does not mean that certain in-groups are not favored discriminatorily in the real world, nor does it mean that ethnies are not among the social categories that more easily generate such in-group favoritism. Evidence for both propositions is already overwhelming from the historical and current data on nationalism, etc. What this result suggests, however, is that an abstract 'ingroup favoritism bias', applicable to any and all in-groups is weak at best, and not particularly illuminating as the basis of an account of intergroup discrimination and conflict.

CONCLUSION

The results of the ultimatum experiments in Bulgan Sum support the hypothesis that performance in this game is significantly influenced by local culture and the ideas concerning fair offers and punishment contained therein. Proposers were fearful of possible responder punishment, but a taste for punishment failed to manifest itself among the responders. This is counterintuitive in light of the results which have been obtained in these experiments when conducted with western (or westernized) populations. However, they are plausible and comprehensible when evaluated against the backdrop of a local culture that stresses the importance of one's reputation as a moral person, but considers active punishment itself immoral.

Two major theories in social psychology—Social Categorization Theory and Realistic Conflict Theory—have tried to explain intergroup animosity with experimental setups that involved groups very different, and decision matrices very alien, to the ones that ultimately one wishes to understand (e.g. actors who weigh costs to themselves in the context of interethnic conflict). The results of this experiment suggest Social Categorization Theory has not given us a very good foothold into the cognitive processes important to intergroup conflict, and that Realistic Conflict Theory is incomplete and more attention should be given to the role of monitoring.

In the future, economic experiments will probably offer a better avenue to an investigation of competing claims about the cognitive basis of intergroup conflict. If a good theoretical model must be a good caricature of a real causal process, then a good experiment must be a good caricature of a real situation (Gil-White 2001c). The paradigm of experimental economics has the advantage of allowing for decision matrices involving realistic costs and benefits. So far, however, the experimental literature in economics has mostly neglected the possible effects of social category membership on decisions. Given the fact that many decisions that we make are framed in terms of the roles and categories we inhabit as social actors, this is a question obviously deserving close scrutiny. The present study produces no definitive answers, but it suggests that here lies a rich arena for further work.

APPENDIX A: PROTOCOL FOR PROPOSER
RECRUITMENT IN STUDY 1

Note, I refer to myself (Fran, my nickname) in the third-person throughout because of the role-playing used in the explanations. In the explanations, I pretend to be one of the participants, and Boldoo, my assistant, the other, for illustrative/explanatory purposes.

'Fran is doing an experiment. This experiment is like a game. I will explain shortly. If you participate, I will pay you T1600.'

(1) 'This experiment has been done many times, but always in America or else in Europe, and always with city people. For this reason some anthropologists are going to Asia and Africa and will do this experiment again with country folk.'
(2) 'Okay. Boldoo and I will now show you how to do this. This experiment is like a game, and you can make some money.'
   • 'For example, make believe I am not Fran. Okay? Right now I am this guy Tsatsral, a Torguud. Tsatsral and Boldoo will play together now.'
   • 'Fran gave Tsatsral these T8000. Tsatsral is the proposer, and Boldoo is the responder. Since Tsatsral is the proposer, with this money I will make a partition. I will keep some of the money, and the rest I will offer to Boldoo.'
   • 'Since Boldoo is the responder he will get to decide once I make my partition. If Boldoo allows my partition, he will get the money I offered, and I will get the money that I kept. But if Boldoo does not allow my partition, then Boldoo and Tsatsral get nothing, and Fran will again collect this money.'
(3) [Here I bring the money out and I do the example visually by placing the offer at Boldoo's feet, and my offer at mine.
   • 'For example: After getting T8000 from Fran, I will partition the money thus: I keep T6500, and to Boldoo I offer T1500.'
   • 'Boldoo is the responder, so if he allows this partition, he will get those T1500, and I, Tsatsral, will get these T6500. But if Boldoo does not allow this partition, nobody gets anything and Fran will again take all this money back from us.'
(4) 'All right. Now Boldoo and I will play three examples.' [The examples are all acted out. I pretend to take the money from

an invisible Fran to my left and explain that me, Tsatsral, is taking the money from Fran. Then I proceed to make the partition and, once done, I ask Boldoo whether he will allow it. The partitions and Boldoo's scripted answers are as follows.]

- Offer: T1500. Response: Won't allow.
- Offer: T4000. Response: Will allow.
- Offer: T3000. Response: Will allow.

[After each response, I explain exactly what that means. In the first example, after Boldoo says he doesn't allow it, I collect all of the money and pretend to give it back to the 'air' Fran to my left, explaining that since the offer was not allowed, nobody gets any of this money and it all goes back to Fran. In the second example I explain that since Boldoo allowed the partition, he gets exactly T4000, the money offered, and I get exactly T4000, making a motion for Boldoo to pocket the money and doing the same with my money myself. The third example is as the second except for the quantities apportioned.]

(5) 'Now we will ask *you*.' [This is the test. I present them with the following examples and ask them to tell me what will happen. Every example is acted out in full just like the previous ones.]

- 'If Tsatsral makes the following partition: T6000 for Tsatsral, and T2000 for Boldoo, what will happen if Boldoo allows the partition? (...) What will happen if Boldoo doesn't allow the partition? (...)'
- [As above with T4500 for Tsatsral, and T2000 for Boldoo].

(6) 'Okay. You've understood now. But this is not exactly the real experiment. We will now explain the real experiment.' [At this point I lay on the floor the twenty pictures of the responders.]

- 'You will be a proposer. Among these twenty people is your responder. I cannot tell you which one is your responder because you may not know that. Everybody will play anonymously.'
- 'You will now make a partition. After you make the partition, I will go to the responder's home and will show him/her your partition. [This was explained with role-playing again where I pretended to go to Boldoo's *ger* (who is now standing in for the responder) and went through the

motions of how the partition would be explained to the responder.] Then, that person will decide: he/she will either allow your partition, or not.'

- 'Your responder may not know who *you* are. I will show the responder twenty pictures, including your own, but I will not tell him/her who the proposer is. All participants will always be anonymous.'
- 'Other than who you are, the responder will know everything. He/she will know how many *tögrög* I gave you. I will also tell him, of those T8000, how many you offered and how many you propose to keep. I will also explain to the responder exactly what will happen if he/she allows, or doesn't allow the partition. The responder will know everything. The only thing the responder doesn't know is who you are.'

APPENDIX B: PROTOCOL FOR RESPONDER RECRUITMENT IN STUDY 2

Start with the protocol for responder recruitment used in Study 1. Once finished, administer the test shown below. Every one of the smallest level points represents an item of information that is important for the responder to understand. Every answer following each of these questions is the information that the responder should supply, and the explanation that the tester must give should the responder's answer fail. Only moderately good-to-excellent performance on the first pass is acceptable. Anybody failing badly on the first pass, or showing great difficulty in understanding the points she got wrong, must be excluded from participation in the experiment. Those who fail on the basic points concerning the mechanics of the game should be considered to have failed miserably, and should not be allowed into the experiment. (Note: The test for proposers was essentially identical, with obvious modifications to make it specific to proposers.)

I. Tests whether responders understand that the money is not the proposer's, or mine, but the school's, and that the proposer is offering money because otherwise she may not play.

- **Why will the proposer offer you money?** A: The answer to this question could be anything at all, and will guide which of the following questions is used, or which is used first. If there is long hesitation just jump into the following specific questions.
    A. **What happens if the proposer doesn't want to make a partition?** A: He may not play unless he makes a partition. If he doesn't want to make a partition, he may not play.
    B. **Whose money is the proposer playing with?** A: He got money from Fran to play with. This is not Fran's money. The school gave Fran money to do this experiment with.
    C. **Are we playing with real or pretend money?** A: Real money.

II. Tests whether responders understand the mechanics of the game and the consequences of their decision.

- **What will you do after I show you the proposer's partition?** A: The answer to this question could be anything at all, and will guide which of the following questions is used, or which is used first. If there is long hesitation just jump into the following specific questions.
    A. **After seeing the proposer's partition, may you choose not to allow it?** A: Yes.
    B. **After seeing the proposer's partition, may you choose to allow it?** A: Yes. Whether I allow or not the partition is my decision.
    C. **If you don't allow the proposer's partition, what will Fran do?** A: Fran will not give me any money, but he will not give any money to the proposer either.
        ⇒ **Where does the money go, then?** A: Fran will give it back to the school.
        ⇒ **If you don't allow the partition, does the proposer make another offer?** A: No. We play only once. The proposer only offers once, and after I make my decision that is the end of the game. The proposer cannot make another offer.
    D. **If you allow the partition, what will Fran do?** A: Fran will give me the money offered to me by the proposer,

and he will also go back to the proposer's *ger* and give him the remaining money.

⇒ **Does the school care that it may never see this money again?** A: The school does not care at all. I must not decide out of concern for the school. The school gave this money to do the experiment and it doesn't need the money back.

E. **How much money will Fran give the proposer to play with?** A: T8000.

F. **Does the proposer keep that money?** A: No. Fran gives it to the proposer merely to see the proposer's partition, then Fran takes the money again. The proposer gets nothing unless I allow the partition.

G. **Can the proposer make any partition that she wants?** A: Yes.

H. **Will you and the proposer play with real or pretend money?** A: For real money.

III. Tests whether the responder understands what the proposer knows.

• **What will I tell the proposer?** A: The answer to this question could be anything at all, and will guide which of the following questions is used, or which is used first. If there is long hesitation just jump into the following specific questions.

A. **Does the proposer know who you are?** A: No. Everybody is playing anonymously.

B. **Does the proposer know what happens if you allow the offer?** A: Yes. The proposer knows that if I allow the offer, Fran will give me the money offered, and he will also give the remainder to the proposer.

C. **Does the proposer know what happens if you don't allow the offer?** A: Yes. The proposer knows that if I don't allow the offer, Fran will not give me any money, but he will not give any money to the proposer either, and will return the money to the school.

D. **Will Fran explain to the proposer what the responder knows?** A: Yes. Fran will tell the proposer, 'The responder knows I gave you T8000 to play with.' Fran will also tell the proposer, 'The responder knows what happens if she allows or does not allow your offer.'

    E. **What is the only thing that the proposer doesn't know?**
    A: My name.
    F. **What is the only thing that you don't know?** A: The
    proposer's name.

REFERENCES

Barth, F. (ed.) (1969). *Ethnic Groups and Boundaries: The Social Organization of Cultural Differences*. Boston: Little Brown & Co.

Boyd, R. and Richerson, P. J. (1985). *Culture and the Evolutionary Process*. Chicago, IL: University of Chicago Press.

Diehl, M. (1990). 'The minimal group paradigm: Theoretical explanations and empirical findings', *European Review of Social Psychology*, *1*, 263–92.

Gil-White, F. J. (1999). 'How thick is blood? The plot thickens...: If ethnic actors are primordialists, what remains of the circumstantialist/ primordialist controversy?', *Ethnic and Racial Studies*, *22*, 789–820.

——(2001*a*). 'Are ethnic groups biological "species" to the human brain?: Essentialism in our cognition of some social categories', *Current Anthropology*, *42*, 515–54.

——(2001*b*). 'Sorting is not categorization: A critique of the claim that Brazilians have fuzzy racial categories', *Journal of Cognition and Culture*, *1*, 219–49.

——(2001*c*). 'A good experiment of choice behavior is a good caricature of a real situation', *Brain and Behavioral Sciences*, *24*, 409.

——(2002*a*). 'The cognition of ethnicity: Native category systems under the field-experimental microscope', *Field Methods*, *14*, 170–98.

——(2003). 'Is ethnocentrism adaptive?: An ethnographic analysis under review', *Nomadic Peoples*.

Frank, R. H. (1988). *Passions within Reason: The Strategic Role of the Emotions*. New York: W.W. Norton.

Haidt, J. (2001). 'The emotional dog and its rational tail: A social intuitionist approach to moral judgment', *Psychological Review*, *108*, 814–34.

——Koller, S., and Dias, M. (1993). 'Affect, culture, and morality, or is it wrong to eat your dog?', *Journal of Personality and Social Psychology*, *65*, 613–28.

Henrich, J. (2000). 'Does culture matter in economic behavior? Ultimatum game bargaining among the Machiguenga', *American Economic Review*, *90*, 973–9.

Hirshleifer, J. (1987). 'On the emotions as guarantors of threats', in J. Dupré (ed.), *The Latest on the Best: Essays in Evolution and Optimality*, Cambridge, MA: MIT Press.

Khazanov, A. (1994). *Nomads and the Outside World*. Madison, WI: University of Wisconsin Press.

Mummendey, A., Simon, B., Dietze, C., Grünert, M., Haeger, G. *et al.* (1992). 'Categorization is not enough: Intergroup discrimination in negative outcome allocation', *Journal of Experimental Social Psychology*, *28*, 155–44.

Sabini, J. (1995). *Social Psychology*. New York and London: Norton.

Sherif, M., Harvey, O. J., White, B. J., Hood, W. R., and Sherif, C. W. (1961). *Intergroup Conflict and Cooperation: The Robber's Cave Experiment*. Norman, OK: University of Oklahoma Book Exchange.

Tajfel, H. (1970). 'Experiments in intergroup discrimination', *Scientific American*, *223*, 96–102.

—— (1982). 'Social psychology of intergroup relations', *Annual Review of Psychology*, *33*, 1–39.

—— and Turner, J. C. (1979). 'An integrative theory of integroup conflict', in S. Worchel and W. G. Austin (eds), *The Social Psychology of Intergroup relations*, Monterey, CA: Brooks/Cole, pp. 33–47.

Turner, J. C., Hogg, M. A., Oakes, P. J., Reicher, S. D., and Wetherell, M. S. (1987). *Rediscovering the Social Group: A Self-Categorization Theory*. Oxford and New York: Blackwell.

Smith, E. A. and Bliege Bird, R. L. (2000). 'Turtle hunting and tombstone opening: Public generosity as costly signaling', *Evolution and Human Behavior*, *21*, 245–61.

Szynkiewicz, S. (1993). 'Mongolia's nomads build a new society again: social structures and obligations on the eve of the private economy', *Nomadic Peoples*, *33*, 73–103.

10

Kinship, Familiarity, and Trust: An Experimental Investigation

Abigail Barr

INTRODUCTION

Between independence and 1997 approximately 71,000 Zimbabwean households were resettled into new villages on land previously owned and farmed by commercial farmers. The majority of these households were resettled on an individual basis. Thus, instead of living within villages made up almost exclusively of their kin, as do most other Zimbabweans, they now live in villages almost entirely made up of unrelated households. In this regard, their lives have more in common with their urban compatriots than with other rural Zimbabweans and, for this reason, the programme of land reform can be seen as a rare and useful natural experiment. One aspect of urbanization has been imposed upon these people without the imposition of the many other aspects, such as more crowded living, changing livelihoods, greater dependence on money, greater anonymity, and greater exposure to all sorts of markets, to advertizing and to both local and international media.

One possible outcome of this process could be an erosion of trust, which, in turn, could lead to lower economic efficiency and slower economic development (Arrow 1972, 1974; Fukuyama 1995; LaPorta *et al.* 1997). Here, I use the Zimbabwean natural experiment to investigate whether and why resettlement among non-kin leads to a persistent reduction in trust. I do this by comparing the behavior of people in the resettled villages with that of a control

Many thanks to Michael Shambare, for his tireless efforts in the field. Thank you also to Bill Kinsey, coordinator of the resettlement monitoring exercise in which all of the experimental subjects are involved. Finally, thank you to the participants of the MacArthur Foundation Conference on Cross-Cultural Experimental Economics, and the current and former members of the CSAE who offered insightful comments. All remaining errors are my own.

group of people in non-resettled villages during two economic games. The games are the Trust Game originally designed by Berg, Dickhaut, and McCabe (1995) and the Ultimatum Game (Ultimatum Game). The former provides data on trust and reciprocity. The latter provides data relating to behavioral rules about sharing and fairness, which may also have a bearing on reciprocating behavior. Details of the games are given in Chapter 2.

To the author's knowledge, neither of these games have ever been used to look at the effects of kinship ties on social interaction. Glaeser *et al.* (1999) have used a variant of the Trust Game to investigate the effects of social connectedness on trust: they introduced pairs of players (all Harvard undergraduates) to each other prior to play and then asked whether and how they knew one another. Using the resulting data in conjunction with that generated during the game, they found that greater social connection led to larger investments, that is, more trusting behavior, by first players and concluded that this was because greater social connectedness implied greater opportunities for post play punishment in the event of non-reciprocation. This conclusion, however, calls into question whether their experiment is about trust at all. According to a growing number of researchers, trusting behavior involves making oneself vulnerable to exploitation by potential trustees (see, for example, Hardin 1991; Yamagishi and Yamagishi 1994). A trusting agent accepts this vulnerability because he or she expects that the trustee, rather than exploiting this vulnerability, will respond positively to the trust that has been placed in him or her, that is, will reciprocate. Berg *et al.*'s original design ensures that an investing first player assumes some vulnerability by making the game one-shot and by preserving player anonymity. If the social relations in the Glaeser *et al.* (1999) experiment served to make post play punishment easier, they were reducing the vulnerability of the first players and, hence, the need for trust, rather than increasing the level of trust.

With this in mind, the social contexts, that is, low density of kinship ties in resettled villages and high density of kinship ties in non-resettled villages, were incorporated into the Zimbabwean experiment in such a way that the one-shot, anonymous nature of the original Berg *et al.* (1995) game was maintained. The players were paired with people from their own village and informed accordingly, but they were not told the precise identity of their partners.

Thus, while each player did not know the specific behavioral characteristics of their playing partner, they would have had some idea about the distribution of behavioral characteristics across the population from which their partner had been drawn. To ensure consistency, the same principle was applied in the Ultimatum Game.

The behavior observed in resettled and non-resettled villages in the context of these two games was as follows:

1. *Trust game*: See Figures 10.1 and 10.2. (a) In both subject pools the observed outcomes deviated from those predicted under selfish money maximization. On average first players invested more than zero and the second players gave more than zero back. (b) In both subject pools the proportion given back by the second players did not depend on the amount invested by first players. (c) On average, resettled first players invest significantly less. (d) In contrast, there was no discernible difference in the proportions given back by second players.

2. *Ultimatum game*: See Figures 10.3 and 10.4. (a) In both subject pools the observed outcome deviated from those predicted under selfish money maximization. On average, first players offered more than zero to the second players. In addition, rejections by second players are observed in both subject pools. (b) In both subject pools, one distinct modal offer

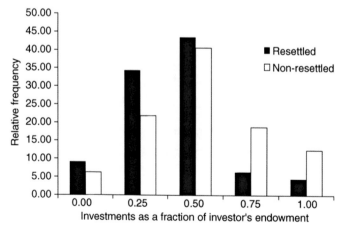

FIG. 10.1. Distribution of investments in the Trust Game in resettled and non-resettled villages (investor's endowment $E = 20$ Zim$)

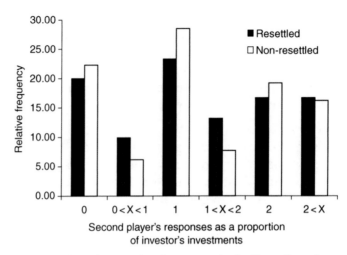

Fɪɢ. 10.2. Distribution of proportional responses in the Trust Game in resettled and non-resettled villages

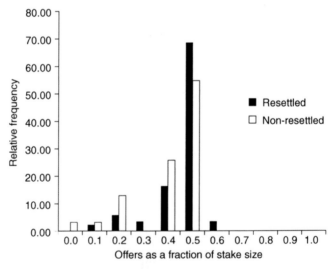

Fɪɢ. 10.3. Distribution of offers in the Ultimatum Game in resettled and non-resettled villages (stake size $S = 50$ Zim$)

corresponding to the 50–50 or fair division of the money was observed. (c) Resettled first players were significantly less likely to make a less than fair offer. (d) In both subject pools the probability of rejection was greater than zero for all

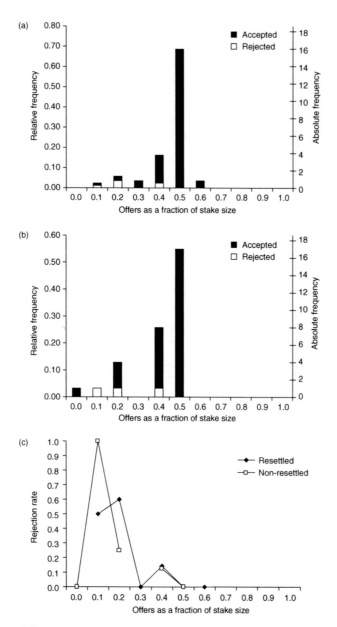

FIG. 10.4. Offers and rejections in the Ultimatum Game in (a) resettled villages
($n = 86$, stake size $S = 50$ Zim\$), (b) non-resettled villages ($n = 31$, stake size $S = 50$
Zim\$), (c) rejection rates as a function of offer size in the Ultimatum Game in
resettled and non-resettled villages (stake size $S = 50$ Zim\$)

less than fair offers and was inversely related to offer size. (e) There was no evidence to suggest that either the overall rate of rejection or the rate of rejection for given offers varied between the two subject pools, although the power of these tests was compromised somewhat by the low number of rejections.

In general, these results are consistent with there being no differences in socially transmitted behavioral rules between resettled and non-resettled villages. They are also consistent with the hypothesis that resettled villagers are neither more nor less altruistic or loyal toward their co-villagers than non-resettled villagers. Finally, they are consistent with the hypothesis that resettled villagers behave more cautiously when in strategic situations with their co-villagers. This might be due to the lower density in kinship ties, they are less familiar with one another's behavioral characteristics.

The experiment was designed to control for a variety of other factors that might lead to observed variations in behavior between the two subject pools (see section on 'Experimental Design'). This notwithstanding, the number and gender mix of people in each experimental session did vary. Econometric techniques were employed to control for these factors *ex post* (see section on 'Results'). There is an issue of self-selection bias that cannot be tackled using the available data. However, it is likely that the bias is acting to suppress rather than create the observed variations in behavior (see section entitled, 'Discriminating between familiarity and loss aversion and the issue of self selection').

EXPERIMENTAL DESIGN

Sample design

The households from which the players in each of the subject pools originate are participants in an on-going monitoring exercise designed to assess the effects of resettlement in Zimbabwe. This monitoring exercise involves households from twenty-two resettled villages spread across three resettlement areas, each with very different agro-climatic characteristics, and six non-resettled villages, two situated on the edge of each resettlement area.

All of the resettled villages in this study were created in 1982, shortly after independence. They were among the first resettled villages to be created. All of the households in these villages chose to resettle. Some squatted before being officially resettled, while the majority awaited the government's approval. Some were escaping landlessness, others, horrific memories associated with the struggle for independence. But whatever the reason for resettlement, it is safe to assume that there were many more households in similar situations who did not resettle, either because their applications were unsuccessful or because they found traditional means of accessing land and dealing with personal trauma more attractive.

Like those in non-resettled villages, the resettled households earn the large majority of their income from cash crop farming. Maize and groundnuts are grown to be sold and for own consumption, cotton, tobacco, and paprika are grown to be sold, and beans, vegetables, and, in some villages, rice are grown for own consumption. In all three areas, but especially in one, cattle rearing provides an additional, important source of income. Collective effort relating to both cash crop production and cattle rearing is rare. Some villagers are involved in collective tobacco growing and drying, market gardening, and small livestock raising projects. However, in all but one village these are peripheral to primary income earning and subsistence activities. Projects of this kind are more likely to be found in resettled villages, while traditional labour-sharing arrangements are more likely to be found in communal villages. These arrangements are of particular importance to households with absent senior males. Until 1992 resettled household heads were not allowed to seek waged employment. This has now changed, but new opportunities for such employment are very scarce.

Where the resettled villages differ most from their non-resettled counterparts is in their kinship structure. The Zimbabwean resettlement exercise in the early 1980s involved individual household applications and placements. Thus, the majority of resettled households live among neighbours who are highly diverse with respect to kin group. This contrasts starkly with the non-resettled villages in which, with few exceptions, every household is related to every other. The two types of village also differ in age. However, here it is unclear what the comparable ages of the non-resettled villages are. All of the non-resettled villages assumed their current locations during the 1940s and 1950s. These dates do not, however, represent the point in time when the village inhabitants or their ancestors started living together. In this sense the non-resettled villages' ages are much greater but indeterminate.

In two out of the three resettlement areas the monitoring exercise involves all the households in each of the randomly selected villages. In the third resettlement area and in the six non-resettled villages a random sample of households is involved. To the extent possible the samples of subjects for the experiment matched the sample of households in the monitoring exercise. Thus, the experiment involved between eight and forty households in each of the twenty-two resettled villages and sixteen and twenty-four households in each of the six non-resettled villages.

Each household was asked to send one adult (above the age of 14) to the experimental session in their village. The chairman or headman of each village was charged with the duty of ensuring both that the volunteers arrived at the session and that between forty and sixty percent of the volunteers were women. Approximately half of the volunteers (53 percent in the resettled villages and 51 percent in the non-resettled villages) were heads of households. Each volunteer played one or other game and was either a first or second player. Allocations of games and roles were determined randomly prior to the start of each session. In sixteen of the twenty-eight villages both games were played. In the remaining twelve the number of households in the monitoring exercise and hence the number of volunteers was less than eighteen and so only one game selected at random was played. The Trust Game was played by 109 pairs in resettled villages and thirty-two pairs in non-resettled villages. The Ultimatum Game was played by eighty-six pairs of players in resettled villages and thirty-one pairs in non-resettled villages.

Procedural design

Experimenters working in developing countries, especially in rural areas, usually find it necessary to adopt procedures that deviate significantly from those typically employed in the United States. This is made necessary by the generally low level of education and the potentially high incidence of illiteracy among subjects and the consequent need to test the understanding of each subject verbally before they play. I adopted a procedural design similar to Henrich's (2000) to deal with these problems. During a pilot in three villages a script for each game was developed in Shona, the local language in all the villages (English translations of full scripts contained in Appendix A).[1] Each script contained three components: a detailed and repetitive description of the game; a set of examples and questions showing how particular combinations of decisions yield particular pay-offs for each player; and, for second players only, a description of what their corresponding first players had decided to do. For the Ultimatum Game the same set of examples was used for each player, while for the Trust Game one set was used for all first players and another for all second players. The sets were designed to demonstrate the key features of the games, while minimizing the extent to which players might be led to behave in certain ways.

Once the pilot was over the scripts were adhered to in every session. When players had questions, the relevant part of the script was repeated. Players who could not demonstrate that they understood the games were not allowed to play. The need to test players' understanding verbally rendered a double blind procedure impractical. Hence, potential subject-experimenter effects need to be considered.[2] It is quite possible, for example, that the relatively large amounts invested by first players and returned by second players as compared with the US undergraduates observed by Berg, Dickhaut, and McCabe (1995), reflect the presence of such effects in the Zimbabwean experiment. To minimize the likelihood of subject-experimenter effects leading to observed differences in behavior between the two Zimbabwean subject pools great care was taken to follow the same procedure with each player. To the extent possible even hand movements were standardized. This notwithstanding different subject-experimenter effects on male and female players could have biased the results.[3] While the proportion of females drawn from each subject pool remained within the prescribed limits, there was some variation: 44 and 56 percent of players were female in resettled and non-resettled villages,

---

[1] Data from the pilot villages (twenty-eight pairs of players, seventeen from resettled villages, eleven from non-resettled villages, sixteen playing the investment game, twelve playing the Ultimatum Game) has been included throughout the analysis. Excluding these observations from the analysis does not alter any of the conclusions.

[2] Hoffman *et al.* (1994) provide evidence that subject/experimenter anonymity affects behavior. However, Roth (1995) reviews several other studies that report the opposite.

[3] Eagly and Crowley (1986) found that subject-experimenter effects can differ for men and women.

respectively. Econometric methods were used *ex post* to control for this possible source of bias.

In each session the players of both games were gathered together. Then one by one they were called to meet with the experimenter and a Shona-speaking research assistant in private. In the first pilot village the private meetings took place in a hut. However, in some villages the players felt that if a hut was used it would be too easy for unobserved eavesdroppers to overhear the discussion. In these instances tables, chairs, and screens hiding both the player's and the experimenter's hands were set up some distance from the waiting players in an area where eavesdroppers could be seen and asked to go away before they had learnt anything. Special measures were taken to prevent subject contamination. Prior to their individual meetings with the experimenter and research assistant, the players were told nothing about what they were going to do save that they would be playing games and could win some money. In addition, an appointed monitor was charged with the duty of preventing those who had already played returning to the group who had not yet played. There was an additional risk of contamination between villages in the few instances were they were close to one another. In these cases, the experimental sessions were held on the same or consecutive days. Interviews with all the players and some non-players indicated that between-village contamination was not occurring. Finally, there were concerns that in the villages where relatively few players were involved in the games, the sense of anomity felt by the players might be partially compromised.[4] While no experimental solution could be applied to this problem, econometric methods were used *ex post* to control for this possibility.

The Ultimatum Game was played with an initial stake of Zim$50 supplied to the first player as ten Zim$5 bills.[5] In the Trust Game each player was given Zim$20, supplied as four Zim$5 bills. These stakes were set to yield an average winning of approximately half a day's casual wage. Used rather than new Zim$5 bills were provided to the players throughout the experiment for two reasons. First, new bills are rarely seen in the areas where the experiments were being conducted and it was feared that their presence might affect

---

[4] Hoffman *et al.* (1994) show that reduced subject/subject anonymity leads to greater observed generosity.

[5] The exchange rate at the time of the experiments was Zim$37.95 per US$.

play. Second, the supply of new Zim$5 bills was limited and uncertain and it could have gravely affected the results had it become necessary to change from new to used bills half way through the experiment.

RESULTS

Village-level trust and reciprocity in the context of an investment decision

The results of the Zimbabwean Trust Game are similar to those of Berg Dickhaut, and McCabe (1995). In both subject pools less than 10 percent of first players made an investment of zero. This result could be seen as lending further support to the conclusion drawn by Berg, Dickhaut, and McCabe (1995). However, both sets of results could also be explained by altruism, defined here as being unconditional other-regarding behavior, while trust is conditional on there being an expectation of reciprocity and trustworthiness is conditional on having been trusted.

The distribution of investments made by the first players in both the subject pools are depicted in Figure 10.1 and corresponding descriptive and test statistics are reported in Table 10.1. While the mode investment is Zim$10 (0.50 of the investor's initial endowment) in both subject pools, only in resettled villages is the distribution of investments skewed to the left. This is reflected in the means which are Zim$8.03 (0.40 of the investor's initial endowment) and Zim$10.47 (0.52 of the investor's initial endowment) for resettled and non-resettled villages, respectively. According to a *t*-test, in which the variances of the two distributions are assumed equal (*p*-value for Levine's test for equality of variance is 0.50), this difference is significant at the 0.02 level. An Epps-Singleton test indicates that the difference in the distributions is significant at the 0.001 level.

The variation in first players' behavior between the two subject pools could be due to a difference in levels of altruism or loyalty toward co-villagers. There are two possible variants of this hypothesis. (1) There could be a lower level of altruism or loyalty in resettled villages due to the reduced density of kinship ties. Alternatively, (2) less altruistic or loyal people could be more likely to resettle. In either case we would expect to see the difference similarly

Abigail Barr

TABLE 10.1. First-player behavior in the Trust Game

	Non-resettled villages	Resettled villages
Number of playing pairs	32	109
Stake size		
(Zim$)	20	20
Sub-game perfect equilibrium plays		
(number of pairs)	2	10
(proportion of pairs)	0.06	0.09
Mode investment		
(Zim$)	10	10
(proportion of stake)	0.50	0.50
Mean investment		
(Zim$)	10.47	8.03
(proportion of stake)	0.52	0.40
Standard deviation of investments		
(Zim$)	5.44	4.57
Levene's test for equality of variance in investments (p-value)	0.504	
t-test for equality of mean investments, equal variance assumed (p-value)	0.012	
t-test for equality of mean investments, equal variance not assumed (p-value)	0.026	
Epps-Singleton test for equality of distribution (p-value)	0.000	

reflected in the behavior of second players; where first players invest less, second players should also return less.

Alternatively or additionally the investments by the first players may reflect their expectations about what their fellow villagers will do when placed in the role of second player, the more they trust them to reciprocate the more they will invest. Bearing this in mind, we can formulate several other hypotheses as to why levels of investment differ between the two subject pools. Average levels of reciprocity could be lower in the resettled villages because: (3a) different behavioral rules apply between kin and non-kin; because (3b) either differences in the behavioral rules relating to reciprocity or differences in levels of adherence to those rules have emerged since resettlement; or because (3c) less reciprocating people are more likely to resettle. (4) There could be a greater variation in levels of reciprocity within resettled villages, perhaps because the inhabitants come from a wider variety of backgrounds. This would add to the uncertainty faced by first players and, assuming that they are loss averse, cause them to be more cautious in their investment decisions. (5) Independent of their being any real difference in the distribution of reciprocating behavior between the two subject pools, players in resettled villages may ascribe a greater variance to their expectations of reciprocity on the part of their fellow villagers because they are less familiar with their behavioral characteristics. This reduced familiarity could follow from the resettled villagers having less experience of each other in strategic situations. Finally, (6) independent of their being either a real or a perceived variation in reciprocal behavior, players in resettled villages could be more loss averse. This would occur if there was a tendency for more loss averse people to resettle.

The responses made by the second players are depicted in Figure 10.2 and corresponding descriptive and test statistics are reported in Table 10.2. The responses are presented as proportions or multiples of the amounts invested by the first players for two reasons. First, while investments and actual money responses are likely to be correlated simply because of the maths of the game, this is not true for proportional responses.[6] This being the case, we need to be wary of drawing inferences about reciprocating behavior from the actual money responses. Second, certain values of the proportional response lend themselves to easy interpretation. A proportional response of zero corresponds to self-interested money maximization, a proportional response of one corresponds to what one might call 'pure reciprocity', that is, returning exactly what was given, and a proportional response of two corresponds to what one might call 'pure sharing', that is, to dividing the total money in the game equally. Note that in both subject pools there are three modes in the distribution, one corresponding to each of these values. Clearly these values were focal points for the Zimbabwean second players in the game. This notwithstanding, we should not conclude

---

[6] The upper bound of the set of actual responses from which the second player can choose is directly proportional to the level of investment made by the first player. The upper bound of the set of proportional responses from which the second player can choose is constant at three, that is unrelated to the level of investment made by the first player.

TABLE 10.2. Second-player behavior in the Trust Game

	Non-resettled villages	Resettled villages
Number of responding second players[a]	30	99
Dominant mode response (expressed as a proportion of investment)	1.00	1.00
Mean response (expressed as a proportion of investment)	1.28	1.28
Rate of reciprocation (proportional response $\geqslant 1$)	0.70	0.72
Standard deviation of proportional response	0.96	1.04
Levene's test for equality of variance in responses (p-value)	0.698	
t-test for equality of mean responses, equal variance assumed (p-value)	0.983	
t-test for equality of mean responses, equal variance not assumed (p-value)	0.983	
Epps-Singleton test for equality of distribution (p-value)	0.906	

[a] A response is made only when the investment by the first player is greater than zero.

that this is because the values have the meanings described above.[7] It could simply be because the maths associated with these responses is easier.

The results provide no evidence of a variation in the distribution of proportional responses between the two subject pools. In both, the dominant mode is at one and a similar proportion of second players (72 and 70 percent in resettled and non-resettled villages respectively) returned at least this amount. Further, in both resettled and non-resettled villages second players returned an average of 1.28 times the investment made by first players. There is a difference in the standard deviations of second players' responses between the two subject pools but it is not statistically significant. Finally, an

[7] The Berg, Dickhaut, and McCabe (1995) data has only one mode at zero, while comparisons with Glaeser *et al.* (1999) are inappropriate because of variations in the maths.

Epps-Singleton test provides further evidence that second players' behavior does not vary between the two subject pools.

This absence of variation in the second players' behavior indicates that we should reject hypotheses (1) and (2). While the behavior of both first and second players may, in part, be driven by altruism or loyalty, there is no evidence that differences in altruism are accounting for the variation in first players' behavior. The absence of variation in the second players' behavior also suggests that we should reject hypotheses (3a), (3b), (3c), and (4). Resettled villagers appear to be no less reciprocating, in the sense that they are neither more nor less willing to return what is given to them, and no more varied in terms of what they return, than their non-resettled counterparts.[8]

Finally, we are left with hypotheses (5) and (6). The lower level of trust observed in resettled villages is due either to less familiarity and consequently greater uncertainty, or to greater loss aversion on the part of resettled villagers. I shall return to these after a discussion about the Ultimatum Game results.

The ultimatum game and behavioral rules relating to sharing and fairness

The Ultimatum Game results also contradict the assumptions of selfish, money maximization (see Figure 10.3 and Table 10.3). In resettled villages no first players offered zero, only two (2.3 percent) made the lowest possible positive offer of Zim$5 (0.10 of the original stake), and one of these offers was rejected. In non-resettled villages one (3.2 percent) first player offered zero and was accepted, while one offered Zim$5 (0.10 of the original stake) and was rejected.[9] In both subject pools the mode offer was Zim$25 (0.50 of the original stake). The dominance of this mode is striking, with 69 and 55 percent of first players in resettled and non-resettled villages, respectively, making such offers. Evidence of a variation in first

---

[8] Counter to hypotheses (3a), (3b), and (3c), one might be tempted to argue that the combination of lower investments by first players and *not* lower proportional responses by second players indicates that levels of reciprocity are in fact higher in resettled areas. Note, however, that neither the original experiment by Berg, Dickhaut, and McCabe (1995) nor the Zimbabwean experiment was a correlation found between the amount invested and the proportional response.

[9] The accepter of the zero offer explained that only someone in dire need of the money would offer zero, so how could she refuse.

TABLE 10.3. First- and second-player behavior in the Ultimatum Game

	Non-resettled villages	Resettled villages
Number of playing pairs	31	86
Stake size		
(Zim$)	50.00	50.00
Sub-game perfect equilibrium plays[a]		
(number of pairs)	2	1
(proportion of pairs)	0.06	0.01
Mode offer		
(Zim$)	25.00	25.00
(proportion of stake)	0.50	0.50
Mean offer		
(Zim$)	20.32	22.67
(proportion of stake)	0.41	0.45
Standard deviation of offers		
(Zim$)	6.94	5.07
Levene's test for equality of variance in offers (p-value)	0.073	
t-test for equality of means, equal variance assumed (p-value)	0.048	
t-test for equality of means, equal variance not assumed (p-value)	0.092	
Epps-Singleton test for equality of distribution (p-value)	0.425	
Offers of less than Zim$25		
(number of pairs)	14	24
(proportion of pairs)	0.45	0.28
Chi-square test for equality of proportion of offers less than Zim$25 ($p$-value)	0.079	
Rate of rejection		
(proportion)	0.10	0.07
Chi-square test for equality of rate of rejection (p-value)	0.629	
Rate of rejection of offers below Zim$25, 50% of stake	0.21	0.25
Rate of rejection of offers below Zim$10, 20% of stake	0.50	0.50
Highest offer rejected		
(Zim$)	20	20
(proportion of stake)	0.40	0.40

[a] First player offers zero or lowest possible nonzero amount and second player accepts.

players' behavior between the two subject pools is mixed. More super-fair offers combined with a relatively low tendency to make less than fair offers led to a mean offer of Zim$22.67 (0.45 of the original stake) in resettled villages compared with a mean of Zim$20.32 (0.41 of the original stake) in non-resettled villages. According to a *t*-test, in which equal variances are not assumed (*p*-value for Levine's test for equality of variance is 0.07), the difference between the means is statistically significant at the 0.10 level. However, the *t*-test may be inappropriate in this context as the underlying distributions may not be continuous. With this in mind, two tests reflecting the discreteness of the distributions were performed. An Epps-Singleton test suggests that there is no variation in first player behavior between the two subject pools, while a Chi-squared test, based on the proportion of first players from the two subject pools who made less than fair offers, yields a statistic that is significant at the 0.08 level. These mixed results can be reconciled as follows: while the 50–50 split is the dominant and probably the only behavioral rule relating to sharing in both subject pools, there is a tendency for some players to deviate from this rule by offering less and that tendency is greater in non-resettled villages.

Roth *et al.* (1991) argued that offers in Ultimatum Game vary between subject pools because either behavioral rules vary or the willingness to risk rejection varies. In the case of the former, higher average offers do not lead to lower overall rejection rates, while any given offer is more likely to be rejected. In the case of the latter, higher average offers do lead to lower overall rejection rates, while any given offer is equally likely to be rejected. The data on first players' behavior favored the latter explanation. Our ability to confirm this conclusion by identifying the prescribed pattern in rejection rates is somewhat hampered by the low overall number and rate of rejections (see Figure 10.4(a–c) and Table 10.3). The overall rates of rejection are 7 percent (six out of eighty-six) and 10 percent (three out of thirty-one) in resettled and non-resettled villages, respectively. The rates increase to 25 and 21 percent, respectively, for offers under Zim$25 (0.50 of the original stake) and to 50 percent in both subject pools for offers under Zim$10 (0.20 of the original stake). One of the more striking results is the greater than zero likelihood of offers as high as Zim$20 (0.40 percent of the original stake) being rejected in both subject pools. These results indicate neither a variation in the overall rejection rate nor a variation in rejection rates for given offers between resettled and non-settled villages. While they must be viewed with some caution, both a Chi-squared test (see Table 10.3) and probit analyses (see Table 10.4) ran on the full sample of 117 second players' responses (nine rejections, 108 acceptances) and the subsample of responses by second players facing offers of less than Zim$25 (0.50 of the original stake, nine rejections twenty-nine acceptance) yield similar results. Given no evidence of a variation in rejection patterns between resettled and non-resettled villages, the expected income maximizing offer can be assumed to be the same for each. The regression analyses indicate that the expected income maximizing offer is Zim$15 (0.30 of the original stake). Thus, most of the Zimbabwean first players in both subject pools are either rejection averse or motivated by something other than selfish money maximization, as are at least some of the second players.

The results of the Ultimatum Game provide additional insights relating to the hypotheses listed above. Resettled first players invest less in the Trust Game, but are more likely to make a fair offer in the Ultimatum Game. If one assumes that the two games tap the same social preferences, this pattern of behavior is inconsistent with

TABLE 10.4. Probit analysis of rejections by second players in the Ultimatum Game (Dependent variable: *reject* = 1 if second player rejects offer, 0 otherwise)

	Full sample			Subsample of those facing less than fair offers		
Constant	− 1.300***	0.752	0.216	− 0.792**	0.217	− 0.131
	(0.31)	(0.56)	(0.76)	(0.38)	(0.63)	(0.84)
Resettled	− 0.177	0.214	1.219	0.117	0.250	0.964
	(0.37)	(0.48)	(1.06)	(0.47)	(0.50)	(1.20)
Offer		− 0.124***	− 0.087**		− 0.074*	− 0.048
		(0.03)	(0.04)		(0.04)	(0.06)
Resettled*offer			− 0.063			− 0.051
			(0.06)			(0.08)
Observations	117	117	117	38	38	38
Pseudo R^2	0.003	0.334	0.352	0.001	0.093	0.104

Note: Standard errors in parentheses. ***—coefficient significant at 0.01 level. **—coefficient significant at 0.05 level. *—coefficient significant at 0.10 level.

hypotheses (1) and (2) both of which state that resettled villagers are less altruistic or less loyal, but is consistent with hypotheses (5), that variations in first players' behavior reflect the degree of uncertainty they face, and (6), that they reflect variations in their degrees of loss aversion. In the Ultimatum Game higher offers are less risky, while in the Trust Game lower investments are less risky.

Controlling for other factors

At several points in the preceding text, I mentioned several factors other than resettlement that might affect player behavior. These include the number of players in a session and whether the players are men or women. In addition, recall that the experimental subjects inhabit three agro-climatic regions. Agro-climatic factors are among the most important exogenous determinants of income in Zimbabwe. Thus, controlling for region will at least partially control for income effects. It may also control for regional variations in socially transmitted behavioral rules.

The investigation involves a series of simple regressions (see Table 10.5). First, the two behavioral variables from the Trust Game, investments by first players (*invest*) and proportional responses by second players (*response*) are regressed upon a dummy that takes the value one for resettled players and zero otherwise (*resettled*) using ordinary least squares. Then a dummy that takes the value one for female players and zero otherwise (*female*), the number of players involved in the session each player attended (*session*), and two regional dummies (*agroclim2* and *agroclim3*) are added to the right-hand side and the effect on the significance and magnitude of the coefficient on *resettled* monitored. For the Ultimatum Game, a similar procedure is followed, although the dependent variable is a dummy variable that takes the value one for offers of Zim$25 (0.50 of the original stake) or above and zero otherwise (*fairoffer*), and a probit is fitted. Finally, where *response* is the dependent variable the regressions are also run with *invest* as an additional right-hand side variable.

When the dependent variable is either *invest* or *fairoffer*, the introduction of the additional variables has little effect on the significance or the magnitude of the coefficient on *resettled*. When *response* is the dependent variable *resettled* remains insignificant. These results support earlier conclusions, while the inclusion of the

TABLE 10.5. Controlling for other factors

	Invest (OLS)	Invest (OLS)	Response (OLS)	Response (OLS)	Response (OLS)	Response (OLS)	Fairoffer (probit)	Fairoffer (probit)
Constant	10.469***	12.423***	1.275***	1.283***	2.705***	2.791***	0.122	0.779
	(0.84)	(2.18)	(0.19)	(0.31)	(0.46)	(0.54)	(0.23)	(0.62)
Resettled	-2.441**	-2.855***	-0.004	-0.003	-0.179	-0.196	0.464*	0.518*
	(0.96)	(0.99)	(0.21)	(0.22)	(0.22)	(0.22)	(0.27)	(0.28)
Female		0.155			-0.312*	-0.313*		-0.248
		(0.82)			(0.18)	(0.18)		(0.26)
Session		-0.021			-0.042***	-0.042***		-0.025
		(0.07)			(0.01)	(0.01)		(0.02)
Agroclim2		-2.810**			-0.557**	-0.571**		0.133
		(1.26)			(0.28)	(0.29)		(0.42)
Agroclim3		-2.019*			-0.488**	-0.498*		-0.111
		(1.12)			(0.25)	(0.25)		(0.31)
Invest				-0.001		-0.007		
				(0.02)		(0.02)		
Observations	141	141	129	129	129	129	117	117
R^2, Pseudo R^2	0.044	0.098	0.000	0.000	0.093	0.094	0.020	0.044

Note: Standard errors in parentheses. ***—coefficient significant at 0.01 level. **—coefficient significant at 0.05 level. *—coefficient significant at 0.10 level.

additional right-hand side variables reveals some interesting patterns in the data. Both *invest* and *response* are lower in agro-climatic regions 2 and 3 than in region 1 (there is no significant difference between regions 2 and 3) and *response* is lower for female players and players in larger sessions. The results relating to agro-climatic region are worthy of note. That both investments and proportional responses are lower in regions 2 and 3 suggests a difference in behavioral rules. Second players provide a lower return on first players investments and first players predict this and invest less as a result. Whether this is due to regional differences in economic factors such as income remains to be seen.[10]

Correcting the standard errors in the regressions for heteroscedasticity using White's (1980) procedure affects the significance of some of the coefficients but does not alter the main conclusions (see Appendix B). Similarly, correcting for the possibility that error terms are correlated within villages because fellow villagers share unobservable characteristics leaves the main conclusions unaltered.

Several other variables were entered as right-hand side variables in the estimated equations but were found neither to be significant nor to affect the results relating to the *resettled* dummy. These other variables included a dummy for household heads and a series of interaction terms between *resettled* and the agro-climatic dummies.

Discriminating between familiarity and loss aversion and the issue of self-selection

The empirical analysis leaves two competing hypotheses, that variations in trust are due to differences in either familiarity between villagers or their levels of loss aversion. The first of these explanations implies that resettlement affected economic behavior, while the second depends on a particular type of person being more likely to resettle.

What sort of behavioral characteristics do we expect resettled villagers to have? Recall that they were among the first to resettle

---

[10] The probit analyses for second player behavior in the Ultimatum Game was similarly augmented. None of the additional variables where significant and the results relating to resettlement remained ambiguous.

following Zimbabwe's independence. They chose resettlement as a solution to their problems at a time when no one knew what the government had in store for resettled families and when others were choosing or having to rely on more traditional solutions to solve similar sets of problems. Given this background, one behavioral characteristic likely to have influenced the resettlement decision is an individual's level of loss aversion. We would expect less loss averse people to have chosen resettlement. But, this cannot account for the observed pattern of behavior. If we assume no difference in levels of uncertainty, then the observed variations are consistent with resettled villagers being more, not less, loss averse. If the self-selection bias described here does exist it will be acting to suppress rather than induce the observed variations in behavior. Thus, we can reject hypothesis (6) with a considerable degree of confidence.

We are left with hypothesis (5), that resettled villagers are less familiar with each other's behavioral characteristics than their non-resettled counterparts. Could this be due to something other than the lower density of kinship ties? Could it be due to the newness of the resettled villages? It could, if we believe that, as a consequence, resettled villagers have less experience of each other in strategic situations. Recall that the resettled villages were created in 1982, 17 years before the experiment was conducted. Most of the participants in the game will have spent all of their adult lives in these villages. It seems unlikely, then, that the resettled villages are still in some sort of disequilibrium—that if we were to return to them in another 17 years, say, we would find less of a difference between their levels of trust and those of the non-resettled control. While it is difficult to reject this hypothesis with the same degree of confidence as we rejected the loss aversion hypothesis, these arguments do tend to favor the lower density of kinship networks as the origin the observed variation in trust.

SUMMARY AND CONCLUSIONS

I started with two questions—does resettlement among non-kin lead to reduced trust and, if so, why? Using an economic experiment involving two games to generate the necessary data, I found that there is, indeed, a lower level of trust within resettled villages, where kinship networks are less dense. Further, by carefully analyzing the behavior of both the first and second players in the two games in conjunction with the history of resettlement, I have been able to rule out various other possible explanations for this result. These alternative explanations included the self-selection of more loss averse individuals into resettlement and the relative newness of the resettled villages. The results of the analysis also rule out the possibility that it is not a difference in trust but a difference in altruism that is being captured. Further, the analysis provides some insights into why the lower density of kinship networks in resettled villages leads to lower trust. Surprisingly, it does not appear to be due to variations in behavioral rules associated with reciprocation. Rules about sharing and fairness do not appear to vary either. The lower trust among the unrelated, resettled villagers appears to be due to a reduced ability to predict their fellow villagers' behavior, that is, they are less familiar with one another's behavioral characteristics than the more inter-related non-resettled villagers.[11] Whether this is because of variations in patterns of social interaction between kin and non-kin or because kinship and empathy are directly related is a topic for future research.

Returning to the current experiment, recall that this reduced familiarity led to less investment. If this effect on behavior is also manifest in everyday life, it could have important economic implications. Where trust is low more complex and potentially more costly institutional arrangements are required to keep transactions costs to acceptable levels. If such institutional arrangements are not forthcoming resettled villagers may have to suffer the consequences of reduced investment and lower resulting economic growth.

APPENDIX A: GAME SCRIPTS

Ultimatum Game

We are gathering knowledge through the playing of games. We would like you to take the games seriously. You may win some money.

Have you heard about the game that we want you to play? If you have, we will not waste time explaining it to you.

---

[11] Gil-White (Chapter 9, this volume) draws similar conclusions from his comparison of inter- and intra-ethnic group behavior in the Ultimatum Game.

I will begin by explaining the game to you. Then I will ask a few questions to check your understanding.

You will be playing this game with someone from your village. However, the identity of each player will remain unknown to the other. The amount of money that will be used in playing the game is $50. We supply the $50. The first player's role is to divide the $50 into two piles, one for himself and the other for the second player. Later on we will show the second player the division made by the first player and indicate which pile has been allocated to him. The names of the players will not be revealed. It is up to the second player to accept or refuse the pile allocated to him. If the second player accepts, both players will be given the money as per the first player's division. If the second player refuses, neither player gets any money. The first player gets nothing and the second player gets nothing.

Note that the first player has the power to divide the money into two piles, while the second player has the power to prevent the first from getting any money. The second player can do this by refusing to accept his allocation. Once the second accepts his allocation both players will get their money.

Example: If the first player, out of the $50, allocates $20 to the second player, who then accepts, the first player gets $30 and the second gets $20. But if the second player refuses the $20, knowing that the first player would get $30 if he accepted, both players get nothing.

Questions: If the first player, out of the $50, allocates $10 to the second player, who then accepts, what does the first player get? What does the second player get? If the second player refuses the $10, knowing that if he accepts the first player will get $40, what will each player get?

If the first player, out of the $50, allocates $30 to the second player, who then accepts, what does the first player get? What does the second player get? If the second player refuses the $30, knowing that if he accepts the first player will get $20, what will each player get?

If the first player, out of the $50, allocates $25 to the second player, who then accepts, what does the first player get? What does the second player get? If the second player refuses the $25, knowing that if he accepts the first player will get $25, what will each player get?

If the first player, out of the $50, allocates $5 to the second player, who then accepts, what does the first player get? What does the second player get? If the second player refuses the $5, knowing that if he accepts the first player will get $45, what will each player get?

First player: You are the first player. Show Dr. Barr the amount of money you want to allocate to the second player. [*At this point $50 is placed on the table in front* *of the player and the player makes the division and indicates which pile he intends for Player 2.*] We shall tell the second player your offer, but not your name. You will not be told the name of the second player either. If the second player accepts the division we will inform you and give you your share.

Second player: You are the second player. Dr. Barr will show you the amount of money that the first player has allocated to you out of the $50. [*At this point the two piles of money are placed in front of the player and the one that is for him indicated.*] Do you agree or disagree with the division that has been made? [*If they agree they are encouraged to take their pile . . .*] Go ahead, its yours!

Finally, please do not reveal how you played to anyone, not even the amount of money you received. Do not tell any other villagers about the game, otherwise you will jeopardize our research. This will make it difficult for us to come back and play more games with you.

Thank you.

Trust game

We are gathering knowledge through the playing of games. We would like you to take the games seriously. You may win some money.

Have you heard about the game that we want you to play? If you have, we will not waste time explaining it to you.

I will begin by explaining the game to you. Then I will ask a few questions to check your understanding.

You will be playing this game with someone from your village. However, the identity of each player will remain unknown to the other. We will give twenty dollars to each player. The first player will be given the opportunity to give back any amount that he wishes from his $20. Whatever amount he gives back, we will increase and then pass it on to the second player. So, if he gives back $5, the second player will receive $35 and the first player will be left with $15. If he gives back $10, the second player will receive $50 and the first player will be left with $10. If he gives back $15, the second player will receive $65 and the first player will be left with $5. If he gives back $20, the second player will receive $80 and the first player will be left with nothing. The first player has the option of giving back nothing, in which case the second player will get and keep his $20. As long as the first player gives back some money, the second player will get the chance give something back to the first player.

I am now going to give/ask you some examples/questions. These are examples only. If, out of his $20, the first player decides to give $5 back to be increased and passed on to the second player, what does the first player have left? We will increase the $5 to $35 and pass it onto the second player. Now, if we ask the second player whether he wishes to give anything back to the first player and he refuses, what does the first player end up with? And what does the second player end up with?

Here is a different example. If, out of his $20, the first player decides to give $5 back to be increased and passed on to the second player, what does the first player have left? We will increase the $5 to $35 and pass it onto the second player. Now, if we ask the second player whether he wishes to give anything back to the first player and he gives back $10, what does the first player end up with? And what does the second player end up with?

Examples for Player 1s

P1 gives	P2 gets	P1 is left	P2 gives back	P1 ends up with	P2 ends up with
5	35	15	0	15	35
5	35	15	10	25	25
10	50	10	0	10	50
10	50	10	20	30	30
15	65	5	0	5	65
15	65	5	30	35	35
20	80	0	0	0	80
20	80	0	40	40	40

Examples for Player 2s

P1 gives	P2 gets	P1 is left	P2 gives back	P1 ends up with	P2 ends up with
5	35	15	0	15	35
5	35	15	10	25	25
10	50	10	0	10	50
10	50	10	30	40	20
15	65	5	0	5	65
15	65	5	20	25	45
20	80	0	0	0	80
20	80	0	25	25	55

Note that the larger the amount given back by the first player, the greater the amount that can be taken away by the two players together. However, it is entirely up to the second player to decide what he should give back to the first player. The first player could end up with more or less money as a result.

First player: You are the first player. Here is your $20. [*At this point $20 is placed on the table in front of the player.*] Will you please give back the amount of money that you wish us to increase and pass on to the second player. Give back whatever you wish, $5, $10, $15, $20, or zero. Remember the more you give back the greater the amount of money at the second player's disposal. Although the second player is under no obligation to give anything back, we will pass on to you whatever he decides to return. [*Now the player hands back his bid.*]

Second player: You are the second player. Dr. Barr will show you what player one has done. [*The player is shown $20 from which is taken what the first player chose to give back.*] The first player gave back $— out of his $20. [*Then the appropriate amout is added to what the first player gave back.*] We have increased this to $—. So you are now getting $—. [*The pile of money showing what the first player currently has left is indicated.*] This means that the first player in left with $—. It is now up to you to decide what to give back to the first player. You can choose to give something back or not. Do what you wish.

Finally, please do not reveal how you played to anyone, not even the amount of money you received. Do not tell any other villagers about the game, otherwise you will jeopardize our research. This will make it difficult for us to come back and play more games with you.

Thank you.

TABLE B.i. Controlling for other factors and using White's procedure to correct standard errors for heteroscedasticity

	Invest	Invest	Response	Response	Response	Response	Fairoffer	Fairoffer
Constant	10.469***	12.423***	1.275***	1.283***	2.705***	2.791***	0.122	0.779
	(0.95)	(2.08)	(0.17)	(0.31)	(0.42)	(0.52)	(0.23)	(0.66)
Resettled	−2.441**	−2.855***	−0.004	−0.003	−0.179	−0.196	0.464*	0.518*
	(1.05)	(1.03)	(0.20)	(0.21)	(0.20)	(0.21)	(0.27)	(0.29)
Female		0.155			−0.312*	−0.313*		−0.248
		(0.84)			(0.18)	(0.18)		(0.25)
Session		−0.021			−0.042***	−0.042***		−0.025
		(0.06)			(0.01)	(0.01)		(0.02)
Agroclim2		−2.810**			−0.557**	−0.571**		0.133
		(1.34)			(0.24)	(0.25)		(0.44)
Agroclim3		−2.019*			−0.488*	−0.498*		−0.111
		(1.06)			(0.28)	(0.28)		(0.30)
Invest				−0.001		−0.007		
				(0.02)		(0.02)		
Observations	141	141	129	129	129	129	117	117
R^2, Pseudo R^2	0.044	0.098	0.000	0.000	0.093	0.094	0.020	0.044

Note: Corrected standard errors in parentheses. ***—coefficient significant at 0.01 level. **—coefficient significant at 0.05 level. *—coefficient significant at 0.10 level.

TABLE B.ii. Controlling for other factors and correcting for within-village correlation in error terms

	Invest	Invest	Response	Response	Response	Response	Fairoffer	Fairoffer
Constant	10.469***	12.423***	1.275***	1.283***	2.705***	2.791***	0.122	0.779
	(1.09)	(2.34)	(0.12)	(0.27)	(0.52)	(0.57)	(0.12)	(0.62)
Resettled	−2.441*	−2.855***	−0.004	−0.003	−0.179	−0.196	0.464**	0.518*
	(1.28)	(0.93)	(0.20)	(0.19)	(0.18)	(0.17)	(0.21)	(0.28)
Female		0.155			−0.312	−0.313		−0.248
		(1.00)			(0.22)	(0.22)		(0.26)
Session		−0.021			−0.042**	−0.042**		−0.025
		(0.07)			(0.02)	(0.02)		(0.02)
Agroclim2		−2.810*			−0.557**	−0.571**		0.133
		(1.50)			(0.26)	(0.27)		(0.42)
Agroclim3		−2.019			−0.488	−0.498		−0.111
		(1.34)			(0.33)	(0.34)		(0.31)
Invest				−0.001		−0.007		
				(0.02)		(0.02)		
Observations	141	141	129	129	129	129	117	117
R^2, Pseudo R^2	0.044	0.098	0.000	0.000	0.093	0.094	0.020	0.044

Note: Corrected standard errors in parentheses. ***—coefficient significant at 0.01 level. **—coefficient significant at 0.05 level. *—coefficient significant at 0.10 level.

REFERENCES

Arrow, K. J. (1972). 'Gifts and exchanges', *Philosophy and Public Affairs, 1*, 343–62.

—— (1974). *The Limits of Organization*, New York: W. W. Norton and Co.

Berg, J., Dickhaut, J., and McCabe, K. (1995). 'Trust, reciprocity, and social history', *Games and Economic Behavior, 10*, 122–42.

Dasgupta, P. (1988). 'Trust as a commodity', in D. Gambetta, (ed.), *Trust: Making and Breaking Cooperative Relations*. Oxford: Basil Blackwell.

Eagly, A. H. and Crowley, M. (1986). 'Gender and helping behavior: A meta-analytic review of the social psychological literature', *Psychological Bulletin, 100*, 283–308.

Fukuyama, F. (1995). *Trust*. New York: Free Press.

Glaeser, E., Laibson, D., Scheinkman, J., and Soutter, C. (1999). 'What is Social Capital? The Determinants of Trust and Trustworthiness', NBER Working Paper no. 7216.

Hardin, R. (1991). 'Trusting persons, trusting institutions', in R. J. Zeckhauser (ed.), *Strategy and Choice*, Cambridge, MA: MIT Press.

Henrich, J. (2000). 'Does culture matter in economic behaviour? Ultimatum game bargaining among the Machiguenga of the Peruvian Amazon', *American Economic Review* 90(4), 973–9.

Hoffman, E. and Smith, V. (1994). 'Preferences, property rights and anonymity in bargaining games', *Games and Economic Behavior, 7*, 341–61.

Hoffman, E., McCabe K., and Smith, V. (1996). 'Social distance and other-regarding behavior in dictator games', *American Economic Review, 86*, 653–60.

Knack, S. and Keefer, P. (1997). 'Does social capital have an economic payoff? A cross-country investigation', *Quarterly Journal of Economics, 112*, 1251–88.

LaPorta, R., Lopez-de-Silanes, F., Shleifer, A., and Vishny, R. (1997). 'Trust in large organizations', *American Economic Review Papers and Proceedings, 87*, 333–8.

Roth, A. E., Prasnikar, V., Okuno-Fujiwara, M., and Zamir, S. (1991). 'Bargaining and market behavior in Jerusalem, Ljubljana, Pittsburgh, and Tokyo: an experimental study', *American Economic Review, 81*, 1068–95.

White, H. (1980). 'A heteroscedasticity-consistent covariance matrix estimator and a direct test for heteroscedasticity', *Econometrica, 48*, 817–38.

Yamagishi, T. and Yamagishi, M. (1994). 'Trust and commitment in the United States and Japan', *Motivation and Emotion, 18*, 129–66.

11

Community Structure, Mobility, and the Strength of Norms in an African Society: The Sangu of Tanzania

Richard McElreath

INTRODUCTION

Both ethnographic and experimental evidence suggest that a significant number of individuals in many, and probably most, human communities have a tendency to punish individuals who violate local norms, often at a substantial cost to themselves and even when the norm violations do not directly cost the punisher anything (Boyd and Richerson 1985, 1992). The first of these lines of evidence is the widespread observation (typically ethnographic or anecdotal) of 'moralistic' punishment, wherein third parties punish violators of social rules. Another, line of evidence has emerged in experimental economics, where human behavior in several economic 'games' has generated unexpected and seemingly irrational results (see Kagel and Roth 1995).

The Ultimatum Game has been a favorite among these games, and the chapters in this volume indicate that the 'non-rational' game behavior is generally cross-cultural, although some societies do approach the standard definition of 'rational' choice. The Ultimatum Game involves an anonymous first player (*proposer*) who splits a pool of money any way she chooses, followed by an anonymous receiving individual (*responder*) who decides whether to accept her portion of the split, giving the remainder to the first player, or to reject the split, giving both herself and the first player none of the pool of money. The classic prediction is that the rational proposer should offer the lowest nonzero amount possible while the responder should always accept any offer greater than zero. However, not only do proposers commonly offer more than the lowest unit of money (mean offers are usually slightly below 50 percent in industrialized settings), but responders sometimes reject low offers (Ultimatum Game data chapters here). To explain these results, some researchers (Bolton and Zwick 1995; Camerer and Thaler 1995; Roth 1995; Konow 1996) have suggested these offers and rejections constitute evidence that humans may have an innate taste for punishment and sense of fairness.

The results in this volume strongly suggest that any such taste is tuned by other factors. The next challenge is to discover which group and individual variables predict these variations in bargaining behavior. One source of relevant models is those developed by evolutionary ecologists and social scientists interested in the problem of cooperation. These models (e.g Axelrod 1984; Boyd and Richerson 1992) have explored how reciprocity and punishment can evolve and stabilize pro-social norms, and such models suggest again and again that stable, long-lasting relationships are important for the emergence and maintenance of both cooperative relationships and punishment (although see Henrich and Boyd 2001), which in turn can stabilize cooperation or any number of norm equilibria.

In this chapter, I present Ultimatum Game results from an African society with substantial internal economic variation. Among the Sangu of southwest Tanzania, a more sedentary and stable community of farmers exhibited more rejections in the Ultimatum Game than a more mobile and compositionally fluid community of agro-pastoralists (individuals who sometimes farm but also derive a substantial amount of their income from livestock). These communities exhibited no differences in the distributions of offers, implying that they share an idealized norm for sharing or, as they said, 'dividing equally', but differ in their willingness or perception of the need to punish norm violations. I examine how individual variables like age and differences in the nature and duration of relationships among the two groups may explain some of the difference in offers and willingness to reject, as well as evaluate the possibility that differences in risk-aversion may account for the differences in rejection rates. In doing so I present a method for describing and comparing rejections rates of different populations (which was used in the introductory chapter). I also discuss how the structure of the Ultimatum Game makes interpretation of data like these problematic, due to the functional ambiguity of rejection behavior.

SANGU ENVIRONMENT, SOCIETY, AND ECONOMY

The Usangu Plains is a 15.5 thousand square kilometer (Pipping 1976; Hazlewood and Livingstone 1978) region of southwest Tanzania which is home to a number of ethnic groups living throughout a gradient between wet and dry environmental zones. In the wetter regions of the south, annual rainfall ranges from 600 to 1000 mm, and is dependable. The dry range lands and northern regions, which comprise most the Usangu Plains, vary widely in rainfall, from 200 to 600 mm annually. This rainfall is comparable to that experienced by the Nuer of the Sudan (Evans-Pritchard 1940) and Mursi of Ethiopia (Turton 1980) in both paucity and unpredictability.

The Sangu numbered about 40,000–50,000 in 1990 (Charnley 1994). At that time, the total population was somewhat greater than 150,000, most of them living in the southern wet zone and many of them immigrant farmers from more southerly ethnic groups, like the Nyakyusa. The dry regions in the north remain sparsely populated, but are increasingly sites of grazing competition, as cattle far outnumber people in those regions. The entire population of Usangu has probably doubled in the last decade (largely from immigration), but poor census estimates and transient residents make it hard to know.

Probably still the single largest ethnic group in the Usangu Plains, the Sangu originated from a mixture of Bantu peoples in the region in the late 1800s and early 1900s, when they united under a hereditary chief and began raiding their neighbors for wealth and livestock (see Wright 1971; Shorter 1972). At the peak of that power, the Sangu were wealthy cattle herders who held considerable military power in the region (aided partly by German colonial administrators). Now, most Sangu are farmers, although probably a few hundred households still keep herds in the Plains. The major crop is corn, which is processed for food as well as sold. Many people have begun to plant rice, which is largely a cash-crop, sold at market and changed into corn for food or disposable wealth. Wage work is very scarce and desirable.

Since 1997, I have been working with two Sangu communities. The agricultural areas of Utengule (Sangu for 'place of peace') and its surroundings is the first. Utengule was once the home of the hereditary chief of the Sangu ethnic group. Utengule residents live in very closely spaced settlements, where there is often less than 10 miles between homes, and the vast majority of them farm. A small number make a living off transport between Utengule and the nearest paved road (about 10 miles) or by selling imported goods (mostly beer) in the market. Very few Utengule households own livestock, and since wealth (traditionally livestock, but now including cash) is required to pay bride fees to the families of women, most men can afford and marry only one wife. Family sizes are typically between four and six children. Most people below 30 years of age in Utengule have had some primary schooling, and most of them can read and write at a basic level.

Ukwaheri ('place of blessings') is less of a town or village and more of a region of interrelated communities. Ukwaheri lies about 20 miles north and east of Utengule, within the dry region of the Plains. Household compounds are very scattered: distances of 1 or 2 kilometers are the norm. In a region with no real roads, I have spent entire days traveling to a single household and back. Some Ukwaheri residents do not own cattle and instead live more densely near a spot where the water table is high (this is Ukwaheri proper). Most, however, own at least some livestock, and those with larger herds (typically more than twenty cattle) practice transhumance. That is, in those households with larger herds, men often spend part of the year away from the main household taking the herds to graze farther north, over great distances on foot. Access to markets is much more restricted in this area, and journeying to Utengule or the regional capital (Mbeya) takes place on the order of days. Family sizes can be considerably larger than in Utengule, as wealthy herders marry as many as five or six wives, each mothering an average of four or five surviving children during her fertile years. Very few people of any age in Ukwaheri region can read or write anything beyond their own names. While many children in Ukwaheri proper (near the high water table) attend school, the instructors are frequently absent and rarely hold classes.

METHODS

In the summer of 1998, I played the Ultimatum Game with twenty pairs of Utengule residents (farmers) and twenty pairs of Ukwaheri residents (herders). I adhered to the standardized procedures followed by other researchers in this volume, wherever possible. What wage work was available in the area paid 1,000–1,500 Tanzanian Shillings per day (in 1998, USD 1 = TSH 650). I thus used, 1,200 shillings as the stakes, approximating one day's wages. These 1,200 shillings were divided into 100 shilling coins, in a stack of twelve. Participants were able to physically manipulate this pile when making and receiving offers. In the case of offering, they physically divided the pile themselves. In the case of receiving, they saw the original pile and then the portion the proposer had set aside for them.

All participants were adults of marriageable age, with equal numbers of males and females. I recruited players by several methods. Initially, I asked individuals to help me with my research about Sangu life by playing a game for money, while I was traveling the communities collecting other data. As word spread about the amounts of money involved (mostly the amounts won in the risk preference/aversion game I was playing concurrently with the Ultimatum Game; see Henrich and McElreath 2002), potential players began to seek me out. About half my samples are these self-recruited individuals, although I often rejected multiple individuals from the same family or household or selected older individuals when I had already played with plenty of young people. If self-recruited individuals altered the results, my intuition is that the risk aversion of the sample is lower than that of the population in general, as those most willing to travel and wait to play the games are overrepresented.

I played several games each day, selecting proposers and responders at random by slips of paper with ID numbers from a plastic bag. Participants got to see this selection process, which I hope helped to convince them of their anonymity and the randomness of the pairings. Each player first heard the translated script and then had to test correctly twice in example games before being allowed to play. Additional instructions, when necessary, were given ad lib in Swahili, with both myself and my best field assistant (who is himself Sangu) teaching them with instruction and examples. Very few participants failed to understand the game, but those who did fail to understand had to leave without playing (much to their disappointment).

I played the games in various locations, but always alone with the participant, my field assistant, and any nursing children. My field assistant spent much of the time keeping onlookers from spoiling the anonymity of player decisions. Despite this, it is unlikely that player decisions were entirely anonymous, as several individuals announced their offers or rewards upon leaving the room in which we were playing the game (as was the case with the Machiguenga, Henrich and Smith Chapter 5, this volume).

RESULTS

The distributions of offers among the Sangu look very much like typical western results (Figure 11.1). The mean offer for the entire sample is 497.5 shillings (41 percent) while the mode is 600 shillings (50 percent). The means and modes for the farmer and herder subsamples are the same: 495 (41 percent) and 600 (50 percent) for the farmers, 500 (42 percent) and 600 (50 percent) for the herders. The minimum offer is 100 (8 percent). The maximum is 800 (67 percent). There are no significant differences between the farmer and herder subsamples.

Variation in offers

Wealth and demographic variables do not seem to explain much of the variation in offers, in either community (Table 11.1). Age, however, explains some of the variation ($\beta = 0.337$, $p = 0.092$). Young individuals made many of the lowest offers.

Variation in rejections

The distributions of rejections, however, look quite different between the two samples (Figure 11.1). The farmer sample shows five total rejections, one each at 100, 300, 400, 500, and 600 shilling offers. The herder sample shows exactly one rejection, at 200 shillings. Figure 11.2 plots the proportions of each offer amount which the farmer and herder samples rejected. These distributions are seemingly quite different, and we might wonder if the difference is real, given how little data I have on rejections. The specific-offer method unfortunately generates little data on rejections, because if people fear rejections and make higher mean offers because of it, we will fail to see many rejections in the data. It would have been better for testing for differences in rejections if I had asked each responder to state the minimum offer they would accept.

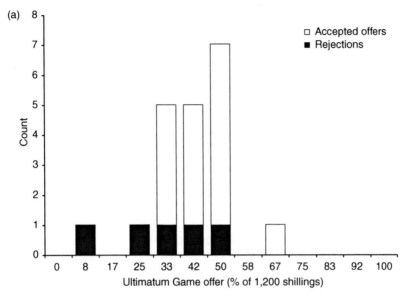

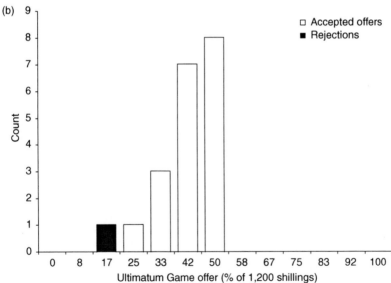

FIG. 11.1. Distributions of offers and rejections for both communities:
(a) farmers ($n = 20$) in Utengule area and (b) herders ($n = 20$) in Ukwaheri area

Notes: Light bars are numbers of offers at each amount which were accepted. Black bars are numbers of rejections at each amount. Thus the total height of each column is the total number of offers at that amount.

TABLE 11.1. Linear regression of Ultimatum Game offer on wealth and demographic variables

	Unstandardized coefficients		Standardized coefficients		Significance values
	β	SE	β	t	
(Constant)	393.705	160.824		2.448	0.020
Age	2.892	1.668	0.337	1.734	0.092
Education	6.976	10.364	0.197	0.673	0.506
Community	5.792	70.006	0.023	0.083	0.935
Gender	− 35.656	44.367	− 0.137	− 0.804	0.427
Cattle	0.929	1.224	0.140	0.759	0.453

Note: Dependent Variable: Ultimatum Game Offer. In Gender, female = 1, male = 2. In Community, farming village = 1, herding areas = 2, Model = 1.

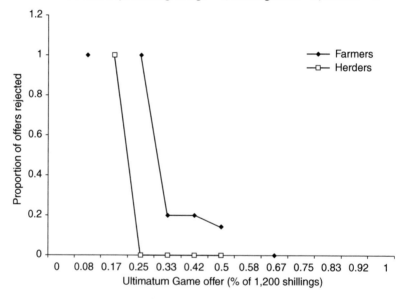

FIG. 11.2. Proportions of offers rejected at each offer amount, for farmer and herder communities

A logistic regression of rejections against offer, community, and individual variables retains only offer, age, and community. However, community and age are highly correlated, and so the model including both together with offer is unreliable (Table 11.2).

TABLE 11.2. Logistic regression of rejections against age, community, and offer

Variable	β	SE	Wald	Significant values	Exp (β)
Age	−10.9565	85.3048	0.0165	0.8978	0.0000
Offer	−0.1208	0.8534	0.0200	0.8875	0.8862
Community (1)	66.8998	808.0509	0.0069	0.9340	1.133E + 29
Constant	266.4470	2240.4449	0.0141	0.9053	

Both age and community are significant when included in a model with only one another. Either is marginally significant ($p < 0.10$) when included in a model with offer. Offer is always either significant ($p < 0.05$) or marginally significant. Offer clearly affects rejections, since lower offers are more likely to be rejected (which is consistent with the overall finding for rejections across all datasets; Henrich *et al.* Chapter 1, this volume). Both age and community may explain portions of the remaining variation in rejections, which is considerable. One of the two bears some actual relationship to the difference in rejections between the two samples.

Informants' explanations of their own behaviors

In postgame interviews, players often invoked a custom of dividing equally in explaining fair offers. Those who made unequal divisions offered no explanations, typically, although two individuals said they felt they were in greater need than the other person. Rejections were always explained as reactions to unfair behavior, except in the case of the farmer who rejected an offer of 600 (50 percent). In that case, the individual said he did not want the money and would provide no further explanation.

In general, as in some of the other chapters in this volume, informants are quite poor at providing explanations of their own behavior, and even when they are facile at it, we probably should not jump to believe them (Fiske n.d.). For this reason, I did not find the postgame interviews to provide good data about what motivated offers, especially given the fact that many people could provide no explanation at all without intense prompting. Explanations of rejections came much more readily, however, and so those data are perhaps more meaningful.

In summary, the farmer and herder samples do not differ with respect to offers in the Ultimatum Game. Individual variables also do not seem to explain much of the variance in offers, although age explains a good fraction. There is evidence as well that the communities differ in the likelihood of rejections, farmers being more likely to reject a given offer amount than herders, although it is unclear if this is really an age effect, since the samples have different age profiles and regression cannot sort of which variable is responsible. In the next section, I attempt to motivate some explanation for these differences.

DISCUSSION

There are several possible explanations for the observed differences in rejection behavior between farmer and herder samples. The crucial thing is to explain how both samples could have very similar offer distributions but different rejection patterns.

1. Farmers are more likely to reject than herders (for an unknown reason), but more risk-aversion among herders leads them to make similarly high offers as farmers.
2. Rejection rates differ perhaps because structural features of farmer and herder life are different, and these differences may affect the benefits from punishment.
3. Age differences could explain the majority or a substantial amount of the difference in rejections, in which case younger people were more likely to reject than older people. Note that younger people were also more likely to make smaller offers than older people ($p < 0.10$, $\beta = 0.33$).
4. Farmers might also have different rejection rates than herders but offers may be unrelated to rejection behavior, as the game might confuse several functionally unrelated aspects of their social lives. That is, proposers and responders may be mapping the Ultimatum Game onto different social experiences and therefore playing different games.

In this section, I briefly explore each of these interrelated possibilities.

Similar offers may be due to risk-aversion

One way to go about testing if differences in risk-aversion could produce the same offer distribution is by estimating the functions which might generate the different rejection distributions and calculating the amount of risk-aversion necessary to produce the same distribution of offers.

First, assume that individuals reject a specific offer with probability

$$p = 1 - \frac{\exp(\alpha + \beta x)}{1 + \exp(\alpha + \beta x)}$$

where

$$x = \frac{\textit{offer}}{6} - 1.$$

This function is logistic, and α and β describe its shape. The logistic is a good start for imagining such a function, since it provides for a transition between a high probability of rejection at low values and a low probability of rejection at higher or middle values.

We can estimate the separate functions for farmer and herder data with maximum likelihood estimation. The maximum likelihood function is the one with the greatest chance of producing the observed data. In general, one can find nonlinear maximum likelihood functions only by computer iteration, testing different values of function parameters (α and β in this case) and remembering those values which match the data best.

I estimated the maximum likelihood functions for independent farmer and herder data, as well as the pooled dataset. I estimated each function at 0.05 intervals, using an exhaustive search of positive parameter values. Figure 11.3 shows the independent farmer and herder functions. The pooled estimation allows me to test if the independent estimates are significantly more likely than a single function which estimates both distributions of rejections. That is, it allows me to test whether a null hypothesis that a single function estimated from the pooled data (farmer and herder data together) can explain the two distributions of rejections, or whether two independent estimates derived from the farmer and herder data separately fit the data better. Table 11.3 shows the significance test using the three estimated functions: the farmer, herder, and pooled estimates. Using these estimates, the difference is significant at the 5 percent level.

The trouble with these estimates, however, is that portions of the herder function have greater probabilities of rejection than the

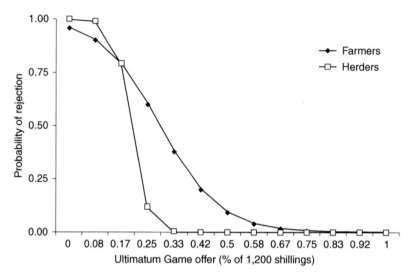

FIG. 11.3. Maximum likelihood rejection functions for independent farmer and herder data

Notes: Farmer function is $\alpha = 2.30$, $\beta = 5.40$. Herder function is $\alpha = 12.0$, $\beta = 20.0$. (Both estimated at 0.05 intervals.)

TABLE 11.3. Test of significance of function estimates

Data	α	β	Likelihood function
Farmers	2.3	5.4	− 8.9758
Herders	12.0	20.0	− 0.3766
Pooled	3.4	6.6	− 12.4665

Notes: $\chi^2 = 6.2282$; $p = 0.04$.

farmer function. That is, as you can see in Figure 11.3, for some offer amounts, herders are *more* likely to reject than are farmers. This odd estimate results from the poor nature of the data: there is only one rejection in the herder sample, and that rejection was 100 percent of offers at that amount (200 shillings). The maximum likelihood routine attempts to maximize (to 100 percent) the chance of rejection at this data point and minimize (to 0 percent) the chance of rejection above it, where there were no observed rejections. In fact, the parameters α and β in this herder estimate will climb as high as I allow them. The slope of the function between 200 and 300 shillings is only limited by the size of the parameter search space, which I specify.

The reason this result is troubling is that it does not match the hypothesis about the difference between the two samples. The proposition is that the herders are less likely to reject offers in general, not just above 200 shillings. Another way to estimate the herder function is to restrict it such that it must always have a less than or equal chance of rejection as the previously estimated farmer function ($\alpha = 2.3$, $\beta = 5.4$). I estimated the herder function again with this restriction, and Figure 11.4 shows the new function comparison. Table 11.4 shows the new significance test, using the new estimates. The result is no longer significant at the 5 percent level. Since the small amount of data in the sample creates such low power, however, significance at the 10 percent level is still a rather compelling result, and it matches the result from the earlier logistic regression.

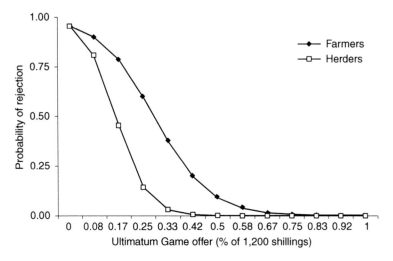

FIG. 11.4. Maximum likelihood rejection functions for independent farmer and herder data

Notes: Herder function is restricted to always have a lower probability of rejection than the maximum likelihood farmer function. Farmer function is again $\alpha = 2.3$, $\beta = 5.4$. Herder function is now $\alpha = 6.65$, $\beta = 9.70$. (Both estimated at 0.05 intervals.)

TABLE 11.4. Test of significance of
function estimates, using restricted
herder function

Data	α	β	Likelihood function
Farmers	2.3	5.4	− 8.9758
Herders	6.65	9.7	− 1.0847
Pooled	3.4	6.6	− 12.4665

Notes: $\chi^2 = 4.7920$; $p = 0.09$.

Using these estimated functions, one can derive the offer which maximizes expected utility (payoff adjusted for risk-aversion) for playing with someone who rejects using either function. The Utility Maximizing Offer is the offer which maximizes

$$U(offer) = (1 - p_o)(1{,}200 - offer)^r,$$

where p_o is the probability of rejection of *offer*, given by the rejection function, and r is a fractional exponent specifying the amount of risk-aversion for the player making the offer. Assuming proposers make offers rationally in order to maximize their returns, we can simulate a distribution of offers by bootstrapping from the paired observed offers and rejections and estimating a new rejection function each time. This is meant to simulate a process by which individuals estimate the rejection function of those they play against by some sampling process. Thus there will be variation in individual estimates of rejection functions, and this will produce a distribution of offers as individuals make Utility Maximizing Offer's according to their personal estimates of these functions.

We can then estimate the difference in values of r necessary to produce the same distribution of observed offers. This is possible by varying r for each sample and creating bootstrapped offer distributions until we find the value of r that minimizes the largest deviation (D statistic, Z-test) between the bootstrapped Utility Maximizing Offer distribution and the observed distribution for that sample. This procedure is explained again in the appendix (McElreath and Camerer Appendix, this volume).

Following the above procedure, the value of r for the farmer sample which minimizes the deviation between observed and simulated offer distributions is 0.51. The value of r for the herder sample is 0.02. This means that in order for risk-aversion to produce similar offer distributions for farmers and herders, given the estimates we have of the different rejection functions, herders would have to be more than 20 times more risk-averse than farmers—this finding is consistent with that of other groups discussed in the introductory chapter.

There are two obvious reasons to doubt that such a huge difference exists. First, my risk-aversion experiments with the same samples indicate little or no difference between farmers and herders in their likelihoods to accept equal-expectation gambles over fixed amounts of money (Henrich and McElreath 2002). Second, while the estimate of r for the farmer sample is perhaps plausible, the estimated risk-aversion for the herder sample is outrageously high.

Stable relationships and pro-social behavior in Usangu

The stability and longevity of relationships are important in the evolution and maintenance of reciprocity and cooperation. There are two ways such stability might affect the persistence of norms for fairness and, more importantly in the case of the Sangu, for punishment.

First, in classic models of reciprocal altruism (see e.g. Axelrod 1984), the probability of a relationship between two individuals continuing (w) strongly affects the likelihood that cooperative strategies will perform well. Clutton-Brock and Parker (1995) identify negative reciprocity, where an actor returns a retribution for a defection in cooperative behavior, as a natural form of 'punishment' which results from the evolution of reciprocal altruism. However, there is reason to believe that these models are not relevant to the evolution of third-party punishment as observed in human groups. It seems unlikely for negative reciprocity to be important in the evolution of human punishment, such as many think operates in the Ultimatum Game. First, reciprocity may be a strong source of cooperation in pairs of individuals, and stern behavioral rules which do not tolerate defections do well

(Axelrod 1984). However, reciprocity alone is unlikely to be a real source of large-scale cooperation, since groups larger than about three or four individuals have a very hard time evolving or maintaining reciprocal altruism (Boyd and Richerson 1992). Additionally, pair-wise reciprocity does not easily resemble the type of third-party punishment humans often perform. For these reasons, the evolution of pair-wise reciprocity appears tangential to the problem of how punishment in large groups evolved. Negative reciprocity is of course just as tangential (e.g. Clutton-Brock and Parker 1995). Models of the evolution of cooperation and punishment in sizeable groups, all of which resemble Boyd and Richerson 1992, indicate that third-party punishment evolves under quite different dynamics than pair-wise reciprocity, negative or positive.

Punishment in groups ('punishment' from here on), however, can maintain large-scale cooperation among many unrelated individuals, as well as stabilize any behavior for which individuals punish deviations from a norm (Boyd and Richerson 1992; Henrich and Boyd 2001). In this body of theory, as well, stability of interactions affects the strength of norms and of punishment behavior. Although it is unclear how punishment might get started, since it seems incapable of invading a population of non-punishers, longer lasting interactions promote the stability and strength of punishment even in quite large groups. Thus, whether one takes models of pair-wise reciprocity as the basis (a likely mistake) or models of punishment in large groups, the stability of relationships and community structure strongly impact the profits to be had from punishment.

Among Sangu farmers, life is rather predictable. The rains most always come, same time, same place. Individuals live very close to unrelated individuals and continue to do so for most of their lives, as they are tied to specific pieces of land. Land is becoming scarce, making tenure more pronounced. Relationships with one's neighbors, for a farmer, are very important. The farmer has nowhere else to go. All of these factors create very long tenure and stable community composition, both of which promote the relative effectiveness of pro-social behaviors, as well as punishment as a regulating behavior which maintains pro-social (or any, cf. Boyd and Richerson 1992) behavior.

Among Sangu herders, life is much less predictable. No one knows when the rains come, or where. Individuals live very closely with kin, but quite far from non-kin. Residence also shifts, as households look for better locales. Polygynous herders often maintain multiple households, spending long periods of time away from one community to be in another. During part of the year, most of the unmarried and newly married men are away with herds in the north, largely isolated from any community. When disagreements occur, angry parties can simply move away. No one is tied too closely to the land, after all. All of these factors attenuate relationships and bring into doubt the chances of the same group memberships forming in the future. These shorter and less dependable interactions then weaken the advantages and feasibility of punishment.

If these differences in community structure and mobility do indeed influence rates of rejection, the problem of explaining how the two communities have the same offer distributions remains. Another explanation is needed for that substantial problem.

Age may explain differences in rejections and offers

I showed earlier how younger individuals both made lower average offers and were more likely to reject. One way to interpret these results is to imagine that younger subjects are better educated, and therefore better able to understand the game and play 'rationally', at least with respect to offers. This cannot be true, however, since education, while it varies quite a lot within the samples, explains little variation in either offers or rejections. A bigger problem with such an explanation is that it leads us to explain offer behavior as 'rational' while younger people are also more likely to reject positive offers, which is surely the most 'irrational' behavior possible in the Ultimatum Game.

It might be true, however, that younger subjects are more experienced with markets, wherein anonymous or functionally-anonymous interactions are common. This could be true regardless of educational level. Such exposure would then lead them somehow to play the Ultimatum Game more like peoples from industrialized areas. Again, however, this will explain higher rejections, but not lower offers, since offers appear to rise with industrialization or sociopolitical complexity (see Chapter 1). The trouble with this explanation is that we might then expect gender to explain some of the variation, since men have considerably more experience with markets than women. Women in Usangu travel far less than male peers, are less likely to speak the national language (Swahili), and generally spend more time, both in production and recreation, at the homestead. Despite these substantial differences and exposure to markets, gender does not explain any substantial variation in either offers or rejections. It might be, of course, that a small amount of market exposure is just as good as a lot, and therefore gender explains little of the variation. If that were true, however, it is difficult to see how the differences in exposure between older and younger subjects could produce offer and rejection variation when comparable differences in market exposure do not produce similar variation based on gender.

A final possibility is that the younger subject are less risk-averse. This would produce lower mean offers, but it is unclear how less risk-aversion would produce more rejections as well.

Ultimatum Game possibly conflates punishment and retribution

The results of the many Ultimatum Game experiments, even without those in this volume, have motivated some to suggest that humans have an innate sense of fairness or taste for punishment (Camerer and Thaler 1995; Roth 1995; Konow 1996). In light of the cross-cultural results in this volume, it is clear that any such tastes are not entirely universal, however. They are widespread and vary with institutional setting and other unknown variables. One of the interpretations I have made above is that intracultural variation in social structure and residential patterns might explain differences in rates of rejection in the Ultimatum Game.

Yet while all these results provide a great deal of evidence that considerations including sharing, retribution, and punishment of norm violations strongly influence economic behavior, the game does little to help us disentangle the relative contributions of these considerations or clearly relate our theoretical variables to our game data. Some of this difficulty arises from the functional ambiguity of player behavior in the Ultimatum Game. Here are two examples of how that ambiguity complicates interpretation.

Actual (rather than observed) farmer and herder norms may be different Perhaps farmers have a weaker sharing norm (which generates offers), but high rejection rates push up their modal offer so it resembles the herder norm, which is more fair and requires less punishment (rejection) to maintain. This interpretation is consistent with the argument above that stability of relationships contributes to different rates of punishment. These different rates of punishment then create the illusion that the sharing norms (the offer behaviors) are the same for both farmers and herders. Playing the Dictator Game (which only involves offers with no chance of rejection) with the same population can help determine if the sharing norms are different, but it cannot resolve the role of rejection in altering these offers, especially if players' *expectations* of rejection are altering their offers. In light of Fehr and Gächter's (2000) data, which show that individuals begin to contribute more to a public good even before they are punished, we might easily expect that players alter their offers in response to imagined rejections.

Rejections may have little or nothing to do with the sharing norm   It is unclear if rejections function to promote sharing behavior, since retribution (desire to get revenge) may motivate part or the majority of rejections. It is important to distinguish punishment (a cost imposed on actors for violating a norm where the punisher pays a cost herself) from retribution (negative pair-wise reciprocity intended to preserve reputation) because models of the evolution of cooperation suggest that reciprocity and negative reciprocity (what I am calling 'retribution' here) have little or nothing to do with the formation or maintenance of public goods. It is possible, for example, that farmers 'punish' just as much as herders, but are more likely to pursue retribution. This would produce different levels of rejections, even though the actual functional rejections, punishments, were rare in both groups and maintained the same levels of sharing. Essentially, the Ultimatum Game cannot separate retributive motivations ('That bastard cheated me, and I can't let him get away with that.') from desire to punish norm violators ('That is a bad person.'), since the player receiving the offer owns all reputational effects from accepting or rejecting. In this case, that plausible differences in rejections do not lead to different offer distributions would result from the fact that many rejections are retributive and have little to do with the maintenance of norms about sharing, which might still generate the observed offers.

These problems in interpretation arise from limitations of the structure of the game. To explore questions about the nature of public goods and punishment, more complex multiparty games (such as Fehr and Gächter 2000, 2002) are more appropriate. The drawback is that such games may be nearly impossible to efficiently organize in the field.

REFERENCES

Axelrod, R. M. (1984). *The Evolution of Cooperation*. New York: Basic Books.
Bolton, G. E. and Zwick, R. (1995). 'Anonymity versus punishment in ultimatum bargaining', *Games and Economic Behavior*, 10, 95–121.
Boyd, R. and Richerson, P. J. (1985). *Culture and the Evolutionary Process*. Chicago, IL: University of Chicago Press.
—— —— (1992). 'Punishment allows the evolution of cooperation (or anything else) in sizable groups', *Ethology and Sociobiology*, 13, 171–95.
Camerer, C. and Thaler, R. H. (1995). 'Anomalies: Ultimatums, dictators and manners', *Journal of Economic Perspectives*, 9, 209–19.
Charnley, S. (1994). Cattle, Commons, and Culture: The Political Ecology of Environmental Change on a Tanzanian Rangeland. Ph.D. Dissertation, Stanford University.
Clutton-Brock, T. H. and Parker, G. A. (1995). 'Punishment in animal societies', *Nature (London)*, 373, 209–16.
Evans-Pritchard, E. E. (1940). *The Nuer: A Description of the Modes of Livelihood and Political Institutions of a Nilotic People*. Oxford: Clarendon Press.
Fehr, E. and Gächter, S. (2000). 'Cooperation and punishment in public goods experiments', *American Economic Review*, 90, 980–94.
—— —— (2002). 'Altruistic punishment in humans', *Nature*, 415(10), 137–40.
Fiske, A. P. (n.d.) *Learning a Culture the Way Informants Do: Observation, Imitation, and Participation*.
Hazlewood, A. and Livingstone, I. (1978). *The Development Potential of the Usangu Plains of Tanzania: A Study*. London: Commonwealth Secretariat.
Henrich, J. and Boyd, R. (2001). 'Why people punish defectors: Weak conformist transmission can stabilize costly enforcement of norms in cooperative dilemmas', *Journal of Theoretical Biology*, 208, 79–89.
—— and McElreath, R. (2002). 'Are peasants risk averse decision-makers?', *Current Anthropology*, 43(1), 172–81.
Kagel, J. H. and Roth, A. E. (eds) (1995). *The Handbook of Experimental Economics*. Princeton, NJ: Princeton University Press.
Konow, J. (1996). 'A positive theory of economic fairness', *Journal of Economic Behavior and Organization*, 31, 13–35.

Pipping, K. (1976). *Land Holding in the Usangu Plain. Scandanavian Institute of African Studies Research Report No. 33.* Uppsala: Scandanavian Institute of African Studies.

Roth, A. (1995). 'Bargaining Experiments', in J. H. Kagel and A. E. Roth (eds), *The Handbook of Experimental Economics*, Princeton, NJ: Princeton University Press, pp. 253–348.

Shorter, A. (1972). *Chiefship in Western Tanzania.* Oxford: Clarendon Press.

Turton, D. (1980). 'The economics of Mursi bridewealth: A comparative perspective', in J. L. Comaroff (eds), *Meaning of Marriage Payments*, London: Academic Press.

Wright, M. (1971). *German Missions in Tanganyika.* Oxford: Clarendon Press.

12

Market Integration and Fairness: Evidence from Ultimatum, Dictator, and Public Goods Experiments in East Africa

Jean Ensminger

It is now well established that people in developed economies behave very differently in economic experiments than narrow economic self-interest would predict. Specifically, people appear to be more fair-minded and cooperative than predictions based on *Homo economicus* would lead us to assume (Fehr and Schmidt 1999; Henrich *et al.* Chapter 2, this volume). Intriguingly, the first data from a less developed society, namely the Amazonian Machiguenga study of Henrich (2000), which was a pilot for this volume, demonstrated far less fair-mindedness. Many of the other less developed societies represented in this volume also have means and modes in the Ultimatum Game that are below those for developed societies. Indeed, one of the hypotheses that holds across these less developed small-scale societies is the positive relationship between Market Integration and offer size in the Ultimatum Game (see Henrich *et al.* Chapter 2, this volume). While the cross-cultural evidence alone justifies a closer look at this relationship, it is also worth pursuing studies of intracultural variation in societies that have significant variation in market involvement. The Orma of East Africa is one such society.

To most people the notion that individuals in market societies might be more fair-minded seems counterintuitive. My highly anecdotal survey of such opinion demonstrates that this may hold

The author is particularly grateful for the constructive comments of Sam Bowles and Herb Gintis and for seminar participants at Washington University and the University of Cologne, where this chapter has been presented. The author also wishes to thank the MacArthur Foundation for generous support of this research. While conducting research in Kenya the author was affiliated with the Institute for Development Studies at the University of Nairobi. Members of the Institute provided much encouragement and valued critiques of this work in an informal seminar. Finally, the author also would like to thank the Government of Kenya for granting research clearance for this project.

true for economists, anthropologists, and lay people alike (see David Wessel, WSJ January 24, 2002: 1). Thus it is with good reason that we may wish to approach any data to the contrary cautiously. In defense of the counterintuitive, however, it is worth noting that the argument is not without its sympathizers (Hirschman 1982). Nor, I would argue, is it entirely implausible.

Hirschman (1982) traces the history of thought on the effects of commerce on the citizen and civil society. Hirschman begins with Montesquieu (1973 [1749], Vol. 2: 8), who notes that, 'wherever there is commerce, manners are gentle'. And again, 'Commerce... polishes and softens (*adoucit*) barbaric ways', (p. 81). Particularly prominent in Hirshman's review of these early scholars is the increasing premium on honesty and reputation attributed to market economies due to the requirements of repeat dealing. In contrast, the early nineteenth century, according to Hirschman, brought the contrary view represented by Marx and others, that markets undermine the moral foundations of society. The new view placed more emphasis upon the corrosive effect of self-interested behavior that was encouraged by the market and which eroded traditional values. Hirschman himself concludes (1982: 1483) that both forces are likely at work in market societies. Thus, 'the constant practice of commercial transactions generates feelings of trust, empathy for others, and similar *doux* feelings, but on the other hand, as Montesquieu already knew, such practice permeates all spheres of life with the element of calculation and of instrumental reason'. While he notes the loss of predictive power associated with accepting the complexity of this duality, Hirschman concludes that it is probably the most accurate perspective. If Hirschman is right, then we might expect to see something of this bimodal distribution (between pure self-interest and pure altruism) in experimental data from market societies, which indeed we do.

Hirschman's argument for the socializing effects of the market hinges upon the increasing importance and value of reputation in market societies. One avenue for extension to behavioral predictions in economic experiments is to propose that a powerful way to signal one's reputation is to engage in fair-minded behavior. This leads to the hypothesis that we would expect more fair-minded offers among those most involved in the market. This is indeed consistent with the findings that will be presented below for the Orma, and also consistent with our cross-cultural results in this volume.

One problem that needs to be addressed if we are to entertain a reputation-building explanation for fairness in these experiments concerns the anonymous and one-shot nature of these games. In the games there is no reputation-building built into the game because they will not be repeated, and there are no possible spillover effects from the game to everyday life because they are played anonymously. A number of accounts from behavioral economics and elsewhere can help us understand why even under these conditions we could see people invoking 'rules of thumb' learned in the everyday life of repeated interactions. Gabaix and Laibson (2000) provide a psychologically plausible model of how people make complicated decisions. In their account it is assumed that cognition is costly and that accurate calculation is impossible. People economize by not considering decision alternatives of low probability. It is conceivable that in the context of many small-scale societies, if not all societies, guaranteed perfect Anonymity is a rare event—so much so that people behave in many contexts as if their behavior will be known. Thus, we might find behavior in one-shot games consistent with behavior more appropriate to repeated games. Put simply, people invoke 'rules of thumb' cued by reminders of familiar circumstances when faced with a completely novel situation, as might occur in an economic experiment.

Robert Frank's work (1988) is also relevant here. He argues that, while it might pay for an opportunist to fake cooperative behavior, there may be physical limitations to our ability to deceive consistently, such that it does not pay to try to do so. This would also explain why behavior learned in a repeated environment cannot be easily turned off in a one-shot context.

Both cognitive and psychological explanations can help us understand how even self-interested individuals could exhibit fairness in one-shot games and also how behavior designed primarily to promote reputation could emerge there. But it is quite likely that something more profound is surfacing in these data that points to the internalization of fairness norms in more market-oriented societies. Such internalization would require that fairness is learned in the course of market exchange and we have evidence that this is the case across the developmental life cycle. Camerer and Thaler (1995) agree that norms of fairness are learned, noting that kindergarteners are the most selfish in economic experiments, while by the sixth grade, more fair behavior towards one's peers emerges.

One of the curiosities of the relationship between Market Integration and fairness is that we have much ethnographic evidence from the least market oriented societies (especially hunters and gatherers/horticulturalists) that emphasizes a tremendous amount of sharing. The fact that such societies show up in this cross-cultural study as often the least generous in the Ultimatum Game appears superficially to be inconsistent with real life. One explanation for this anomaly is that the high degree of sharing we observe in many of these societies is the result of precise rules specifying behaviors such as meat sharing, and the considerable monitoring that occurs naturally in close-knit small-scale societies. In other words, despite the apparent presence of sharing, it may not be the case that a 'norm' of generalized sharing has been internalized that can apply to new opportunities and circumstances. Self enforcement need not develop when second party enforcement is ever-present. In market societies, however, where social monitoring is less efficient and rigid rules mandating sharing do not exist, cooperation may require the internalization of basic norms such as fairness that may have their origins in reputation building.

Although I have had a long-standing interest in the effects of Market Integration on small-scale societies, I did not set out to test hypotheses concerning Market Integration when I was asked to join the cross-cultural experimental project upon which this volume is based.[1] Like many of the others, my first venture into experimental economics in the bush was largely theoretically inductive and methodologically exploratory. I was not confident that controlled experiments with the Orma would even be logistically possible. In the end, I learned a great deal about feasible methods for conducting experiments in the bush, and returned with a modest sample of ultimatum bargaining games ($n = 56$), Dictator Games ($n = 43$), and Public Goods Games ($n = 24$), from which to develop hypotheses for future testing.[2] These results are presented below, together with some analysis that points to directions for future research and theory testing.

[1] I began research with the Orma in 1978 and have returned on numerous occasions (1978–1981, 1987, 1994, 1996, 1998–2000) to study changes in the political economy that have accompanied the steady increase of market participation (see especially Ensminger 1992).

[2] I also ran some investment (also known as trust) games on this trip, but those results will not be discussed here.

ETHNOGRAPHIC CONTEXT—THE POLITICAL
ECONOMY OF THE ORMA

In this section of the chapter I highlight some aspects of Orma life
that may be relevant to their behavior in the experiments (for more
details see Ensminger 1992). The picture is necessarily broad brush,
but the attempt is to at least touch upon issues in the political
economy and social arena that may be salient to the analysis.

The pastoral Orma share Tana River District in northern Kenya
with the Pokomo, who farm the narrow flood plain of the Tana
River, and lesser numbers of Wardei and Somali pastoralists. The
Orma are divided geographically from north to south into three
sections and this research took place among the geographically
central Galole Orma. No accurate population statistics for the
entire Orma ethnic group exist, but I would estimate the total to be
between 30,000 and 60,000. The Galole population is roughly
10,000–20,000.

The Orma are a pastoral–nomadic group dependent primarily
upon cattle, though many households also keep sheep and goats
and an increasing number each year diversifies into trade and wage
labor. Most sedentary households are now also pursuing opportunistic flood plain agriculture, which yields a harvest once every two
or three rainy seasons. A local stone quarry also provides income to
those who dig stones for builders in the district capital. Regardless
of these efforts at diversification, even sedentary households are still
heavily tied to the livestock economy.

Historically, the Orma were quite wealthy pastoralists largely due
to their military prowess and the lush riverine environment they
inhabited along the seasonal rivers and delta of the Tana River.
But given substantial losses of territory to game reserves, private
ranches, irrigation schemes, and immigrant Wardei and Somali,
coupled with a healthy population growth rate, the Orma are not
nearly as well off on a per capita basis as they were even 20 years
ago. One consequence of these trends has been an increase in
sedentarization. While this process began in the 1950s, it accelerated
substantially in the 1970s, perhaps in large part as a consequence of
the devastating Sahelian drought. The rich are drawn to settled
living for an easier life (including proximity to transport and the
dispensary), to pursue economic diversity in the form of trade and

wage employment, and to educate their children. Many of the poor settle to pursue opportunistic flood plain agriculture along the banks of the seasonal rivers and because there are no longer sufficient numbers of rich pastoralists to support them in a nomadic lifestyle.

It is widely recognized by the Orma that sedentarization is associated with a more commercially oriented lifestyle. Sedentarization usually involves the removal of livestock far from the overgrazed permanent village to places where grazing conditions are superior. This means that virtually all food must be purchased, and this in turn involves the sale of a great deal of livestock; many have found it difficult to increase their herds under these conditions. Meanwhile, those who persist as nomads are attempting to live a more subsistence lifestyle based upon the products of their herds, which they hope will grow in size as they avoid cattle sales. Since the late 1970s, approximately two-thirds of the Orma have been sedentary.[3] Given this variation in economic strategy, the Orma afford a broad continuum of market orientation, as there are many households that engage in wage labor and purchase virtually all of their daily foodstuffs, and others that go half the year living exclusively off the milk and by-products of their herds and do so at remote distances from towns and trade of any sort.

Even today, outward signs of development are absent in the Orma interior. There is no running water, no electricity, roads are scarce, and people live in grass houses with few personal possessions beyond clothing and cooking pots. Most sedentary households send their sons to primary school, fewer send daughters, but even fewer attend school for more than 3 years; almost all of the adult population is illiterate.

Like most East African pastoralists, the Orma are patrilineal and largely patrilocal. Inheritance norms are gradually drifting from primogeniture to equal inheritance for sons, possibly as a consequence of Islamic influence. While the ideal is for brothers to stay together even after their father's death, this is now the exception rather than the norm. Most sons split off to set up independent households even before the father's death. This and many other

---

[3] There has been a small movement back toward nomadism by rich and poor. I believe this can be explained by the general decline in the Kenyan economy such that the benefits of market exchange have diminished in comparison to the gains from a nomadic lifestyle.

social changes are likely related to the increasing bargaining power of young men, who through wage labor and diversification of the economy in the sedentary sector, have independent means such that they are no longer completely dependent upon their father's monopolistic control of household wealth in the form of the family herd.

Politically, the Orma are subject to the institutions of Kenya. The highest ranking local civil servant resident among the population is the government appointed Chief, who resides in one of the sedentary towns where this research took place. The Chief's major functions have to do with the rule of law and the interface between the local population and the government of Kenya. He both adjudicates many disputes locally in consultation with the council of elders and refers other cases, mostly criminal ones, to the national court structure in the district headquarters. The Chief is also responsible for the distribution of government famine relief and the organization of local *harambee* fund raising activities for the schools and other community development efforts (see below under the Public Goods Game for more details on this institution). To a remarkable degree (and contrary to the experience of other parts of Kenya and even other parts of Ormaland), these government sponsored initiatives and the adjudication process are run in a disciplined and largely uncorrupt manner in this particular local area. This was also the case under the previous two chiefs going back at least to the 1950s.

The Orma have strong clan affiliations, though these had greater significance in the past than they do today. Beginning around 1990, the practice of clan exogamy broke down. This is probably a consequence rather than a cause of the demise of clans. Clans and lineages are influential in the adjudication of disputes. Minor family and property matters are resolved between the senior lineage elders of the disputing parties. When they are unable to agree, the case is brought to the Chief's office. He then convenes what he deems to be an appropriate assortment of more senior clan and lineage elders representing both sides and the case is usually resolved. Very few domestic cases make it past this process and move up to the national court system.

In addition to the Chief's office, other signs of government infrastructure in the area include a local dispensary, three primary schools, security forces at the disposal of the Chief, and veterinary agents. The presence of the 'state' is increasingly felt in this remote part of Kenya. Nevertheless, it is fair to say that relative to the rest of Kenya, Ormaland remains considerably autonomous. One example of this is that despite a mandate in 1978 that all children must attend primary school, less than 50 percent of Orma school aged children attend school even to this day, some 25 years after the Presidential edict.

Property rights among the Orma are quite clearly specified. Land is held in common by all Orma, while livestock are owned individually, mostly by male heads of lineages. Women generally do not own many livestock, but may acquire some as gifts from their fathers, husbands, or close friends, in dowry, in bridewealth payments, in inheritance from husbands, and occasionally in trade. Women own all of the milk from their allocated milking stock and are free to market it as ghee when there is a surplus. Women also own the skins of all livestock and regularly market sheep and goat hides, while they retain all cattle skins for personal use. Most individuals control all income from the marketing of any craft they sell or any profits from trade. The exception here is the income of sons still dependent upon their fathers. This is a gray area that leads to frequent disputes and often results in sons taking early separation from their father once their income is sufficient to 'go it alone'. Generally speaking, cash is viewed as a private good, and that is also true for cash earned in these experiments. This is especially the case with the experimental cash because the amounts were relatively small compared with say a dependent son's monthly salary, for example, which fathers almost always attempt to tax. Women do have access to cash through the sale of ghee, skins, and handicrafts. Their rights to private control of cash are well protected, and husbands are subject to severe punishment if they encroach upon the 'private bag' in which a woman keeps such items. Increasingly, women use a locked trunk for this purpose.

Between 1920 and 1940 the Orma made a universal conversion to Islam. This involved some dramatic initial changes in lifestyle that attest to the sincerity with which this mass conversion took place. Most remarkably, the population gave up alcohol, which had been central to many indigenous ceremonies, as it is today among most other East African pastoralists. By the 1950s a number of wealthy Orma were making the Hajj. Virtually all Orma today fast during Ramadan. Nevertheless, some Islamic institutions have been more difficult to meld into traditional Orma custom. For example, while the Orma are well aware that Islam mandates inheritance for women, this is not practiced among any households I know. Wealthy fathers often make presents of cows to their daughters, but I know of none who have given daughters the mandated half shares of each of their sons. There is, however, an increasing movement toward indirect dowry payments to the bride (mandated by Islam) and away from bridewealth payments to the bride's parents (see Ensminger and Knight 1997 for more details).

The status of women has certainly not declined since the Orma converted to Islam, and an argument could be made that it has risen substantially. However, many of the changes are a consequence of government initiatives. Most particularly, widowed women are increasingly refusing levirate marriage and remaining on their own. The Chief has heard many cases where the widow has been allowed to keep her deceased husband's property rather than return it to his brother. Both Islamic law and Kenyan law have been invoked in a number of women's rights cases.

Tithing is a fundamental requirement for Muslims, and indeed, the Orma do practice the annual tithe. As in all societies, some follow the letter of the law more precisely than others, and there is some self-serving reinterpretation of the rules at the margins. For example, it has become common practice to give a second cow (one more than the contracted annual fee) to one's hired laborers and count this against the annual tithe, when in fact it should be considered salary.

Noblesse oblige is a value system among the Orma that predates conversion to Islam. The notion that the rich have a responsibility to the poor has deep roots in Orma society. In the past, and even today among the nomads, there are reciprocal relationships between herd owners who are cattle rich and labor poor and those who have complementary assets and deficits. Until relatively recently there was also strong sentiment that clan and lineage members had an obligation to help those who suffered heavy losses in droughts by providing animals to facilitate restocking. Such sentiments have fallen as relatively few people perceive themselves to be wealthy enough to give so freely. This is also compounded by the early splitting up of large well-stocked households into many smaller units of independent sons. In short, conversion to Islam has not led to any major change in values among the Orma regarding relationships between rich and poor and generalized obligations of giving and wealth redistribution.

Sharing norms, especially regarding food, differ considerably from village to village. One relevant variable is whether the household lives a primarily subsistence strategy through nomadism or has converted to commercial cattle production and lives as a sedentary household purchasing most of its food. This distinction derives from the fact that nomads have better access to good grazing and water, and live with their herds where they are able to consume the milk. Milk yields are far higher than in sedentary villages and surplus milk has, relatively speaking, much less value. Thus, the costs of sharing are considerably lower. Grazing conditions around sedentary villages are poor and necessitate that stock is sent far away to better grazing, thus reducing the milk available for consumption. Families must purchase almost all of their food. Because all food is purchased at considerable expense in sedentary villages (it may easily make up 80 percent of a household's expenditure), and because such villages tend to be far larger than nomadic camps, there is less food sharing and what there is tends to be among tight networks.

METHODS

This cross-cultural project adds a great deal of diversity to our data base of experimental economics by expanding into non-western and less developed societies. Another advantage of these study sites is that it is easier to draw samples more representative of the population at large than is often the case in laboratory studies. While I make no claims that the sample used in this project is representative of all Orma, it almost certainly is more so than American university undergraduates can be said to represent the US population at large. However, this clear advantage of getting out of the university and out of the laboratory is counterbalanced by some of the problems associated with working with populations less adept at experiments, and in environments where controls are challenging.

Before turning to some of the more problematic issues facing experimentalists outside the laboratory, it is worth recording a few issues that one might expect to have been problems, but that in fact were not. There was no resistance by the Orma to playing the games; on the contrary, people loved them—by the end they were imploring me to make arrangements to come back as soon as possible and play more games. Of course they enjoyed the remuneration component of the games, but they also actually enjoyed the play itself and were intellectually amused. I received many jovial comments such as the following, 'I will be spending years trying to figure out what this all meant.'

While I began the games with concerns about logistics, these were ill-founded. Grass houses are not at all a hindrance to running experiments. In fact they were the perfect size for isolating small groups from one another during the course of play, and one research assistant seated by the door was able to keep groups from talking about the game, exiting, or chatting with visitors. 'Crowd control' turned out to be relatively simple. People never had to wait more than 3 hours to finish their play, but many were willing to do so. When I explained that they could not talk about the game during the play, there was remarkably disciplined compliance.

Prior to beginning the experiments I held a large public meeting to explain the work. This meeting was well attended by elders and young men, though fewer women showed up, as is the norm. I explained that this work would be quite different from my previous work, and that it would involve playing 'fun games for real money'. I purposely said nothing in this open forum about the content of the experiments, so as not to steer behavior in any way. But I explained that these were games being carried out around the world to study economic decision-making, and that they have been played many times in the United States and Europe. The discussion that ensued was one of great amusement at the 'insanity' of western ways. Most people seemed both at this point and after the games were played, to interpret them in this light; that is, westerners 'had money to throw away on such foolishness'. Some seemed to have a true under-standing of the nature of research and that this would somehow teach us something about human behavior. An alternative hypo-thesis that also floated around, perhaps never taken completely seriously, was that I wanted to provide aid to the community so I dreamt up this complicated scheme to provide an excuse to do so. One thing is certain: there was never any hesitation about accepting the money, whatever the reason assumed to explain the windfall.

I explained that I would be approaching every household in each of five villages with a household economic and demographic survey very similar to those I had administered in 1978 and 1987. No household was required to participate either in this survey or in the games that would follow. From the surveyed households I promised to try to invite at least one adult from each household to play a game.

Six native-speaking Orma research assistants with Form 4 education carried out the household economic surveys with 205 households in these five villages. Village size ranged from thirteen for the one nomadic village to 36–69 households in the four sedentary villages, with an average of 8.1 individuals per household, totaling 1,669 individuals in all. A three-generation genealogy was drawn for each household and individual demographic statistics for all household residents were gathered on relationship to head of household, age, sex, education, work, and income by source. Household level data on migration history, length of residence in the community, and wealth of household were also elicited. Voluntary compliance with this survey was 100 percent. At least one individual from almost all surveyed households played 1 of the 144 games (262 players).[4] Of those who made offers in the games reported here, the mean age was 37.7 and mean education was 1.4 years. Mean household wealth measured in cattle equivalents was 19.8 and individual income other than that from the sale of one's own stock averaged 665 Kenyan shillings per month.

All games were run jointly by a bilingual, native-speaking research assistant (the games master) and me. The school teacher I chose for this purpose was amazingly patient with 'slow learners', and has a reputation in the village for trustworthiness. Numerous native speakers were also used as monitors, but they were not in the room with individuals at the time offers were made. Given that the games master is known to many of the individuals playing the games, I had him turn around at the time offers were made to ensure that only I had access to that information, thus enhancing anonymity.

Many conditions of the experimental design for my study were set by the group project in order to standardize across the research sites. The stakes were set at approximately 1 day's casual labor wage, with a show-up fee of one-third of a day's wage for all sites.[5] In the Orma case, this translated into games played for 100 shillings or roughly the equivalent of $2; this was the local daily casual wage

---

[4] This includes the trust games that are not discussed in this chapter.
[5] I had no choice but to lower the show-up fee from one-third to one-fifth of a day's wage due to the shortage of currency in the necessary denominations.

rate at the time. Each player received a show-up fee of 20 shillings at the very beginning of the game instructions. This drove home the fact that they were playing for real money, and served as partial compensation to those who might not earn much in the games. Each of the game texts was back translated; that is, one native speaker translated it from English to the local language and another one, unfamiliar with the English text and the game, translated it back into English to ensure precision and clarity of meaning. All games were one-shot with no repeat play. I was careful to do exactly what I promised in each game to ensure that people did not distrust my intentions, and to facilitate understanding of the game; there were no sham offers. Feedback from trustful participants indicates that neither distrust of the experimenters, nor fear of losing anonymity were a problem.

Efforts were made to be as systematic as possible in sampling, but because the games had to be played en masse, there were biases toward availability. Given the enthusiasm that most people had for participating, however, this was less than one might expect. Young men who herd were underrepresented, but those working on their farms chose to take time out from their field preparations rather than miss the game. Undoubtedly, those who travel more and happened to be away are slightly underrepresented, though if they missed one opportunity to play they were often called a second time, as were herders. A major effort was made to include at least one adult from each household and often both a man and woman were included.

People were notified the night before a morning game that they could show up at a certain location to play. For the Ultimatum Game and Dictator Game I usually called twenty people for this purpose. In the largest two villages where school buildings were available, I ran through the game instructions with the entire group together. No one knew at this point whether they would be player one or player two. The game master read the instructions twice and I then demonstrated the play with a set of ten shilling coins. I ran through a randomly generated series of hypothetical possibilities of play, including rejections in the Ultimatum Game. Each person in the room was then quizzed with a hypothetical example to test for comprehension. The group was then left with two or three research assistants monitoring them with instructions that they could not discuss the game. Individual players were then brought in one by one to a separate room where only the game master and I were located. The order of play was determined publicly by drawing slips of paper from a hat with each player's name on it. This served to emphasize both the randomness in the order of play (which affected waiting time) and in the assignment of roles. Once alone, we ran through the rules of the game again until the individual understood the play. At this point they were told whether they were player one or player two. They made their offer by pushing whatever coins they wished to offer to one side of the table while the games master had his back turned. Once they had made their offer or declared their response to an offer, they were allowed to return home, but could not talk to any of those who had not already played the game. In the case of the Ultimatum Game, a second appointment time was set for first players to return and learn whether their offer had been accepted.

Four individuals had to be eliminated from play because they did not understand the game. One was blind, one was deaf, and two were rather slow. Once we were in private I paid them as if they had played and no one knew that they had actually not played the game.

One of the main differences between the studies represented in this project and those most often carried out in US laboratories, is that we are running them in small communities where most people know one another or at least have a high probability of having future repeat dealings. There is also a high level of interrelatedness. This characteristic may affect play in a number of different ways. People who live in small communities may habitually share more in every day life (as I discussed above), they may have different conceptions of privacy and anonymity, and there are more serious problems associated with contagion of the population if games are played over time.

I have a bit of anecdotal evidence that bears on the anonymity question. About a week after the play was finished in one large village, I made inquiries about what people knew about how other people had played. I was told that while some had told their close friends how they had played, most had not. They discussed the games in a general sense, but did not reveal their actual offers. A very close friend also approached me approximately a week after his wife had played the Dictator Game. The friend was curious how his wife had played because, 'She won't tell me'. Finally, three women who played the Dictator Game and kept the entire pot for themselves were so proud of the fact that they immediately ran into the village and told their neighbors. It is also entirely possible that some Orma lied about how they played, knowing fully well that there was no way anyone could challenge their assertion. Several people reported to me that the steps taken to ensure anonymity were obvious and that no one in the village was concerned about being found out.

I was especially concerned with the problem of contagion across the games once anyone in the village had played. People in small communities share information rapidly and freely within the community. These games raised a great deal of interest and it stands to reason that people talked about them. If one assumes that people talk, then those coming to play a game after the first round in a given village might have heard how the game was played and might also have heard discussion about the 'proper way to play the game'. I tried to get around these problems by calling large groups of people for a game and holding them all until the group was finished. I also moved from village to village as rapidly as possible to try to beat any news that might travel. Finally, I changed games and never announced which game people were being called for on any given day.

Another characteristic of this population that bears emphasis is that they are largely illiterate and unfamiliar with experiments. While extensive efforts were made to ensure that all participants understood the games clearly, and relatively simple games were chosen, the possibility remains that there is more 'noise' in these results stemming from misunderstanding the task than one often finds in experiments run in developed societies.

I turn now to a discussion of each game in turn.

THE ULTIMATUM BARGAINING GAME

It was Henrich's (2000) study of the ultimatum bargaining game among Machiguenga Indians that served as a pilot for this project. The Machiguenga made low offers and these were not refused. I also expected the Orma to make very low offers and for there to be almost no refusals. I was half right (see Figure 12.1). Orma mean offers were a high 44 percent (exactly in line with the US range), far higher than the 26 percent mean offer observed in the Amazon. Orma behavior departed from the US pattern, however, in the

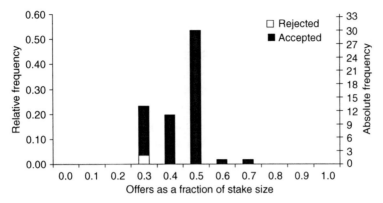

FIG. 12.1. Distribution of offers in the Ultimatum Game ($n = 56$, stake size $= 100$ Kenyan shillings)

distribution. In the United States it is common to have low offers (below 25 percent), and there is a significant rejection rate in this range (Camerer 2003). For the Orma the lowest offer out of fifty-six games was 30 percent, and there were only two refusals among the thirteen who received 30 percent offers. It may be significant that the only two rejecters were both educated men from rather wealthy families. It is difficult to make much of this, but the role of such individuals as the 'defenders' of social norms in society is so important that it bears further investigation. Notably, there is anecdotal evidence from a variety of the research sites reported in this study that rejecters in some of them also bear these characteristics.

In my postplay interviews with players, almost every player who offered 40 or 50 percent indicated that they did so because of fairness. In the formal interview immediately after the play, no one owned up to being strategic or fearing that a lesser offer would be rejected. Furthermore, virtually every responder indicated that he or she would have accepted an offer of even 10 percent, the lowest possible short of zero. While the fairness explanation was consistent with the willingness to accept low offers, I was still suspicious of proposers' motivations for giving high offers. I sought out a few reliable informants I knew I could trust to fill me in on 'the talk in the village'. The 'talk' revealed that people were *obsessed* with the possibility that their offer might be refused, in spite of the fact that they thought (correctly) that it was unlikely that people would refuse even a small offer. But very few wanted to take such a chance. Henrich and Smith (Chapter 5, this volume) report similar strategic thinking among the University of California, Los Angeles graduate students who feared there might be some people (albeit very few) out there who would reject any offer below 50 percent, and they did not want to miss their $80 (half of the $160 stake).

Table 12.1 presents the findings from the linear regression analysis. Both education and income are represented as dummy variables because the distributions are highly skewed toward zero in both cases (78 percent for education and 67 percent for income) and, in the case of income, there is a large lump in the middle of the positive distribution that represents the income shared by all in a common form of employment. Wealth is measured in cattle equivalents (with five sheep or goats equal to one steer). Virtually all wealth in the society is held in livestock. It is worth noting that the correlation between income and wealth is extremely low, as the income measure used here reflects income other than that acquired by the sale of one's own stock. Those who are wealthy in livestock often do not pursue employment in the wage market and/or trade, and thus do not have such incomes. The examination of individual level effects in a regression analysis demonstrates that the income dummy is the only variable that predicts size of offer at the 0.05 probability level or above. While education is not technically statistically significant, it is close, and furthermore, the sign is negative. One explanation for this could be that more educated individuals are cuing on the 'strategic' nature of the game (i.e. what is the lowest offer I can get away with) and making lower offers as a consequence. Following the discussion of all of the games, I shall

TABLE 12.1. Linear regression of Ultimatum Game offer

Variables	Coefficient	SE	β	p value
Age	−0.064	0.102	−0.096	0.533
Sex	0.569	2.990	0.030	0.850
Education dummy	−5.886	3.037	−0.289	0.058
Wealth	−0.033	0.0459	−0.102	0.474
Income dummy	6.216	2.933	0.335	0.039
Constant	45.953	4.966		0.000

return to the implications of the wage market effect demonstrated in these results.

While we cannot differentiate fairness from strategic economic self-interest in the ultimatum bargaining game, the Dictator Game does facilitate this disaggregation.

THE DICTATOR GAME

The Orma mean offer for the Dictator Game was 31 percent (see Figure 12.2). While this is high for comparable experiments from the developed world, which range from 20 to 30 percent, it is not far out of bounds and is significantly lower than their offers of 44 percent in the Ultimatum Game. It would appear, therefore, that contrary to Orma statements that all of their offers in the Ultimatum Game were driven by fairness, some appear to have been influenced by strategy. What is most striking in the Orma case is the distribution of offers. While it is common to find 30–40 percent of players taking all of the pot in the United States and Canada, one finds a much smaller percentage of purely self-interested players among the Orma (9 percent). This may result from an aversion to giving nothing, or taking all, which also appears to be evident among the Hadza (see Marlowe, Chapter 6, this volume). The

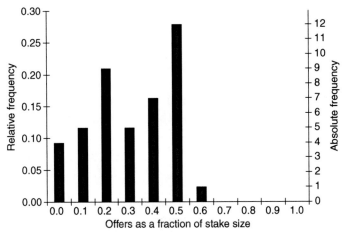

FIG. 12.2. Distribution of offers in the Dictator Game ($n = 43$, stake size $= 100$ Kenyan shillings)

TABLE 12.2. Linear regression of Dictator Game offer

Variables	Coefficient	SE	β	p value
Age	−0.277	0.204	−0.2109	0.179
Sex	0.518	7.204	0.015	0.943
Education dummy	−9.413	9.608	−0.158	0.334
Wealth	0.113	0.110	0.161	0.308
Income dummy	16.786	7.304	0.478	0.027
Constant	33.073	10.858		0.004

Note: $n = 43$; Adjusted $R^2 = 0.0884$.

number playing for fairness, at 40–50 percent, is about the same for the Orma and US samples. Thus, while there are two modal strategies in the developed world—pure fairness and pure self-interest—there is less consensus among the Orma. In other words, behavior is not driven by a dominant or by two competing norms. The bulk of the distribution for the Orma falls between pure self-interest and pure fairness.

As was the case in the Ultimatum Game, the only variable that is a statistically significant predictor of offer size is a dummy variable for presence or absence of wage/trade income (Table 12.2). Age, sex, education, and wealth of household are all insignificant as predictors of offer size. I discuss the wage/trade income effect below following the discussion of the Public Goods Game.

It is worth commenting that in the Dictator Game the effect of education that was noted in the Ultimatum Game is considerably less strong here. Again, this would be consistent with the fact that among the educated the Ultimatum Game may cue strategy, while the Dictator Game may cue fairness for both educated and uneducated (cf. Henrich and Smith, Chapter 5, this volume).

THE PUBLIC GOODS GAME

I ran a version of the Public Goods Game with four players. For this game I purposely chose a sample of younger men (mean age of thirty) with and without formal education. I was concerned that this game would be difficult for uneducated people to understand and

I wished to stratify the sample to test whether or not competence in math might make a difference in their play; it did not. As there are very few educated women, I did not use women in this game. Four to twelve individuals were called at a time from each village. Once people had played they were not allowed to have any contact with those who had not played. No instructions were given to the group as a whole and each group of four was called in to a separate room to play the game. The instructions were read twice, numerous examples were demonstrated, and players were allowed to ask questions related only to the rules and mechanics of the game. No discussion of the play itself was allowed. Each individual was endowed with 50 shillings and given the opportunity to contribute any or all of it to a 'group project'. All contributions were made privately in an envelope so that no one but the experimenter knew the amount of each contribution. The envelopes were shuffled before they were opened to be sure that no one could tell who had contributed what. I had previously numbered the inside of each envelope and was therefore able to record the contributions by individual to capture the demographic correlates. The sum of all their contributions was counted by a member of the group, doubled by me, and divided equally among all four players.

Orma contributions to the Public Goods Game were on the high end of the spectrum relative to US populations, coming in at 58 percent (see Figure 12.3). US contributions range from 40 to 60 percent (Ledyard 1995). The ethnographic context is enlightening

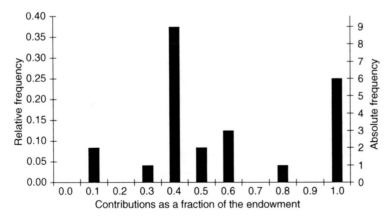

FIG. 12.3. Distribution of offers in the four-person Public Goods Game ($n = 24$, endowment = 50 Kenyan shillings with doubling of contributions by experimenter)

here. When this game was first described to my research assistants, they immediately identified it as the '*harambee*' game, a Swahili word for the institution of village-level contributions for public goods projects such as building a school. The government of Kenya has for many years encouraged the formal use of *harambee* fund-raising as a means of community development. This institution did not become adopted by the Orma until relatively recently. In the 1990s its importance rose as the Orma became increasingly seden-tary and began to appreciate education at exactly the same time that the government could no longer afford to build schools. *Harambee* is much encouraged by the government, which provides receipt books and some oversight of accounts.[6] There was in fact a major *harambee* collection ongoing at the time of these games. After these games it was clearly evident from the comments of participants that many made the association between this game and the institution of *harambee*.

I suggest that the Orma were more willing to trust their fellow villagers not to free ride in the Public Goods Game because they associated it with a learned and predictable institution. While the game had no punishment for free riding associated with it, the ana-logous institution with which they are familiar does. A social norm has been established over the years with strict enforcement that mandates what to do in an exactly analogous situation. It is possible that this institution 'cued' a particular behavior in this game.

In a recent paper, Ochenfels and Weimann (1999) present data from common goods and solidarity games played in East and West Germany. They find West Germans to be considerably more cooperative than East Germans, and make the case for culture-specific norms resulting from differing economic and social histories in the two parts of Germany. It is a fascinating cross-cultural case because so many often-confounding variables are controlled for; namely: language, currency, and the experimenters. The work is relevant to this discussion because it is also conceivable that the West Germans are more cooperative as a direct result of their experiences with formal institutional structures in much the same way that I am speculating about the Orma case.

---

[6] It should be noted that these highly localized *harambee* collections in which the Orma participate are largely (though not entirely) free of the corruption that usually accompanies these efforts when they are conducted at the national level or cross-regionally.

TABLE 12.3. Linear regression of Public Goods Game offer

Variables	Coefficient	SE	β	p value
Age	0.297	0.480	0.139	0.544
Education dummy	−0.137	6.623	−0.005	0.984
Wealth	0.637	0.303	0.500	0.050
Income dummy	10.281	7.124	0.350	0.166
Constant	2.634	17.840		0.884

Note: $n = 23$; Males only; Adjusted $R^2 = 0.0559$.

Bearing in mind that the sample used for this game was less systematically representative than that used for the other two games, and the sample size was quite small ($n = 24$), the overall regression analysis turns up some interesting results that speak to the role of this institution in the context of Orma society (Table 12.3). While market involvement (as measured in the income dummy) was significant in both the Ultimatum Game and Dictator Game, it is not significant here. Furthermore, wealth of household is significant, while it was not in either of the other games. Again, this might have to do with the particulars of the *harambee* institution that this game so closely mimics. As practiced today, *harambee* fund raisings, while modeled on the pattern of 'voluntary' contributions to public goods, are actually more akin to progressive taxation. Households are assessed specific amounts which they are required to pay toward the community development project. This process is quite open, and there is a graduated scale, going from the poorest members of society, who pay nothing, to those who are required to pay 5,000 Kenyan shillings ($83). The fact that wealthier members of the community voluntarily contributed more in the Public Goods Game is actually consistent with real behavior in the society.

THE EFFECTS OF WAGE/TRADE INCOME IN THE ULTIMATUM AND DICTATOR GAMES

The most significant and potentially interesting finding to come out of this set of games has to do with differences between those who earn income other than from the sale of their own livestock and those who do not. Wage/trade income in this context includes: casual wage labor, civil service employment, profits from trade in livestock or other products that are not one's own, digging stones at a local quarry for sale to builders, or production of handicrafts for sale. The argument for excluding income from household stock sales is to better highlight the difference between those who engage directly in market exchange beyond the marketing of surplus production from their subsistence herds, and those who do not. This distinction also allows for the disaggregation of wealth and income effects. Income from livestock sales is far more closely correlated with wealth (measured in livestock) than is the income measure used here. Income, absent own stock sales, is not correlated with wealth, as many of those who are driven to market their labor do so because they cannot support themselves from subsistence livestock production or sales from their herds.

In the Ultimatum Game and Dictator Game, the presence or absence of wage/trade income is a highly significant predictor of offer size. In Figures 12.4 and 12.5, for each game we see that those with wage/trade income clearly favor 50–50 splits in both games. While 50 percent offer half in the Dictator Game, nearly 80 percent do so in the Ultimatum Game. These norms are in dramatic contrast to the absence of any such spike among those without such

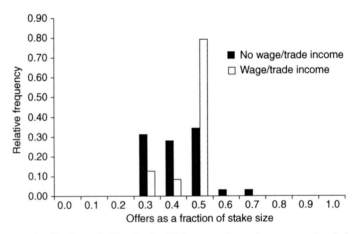

FIG. 12.4. Distribution of offers in the Ultimatum Game by no wage/trade income ($n = 32$) and positive wage income ($n = 24$), stake size = 100 Kenyan shillings

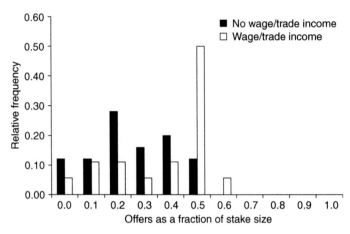

FIG. 12.5. Distribution of offers in the Dictator Game by no wage/trade income ($n = 25$) and positive wage income ($n = 18$), stake size = 100 Kenyan shillings

income. Indeed, it is striking that among those less integrated in the market there is no clear normative tendency whatever, nor do we find the bimodal pattern so typical in developed societies where both pure selfishness and pure altruism compete to form two modes. Epps-Singleton tests were run on each of these games individually and on the sum of both games together. In the Ultimatum Game ($n = 56$; no income = 32, positive income = 24), the Epps-Singleton for high versus low market is significant at the 0.017 level. In the Dictator Game ($n = 43$; no income = 25, positive income = 18), the Epps-Singleton is significant at the 0.050 level. If one lumps the offers in both games ($n = 99$; no income = 57, positive income = 42), the Epps-Singleton is significant at the 0.001 level.

The tendency for more and less market-oriented individuals to play differently does not hold in the Public Goods Game. However, it is worth noting that the sample size is small ($n = 24$), it represents younger men (average age of thirty versus thirty-nine and forty respectively for the Dictator Games and Ultimatum Games), and there are considerably fewer of them with income ($n = 9$) than in the other games.

Discussions with the Orma clearly indicate that the Public Goods Game was cueing associations to the real life *harambee*. That being the case, the appropriate response was for the wealthy to contribute more, as indeed they did. There would have been no reason for those with wage/trade incomes to feel compelled to offer more, as these are often poor individuals. The Dictator Games and Ultimatum Games were certainly cueing 'fairness' based upon my one-on-one interviews postplay. Obviously, the Ultimatum Game was also cueing strategic behavior, as the offers were substantially higher than were those in the Dictator Game when the rejection possibility was relaxed. What remains to be explained is why those engaged in wage labor and trade were more prone to engage in fair behavior than those more engaged in subsistence production.

These Orma results are consistent with the general finding from the overall cross-cultural project that shows fairness increasing with market integration. Something appears to trigger fair-mindedness in association with exposure to market institutions. I suggested at the beginning of the chapter that among those selling either their labor or their goods, there may be a higher premium placed upon reputation, and that one way of signaling a good reputation is to behave fair-mindedly. Eventually, this norm appears to be internalized, as is evident from its emergence in the anonymous, one-shot, economic experiments. This hypothesis warrants future replication in tightly controlled experiments with even more cross-cultural samples and also with cases similar to the Orma that offer a broad spectrum of variation in market integration within one society, thus helping to control for a vast array of potential confounds.

REFERENCES

Camerer, C. F. (2003). 'Dictator, Ultimatum, and Trust Games', Chapter 3, *Behavioral Game Theory*. New York: Russell Sage Foundation.
—— and Thaler, R. (1995). 'Ultimatums, dictators and manners', *Journal of Economic Perspectives*, 9(2), 209–19.
Ensminger, J. (1992). *Making a Market: The Institutional Transformation of an African Society*. New York: Cambridge University Press.
—— and Knight, J. (1997). 'Changing social norms: Common property, bridewealth, and clan exogamy', *Current Anthropology*, 38(1), 1–24.
Fehr, E. and Schmidt, K. (1999). 'A theory of fairness, competition, and cooperation', *Quarterly Journal of Economics*, 1114(3), 817–68.
Frank, R. (1988). *Passions within Reason: The Strategic Role of the Emotions*. New York: W. W. Norton & Company.
Gabaix, X. and Laibson, D. (2000). *AEA Papers and Proceedings*. May 2000: 433–8.

Henrich, J. (2000). 'Ultimatum game bargaining among the Machiguenga: Why culture matters in economic behavior', *American Economic Review*, 90(4), 973–9.

Hirschman, A. (1982). 'Rival interpretations of market society: Civilizing, destructive, or feeble', *Journal of Economic Literature, XX*, 1463–84.

Ledyard, J. O. (1995). 'Public goods: A survey of experimental research', in A. E. Roth (ed.), *The Handbook of Experimental Economics*, Princeton, NJ: Princeton University Press.

Montesquieu, C. 1973 [1749] *De l'esprit des lois*. Paris: Garnier.

Ochenfels, A. and Weimann, J. (1999). 'Types and patterns: An experimental East–West-German comparison of cooperation and solidarity', *Journal of Public Economics, 71*, 275–87.

13

Economic Experiments to Examine Fairness and Cooperation among the Ache Indians of Paraguay

Kim Hill and Michael Gurven

INTRODUCTION

Economic experiments in modern societies suggest that people often cooperate in anonymous one-shot games where non-cooperation would lead to highest payoff for any individual player, but cooperation leads to the highest mean payoff for all players (Camerer and Fehr, Chapter 3, this volume). Such results are referred to in economics as 'anomalies' (Thaler 1992) because they are not consistent with rational self-interested decision-making that is the basis of most modern economic theory. In such experiments cooperation is especially high whenever interactants know each other, or when strangers are allowed to become somewhat familiar prior to interacting (Bohnet and Frey 1999), when responses of fellow interactants are known (Gächter and Fehr 1999), when interactants belong to the same artificially created group (Dawes, van de Kragt, and Orbell 1988), if they are allowed to communicate with fellow interactants before or during the experiment (Dawes and Thaler 1988; Orbell, Dawes, and van de Kragt 1988), or if interactants can punish non-cooperative interactants (Fehr, Fischbacher, and Gächter 2002). In almost all cases listed above strong incentives for cooperation come from group approval or disapproval. Consistent with this are the results of recent theoretical modeling (Boyd and Richerson 1992) showing that punishment alone is sufficient to obtain evolutionary stability for almost any costly social norm.

These results may imply an evolved tendency to cooperate that is unique to our species. If so, cooperative outcomes may be even more ubiquitous traditional hunter–gatherer societies, which are characterized by economic systems that more closely resemble those in which most human psychological mechanisms behind economic choice, fairness, and cooperation probably evolved. On the other hand, it is possible that the observed cooperative outcomes reflect primarily the conditions of large modern societies where unfamiliar actors learn to interact cooperatively because of rigidly enforced cooperative regulations backed up by state level power structures.

To examine these issues two widely studied experimental economic games were carried out with the Ache, a tribal group of recently contacted hunter gathers living in South America. The games were the Ultimatum Game and the Public Goods Game. In the Ultimatum Game an individual (the 'proposer') is given a stake and then must offer some amount of that stake to the 'responder' who can chose to accept the offer or reject it. If the responder accepts the offer, he/she keeps the amount offered and the proposer keeps the remainder of the initial stake. If the responder rejects the offer neither individual gets anything. In the Public Goods Game, a group of n individuals are told they are playing together and each is given a stake. Each individual is given the opportunity to put some amount from their stake into a common pot. After all individuals have contributed their chosen amount to the pot, the amount in the pot is multiplied by a factor k ($n > k > 1$) and then divided out equally to the n members of the group.

In this chapter we examine how individual choices in the two games are affected by methodological permutations of the game and how the choices on one game are associated to choices in the other. We also consider how choices in the games are associated with other relevant characteristics of the individuals who played the games. The results of these games are especially interesting because the Ache are well known in the anthropological literature for their extensive food sharing (Kaplan *et al.* 1984; Kaplan and Hill 1985) and high levels of cooperative food acquisition (Hill 2001).

THE ACHE

History

The Ache are an isolated population of about 900 people living in the forested areas of Eastern Paraguay. Until the 1970s they were nomadic hunter–gatherers who had lived for centuries in the headwaters and foothills regions between the Parana and Paraguay Rivers. In the pre-European period, they shared their geographical range with Guarani village horticulturists who favored larger rivers and semi-open cerrado grassland areas for their settlements. The earliest reports about the Ache come from Jesuit chronicles of the seventeenth century, where they are described as 'living like animals' roaming naked in the forest with no agriculture or domestic animals and very few material possessions. They had no peaceful interactions with the Guarani at the time of Spanish conquest. In the twentieth century, the Ache finally made first peaceful contact with outsiders, and at that time they were divided into four linguistic groups that were geographically separated by regions of colonization. This study took place with the Northern group of Ache, which is the largest, the last to be contacted, and the best studied of the groups.

The Northern Ache consisted of about 550 people who roamed an area of about 15,000 km^2 just prior to peaceful outside contact in the 1970s. They have been the subject of extensive ecological studies focusing on foraging decisions, time allocation to activities, the sexual division of labor, food sharing, mating patterns, demography and life history parameters (see Hill and Hurtado 1996 for review). Prior to contact these people resided in about 10–15 different bands, whose membership was highly fluid. All adults knew and occasionally interacted with all other adults in the population. All people outside this population were considered enemies. Typically bands were made up of between 15–60 individuals who moved camp every day at times, but more frequently remained in a single spot for a few days or even a week. Band members often split up for a day or two to forage for specific resources in known locations, and then reunited to share the proceeds of their forays.

Traditional economy

The Ache forest economy is based on hunting wild game, and extracting palm starch, growing shoots and larva from palms that are purposely cut to provide a substrate for the larva. During the wet season honey extraction is also important and gathering activities are focused on fruit collection for a few weeks each on four or five species each year. During the peak dry season palm fruit and wild volunteer oranges (originally brought by the Jesuits) are collected.

Energetically the most important component of the Ache diet is wild game, which made up about 78 percent of the daily caloric intake in the forest during the 1980s and 1990s (Kaplan *et al.* 2000). During this sample period the most important game animals by biomass were nine-banded armadillos (35 percent), cebus monkeys (13 percent), paca (16 percent), white lipped peccaries (8 percent), coatis (6 percent), and tapir (10 percent). Typically men acquire about 4 kg of meat (live weight) per day. However, the probability of a single hunter not killing any game on a particular day is about 40 percent (Hill and Hawkes 1983); thus, families are interdependent on each other for food on a daily basis. We have only seen a few days with no game killed by any of the hunters in a residential band during a sample of over 300 days of forest foraging.

Cooperation during hunting is common and critical to success for some species. Men usually coordinate their prey search patterns to stay within earshot of each other. They call other men to help them when they find paca, monkeys, white-lipped peccaries, coati, and sometimes armadillo, or when there is a complicated pursuit of any species. They also call for help in tracking wounded large game. It is not yet known whether the help provided increases the expected hunting return rate of the individual calling, the individual who responds, or if such cooperation only increases the total food available to the band. Preliminary analyses suggests that men spend about 17 percent of their foraging time engaged in activities that appear to be designed to increase the foraging gain rate of another adult, at a cost to themselves (i.e. altruistic cooperation). About 80 percent of that time is dedicated to cooperation during hunting. Women also spend about 11 percent of their foraging time helping other individuals during food acquisition and 80 percent of that time is spent in hunting activities (usually helping their husbands hunt) (all results from Hill 2002). These cooperative food acquisition patterns are probably critical for understanding subsequent food sharing.

Palm starch is extracted by women from trees which are felled by men. When a good patch is found, about 15–20 trees must be felled in order to discover one with trunk fiber high in starch content. The trees are usually cut by one man who is accompanied by all the women in the band who wish to extract palm starch. The man who cuts the trees extracts the growing shoot of each, while women accompanying the man test each tree for starch. Starch content cannot be determined without felling a prospective tree and cutting open a section about $\frac{3}{4}$ of the way up the trunk, pounding the trunk fiber with the back of an axe to soften it, and then tasting the pounded fiber. When a tree high in starch content is discovered the trunk is split open and one or two women extract all the fiber along about a 5–7 meter section of the trunk. The extracted fiber is then taken back to camp, usually in loads of about 20 kg per woman, and then mixed with water and hand-squeezed to extract the starch into the water. This starch water is boiled, and mixed with meat, honey, or insect larva. When the mix is allowed to cool it results in a pudding-like consistency of mildly sweet, but greasy 'bre'e', which is the main carbohydrate staple of the Ache.

Hunters usually call other men to help them when they find honey while searching for game. Honey is extracted using fire to avoid getting stung. In pre-contact times, men often climbed trees to extract honey high in the branches using scaffolding or vines to tie themselves in place while chopping. Now more commonly men take turns chopping down the tree, chopping open an access window, and pulling out the honey comb. The whole process usually takes 1–3 hours for two or more men and nets up to 20 liters of honey in the peak season.

Fruits are gathered opportunistically by women and children during the wet season, and occasionally by men while hunting. All individuals who find a good fruit tree call to others nearby to collect with them. Usually a teenage boy or older man will accompany the women and children's foraging group to climb fruit trees and shake down fruits that are collected by all on the ground below. Men and children usually collect only enough for consumption on the spot, whereas women will often collect for longer periods and stash some fruit in a container which is later shared with their children or their husband when he returns from hunting. When the collectors consist of only a subset of the band's women and children they are more likely to collect in large quantities which are brought back to be shared with band members who have remained behind.

Larva are generally extracted from trees that have been previously cut (often for the specific purpose of providing a larval substrate). These trees are considered to be 'owned' by the person who cut them, and taking larva without permission can cause social conflict. Men return to a stand of palms previously cut for palm starch when they think that larva will be plentiful (usually after a few months). Sometimes men and women work together to extract larva by splitting open the palm trunks and searching through the rotting fiber. When working as a couple the man does the chopping and the women search for the grubs. If women and children extract larva without the help of a man, a strong woman will do the chopping while other (younger and weaker) women and children search for the grubs. Whenever larva is found in large quantities much of it is tied up in leaves and taken back to the main camp to be shared out to members who were not present at the extraction site.

The food sharing patterns of forest living Ache have been described in previous publications (Kaplan *et al.* 1984; Kaplan and Hill 1985). Ache hunters typically abandon killed game at the edge of camp, and enter silently without comment on their hunting success. Hunters do not converse with anyone for about 5 minutes (a cooling down period of hunter modesty about the kill), but children and women noticing blood on the hunter or his arrows may quickly search in the direction from which he entered camp to discover the game he has deposited in the forest outside camp. Animals are cooked by a man's wife or other women (especially pregnant women who name their unborn child for the animal species that they cook). When the meat is cooked an older male (not the hunter) usually divides it up into pieces, or piles of pieces, and hands them out, often with the help of other adults who call out the names of each family that should receive a share. Other band members are quick to remind the distributors who has yet to receive a share (they never mention themselves, only others that they know have not eaten yet).

All meat is pooled and shared equally among adult band members. However, the hunter of the game is not supposed to eat from his own kill. Wives and children of hunters receive no greater portion of meat than any other individual in the band. Single men and women are given smaller portions and families are given larger portions depending on how many children they have. Children between the ages of about 7–20 with no resident parents may be slighted and receive no share or a very small share, especially if their biological father is dead. Teenage boys who do not hunt are not guaranteed a share, but those that hunt seriously (i.e. all day long) receive an adult share.

Palm starch pudding is also shared in the same pattern as meat except that the husband of the woman who cooked the pudding usually distributes the portions. All other resources are shared differently with no taboo against eating one's own production, a tendency for the producer to keep more for his/her family than is given to other band members, a strong trend for sharing to increase with package size, and a statistically significant relationship between the amount shared to specific nuclear families and the amount received from them (Gurven, Hill, and Kaplan 2002). There are no sex differences in the sharing patterns once these factors are controlled.

Recent economy

Although the Ache still spend about 20 percent of all days living in the forest from wild resources, they now spend most of their time at permanent reservation settlements. At those settlements they live in small wooden board houses (about 4×4 meters) spread out about 5–15 meters from their nearest neighbor. Most activities are carried out in front of the house, and usually in full view of at least three or more neighboring families. Reservation Ache farm small plots of land where they plant manioc, corn, beans, peanuts, bananas, and a few other minor crops. They also raise chickens, pigs, a few cows and horses, and a large variety of wild 'pets' which are later eaten. Wage Labor is practiced mainly by young single males, but occasionally by all men in the population when seasonally available and high paying. Money is spent mainly to buy clothes, batteries, sugar, yerba mate tea, hard bread rolls, rice, and noodles. A few Ache men who have long-term employment purchase radios and bicycles. But, mean nuclear family net worth in 1992 was only \$12 per family summing the value of all possessions, housing, and livestock. Firearms are still rare with most hunting carried out using bow and arrow, or by hand. Fishing is now a popular activity during the warm, dry months of the year.

Cooperation in the reservation economy is also common. This includes working together to clear forest for gardens, helping to transport heavy items, caring for each other's livestock, helping each other on house construction, sharing tools, and inviting other individuals along when good Wage Labor opportunities are discovered.

The reservation food sharing pattern is quite different from that on forest treks. About 50 percent of cultivated and store-bought foods are shared out to other nuclear families when acquired, whereas 75 percent of foods brought in from the forest and meat from domestic animals are shared to other families. But, typically, the number of recipient families was only 2–4 despite the fact that the study settlement had twenty-three families during the study period. Small groups of families mainly exchange foods with each other. This sharing shows a strong bias favoring close kin, those who live nearby, and favoring those families who share back in turn. Only when a very large animal is killed do all community members obtain a share (Gurven *et al.* 2001).

EXPERIMENTAL METHODS

Economic experiments were carried out at two Ache settlements in 1999. The large Chupa Pou settlement contained nearly 500 individuals living spread out over a 5-km linear strip. The smaller Arroyo Bandera settlement contained about 110 individuals living in a circular pattern within about 100 m of each other. Individuals in both settlements are closely related (to each other and to those in the other settlement) and have a long history of social interaction. Most adults have known all other adults their entire lives. The study population also contained a few individuals who had married into the community and had only a short time span of acquaintance with other adults. These individuals included several Ache from distant reservations as well as one Paraguayan woman who had married into the community, and a Guarani Indian schoolteacher.

All individuals, except the newcomers, had known the interviewer (K. H.) for at least 20 years (or their entire life for those under age 20) and were well acquainted with scientific studies and occasional experiments. The study population had participated in a variety of foraging experiments (e.g. trying to hunt monkeys alone, different ages of girls trying to extract palm fiber) and also hypothetical scenario building (e.g. asking who is more attractive of a set of photos, who would make a better spouse for one's offspring, which foraging band would the interviewee chose to join under various conditions). In the past it had been explained that these 'experiments' were games that Americans set up in order to learn something about other people. The Ache were comfortable with this explanation and had always been paid for participation and debriefed after experimentation. The relationship between the interviewer and the study subjects was relaxed with frequent joking throughout the experimental session.

Several days prior to the day of the experiment it was announced that all adults who wished to participate in a game where they could win money should arrive at the school building at the indicated time. We were careful to specify that no children would be allowed to attend (because of noise and distraction) and that women should arrange for childcare if they wished to participate. We also suggested that the instructions of the game were somewhat complicated and that the old people and those of limited intellect (there are some mildly retarded people in the study population) would probably not understand the game. Four rounds of games were run in each of the two study communities. They were carried out in the following order: (1) anonymous Ultimatum Game; (2) anonymous Public Goods Game; (3) public Ultimatum Game; and (4) public Public Goods Game. The first two games were played about a week apart and the third and fourth rounds were done on a single day about a week later.

Both types of games were explained to all prospective players congregated in a one-room school building, using the blackboard to illustrate specific examples. The details of how each game was explained are given below. During and after the explanations of the games participants were encouraged to ask questions, and K. H. occasionally asked them questions in order to determine if they understood the game. After the explanation period was over we announced that all individuals who had attended would be given $\frac{1}{2}$ the stake (worth about 50 percent of a days wage) whether they played or not, but that all individuals who felt they didn't understand the game should take the participation fee and leave.

The Ultimatum Game

(A1) First round, anonymous version—the rules of the game were read in Spanish (translation provided by J. Henrich), and then read translated into the Ache language (previously translated by K. H. and written down). Following the reading of the rules K. H. slowly explained the rules again in the Ache language in a manner that he believed was likely to be fully understood. The game in the Ache language was called 'pire bowo' which has a double meaning of 'dividing up the money' or 'dividing the skin'. This latter phrase in Ache is used to refer to the division of animal skin with sub-cutaneous fat which is cut into strips and shared after successful hunting. The player who divides the initial stake was called the 'divider' and the respondent was called 'the one to whom it will be given'. We are not certain whether the Ache terms for the game and the two roles have implications for how the game should be played.

After the explanation, we gave some examples of hypothetical offers and responses to those offers and asked participants in the room to tell us the earnings of each player. After about five examples, it appeared that all participants could correctly assess the payoffs to each player in a hypothetical situation. The hypothetical examples included high and low offers and acceptance or rejection of the offer. Because some participants seemed puzzled about why one might reject an offer, we specifically stated that if the respon-dent believed that the division of the stake was unfair (e.g. if he were angry, disappointed, upset), he might reject the offer in order to punish a player who had made an unfair (stingy) division. The term 'unfair' does not exist in the Ache language, but the word 'stingy' does. When this was mentioned as a hypothetical reason why one might reject an offer, most participants nodded in apparent understanding.

After an hour and a half explanation session all players were asked to draw a number from a hat which determined which role they played in the game (proposer or responder) and in what order they would be called to make a decision. All participants were asked to leave the building and then were called in one by one, told what role they had been assigned, and asked to make a pro-posal or respond to one. The initial stake was 10,000 Guaranies (about US$ 3.70, one day's wage). Any amount could be offered in 1,000 Gs increments. Proposers were called in first and then responders were randomly assigned to an offer, although players were not aware of this fact and did not know who was assigned what role. Responders had no way of knowing who had made the offer that they were presented. After all choices had been recorded individuals were called in again in random order and paid in cash.

(B1) Second round, public version—participants arrived at the schoolhouse and it was announced that the 'pire bowo' game would be played again. A much shorter explanation session was provided since most had played the game a week earlier and all had heard about the game in the intervening week. It was then stated that all offers and responses would be announced publicly in the school in front of all other players, but proposers would not know who would receive their offer until after the offer was made. This led to nervous laughs by many players. Again each participant drew a number from a hat which determined their role in the game and the order in which they would be called on to play. All proposers were required to state their offer in turn, and this was done in a loud voice and repeated in front of all players in that round. After all proposals had been made, those individuals who were responders were matched up at random with an offer and asked to announce to all whether they would accept or reject the offer.

The Public Goods Game

(A1) First round, anonymous—the rules of the game were read in Spanish and then in a previously prepared written translation in the Ache language. After the reading, we spent about a half hour explaining the game slowly in the Ache language and giving examples. The game was called 'contribution' in Spanish, a word which most Ache understand because communal 'contributions' are sometimes requested by tribal leaders to pay for public goods (a feast, school repairs, etc.). The initial stake was 10,000 Gs which was presented as play money in 1,000 Gs notes inside an envelope. It was explained that the contribution to the 'pot' would be done anonymously by leaving any amount of money that one wished in the envelope (including zero) and then depositing the envelope in a slotted box. Players were grouped in sets of five with each envelope marked (e.g. Group one player A, B, C, etc.) which allowed us to assign each contribution to an individual (thus, the contributions were not anonymous to the experimenter). It was explained that the contribution pot would be doubled and then re-divided amongst all five members in each group.

Because the Ache have no formal mathematical training, only some could calculate the double of a specified amount and none could divide the final pot by five to calculate their exact share of the public good. But extensive practice with examples gave them a good sense of the form of the payoffs. Specifically we showed them that: (1) if all players contributed everything they each earned twice as much as if all contributed nothing; (2) if only one player failed to contribute and all others contributed everything, the non-contributor gained more than any other player and more than the players in scenario (1) above; and (3) if only one player contributed all and the other four contributed nothing, that contributor would gain less than any of the players in his round or any other players in any of the above scenarios. It was then restated to the participants that (i) if all contribute they earn more than if all fail to contribute; (ii) if most contribute but a few do not, those non-contributors gain more than anybody; and (iii) if most fail to contribute but a few do, those few contributors get the lowest payoffs possible. We believe that most participants at this point grasped the essence of the game in a qualitative fashion even though they could not calculate the exact payoff to players in any given scenario. We then pointed out to them that this problem was analogous to many common public goods problems at their settlement and we named a few examples (the Ache engage in many communal projects for the common good). At that point all players seemed to have a good under-standing of the game.

Each participant then drew a random number from a hat which determined the group to which they were assigned. They were called into a room one by one and given an envelope containing money that they took to a corner. They secretly extracted whatever amount they wished not to contribute, and then deposited the remainder in a slotted box. None of the players knew the identity of other players in their group.

(B1) Second round, public—A much shorter explanation session was required since most participants had played in a previous round or had heard about the game prior to this last session. After the explanation it was stated that the contributions would be announced in public. Each individual drew a number and was assigned to a group. Players were not informed who was in their group. Then individuals were asked to announce one by one how much they would contribute to a common pot. They did not know which other individuals were assigned to their group, but as the offers were announced they were able to assess the general level of cooperation exhibited by other players on the same day. Those who played first had no information about the level of contribution of others, whereas those who played last had a general sense of whether prior players had contributed a lot or a little.

Anonymity

Players of both games were given a hypothetical stake (on the books or in paper play money) and made decisions about how they wished to play each game. The decisions were recorded by us and after calculations about the payoffs, each individual was called into a room and paid in paper play money. After the payoff to all participants a bank was set up to convert play money into real money. This payout was done in a semi-private setting. The use of play money was necessary because it was impossible to obtain enough currency in small denominations to play all games with all participants using real money. Because winners often were required to pool their play money at the bank (e.g. a winner of 20,000, 17,000, and 13,000 Gs together might be paid in a 50,000 G note which could then be taken to a store and cashed for each to receive his share), some individuals were able to determine how much some other individuals won. This, in combination with some information about the game and what role was played by each individual, could allow some individuals to calculate how other individuals might have played the game. While we have no evidence that anybody actually carried out such calculations, the experimenter (K. H.) was able to do them quickly. Thus, even the anonymous rounds of the games were not perfectly anonymous in the end.

However, greater erosion of Anonymity was due to the fact that many people talked about the games afterwards in small groups and divulged how they had played, and the fact that K. H. had recorded all choices by all participants and that they knew that he was doing so. Because K. H. has a long history in the community and participates in social activities and political decision-making, and because he is known to have allies and enemies in the community and is often involved in distributions of other goods and services, it would be naïve to assume that players were indifferent to the fact that K. H. knew how they played. It is not clear how this effect could be eliminated since K. H. is the only outsider who can speak the language well enough to conduct the games, and since participants cannot read and write, meaning that they must verbally report their choices to someone who then records them.

RESULTS

The Ultimatum Game

About 195 individuals heard all the instructions for both rounds of the game. Four of these chose not to play because they did not understand the game. Of the 95 who had the role of proposer, four were eliminated from analysis because they looked and acted confused and/or their offer seemed to indicate that they did not understand the game (they offered 100 percent of the stake to the responder). However, we are still not completely certain that the two individuals who offered the entire stake to the responder did not understand the game. They looked embarrassed when they made the offer and in debriefing sessions were embarrassed to talk about their offer. This could either mean that they were embarrassed to admit they didn't understand the game, or embarrassed that their offer might seem silly to us. Scaled to 10, the mean offer in the anonymous version of this game for first time players was 4.65 ($n = 47$, $SE = 0.15$). The mean offer for first time players in the public version of the game was 4.45 ($n = 29$, $SE = 0.30$). The frequency distributions of offers for first time players in the anonymous and public versions of the game are presented in Figure 13.1.

While the mean offers in both versions of the game are similar, the spread of offers is greater in the public version of the game. In the anonymous version, 81 percent of all offers are four or five whereas in the public version only 55 percent of the offers are four or five. The most notable thing about the distribution of offers is that 14.3 percent of all offers were greater than five, and only 6.6 percent were less than three. Surprisingly, two offers of nine were made by individuals who, when debriefed, clearly understood the game. And interestingly, all five offers of seven or above were made by women (as were the two offers of ten that were eliminated).

Five variables could potentially associate with the amount offered by the proposer in our data set. They are age (range 14–57), sex (male = 1), settlement size (Settlement Size) (large = 1), number of times played (one, two), and type of game (anonymous = 0, public = 1). In a multivariate regression none of these variables was significantly associated with the size of the offer (Table 13.1), and in univariate analyses none of these variables were significant except

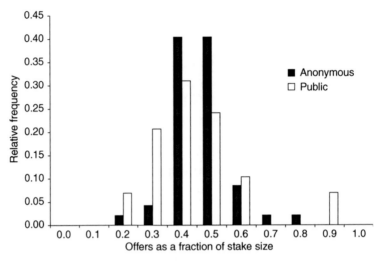

F$_{IG}$. 13.1. Frequency distribution of offers by first-time players in the Ultimatum Game played anonymously ($n = 47$) and in public ($n = 29$)

number of times played.[1] The mean offer in the public version of the game, when only first time players are examined, was almost identical to the mean offer in the anonymous version of the game (see above). Thus, playing the game in public did not seem to affect the mean size of the offer. For the fifteen individuals who were proposers in both rounds of the game the average first offer was 4.27 (SE = 0.27) and the average second offer was 3.73 (SE = 0.42). The reduction in offer size for individuals who played a second time was not statistically significant,[2] but the sample size is very small here and the effect (a 15 percent reduction in offer) seems economically important.

Ninety-six individuals were responders in these two rounds of the Ultimatum Game. Eight of those individuals were eliminated

---

[1] Least squares multiple regression, for Ultimatum Game offer, independent variables are yearborn, sex (1 = male), large settlement (1 = large), game type (1 = public), times played (1,2) showed the following coefficients and p values: yearborn -0.0159, $p = 0.25$; sex -0.145, $p = 0.65$; large settlement 0.417, $p = 0.17$; public play -0.271, $p = 0.41$; times played -0.587, $p = 0.18$. In univariate regressions the only variable with a p value less than 0.10 is times played, coefficient -0.839, $p = 0.031$.
[2] Paired t-test, one-tailed $p = 0.15$.

TABLE 13.1. Multiple regression models for offers in the Ultimatum Game and contributions in the Public Goods Game

Ultimatum Game	Model 1: (adjusted R square $= 0.0418$, $F = 1.785$, $p = 0.124$, obs. $= 91$)	
Variable	*Coefficient*	*p value*
Intercept	36.279	0.1843
Yearborn	−0.016	0.2522
Male	−0.145	0.6470
Large settlement	0.417	0.1735
Public	−0.271	0.4064
Times played	−0.587	0.1835
Public Goods Game	Model 2: (adjusted R square $= 0.175$, $F = 6.91$, $p < 0.001$, obs. $= 140$)	
Variable	*Coefficient*	*p value*
Intercept	48.688	0.1679
Yearborn	−0.022	0.2236
Male	0.671	0.0788
Large settlement	0.228	0.5305
Public	2.385	0.0000
Times played	−1.942	0.0002

from analyses because they acted very confused, rejected, or accepted the offer before the amount was stated, changed their response several times looking to K. H. for guidance, or tried to make an offer as the proposer rather than playing the responder. Eighty-six of the remaining eighty-eight were matched with offers chosen randomly from those made by Ache proposers. None of the offers were rejected. In the remaining two cases we fabricated a sham low offer (one, or two) in order to see if we could elicit a rejection. Both of these low proposals were accepted. Thus, *all* proposals were accepted by the responders, including one proposal of one, seven proposals of two, and fourteen proposals of three.

The Public Goods Game

There were 140 individuals who played the Public Goods Game in twenty-eight groups of five. A handful of individuals who heard the instructions chose not to play. Again, the initial stake was 10,000 Gs. Scaled to 10, the mean contribution for first time players in the anonymous version of the game was 4.48 (SE $= 0.22$). The mean contribution for first time players in the public version was 6.47 (SE $= 0.35$). The frequency distributions of contributions for first

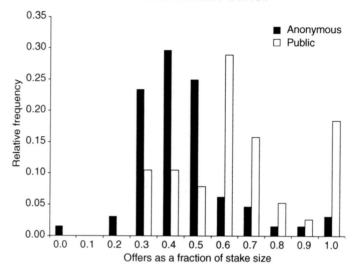

F<small>IG</small>. 13.2. Frequency distribution of contributions to the Public Goods Game played anonymously ($n = 64$) and in public ($n = 38$)

time players in the anonymous and public versions of the game are presented in Figure 13.2.

Again, the most notable thing about the frequency distribution of the contributions is the high proportion of contributions greater than five (17 percent in the anonymous version, 71 percent in the public version) and the low proportion of contributions less than three (4.6 and 0 percent, respectively). Again, many of the highest contributions were from women (7/10) of the individuals who contributed their entire stake to the pot.

The same five independent variables listed above were regressed with the size of contribution. Because, Settlement Size, sex, time played, and public versus anonymous were all strongly colinear (one round of the game was played in public with only women at the large village), univariate analyses are multiply confounded and not instructive. However, the multivariate model with all five independent variables entered together showed strong significant associations between contribution and sex, number of times played, and anonymous versus public (Table 13.1). Men contributed a mean of 0.7 units more to the public pot. Playing a second time reduced the mean contribution by about 1.9 units, but playing in public increased the contribution by about 2.4 units (with all other variables controlled).

Associations with other measures of cooperative tendency

We also looked at the relationship between the choices on each game and several other individual characteristics potentially relevant to cooperation. The first analysis was simply a correlation between how individuals played the two games. Specifically, we examined whether those that made high offers in the Ultimatum Game were more likely to contribute more in the Public Goods Game. Because no methodological variables were significantly associated with offer in the Ultimatum Game, we pooled all Ultimatum Game offers together. The results of the analyses are mixed. There is no relationship between offer in the Ultimatum Game and contribution in the anonymous version of the Public Goods Game, but there is an almost statistically significant positive relationship between offers in the Ultimatum Game and contribution in the public round of the Public Goods Game[3] (Figure 13.3).

Second, we examined the relationship between the offers or contributions in the two games and the measured time discounting rate for money for a handful of individual players. The preferred discount rate was determined by examining the response to differing amounts of money offered at different points in time. Respondents were asked to choose between 3 days' salary now and increasing multiples of that amount after a 15-day delay. The options varied from a 1.5 percent increase to a 150 percent increase on top of the initial offer if the respondent was willing to delay the payoff date. The interest rate at which respondents switch from a preference for immediate payoff to preference for the delayed higher payoff is used to estimate the preferred discount rate. It has been previously suggested that a lower time discount rate is more likely to be associated with a willingness to engage in cooperative economic strategies since some forms of cooperation are simply preferences for a higher payoff after a time delay rather than immediate payoff (Clements and Stephens 1995). Because we observed cross-overs in time discounting preference during our field trial, we assigned all respondents to three rankings: low time discounting (always preferred the higher

---

[3] Analyses of Ultimatum Game offers and contribution in the anonymous version of the Public Goods Game: least squares regression $n = 45$, coeff. $= 0.042$, $p = 0.75$. Analyses of Ultimatum Game offers and contribution in the public version of the Public Goods Game: least squares regression $n = 66$, coeff. $= 0.143$, $p = 0.073$.

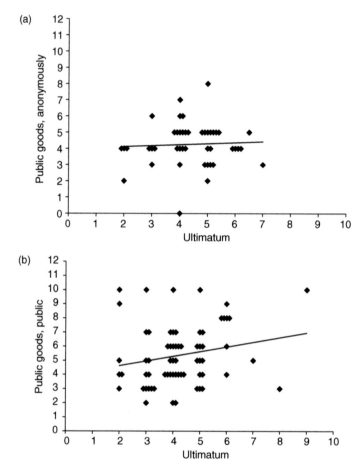

Fig. 13.3. The relationship between offers made by single individuals in
the Ultimatum Game and their contributions in the Public Goods Game played
(a) anonymously, or in (b) public

payoff after a delay), high discounting (never preferred the
delayed payoff), and intermediate (preferred the delayed payoff
depending on the increase associated with the delay). We found
no association between the preferred discount rate of individuals
and their offers or contributions in the Ultimatum Game and
Public Goods Game[4] (Figure 13.4).

[4] Rank regressions of Ultimatum Game offers of Public Goods contributions by
time discounting category $p > 0.5$ for both.

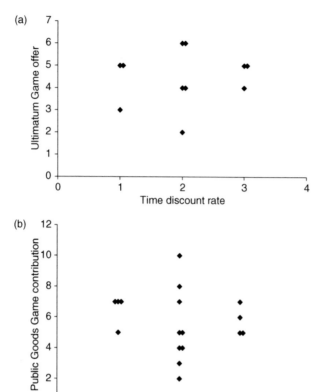

FIG. 13.4. The relationship between the measured discount rate for individuals and their offers in the (a) Ultimatum Game, or (b) their contribution to the Public Goods Game. Discount rates as defined in the text are low (1), medium (2), and high (3)

Finally, we examined the relationship between observed food production and sharing patterns and Ultimatum Game offers or Public Goods Game contributions by individuals in the Arroyo Bandera settlement. Food production and distribution were monitored in detail between January and May 1998 at the Arroyo Bandera settlement (Gurven *et al.* 2001). These data provide information of individual and family total food production (measured in kg produced during sample period) and the percentage of

TABLE 13.2. Regression of individual play in economic games by observed food production or food sharing patterns

	Individual		Household	
	% food kept by family	Total kg food produced	% food kept by family	Total kg food produced
Anonymous trials				
Offer in UG				
p value	0.85	0.64	0.49	0.24
Coefficient	− 0.06	− 0.13	− 0.14	− 0.09
n	16	16	16	16
Contribution in PGG				
p value	0.23	0.36	0.54	0.63
Coefficient	− 0.41	0.11	0.13	− 0.04
n	24	24	24	24
Public trials				
Offer in UG				
p value	0.53	0.65	0.27	0.58
Coefficient	− 0.19	− 0.06	0.17	− 0.04
n	18	18	18	18
Contribution in PGG				
p-value	0.98	0.61	0.61	0.43
Coefficient	− 0.01	− 0.07	− 0.11	− 0.06
n	30	30	30	30

foods acquired that were shared to individuals outside the nuclear family of the acquirer. Offers in the Ultimatum Game appear to measure willingness to divide a valuable resource, and contributions in the Public Goods Game may indicate willingness to cooperate in an arrangement of reciprocal altruism. To test this hypothesis we regressed the observed offers and contributions against the level of food sharing exhibited by the same individuals approximately 1 year earlier. No significant relationships were found (Table 13.2). Likewise, although overall food production rates vary quite substantially among study subjects, and this may effect their willingness to offer resources in the Ultimatum Game, or to contribute in the Public Goods Game, our data show no relationship between food production patterns and choices in the two economic experiments (Table 13.2).

DISCUSSION

The results from these economic experiments provide some interesting insights into concepts of fairness in human societies and some of the social forces behind observed resource sharing patterns. We suspect that the Ache, like many other groups with little experience in such unique conditions for interpersonal interaction, are likely to play the games in ways that to some extent reflect real life patterns of interaction that are favored or at equilibrium in the Ache context. We do not mean to imply that economic behavioral patterns are inflexible to changed conditions, but only that the adoption of behaviors far outside the typical daily range and in contradiction to internally incorporated systems of ethical and moral behavior might require some time to emerge.

In the Ultimatum Game, a significant proportion of offers were greater than five and almost none less than three despite the fact that no offer was ever rejected. If we assume that proposers anticipated that responders were unlikely to reject low offers, then the experiment constitutes a Dictator Game (Dictator Game) (Forsythe *et al.* 1994) in some sense. The offers did not vary by age, sex, settlement, or whether the game was played in public. There may have been a slight decrease in offers by second time players. Although this provides only sketchy information with many possible interpretations, we will suggest a few qualitative insights. First, the Ache are not familiar with the possibility of anonymous behaviors without social consequences and we believe that a number of trials would be required before this possibility would be accepted and incorporated into behavioral decisions. Indeed there is a serious question as to whether true guaranteed Anonymity ever exists even in large scale modern societies. We do expect, however, that offers might erode over a period of time as the Ache began to appreciate the apparent lack of social consequences of making a high or low offer in the game (see Fehr, Fischbacher and Gachter 2002). In addition, it must be remembered that all players live together in a very close community. General lack of fairness in the game context could affect overall community relations in a negative way as players began to realize their neighbors were not cooperating in the game. This might motivate anonymous fair offers by those who are concerned with the 'social environment' of the community, which favors frequent cooperation. Also, detailed discussion of the game after it ended might sometimes reveal those who made 'unfair' offers if it is difficult for the Ache to lie convincingly to close friends and relatives. Certainly, all Ache would be very uncomfortable at the thought of having to lie under these circumstances, and might therefore make fair offers because they knew they would be asked about their offer after the game ended.

Second, we believe that the high number of extra-fair offers (offer > 5) is related to the fact that in Ache society food producers often share out more than 50 percent of what they acquire in a particular patch (and Ache men generally don't eat from their own kill after a successful hunt). Indeed, giving more than half of what one acquires is so typical, that it may even be expected in some cases. One proposer who offered 6.5 in the anonymous Ultimatum Game session spent a long time thinking about his offer and then commented to us during his offer that he was concerned the responder might be angry *if he offered less*. The forces behind the Ache sharing pattern are complicated, but it is important to note that the Ache probably conceive of the Ultimatum Game as a 'sharing' context since there is a clear opportunity to divide that which has been acquired. Extra-fair offers are likely to be related to both the desire to display generosity, and the concern over social approval and disapproval. It must be remembered that K. H. was an observer to all distributions and the Ache were quite aware of that fact. Also, the offers were discussed publicly after the game ended (and lying may be difficult here, as mentioned above). An extra-fair distribution in real life is in fact the only distribution (offer) that would be universally approved. It was K. H.'s sense that those individuals who would score highest in the personality dimension of 'concern about social approval' were also those who made the highest offers in the Ultimatum Game.

Low rates of rejection in Ultimatum Games have been previously interpreted as illustrative of the gain maximizing strategy that should characterize responders. However, we suggest that this is not the correct interpretation of the Ache pattern. Ache proposers behaved in a manner very different from that predicted on the gain maximizing principle. Would these same people turn around and adopt strategies of pure gain maximization as responders? This seems unlikely and instead we suggest that the Ache failed to reject offers because to do so would be a form of serious interpersonal confrontation. According to Ache custom it is bad manners to show anger or disappointment in public. It would be unacceptable in Ache society to refuse a piece of shared meat because the share appeared to be unfairly small. Although distributions are indeed sometimes perceived as unfair or 'stingy', the recipient never confronts the divider over such an issue. Instead the recipient grumbles to other members of the social group about the size of the share, thus damaging the reputation of the divider who ultimately hears about the recipient's displeasure. Such a process constitutes social punishment and may be sufficient to motivate most dividers to seek fair (and even extra-fair) solutions. Thus, the Ache may view rejection of an offer as extraordinarily confrontational. This interpretation is strengthened by the comment of one responder. He was asked to respond to an offer of four. He looked at K. H. and smiled and said, 'could you tell me one more time what will happen if I reject this offer'. K. H. was surprised by his question since he knew that the man had understood the game very well during the explanation phase. K. H. repeated the consequences of rejection by the responder and he said, 'so if I say no, the proposer will get nothing—in that case I had better accept, because (my rejection) would cause problems'. This comment was overheard by another observing anthropologist who had been working with the Ache for over 10 years. He interpreted the lack of rejection as due to a fear of social confrontation (just as we have).

The results from the Public Goods Game also reflect aspects of typical Ache behavior. Public goods dilemmas are common on current reservation settlements. Indeed, when the game was called 'contribution' the Ache immediately recognized its basic form. Chiefs often ask for contributions for public projects, to pay the electric bill for the water pump and school, to pay for medicines at the clinic, to work together fixing the community soccer field, to help care for communally owned domestic animals, to plant and harvest communal fields, etc. Many public goods projects partially succeed, but with a high rate of free riding unless individuals are singled out one at a time to elicit contribution. The rules for participation in generating public goods are much more flexible (less morally rigid) than food sharing rules in Ache society, and adults have a good deal of experience in assessing how much participation serves their interests. The Ache also have a long history of experience informing them that many individuals are 'free riders' in public goods situations. Again, however, there is also a strong social display component to contribution. In real life contexts, individuals who fail to 'contribute' usually invoke important excuses, and when no easy excuse is at hand they usually contribute, sometimes excessively and with vigorous and overt attempts to draw attention to their cooperative behavior (e.g. singing very loud while working on a public goods project).

In the first round, when the Public Goods Game was played anonymously, almost everyone contributed something (because there was no 'excuse' not to and the game was probably not really anonymous in the Ache view). The 'chiefs' of both communities were high contributors (mean 6.2), just as they would be expected to be in a real life situation.

In the second round played in public, there was a lot of verbal encouragement to cooperate during the explanation period. Because all players could monitor the contributions of all others, not surprisingly the mean contribution increased significantly. Even in the first few public plays, before participants could assess how much others would cooperate, the offers increased by about 20 percent (mean 5.7 for first five plays at each settlement). There was no significant trend in contribution by order of play in the public version of the game ($p = 0.71$ for AB and $p = 0.22$ for CP). In the public version, nobody offered less than three and nearly 20 percent of the players contributed the entire stake. The highest *monetary* payoff went to those who contributed the least, but high contributors looked happiest after the game when we were distributing the winnings. In order to understand the high offers, one must realize that long discussions of the game took place in the days following it, and those who had contributed the full stake were mentioned over and over and became known by most of the community, including individuals who did not attend the session. Indeed, we got the impression that the big 'winners' from the game (in social utility rather than the monetary payoff of the game) were those who had contributed the full stake.

In a more general sense the most interesting thing about the results from both games is the suggestion that players seem conditioned to treat them as part of an iterated sequence of interpersonal interactions even when they are explained as one time anonymous choice experiments. The payoff matrix in our version of the Public Goods Game is a classic prisoners dilemma in which money contributed can never be recovered fully from the pot, (since the payoff for a contributor is only $\frac{2}{3}x$ when x is the contribution). But money contributed does increase the payoff to fellow players. If the game is clearly understood as a one time prisoners dilemma (which it is) all players should contribute nothing. The fact that contributions are often quite high may suggest that individuals treat the experiment as if it were part of a much longer set of social interactions. We believe that this perception is correct for the Ache. All participants continued to interact intensively after the game was concluded. Defection during the game, while not detectable on an individual basis (in theory) is quite detectable on a community level. We suspect that all players were concerned that an erosion of the high levels of cooperation characteristic of the community due to defection during the game, would have negative consequences for the whole community long after the game had ended. In other words players acted as if future harmonious (cooperative) community interactions were at stake rather than just the prize money in the game.

The lack of relationship between offers in the Ultimatum Game and contributions in the Public Goods Game is somewhat puzzling. Equally puzzling is the lack of a relationship between choices in the experiments and real life economic parameters. Both experiments seem to measure some commitment to fairness and cooperation between players. It is possible that high offers in the Ultimatum Game are simply motivated by the fear of rejection (and therefore motivated by gain maximization), but this seems incongruous with the total lack of rejection of low offers by Ache participants. It seems difficult not to conclude that contribution to the Public Goods Game indicates a willingness to cooperate with others, but perhaps some Ache misunderstood the payoff matrix and interpreted the game as an opportunity to gamble. Those who contributed most may have hoped to double their money by gambling that other players would also contribute a lot. They may have mistakenly calculated that their contribution had the possibility of paying back more than they gave up, or perhaps believed that their contribution would influence the contribution of others. One of the most notorious gamblers in the community contributed 0.9 of his initial stake and was heard commenting after the game that he had really hoped to double his money. In this case, however, many of the Ache seem to have learned after the first round of the game that other individuals were less cooperative than they hoped, since second round contributions declined significantly.

Most troublesome, however, is the issue of what individual variation in game play actually indicates about individual behavioral tendencies. Not only did responses in the two games show no correlation, but responses in the games shows no significant association with real life behaviors such as measured time preference, previously measured food-sharing generosity, or variation in food production. Some economists have treated individual responses as indicators of individual variation in fairness or a tendency to cooperate. Thus, not only mean responses are reported, but the frequency distribution of various response categories are often reported and compared. However, the Ache data suggest that variation in responses by single individuals the first time they are exposed to the game may indicate little about the variation in those same individual's generosity or tendency to cooperate with others in real life. Is this because responses at one point in time are too influenced by a variety of other factors (e.g. mood, current financial situation, rapid understanding of the game, etc.) that do not necessarily indicate long term characteristics of the individual? This should be examined in more detail, perhaps by regressing play in the first exposure to a game with subsequent play during longer periods of time. Does play in any round predict play in any other round. How strong is the correlation? Perhaps food-sharing patterns would correlate with the average offer in the Ultimatum Game over many trials but not with any one particular offer.

Despite our invocation of culturally specific explanations for some aspects of the Ache results, we are aware that most patterns observed amongst the Ache may be found in many other settings. The mean Ache offers and contributions are not particularly different than those found elsewhere. Extra-fair offers above five in the Ultimatum Game (and even the Dictator Game) are observed in societies that probably have very different food sharing patterns than those of the Ache. Complete lack of rejection of Ultimatum Game offers may be rare but have been found in other societies as well (see Henrich and Gurven, Chapter 5 this volume). The mean Ache contribution to the Public Goods Game is also not exceptional, nor are the findings that offers decrease in subsequent rounds of play, and increase in more public contexts (Dawes and Thaler 1988). Thus, our comments on the Ache may be relevant to other societies as well. Perhaps most individuals have an initial expectation of human interaction based on real life and feel uncomfortable being unfair or stingy even when special contexts are set up that allow or favor such strategies. Optimal behavior in a one time interaction may take some time to fully incorporate, especially for those with no prior experience that such a thing is possible. Frank (1988) has hypothesized that sticking to a moral 'rule of thumb' such as 'always divide fairly' may be an adaptive response under some conditions. Perhaps the rule of thumb includes always behaving in a fair and cooperative manner initially until one can truly determine that behaving otherwise is appropriate (e.g. learning that other individuals will defect, or that one's own defection truly cannot be detected).

At this point we think more investigation into the effects of changed experimental conditions will teach us more about cross-cultural variability than we can learn by simply increasing the sample size of different cultures tested. Multiple trial experiments should be especially interesting as they can remove any doubts about the subjects understanding of the game, or familiarity with its novel conditions relative to their daily lives. If offers and contributions decline it is important to determine whether this is due to learning about the game (e.g. understanding that it really can be played anonymously or that no punishment is possible) or learning about the tendencies of other players (e.g. if the optimal play is to always defect just a tiny bit more than others, this will drive offers and contributions down through time when information is acquired).

In a review of results from the Public Goods Game, Dawes and Thaler (1988) give an example of farmers who leave fresh produce on a table with a box that is attached in which clients can insert (but not extract) payment. They conclude that the farmer's view of human nature is that most people will cooperate but that one must always protect oneself from the few who will exploit the situation. We believe the Ache enter the Ultimatum Game and Public Goods Game with the same general attitude but have higher expectations of fairness and cooperation than are found in some other societies. Perhaps Ache expectations lead them to play these games slightly differently than other human groups. However, the most striking thing about these games is the pan-human pattern of fairness and cooperation which seems so different from that of other primates. The question we are left with is how we got to be this way.

Regardless of the explanations and the amount of cultural variation, humans seem to have tendencies toward fairness and cooperation that are stronger than those of other animals. Reciprocal altruism is rarely observed in nonhumans. The conditions of the Dictator Game are replicated over and over among animals in captivity and in the wild, and 'dictators' rarely voluntarily hand over much of their original stake (acquired food) to neighbors (see DeWaal 1997; DeWaal and Berger 2000 for exceptions in experimental conditions allowing for reciprocity in primates).

Human cooperation is so ubiquitous that people appear to have a sense of 'fairness' that contradicts predictions from rational self-interest models in economics and is unparalleled in nonhuman organisms. This is illustrated by several outcomes in recent economic experiments, such as: (1) the willingness to divide resources with anonymous partners who cannot retaliate if no division takes place ('Dictator' Game, Forsythe *et al.* 1994), or who are known to be unlikely to retaliate (Ultimatum Game without rejections, this chapter; Henrich and Gurven, Chapter 5, this volume); (2) the willingness of a Respondent to reject resources from divisions in which the Proposer keeps a large fraction of the total stake split between a Proposer and a Respondent if rejection punishes the divider; and (3) the willingness to pay a cost to punish individuals who do not cooperate in the production of public goods, even if no further interaction with those individuals is possible (public goods games with punishment in the final round, Fehr, Fischbacher, and Gächter 2002). Particularly notable is the willingness to punish those who behave unfairly even at an extremely high cost to the punisher. For example, Cameron (1999) shows that a substantial number of players will reject offers in the Ultimatum Game that they consider unfair even when the initial stakes are 3 months' salary!

In addition to the above results, studies on the development of cooperative behavior in children suggests that children go from noncooperative to a hyper-cooperative phase prior to reaching an adult phase of contingent cooperative behavior (Murningham and Saxon 1994). Thus, the available data on human cooperation suggests the possibility that humans have an evolved predisposition to: (1) seek cooperative solutions which will benefit all interactants relative to the alternative payoffs from noncooperation; (2) share the resources cooperatively acquired by groups of individuals who are defined as belonging to the same economic 'group', or to share resources individually acquired in which the identity of the initial acquirer of the resource is partially or wholly determined by luck; and (3) punish noncooperative exploitation and unwillingness to divide gains that are understood to belong to all, even when punishment is costly. These traits characterizing interactions between adult non-kin seem particularly well developed in humans relative to any other mammal and are probably ultimately based in evolved psychological mechanisms unique to our species.

REFERENCES

Bohnet, I. and Frey, B. (1999). 'The sound of silence in prisoners dilemma and dictator games', *Journal of Economic Behavior and Organization, 38*, 43–57.

Boyd, R. and Richerson, P. (1992). 'Punishment allows the evolution of cooperation (or anything else) in sizable groups', *Ethnology and Sociobiology, 13*, 171–95.

Camerer, C. and Thaler, R. (1995). 'Anomalies: ultimatums, dictators and manners'. *Journal of Economic Perspectives, 9*, 209–219.

Cameron, L. (1999). 'Raising stakes in the ultimatum game'. *Economic Enquiry, 37*(1), 47–59.

Clements, K. C. and Stephens, D. W. (1995). 'Testing models of animal cooperation: feeding bluejays cooperate mutualistically, but defect in a massively iterated Prisoner's Dilemma', *Animal Behaviour 50*, 527–35.

Dawes, R. and Thaler R. (1988). 'Cooperation', *Journal of Economic Perspectives, 2*, 187–97.

—— van de Kragt, A. J. C. and Orbell, J. M. (1988). 'Not me or thee, but we: the importance of group identity in eliciting cooperation in dilemma situations—Experimental manipulations', *Acta Psychologica, 68*, 83–97.

DeWaal, F. (1997). 'The Chimpanzee's Service Economy: Food for Grooming', *Evolution and Human Behavior, 18*, 375–86.

—— and Berger, M. (2000). 'Payment for labour in monkeys', *Nature, 404*, 563.

Fehr, E., Fischbacher, U., and Gachter, S. (2002). 'Strong reciprocity, human cooperation, and the enforcement of social norms', *Human Nature, 13*(1), 1–26.

Forsythe, R., Horowitz, J., Savin, N. E., and Sefton M. (1994). 'Fairness in simple bargaining experiments', *Games and Economic Behavior, 6*, 347–69.

Frank, R. (1988). *Passions Within Reason*. New York: Norton.

Gächter, S. and Fehr, E. (1999). 'Collective action as social exchange', *Journal of Economic and Behavioral Organization, 39*, 341–69.

Gurven, M., Hill, K., and Kaplan, H. (2002). 'From forest to reservation: transitions in food sharing behavior among the Ache of Paraguay', *Journal of Anthropological Research 58*(1): 91–118.

——, Allen-Arave, W., Hill, K., and Hurtado, A. M. (2001). 'Reservation food sharing among the Ache of Paraguay', *Human Nature, 12*(4): 273–98.

Hill, K. (2002). 'Cooperative food acquisition by Ache foragers', *Human Nature, 13*(1):105–28.

—— and Hawkes, K. (1983). 'Neotropical hunting among the Ache of Eastern Paraguay', in R. Hames and W. Vickers (eds), *Adaptive Responses of Native Amazonians*, New York: Academic Press, pp.139–88.

—— and Hurtado, A. M. (1996). *Ache Life History: The Ecology and Demography of a Foraging People*. New York: Aldine Press.

Kaplan, H. and Hill, K. (1985). 'Food sharing among Ache Foragers; Tests of explanatory hypotheses', *Current Anthropology, 26*(2), 223–45.

—— ——, Hawkes, K., and Hurtado, A. (1984). 'Food sharing among the Ache hunter-Gatherers of eastern Paraguay', *Current Anthropology, 25*, 113–15

—— ——, Lancaster, J., and Hurtado. A. M. (2000). 'The evolution of intelligence and the human life history', *Evolutionary Anthropology, 9*(4), 156–84.

Murningham and Saxon (1994). 'Ultimatum bargaining by children and adults', MS cited in Camerer 1999.

Orbell, J., Dawes, R., and van de Kragt, A. (1988). 'Explaining discussion-induced cooperation', *Journal of Personality and Social Pyschology, 54*, 811–19.

Thaler, R. H. (1992). *The Winner's Curse: Paradoxes and Anomalies of Economic Life*. Princeton, NJ: Princeton University Press.

14

The Ultimatum Game, Fairness, and Cooperation among Big Game Hunters

Michael S. Alvard

THE FIELD SITE

The Ultimatum Game was played with a group of traditional big game hunters, the Lamalera whalers of Nusa Tenggara, Indonesia. The village of Lamalera is located on the island of Lembata, in the province of Nusa Tenggara Timur, in the country of Indonesia. The inhabitants of Lamalera speak Lamaholot, a language ranging in distribution from east Flores to central Lembata. The village is culturally similar to other Lamaholot speakers, sharing a system of patrilineal descent, and asymmetric marriage alliance between descent groups. The village population is approximately 1,200, divided into twenty-one major patrilineal clans (*suku*), the larger of which are further divided into subclans (*lango béla*—see Barnes 1996 for detailed ethnography).

Although whaling occurs throughout the year, two separate seasons are recognized. *Léfa* refers to the primary whaling season from May until October. This is the dry season and the period when sea conditions are best. During léfa, boats go out daily, weather permitting. *Baléo* refers to the opportunistic pursuit of whales during the balance of the year. It also corresponds to a season of fewer resources. Boats are kept in their sheds, and hunts only occur if prey are spotted from shore. It seems clear that sea conditions increase the costs of search—winds drop in this season and boats must be rowed during search (Barnes 1996: 152). Whether prey are also scarcer is unknown. The primary prey for both seasons are sperm whale (*Physeter catadon*), and ray (*Manta birostris, Mobula kuhlii*, and *Mo. diabolus*). They also pursue other toothed whales, including killer whale (*Orcinus orca*), pilot whale (*Globicephala macrohynchus*), several species of dolphin as well as shark, and sea turtle. Interestingly, Lamalera hunters taboo baleen whales (suborder *Mysticeti*). The mean number of whales taken by Lamalera hunters per year during from 1959 through 1995 was 21.4 (SD = 13.8; range 2–56; data from Barnes 1996: table 15). For ray for the same period the mean taken per year was 144.7 (SD = 95.7; range 10–360; Barnes 1996: table 15).

Twelve clans are associated with corporations that own, maintain, and operate whaling operations focused around vessels called *téna*. These craft measure about 11 meters in length and 2.5 meters at the beam, have thick wood hulls, are propelled by either oars or large rectangular woven palm sails, and are steered with a rudder. *Killing prey with a téna is a manifestly cooperative activity, impossible to accomplish alone.* The *téna alep* (téna owner) organizes téna activities. His role is in some ways similar to that of the *umialik* or whaling captain of the Inuit bowhead whale hunters of north Alaska (Spencer 1959). In spite of the name, the téna alep does not own the téna in a real sense. Rather, he works like a coach or manager, and does not necessarily go out to sea. The téna alep acts as a nexus for the whaling operation as he functions to coordinate three specialized and overlapping interest groups—crew members, corporate members, and technicians who all receive shares of the harvest according to their roles (see below).

Crewmembers tend to be clansmen of the corporation that owns the boat, but this is not a prerequisite. Within crews, the specialized roles are harpooner, harpooner's helper, bailers, helmsman, and crew. Corporate members are usually clan members who underwrite the construction and maintenance of the téna. They may or may not act as crewmembers. The technicians—the carpenter, sail maker, smith, and harpoon bamboo provider (often the harpooner) may or may not be clan members or crew.

Crews of at least nine and up to fourteen or more man the boats. During the whaling season a fleet of boats leaves daily at sunrise (weather permitting) to search an area directly to the south of the coast at a distance of up to 13 km. When a whale is sighted, the sails are dropped and the crew rows furiously to catch up with the whale. Once the boat is in range, the harpooner leaps from the small harpooner's platform on the bow of the boat, to drive the harpoon into the back of the whale. The whale then dives or tows the boat about until it is exhausted. By almost any standard whale hunting is dangerous. Boats can be towed out to sea, and often capsize.

Barnes (1996: 307–9) describes a litany of woes that have befallen hapless Lamalera whalers. For a good narrative describing a Lamalera whale hunt, see Severin (2000).

The téna travel in a diffuse group and cooperation between boats is common. Large whales (e.g. adult male sperm whales) are difficult animals to catch and more than one téna is often required to subdue one. A mutually agreed upon norm dictates that additional téna will not assist unless the téna that has struck the whale first requests help. Requesting help is made with careful calculation, because each additional téna that participates in the kill has an equivalent claim to the carcass. After help is requested, the helping téna may attempt to place additional harpoons or they may tie on to the first boat. The téna then act as drogues to tire the whale. During the course of a whale pursuit, téna are often swamped or capsized. Téna also assist one another by recovering hunters who have been thrown overboard. Cooperation among téna is not required for smaller prey such as ray.

The type of systematic norm-based sharing of game found at Lamalera is not uncommon among hunting people (Gould 1967; Damas 1972; Robbe 1975; Ichikawa 1983; Altman 1987; Cassell 1988). In the Lamalera case, I define the primary distribution as the distribution of meat to shareholders that occurs during and immediately following the butchering of the prey. Secondary distributions refer to transfers between households subsequent to the primary distribution. The primary distribution proceeds according to complex norms that are generally consistent between corporations, but may vary in detail with prey species. During the primary distribution, the prey is divided into whole shares with names that correspond to anatomical parts of the prey. For example, for a whale, there are fourteen major whole shares that vary in size and quality. Each whole share has one or more shareholders to what I call individual shares. For more detail on the norms of distribution see Alvard (2002) and Barnes (1996).

Whole shares can be described by the nature of the recipients. First, crewmembers receive shares. These shares go to the active hunters that were crewmembers on the téna when the prey was captured. Second, certain corporate members receive corporate shares as part of hereditary rights. Third, shares go to the craftsmen who may or may not be clan members or crew. Fourth, there are shares that go to two clans whose members are descendants of the original inhabitants of this part of Lambata Island. These shares are given only from sperm whale and represent concession given in exchange for use of the land. Finally, there are small discretionary shares usually given out by the téna alep.

Within whole share types, division becomes complex. Within a crew, for example, there are five positions: harpooner, harpooner's helper, two bailers, helmsman, and crew—who may receive special shares depending on the species. Bailers, for example, receive the *fai mata* share from ray. This is a share similar to a standard crew share with portions from the head instead of gill sections. Corporate shares also vary—for a whale there are six corporate whole share types. Some are small in size with many shareholders; others are larger with few shareholders.

Finally, it is important to note that multiple shareholders receive all their shares. That is, being a technician and corporate shareholder does not preclude one from crewing and receiving crew shares as well. For example, a man who is a crewmember, has a corporate share, and is the sailmaker for a téna that kills a whale, receives all three shares.

Besides whaling, there are few alternatives for acquiring meat or other forms of animal protein. Little animal husbandry is practiced. Some goats, chickens, and pigs are kept, but grazing is poor. The common alternative to whaling is the relatively non-cooperative hook-and-line or net fishing with small boats called *sapã*. Sapã fishing occurs commonly during the baléo season, but also occurs during the léfa season. Some men specialize in sapã fishing year around. Sapã fishing is accomplished alone or in teams of two. While sapã fishing is much less cooperative than whaling and can be accomplished alone, in practice it often involves cooperation among a small number of men. The fishermen often cooperate with sapã and net owners. When this happen, each fishermen and each owner claims a share. Share size is proportional to the number of claimants (Alvard and Nolin 2002). Other less common methods to obtain marine resources include spear gun fishing and fish trapping. Women also gather shellfish and seaweed.

The village of Lamalera is located on the side of a collapsed volcanic caldera, the soil is extremely rocky and steep, and little agricultural land is available. A few villagers have obtained land outside the village (Barnes 1986) or attempt to grow a minimal amount of produce in the rocky ground between houses

(Barnes 1974). Villagers largely depend on trade to secure agricultural goods. The women of Lamalera trade fish and whale meat, and to a lesser degree salt, lime from coral, and dyed weavings with the agricultural communities of the interior of the island. In exchange they receive maize, other carbohydrates such as rice and cassava, as well as other foodstuffs such as coconuts, coffee, sugar cane, citrus fruits, and green vegetables. Women generally conduct trade on a barter basis without the mediation of cash (Barnes and Barnes 1989). Nonagricultural goods like pots and cloth are obtained in markets located in larger towns on the island. However, few people—such as schoolteachers—have a steady source of cash income. A primary source is from villagers who leave to work for cash elsewhere and send money back to the village. Tourists also provide cash income for some villagers.

METHODS

The data were collected in August of 1999. Data were collected with three groups: one group of eleven proposers (mean age = 39.4 years, all male), one group of nine proposers (mean age = 33.4, all male), and one group of twenty responders (mean age = 38.14 years; seventeen males, three females), for a total of forty individuals. Players were explained the rules of the game as groups. The rules were read in Indonesian. All adult Lamalerans are fluent in Indonesian. After all players assured me that they understood the game, numerous sample offers and responses were presented until I was confident that all understood the game. One individual was rejected because he did not understand the game. Each player was presented with a numbered slip of paper. The left half of the slip has a space for the proposer to write his or her offer. The right half of the slip has two checkboxes, marked reject or accept. Proposers were asked to write the number of their offer in the space provided on the slip. The slips were then collected. Players were told to return at a later time to see if their offers were accepted and collect possible winnings.

Responders were given slips with offers indicated on the left side. They were asked to examine the offer, decide to accept or reject, and indicate their choice by checking the appropriate box. After all had indicted their decisions, slips were returned to me and payment was made immediately.

The pot consisted of one carton of ten cigarette packs. Proposers were told they could make any offer between 0–10 packs. Cigarettes were used so that people would not associate the activity with gambling. Cigarettes are highly valued by all people. Eighty percent of the players smoked and cigarettes could easily be given or sold to someone for money or favors. Packages of sixteen cigarettes were priced at approximately Rp3,500, and a carton costs about Rp35,000. At the time, the exchange rate was approximately Rp7,400 to one dollar, so the pot was equivalent to $4.73. This amount is equivalent to approximately 10 days wages, although wage labor was generally not available in the village. A schoolteacher who has worked for 5 years in Lamalera earns around Rp200,000 per month. A minibus driver in the island town of Leoleba makes around Rp100,000 per month. I paid our cook/house person Rp90,000 per month. For comparison, the price of 1 liter of rice is approximately Rp2,600 ($0.35), 1 liter of kerosene cost Rp400 ($0.05), 5 liters of cooking oil cost Rp28,000 ($3.78), and one egg cost Rp700 ($0.09); local markets charged Rp2,500 ($0.34) per liter of onions.

After the first round of data collection with the first group of eleven proposers, it was apparent that a range of offers would not be forthcoming. For the first group of eleven proposers, ten offered five packs and one offered eight. In order to examine responses to a range of offers, I created twenty sham offers consisting of four offers each of 1–5 packs. These sham offer slips were presented as genuine to the twenty subjects acting as responders.

Members of the groups involved in any particular trial were able to communicate with one another. It was impossible to prevent players from talking to one another before and after the sessions. After data collection began, the game became a hot topic of conversation, especially among the crews who spend long hours together on uneventful foraging trips. Players were not, however, able to communicate with their partners in the game, who remained anonymous.

RESULTS

The results of the Ultimatum Game with the whalers were consistent in some ways with the results obtained from trials in western

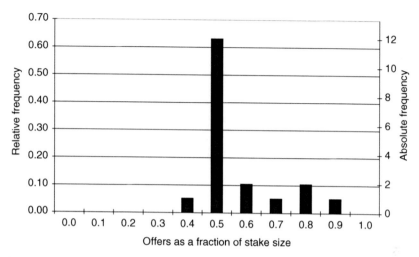

FIG. 14.1. Distribution of offers in the Ultimatum Game ($n = 19$, stake size $S = 10$ packs of cigarettes)

societies. Figure 14.1 presents the offers for the sample of nineteen proposers. Like most previously reported trials, the modal offer was 50 percent (twelve out of nineteen). There was one offer of four packs. Compared with standard western results, the primary difference at Lamalera was that there were a number of cases of hyper fairness. Over 31 percent of the offers (six of nineteen) were greater than five packs; the mean offer was 5.8 packs. Hyper-fair offers also occurred in the crosscultural sample with the Ache of Paraguay (Hill and Gurven, Chapter 13, this volume) and the Au and Gnau of Papua New Guinea (Tracer, Chapter 8, this volume). There was a slight effect for age with respect to offers. Youth was associated with greater offers. Individuals that made offers over 50 percent were more likely to be in their twenties ($R^2 = 0.20$, $p = 0.05$, $F = 4.25$, $df = 17$).

Responses were consistent with previous results in the sense that the rate of rejections increased as the size of offers decreased (Figure 14.2). Twenty-five percent of offers consisting of three packs or less were rejected. The mean rejected offer was two packs. In spite of the tendency for low offers to be rejected, many low offers were, in fact, accepted—75 percent of three packs offers or less were accepted. Men who were wealthy by Lamaleran standards made two of the four rejections. One is a schoolteacher who, in

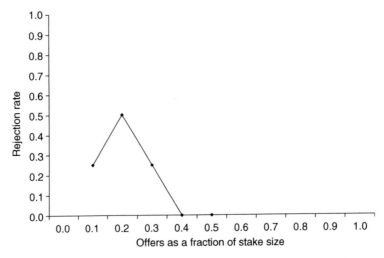

FIG. 14.2. Rejection rates as a function of offer size in the Ultimatum Game
($n = 20$) (stake size $S = 10$ packs of cigarettes)

addition to having a salary, runs a home-stay for tourists who visit
the village. The other was an ex-village head. He worked most of the
year for cash in Leoleba, the largest town on the island, and was
reported by some to be 'the wealthiest man in the village' (this
anecdotal finding parallels that of Ensminger, this volume). The
other two rejecters were our neighbors. They may have been more
concerned about reputation than others. In fact, one neighbor made
sure to tell me that he had rejected the offer and that he did so
because he considered the offer of two packs to be unfair. In the
same breath, however, he lamented the loss of the two packs of
cigarettes, which he would have dearly enjoyed smoking. It is also
possible that our neighbors may have valued the cigarettes less than
others since they regularly obtained smokes from us via inter-
household demand sharing (Peterson 1993). The players who
accepted low offers were téna crewmembers with little opportunity
to obtain cash or other forms of wealth.

DISCUSSION

One easy interpretation suggests that the Lamalera whale hunters
made strategic decisions when they made 'fair' offers (Forsyth *et al.*

1994; Hoffman, McCabe, and Smith 1996*a*, *b*). In this case, when proposers offer fair amounts, they are acting to mitigate the risk that responders will reject the offer. If this hypothesis is true, the whalers' 'fair' proposals are not anomalous from either an economic or evolutionary point of view because fair offers are predicted from an assumption of self-interest. Bodega owners cooperate with the mafia—because if they do not, their legs may be broken. This makes intuitive sense when we think about the success of the mafia and other coercion-based organizations that use intimidation and threat of reprisal as powerful methods to induce cooperation. In this interpretation, the proposer 'cares' about the responder's welfare to the extent that their two interests are linked. In the Ultimatum Game, the proposer's fate is linked to the responder's. If the proposer cannot induce the responder to cooperate and accept the offer, the proposer receives nothing.

Data from Dictator Games support the idea that offers in the Ultimatum Game are high in order to avoid rejection. In the Dictator Game (see Camerer and Fehr, Chapter 3, this volume for details), proposers have no expectations about the behavior of responders. Since there is no risk of rejection, very low offers are expected. Experiments show that offers *are* significantly lower when the risk of punishment is removed (Forsyth *et al.* 1994; Hoffman *et al.* 1994; Hoffman, McCabe, and Smith 1996*a*). It seems that proposers 'care' less about the responder when their fates are not linked. Support for the strategic hypothesis also includes the work reviewed by Roth (1995) that showed that offers are often optimal in the sense that they maximize the payoff *given the probability of rejections*. Using the crosscultural data set, analysis by Henrich *et al.* (this volume), however, does not point to the same conclusion. In all but two cases, the mean offer was higher than predicted given the probability of rejection. In the Lamalera case, given the observed range of rejections, the expected income-maximizing offer is predicted to have been around 31 percent of the pot (Henrich *et al.*, Chapter 2, this volume). It seems clear that in the Lamalera case, the mean of 58 percent cannot result from risk aversion.

The fact that Henrich *et al.* (Chapter 2, this volume) shows that most of the mean offers in the crosscultural sample were greater than the income-maximizing optimal, given the distribution of rejections, suggests there may be more to the issue than strategic offers. Additional evidence comes from the Dictator Game. While offers in the Dictator Game are lower than offers in the Ultimatum Game, they are still not what is predicted by selfish rationality. Even when rejection was not an option, a nontrivial proportion of players give substantial portions of the pot away (Hoffman *et al.* 1994; Hoffman, McCabe, and Smith 1996*a*). Results with the three Dictator Game played in the crosscultural sample also indicated that many people gave shares away (Henrich *et al.*, this volume).

Hoffman, McCabe, and Smith (1996*a*) created a number of additional treatments to the Dictator Game designed to increase the degree of 'social distance' between players and experimenters. Offers were substantially lower when the experimental design was such that complete anonymity was assured to the proposers. In these trials, nobody, including the experimenter, knew the offer. Only 11 percent of the subjects gave 30 percent or more to their partner. Hoffman increased assurance of social anonymity in these cases, and 'fair'; behavior essentially evaporated. Similar results were obtained when the experiment was repeated—64 percent of offers were $0 (Hoffman, McCabe, and Smith 1996*a*).

Hoffman *et al.* (1994) suggest that players are not only strategically motivated to avoid rejection, but also play as if they are concerned about what others think of them. This implies that in the standard Ultimatum Game, some players make their offers as if there may be future interactions, in spite of the fact that the game is designed in a way to get subjects to exclude these possibilities. A number of other researchers have also hypothesized that at least some portion of the results are due to players behaving as if their reputations are at stake (Baird, Gertner, and Picker 1994; Eckel and Wilson 1998, 1999; Tullberg 1999). This may be particularly true in games played with non-western, traditional peoples who have little experience with experimental methods.

These results suggest that the subjects and the experimenters that run the games are playing by different rules (Kollock 1998). Experimenters simplify the real world, create the rules of a game, and have faith that their subjects play by them. Players may view the experiment in a different way—as a game within a game (Burnell, Evans, and Yao 1999). That is, one possible hypothesis to explain 'fairer' than optimal offers is that players make decisions as if the game is part of a larger game where reputation is important—the larger game does not end with the experiment (Hoffman, McCabe, and Smith 1996*a*). The whale hunters and others who make fair offers may do so because they are considering how their decision will have impacts beyond the scope of the game.

The best evidence from the crosscultural sample is Tracer's (Chapter 8, this volume) work with the Au and Gnau of New Guinea. These people rejected both fair and hyper-fair offers in the Ultimatum Game. Tracer interprets this to be the result of a pattern of politics through gift giving common in these societies. Among these groups accepting gifts obligates one to reciprocate—a situation that people work hard to avoid. As Henrich *et al.* (Chapter 2, this volume) point out: 'With this knowledge, the New Guinea result makes perfect sense.' I agree with this interpretation, but it is true only if either the Au and Gnau have a sense that their play is not anonymous, or believe the anonymity but bring non-selfish preferences into the game that they acquired from daily life outside the game (in other words, in the context of the game, the anonymity of the player does cause them to ignore their non-selfish preferences: see Henrich *et al.*, Chapter 2, this volume and Ensminger, Chapter 12, this volume). If the Au and Gnau players 'believed' the games were anonymous and they have only selfish preferences, they should have harbored no fear that they would be obligated, and they should have accepted fair offers. On the contrary, it appears that they rejected offers because they did not want to risk having to reciprocate.

Of course, while anonymity may have affected behavior in certain cases, it remains difficult to explain why groups like the Hadza, Tsimane, Machiguenga, and Quichua, who live in places in which anonymity is nearly non-existent, made such low offers. Further, along these lines, both Henrich and Smith (Chapter 5, this volume) and Hill and Gurven (Chapter 13, this volume) compare treatments in which player decisions were publicly known to standard anonymous versions of the games and find no difference.

WHAT ABOUT THOSE REJECTIONS?

Rejections in the Ultimatum Game have been interpreted to indicate a willingness to punish, at a cost, those who are unfair in economic relations (Bolton and Zwick 1995). Above, I noted that some researchers believe that 'fair' offers may be due to players acting as if the game is a subgame of a larger game where reputation is important. Responders' spiteful punishment observed in the Ultimatum Game might also be part of a general phenomenon related, at least in part, to signaling a willingness to punish noncooperators. Indeed, in addition to assortative interactions among cooperators, punishment of noncooperators has also been suggested to be critical for the development of cooperative outcomes (Boyd and Richerson 1992; Clutton-Brock and Parker 1995; Bowles and Gintis 1998). From this perspective, responders who reject low offers are concerned with their reputations—of course, this still leaves us with the puzzle of why individuals in about half the groups in our sample were unwilling to reject, or only rejected very low offers with low probability.

There are theoretical reasons as well as recent empirical research by evolutionary ecologists to support this idea. Many nonhuman organisms make costly displays to signal their qualities to others. Costly signaling theory suggests that advertising costly traits indicates phenotypic quality because only individuals of such quality can exhibit maximal expression of these traits. Also called the handicap principle (Viega 1993; Zahavi 1997), the most notable example is mating displays like those found in peacocks. Male peacocks have enormous feather displays that are used to attract females to mate. The display is costly because it attracts predators, takes resources to maintain, and restricts mobility. According to the handicap principle, the males that can maintain such displays are signally their quality as mates.

Costly displays have been suggested to work in a similar way in humans. Smith and Bird (2000) argue that a wide variety of seemingly inexplicable and maladaptive behavior in humans may be understood in terms of costly signally theory. Smith and Bird cite such behaviors as genital mutilation and foot binding (Mackie 1996), monumental architecture (Neiman 1998), and expensive public rituals like the potlatch among the Kwakiutl (Boone 1992). For such behaviors to be stable signals, they must be observable, costly, reliable in the sense that they must vary with the quality of the trait being communicated, and of course, they must ultimately provide some benefit to the sender.

What might low-offer rejection in the Ultimatum Game signal? One possibility is that they signal an unwillingness to cooperate with noncooperators. If a low offer represents a defector move, accepting such an offer is essentially cooperation in the face of defection. In games of reciprocity, in which some have argued that the Ultimatum Game is actually embedded, cooperating with a defector is essentially a sucker move, and returns a lower payoff than any defect move. If people behave as if these games are not anonymous, rejecting low offers communicates the fact that they are not dupes. While costly in the short term, such a reputation could be critical in economies where cooperation is vital yet where a perception by others of weakness could be exploited and result in loss.

Subjects in Lamalera are quite willing to punish others for norm transgressions. Here is an example. Bob was the téna alep or boat leader for Ibu Téna, one of the whaling vessels. At a party, Fred became drunk and punched Bob's daughter in the head. The reason was unclear. Fred is the harpooner for Ibu Téna. For a period of weeks, Bob would not allow Fred to harpoon from Ibu Téna. This punishment acted to ground Ibu Téna, because a téna cannot go to sea without a harpooner and no other harpooner was willing to replace Fred. Harpooning is a very specialized skill that few men possess. Not only was Fred punished, but so were the crew and corporate members of Ibu Téna, as well as Bob himself. They failed to obtain any resource that might have been harvested if Ibu Téna had not been grounded. What is even more interesting is that since harpooners are in short supply, Fred was able to harpoon for another boat and did not suffer.

Another example comes from Barnes (1996: 79) who anecdotally describes what might be described as a cheater clan named Lefo Sefo that existed in Lamalera until the turn of the nineteenth century. Their téna, the Fao Puka, was very successful but would only allow clan members as its crew. They also would not return their harvest to the normal beach spot where all other téna butchered and distributed prey. They would butcher at a spot called Lodo Ika. Subsequently, they were punished when other boats did not offer assistance after the Fao Puka capsized during a hunt, and as a result many of her crew drowned. The clan was ostracized afterwards and the last clan member died in the 1920s.

FAIRNESS AND BIG GAME HUNTING

I have not yet addressed any of the variance seen in the crosscultural sample. Yes, perhaps strategic risk reduction explains fair offers—when offers are fair. And, perhaps reputation effects explain costly rejections—when rejections occur. But as the various chapters in this volume attest, not all people play fair and not all low offers are rejected. The whale hunters represent only one extreme in terms of play in the Ultimatum Game. What explains the variance? One hypothesis is that players play fair in the game to the extent that cooperation is an essential aspect of their economic lives (see Hoffmann, Mc Cabe, and Smith 1996*a*: 654; Henrich *et al.* Chapter 2, this volume). If the payoffs to cooperation are high in day-to-day economic life, cooperative payoffs will be valued, norms of cooperation will be strong, reputation as a cooperator, and punisher will be important, and people will be disposed to play fair in the Ultimatum Game. If payoffs to cooperation are low, as Henrich argues is the case for the Machiguenga (this volume), a lack of fairness will be expressed in the game.

This hypothesis is supported by the crosscultural data (Henrich *et al.* Chapter 2, this volume). We rank-ordered the fifteen societies according to their degree of market integration, privacy, anonymity, and payoffs to cooperation. We regressed mean Ultimatum Game offers on these variables and found that the best model incorporates market integration and payoff to cooperation. I will discuss the market integration parameter below and focus for the moment on the role of cooperation. The Lamalera whale hunters are in a unique position. Lamalera represents the extreme within the crosscultural sample with respect to payoffs to cooperation in the peoples' daily lives. They also had the highest mean offer in the Ultimatum Game.

Humans are by far the most cooperative of the primates as well as the most variable. In many societies, people engage in cooperative tasks that either provide greater per capita returns when accomplished in groups, or simply cannot be accomplished alone. I have argued elsewhere that in many cases of cooperation, individuals have immediate common interest and cheating does not pay. Such joint activity is not readily modeled by the Prisoner's Dilemma payoff schedule, and is best described as mutualism or coordination (Alvard 2001; Alvard and Nolin 2002; see Camerer and Fehr, Chapter 3, this volume, for a discussion of the Prisoner's Dilemma and coordination games).[1]

---

[1] It should be noted that there are two types of mutualism—a point not often appreciated in the literature (Alvard 2001). According to Brown (1983), by-product

In contrast to the payoff schedule of a Prisoner's Dilemma, in a coordination game, cooperating with a cooperator is better than cheating with a cooperator. These games are sometimes called 'trust games' or assurance games (Sugden 1986; Binmore 1994). Coordination games can be structured in the same way as a Prisoner's Dilemma, but with a different payoff matrix. In a Prisoners Dilemma it pays to cheat no matter what a partner does; in a coordination game it pays to cooperate when partners cooperate.

The Lamalera whalers are a perfect example. Unless eight men can coordinate to crew the boat, no one goes to sea. In Lamalera, the mean return for cooperative whale hunting is significantly higher than solitary fishing 0.66 kg/h versus 0.37 kg/h (for details see Alvard and Nolin 2002). In the whaling coordination game, choosing to whale is the best choice, unless your partners choose to fish and you are left whaling alone with a zero payoff. In other words, to the extent that individuals receive benefits from cooperation, we expect them to cooperate—provided they have assurance of their partner's behavior. In Lamalera, there is also a complex division of labor and task specialization that provides economies of scale. For payoffs to be realized, however, significant coordination problems must be solved (Becker and Murphy 1992). Sailmakers, for example, must trust that crews will form and go to sea. Oarsmen must be assured that harpooners will attempt to kill prey. If multiple téna are involved in a kill, distribution norms must be coordinated or different boats could lay claim to the same shares. Such coordination is not always as easy as one may intuitively think. Experimental evidence shows that even in coordination games where there is one pareto-dominant Nash equilibrium, players do not always converge (van Huyck, Battalio, and Bei 1990).[2] How the coordination is obtained in Lamalera is unknown, although there are some suggestions (Alvard and Nolin 2002).

---

mutualism involves behaviors that ego must accomplish regardless of whether others are present or not. Whale hunting, however, is not something a hunter can accomplish unless he is in a group. A second kind of mutualistic cooperation is called synergistic mutualism by Maynard-Smith and Szathmary (1995). The difference between synergistic mutualism and by-product mutualism lies with the returns obtained from going it alone. In this case, the payoffs of hunting large game alone are lower than small game alone and hunters must coordinate to receive the greater payoff. This is not the case for by-product mutualism.

[2] A Nash equilibrium is a game theoretical concept that describes a combination of players' strategies that are best against one another. At a Nash equilibrium, no players

Among many big game hunters, Lamalera included, distribution and pursuit norms seem designed to assure participants of how others will behave and the payoffs they themselves will receive. The entire system does seem premised on the implicit assumption by participants that all will receive the payoff prescribed by the norm of entitlements. Ellickson (1991) argues that norms function to reduce transaction costs for achieving cooperative outcomes. Transaction costs are the costs of establishing and maintaining property rights and include such activities as inspection, enforcing, policing, and measurement (Allen 1991). Imagine the transaction costs for determining claims to téna harvests if norms of distribution did not exist for the whalers at Lamalera. For the whale that was killed on 11 June 1999, three téna participated and at least ninety-nine individuals were due and received shares according to the norms of the primary distribution (Alvard and Nolin 2002). It seems unlikely that these individuals would have participated in such an activity if transaction costs could not be minimized and payoffs assured.

Mutualistic subsistence strategies similar to that found in Lamalera may be a particularly strong environment favoring the type of fair-minded cooperation displayed by the Lamalerans and others in the Ultimatum Game. The larger set of rules that guides players' behavior during the Ultimatum Game is certainly generalized from norms based on real-world socio-sexual economic exchanges. One working hypothesis is that general learning about fairness (i.e. equity) is common in societies where the payoffs to cooperation are greater. In societies where folks commonly develop norms to solve coordination problems, fairness becomes a focal point (Schelling 1960) because the cooperatively obtained payoff must be divided (e.g. fair meat distributions). This is not a common problem in more solitary and less cooperative systems like the Machiguenga. To the extent that achieving such fairness is critical for subsistence, we expect fairness to be expressed in the Ultimatum Game. In the Ultimatum Game, players must coordinate in the sense that the proposer must make an offer that the responder will accept—if anyone is to get a payoff. In some societies fairness may be a focal point that helps proposers coordinate with responders.[3]

will do better by changing their decision unilaterally. A pareto optimum, in contrast, is the outcome in which no player can do better except at the expense of the other players.

[3] What does fairness mean to a group like the Ache, where meat-sharing norms dictate sharing such that good hunters subsidize poor hunters (see Kaplan and Hill

Coordination may be a key for understanding the fairness that dominates Ultimatum Game results in western societies. Western society is arguably more cooperative than any of the groups in the crosscultural sample discussed in this volume. In societies like the United States, where specialists are critical to the economy, the cooperation that results is mutualistic. Assuming that the results in the Ultimatum Game game reflect culturally inculcated norms of fairness, the high degree of mutualistic cooperation found in western societies may explain the Ultimatum Game results found in those groups. This hypothesis is supported by the result obtained when we regressed mean Ultimatum Game offers on market integration. Market activity involves complex norms of fairness. The payoffs of exchange cannot occur unless fair agreements can be reached between players (Moulin 1995). One interpretation is that people who do not have experience with markets do not play the Ultimatum Game as if they are infused with such norms of fairness (Ensminger, Chapter 12, this volume; Henrich and Smith, Chapter 5, this volume).

CONCLUSION

Evolutionary theory assumes that natural selection plays the critical role in the evolution of adaptive responses, especially for behaviors that have a strong bearing on reproductive outcomes, such as mating, parenting, and socioeconomic decisions like those modeled by the Ultimatum Game (Smith 1992*a*, *b*; Smith and Winterhalder 1992; Rose and Lauder 1997). Since neoclassical economics and many evolutionary approaches to behavior share the common assumption of rational selfishness, it is not surprising that researchers who use evolutionary theory to understand behavior share the sense of incongruity with the Ultimatum Game's initial

---

1985*a*)? It may mean that the currency with which fairness is judged varies. Fairness exists when players receive shares from a cooperative venture proportional to the costs they have paid. Benefits and costs are often not paid in the same currency—much to the chagrin of the field anthropologist. Good hunters among the Ache are reported to be disproportionally named as partners in extra-marital affairs (Kaplan and Hill 1985*b*). Warriors who kill among the Yanomamo have more wives and father more children (Chagnon 1988). One can imagine that fairness in such contexts becomes difficult for even the actors themselves to measure (see discussion of Ellickson (1991) above). The fact that 'keeping track' is so difficult may be one of the reasons why norms arise: by acting as easy-to-maintain rules of thumb.

results with western study populations. But as evolutionary theory was preparing to explain the incongruous result of a seemingly human universal preference for fairness, the target moved. As the results in this volume show, people do not universally play fair. The question is no longer why do people seem to have a preference for fairness. The question is now: do people behave more or less fairly in adaptive ways?

Recent approaches that use evolutionary theory for understanding human cooperative behavior have focused on trying to discern the mechanisms important in the development of *Homo sapiens'* understanding of risk and reward in a social context. In other words, knowing the social economics of our ancestors is a key for understanding the results in the Ultimatum Game in living populations. These cognitive and behavioral tools likely evolved during the so-called Environment of Evolutionary Adaptedness (Tooby and Cosmides 1992; Foley 1995). What might the conditions have been in our evolutionary past that patterned the expression of fair or unfair exchange?

If current forager and nonhuman primate models are accurate (e.g. Tooby and DeVore 1987), it seems clear that we evolved in an environment where strangers were rare. A good argument can be made that in our evolutionary past, few economic exchanges were anonymous. This is surely the case among contemporary foragers (e.g. Aspenlin 1970; Bahuchet 1990; Kent 1993; Peterson 1993; Caulfield 1994; Hill and Hurtado 1996). Foraging communities, while fluid, consist of small groups of people who are generally known by all members. Even in Lamalera, with a population of 1,200, the number of men who ever hunted was just over 300—a group where all could easily be acquainted. The social environment was one where most, if not all, economic interactions occurred between non-strangers and relatives, and where reputation was important.

If this is true, there are no good reasons to expect humans to be particularly adapted (in an evolutionarily sense) to anonymous exchanges (but see Fehr and Henrich 2003, for counter argument). There is much to suggest that we have a preference to try to avoid them. Hoffman *et al.* (1994) discusses the anonymity that comes with the 'Great City'. It is cooperation in spite of the supposed anonymity of modern economic exchange that has motivated much research in the field of economics (Bowles 1998). While anonymous exchanges between individuals have become more common with the rise of complex society, people rely on symbols to make the exchanges less anonymous. I do not know the clerk behind the counter at McDonald's, but I know 'McDonald's'. In this sense, the exchange is not anonymous. Such a trademark is a symbol that is very costly to imitate, and identifies and distinguishes the source of the goods or services of one party from those of others (PTO 1989). Trademarks in western economics, like clan totems, language, costumes, scarification, tattoos, rituals, and other identifiers indicate association with groups and decrease anonymity (see Barth 1969).

One hypothesis that has limited support is that outcomes in Ultimatum Game vary across societies with the payoffs to cooperation in the day-to-day life of the members of those societies. In societies where cooperation is commonly mutualistic, individual actors 'need' others to achieve the maximum payoff, fairness norms are common, and reputation as a cooperator is preferred. 'Concern' for the fitness of others displayed when the Ultimatum Game is played with such groups occurs because mutualistic cooperation is so essential to life that it translates to the game. Since such norms are costly, it makes sense that norms of fairness vary in adaptive ways depending on the payoffs to cooperation. In some societies, like the Machiguenga, cooperation is not nearly as integral a part of subsistence...and Machiguenga play the Ultimatum Game very differently than do the whale hunters and members of western society.

Having allies can often be critical to survival—cooperation often *does* pay compared with defection, especially in economic systems like that of the whale hunters. Greater-than-zero offers, even in a context where punishment is unlikely, as is the case with the Dictator Game, may indicate that some people are willing to pay in order to maintain reputations as cooperators. They play as if there exists the threat of punishment even though the game rules disallow it. In other words, humans may prefer not to have a reputation of being a cheater among those whose cooperation is valued. Conversely, in contexts where cooperation does not pay relative to solitary pursuits, players may not be willing to pay the costs associated with maintaining a reputation as a cooperator.

Understanding how cooperation works under realistic conditions is the key next step for understanding the variance seen in the results of the Ultimatum Game game. Indeed, in retrospect, given the costs involved in maintaining and enforcing norms, it makes evolutionary sense that such norms not be fixed but rather vary in adaptive ways. Whether or not this is the case remains to be seen.

REFERENCES

Allen, D. W. (1991). 'What are transaction tosts?', *Research in Law and Economics, 14*, 1–18.

Altman, J. (1987). 'Hunter-gatherers today: an aboriginal economy of north Australia', *American Institute of Aboriginal studies, 35*, 701–9.

Alvard, M. (2001). 'Mutualistic hunting', in Craig Stanford and Henry Bunn (eds), *The Early Human Diet: The Role of Meat*, Oxford: Oxford University Press, pp. 261–78.

——(2002). 'Carcass ownership and meat distribution by big-game cooperative hunters', *Research in Economic Anthropology, 21*, 99–132.

—— and Nolin, D. (2002). 'Rousseau's whale hunt? Coordination among big game hunters', *Current Anthropology, 43*(4), 533–59.

Aspenlin, P. (1970). 'Food distribution and social bonding among the Mamainde of Mato Grosso, Brazil', *Journal of Anthropological Research, 5*, 309–27.

Bahuchet, S. (1990). 'Food sharing among the Pygmies of central Africa', *African Study Monographs, 1*, 127–53.

Baird, R., Gertner, R., and Picker, R. (1994). *Reputation and Repeated Games. Game Theory and the Law*. Cambridge, MA: Harvard University Press.

Barnes, R. (1974). 'Lamalera: a whaling village in eastern Indonesia', *Indonesia, 17*, 136–59.

——(1986). 'Educated fishermen: social consequences of development in an Indonesian whaling community', *Bulletin de l'Ecole Française d'Extrême-Orient, 75*, 295–314.

——(1996). *Sea Hunters of Indonesia*. Oxford: Oxford University Press.

Barnes, R. H. and Barnes, R. (1989). 'Barter and money in an Indonesian village community', *Man, 24*, 399–418.

Barth, F. (1969). 'Introduction', in F. Barth (ed.), *Ethnic Groups and Boundaries*, Boston: Little, Brown, pp. 9–38.

Becker, G. and Murphy, K. (1992). 'The division of labor, coordination costs, and knowledge', *Quarterly Journal of Economics, 107*, 1137–60.

Binmore, K. (1994). *Game Theory and the Social Contract*. Cambridge, MA: MIT Press.

Bolton, G. and Zwick, R. (1995). 'Anonymity versus punishment in ultimatum bargaining', *Games and Economic Behavior, 10*, 95–121.

Boone, J. (1992). 'Competition, conflict, and the development of social hierarchies', in E. Smith and B. Winterhalder (eds), *Evolutionary Ecology and Human Behavior*, New York: Aldine de Gruyter, pp. 301–37.

Bowles, S. (1998). 'Endogenous preferences: the cultural consequences of markets and other economic institutions', *Journal of Economic Literature, 36*, 75–111.

——and Gintis, H. 'The evolution of cooperation in heterogenous populations', *Theoretical Population Biology* (forthcoming).

Boyd, R. and Richerson, P. (1992). 'Punishment allows the evolution of cooperation (or anything else) in sizable groups', *Ethnology and Sociobiology, 13*, 171–95.

Brown, J. (1983). 'Cooperation: a biologist's dilemma', *Advances in the Study of Behavior, 13*, 1–37.

Burnell, S. J., Evans, L., and Yao, S. (1999). 'The ultimatum game: optimal strategies without fairness', *Games and Economic Behavior, 26*, 221–52.

Cassell, M. S. (1988). 'Farmers on the northern ice: relations of production in the traditional north Alaskan Inupiat whale hunters', *Research in Economic Anthropology, 10*, 89–116.

Caulfield, F. (1994). 'Aboriginal subsistence whaling in West Greenland', in M. Freeman and U. Kreuter (eds.), *Elephants and Whales: Resources for Whom?*, Basel: Gordon and Beach, pp. 263–92.

Chagnon, N. (1988). 'Life histories, blood revenge, and warfare in a tribal society', *Science, 239*, 985–92.

Clutton-Brock, T. and Parker, G. (1995). 'Punishment in animal societies', *Science, 373*, 209–216.

Damas, D. (1972). 'Central eskimo systems of food sharing', *Ethnology, 11*, 220–39.

Eckel, C. and Wilson, R. (1998). 'Reputation formation in simple bargaining games', Presented at the Preferences Network Workshop, MacArthur Foundation, Summer Institute, August.

———— (1999). Reciprocal fairness and social signaling: experiments with limited reputations. Presented at the American Economic Association Annual Meetings, January 3–5.

Ellickson, R. C. (1991). *Order Without Law: How Neighbours Settle Disputes*. Cambridge, MA: Harvard University Press.

Fehr, E. and Henrich, J. (2003) 'Is strong reciprocity a maladaptation? On the evolutionary foundations of human Altruism', in P. Hammerstein (ed.), *The Genetic and Cultural Evolution of Cooperation*, Cambridge, MA: MIT Press (in press).

Foley, R. (1995). 'The adaptive legacy of human evolution: a search for the environment of evolutionary adaptedness', *Evolutionary Anthropology, 41*, 94–203.

Forsythe, R., Horowitz, J. L., Savin, N. E., and Sefton, M. (1994). 'Fairness in simple bargaining experiments', *Games and Economic Behavior, 6*, 347–69.

Gould, R. A. (1967). 'Notes on hunting, butchering and sharing of game among the Ngatatjara and their neighbors in the West Australian Desert', *Kroeber Anthropology, 36*, 41–66.

Hill, K. (2002). 'Altruistic cooperation during foraging by the ache, and the evolved human predisposition to cooperate', *Human Nature, 13*, 105–28.

Hill, K. and Hurtado, M. (1996). *Ache Life History*. New York: Aldine.

——(1994). 'Preferences, property rights, and anonymity in bargaining games', *Games and Economic Behavior, 7*, 346–80.

Hoffman, E., McCabe, K., and Smith, V. (1996a). 'Social distance and other-regarding behavior in dictator games', *American Economic Review, 86*, 653–60.

————————(1996b). 'On expectations and the monetary stakes in ultimatum games', *International Journal of Game Theory, 25*, 289–301.

Ichikawa, M. (1983). 'An examination of the hunting-dependent life of the Mbuti Pygmies, Eastern Zaire', *African Study Monographs, 4*, 55–76.

Kaplan, H. and Hill, K. (1985a). 'Food sharing among Ache foragers: tests of explanatory hypotheses', *Current Anthropology, 26*, 223–46.

——(1985b). 'Hunting ability and reproductive success among male Ache foragers', *Current Anthropology, 26*, 131–3.

Kent, S. (1993). 'Sharing in an egalitarian Kalahari community', *Man, 28*, 479–514.

Kollock, P. (1998). 'Transforming social dilemmas: group identity and cooperation', in P. Danielson (ed.), *Modeling Rational and Moral Agents*, Oxford: Oxford University Press, pp. 186–210.

Mackie, G. (1996). 'Ending foot binding and infibulation: a convention account', *American Sociological Review, 61*, 999–1017.

Maynard-Smith, J. and Szathmary, E. (1995). *The Major Transitions in Evolution*. Oxford: W.H. Freeman.

Moulin, H. (1995). *Cooperative Microeconomics*. Princeton, NJ: Princeton University Press.

Neiman, F. (1998). 'Conspicuous consumption as wasteful advertising: a Darwinian perspective on spatial patterns in classic Maya terminal monument dates', in M. Barton and G. Clark (eds.), *Rediscovering Darwin: Evolutionary Theory and Archeological explanation*, pp. 267–290. Washington, D.C. Archeological Papers of the American Anthropological Association, no. 7.

Patent and Trademark Office (1989). *Basic facts about registering a trademark*. Pamphlet.

Peterson, N. (1993). 'Demand sharing: reciprocity and the pressure for generosity among foragers', *American Anthropologist, 95*, 860–74.

Robbe, P. (1975). 'Partage du gibier chez les Ammassalimiut observe en 1972 dans un village de Tileqilaq', *Objects et Monde, 15*, 209–22.

Rose, M. and Lauder, G. (1997). *Adaptation*. New York: Academic Press.

Roth, A. (1995). 'Bargaining experiments', in J. Kagel and A. Roth (eds.), *Handbook of Experimental Economics*, Princeton, NJ: Princeton University Press.

Schelling, T. (1960). *The Strategy of Conflict*. Cambridge, MA: Harvard University Press.

Severin, T. (2000). *In Search of Moby Dick: The Quest for the White Whale*. New York: Basic Books.

Smith, E. (1992a). 'Human behavioral ecology: I', *Evolutionary Anthropology, 1*, 15–25.

—— (1992b). 'Human behavioral ecology: II', *Evolutionary Anthropology, 1*, 50–5.

—— and Bird, R. (2000). 'Turtle hunting and tombstone opening: public generosity as costly signaling', *Evolution and Human Behavior, 21*, 245–61.

—— and Winterhalder, B. (1992). 'Natural selection and decision making: some fundamental principles', in E. Smith and B. Winterhalder (eds), *Evolutionary Ecology and Human Behavior*, New York: Aldine de Gruyter, pp. 25–60.

Spencer, R. (1959). *The North Alaskan Eskimo*. Bureau of American Ethnology Bulletin 171.

Sugden, R. (1986). *The Economics of Rights, Co-operation, and Welfare*. Oxford: Blackwell.

Tooby, J. and Cosmides, L. (1992). 'The psychological foundations of culture', in J. Barkow, J. Tooby, and L. Cosmides (eds), *The Adapted Mind*, New York: Oxford University Press, pp. 19–136.

—— and DeVore, I. (1987). 'The reconstruction of hominid behavioral evolution through strategic modeling', in W. G. Kinzey (ed.), *The Evolution of Human Behavior: Primate Models*. Albany, NY: State University of New York Press, pp. 183–237.

Tullberg, J. (1999). *The Ultimatum Game Revisited*. SSE/EFI Working Papers Series in Business Administration.

van Huyck, J., Battalio, R. and Bei, R. (1990). 'Tacit coordination games, strategic uncertainty, and coordination failure', *The American Economic Review, 80*, 234–48.

Viega, J. (1993). 'Badge size, phenotypic quality, and reproductive success in the house sparrow: a study on honest advertisement', *Evolution, 47*, 1161–70.

Zahavi, A. (1997). *The Handicap Principle*. Oxford: Oxford University Press.

Appendix: Estimating risk aversion from Ultimatum Game data

Richard McElreath and Colin Camerer

In the summary chapter, we presented analysis of the Ultimatum Game offers as explained by risk-aversion, given an estimated rejection distributed. Taking rejection behavior as given, the distribution of offers in the Ultimatum Game might be explicable in terms of utility maximizing against a distribution of rejection probabilities. In this appendix, we explain that analysis in detail.

If proposers in the Ultimatum Game are risk-averse, then even low probabilities of rejection for offers less than 50 percent could drive offers upward. We sought to estimate the amount of risk-aversion needed to explain each set of observed offers as the result of utility maximizing behavior by proposers. Specifically, we assumed that each proposer had an estimate of the rejection behavior in their society, generated from observations of past bargaining behavior. Each proposer then uses her estimate of the rejection probabilities to make an offer which maximizes her expected utility. The estimates for rejection behavior vary, as we will explain below, and so variation in the estimated probabilities of rejection for each offer amount generate variation in Utility Maximizing Offers. These Utility Maximizing Offers taken together constitute a distribution of offers which we then compared to the observed distribution of offers for the given society.

In what follows, we explain in detail how we (1) estimated rejection functions for each sample; (2) generated a distribution of rejection functions for a sample of fictional proposers; (3) generated distributions of Utility Maximizing Offers for each sample with variable amounts of risk-aversion; and (4) used these distributions of Utility Maximizing Offers to find the amount of risk-aversion which best fit the observed data for each sample. This process yielded a best-fit risk-aversion amount for each sample, which we then compared against a plausible amount of risk-aversion measured from empirical studies.

ESTIMATING THE REJECTION FUNCTION FOR
EACH SAMPLE

We treated the function describing the probability of rejection for each given offer as the maximum likelihood logistic. For each of the datasets, we estimated a maximum likelihood logistic rejection function with the form

$$p(x) = 1 - \frac{\exp(\alpha + \beta x)}{1 + \exp(\alpha + \beta x)}$$

where p is the probability of rejection and x is the offer amount, as a proportion of the total stakes. The rejection behavior of each sample then is described by two parameters, α and β.

GENERATING A DISTRIBUTION OF REJECTION
FUNCTIONS FOR EACH SAMPLE

In order to simulate a sample of proposers making offers against assumed rejection functions, we needed to generate a distribution of rejection functions for each sample. These distributions of functions were meant to represent individual estimates of the real rejection function, based on personal experience. One way to generate such a distribution of functions, given the maximum likelihood function for a sample, is to use the estimated standard errors of the parameters α and β. These standard errors plus the correlation between them defines a distribution of rejection functions.

Unfortunately, for many of our samples, the counts are too small to approximate the asymptotically normal assumptions used to generate these Standard Errors. Instead, we used bootstrapping to build new rejection estimates from the observed data. For very large amounts of data, this process would generate the same distribution of rejection functions as using the Standard Errors. Since most of our data sets are small, the distributions of bootstrapped estimates look quite different from the ones derived from the Standard Errors. We bootstrapped rejection functions by sampling with replacement n paired offers and rejections from each data set. We did this 10,000 times for each sample, generating 10,000 bootstrapped data sets for each. For each of these new data sets, we then estimated its maximum likelihood rejection function. This yielded

10,000 rejection functions for each sample of observed offers and rejections.

PRODUCING UTILITY MAXIMIZING OFFERS FOR EACH SAMPLE

Given a rejection function, each proposer in our bootstrapped samples chose the offer amount which maximized her expected utility. We transformed income into utility with a concave function, such that

$$U(x) = (1 - p(x)) \, (m - x)^r,$$

where m is the maximum offer possible (the stakes) and r is a positive real number specifying the amount of risk-aversion. When r is one, the above expression indicates risk neutrality. Smaller values of r indicate increasing amounts of risk-aversion. The Utility Maximizing Offer for each value of r is defined as the offer amount x which maximizes $U(x)$.

COMPARING UTILITY MAXIMIZING OFFERS TO OBSERVED OFFERS

For a given r, we calculated the Utility Maximizing Offer for each bootstrap rejection function and combined all of these Utility Maximizing Offers to form a distribution of offers. We did this for each value of r, from 0 to 1, in increments of 0.05. For each value of r, we then compared this distribution of Utility Maximizing Offers to the observed offers for that population using the Kolmorgorov–Smirnov test statistic (D_{min}). The value of r which minimized the difference between the observed and Utility Maximizing Offer offers (had the smallest D_{min}) was taken as the best estimate of the risk-aversion for that population. Using this best-fit estimate of risk-aversion, we then used D_{min} to calculate the probability that the observed and Utility Maximizing Offer distributions were the same, per the Kolmorgorov–Smirnov test.

Given the lack of precision in some of the estimates, due to rare rejections or small samples, we thought it useful to also compare the best-fit estimate to the fit produced from $r = 0.81$, the amount of risk-aversion Tversky and Kahneman derived from risk-aversion experiments (Tverksy and Kahneman 1992).

We discuss our interpretation of these analyses in the summary chapter.

Index

Lightning Source UK Ltd.
Milton Keynes UK
18 March 2011

169521UK00002B/15/P